HIT REPEAT UNTIL I HATE MUSIC: THE MARCH XNESS ANTHOLOGY

Published by Split/Lip Press
PO Box 27656
Ralston, NE 68127
www.splitlippress.com

ISBN: 978-1-952897-49-8

Cover Art: Africa Studio/Shutterstock.com
Interior Images: kersonyanovicha/Shutterstock.com
Cover and Book Design: David Wojciechowski

HIT REPEAT UNTIL I HATE MUSIC:

THE MARCH XNESS ANTHOLOGY

EDITED BY

ANDER MONSON &
MEGAN CAMPBELL

TABLE OF CONTENTS

LISTEN BEFORE READING

It started by taking a joke too far. We, Megan and Ander, the Official Selection Committee of March Xness, are avid listeners of SiriusXMU, formerly Left of Center, the indie rock station on satellite radio, and in February 2016 one of the DJs made a joke about how next month would be March Sadness, in which they'd play sad indie songs of the college rock era. We loved the idea. We were annoyed when we realized that it was just a joke and in fact they were not going to take over the airwaves with sad vintage jams. We said, hmm, what if we actually did the thing? Like if we actually took 64 classic sad indie/college rock songs and played a tournament of it? What if each game had an essay for each song, and if the game was decided by popular vote based on some mystical combination of essay and song?

We made the bracket, then we made the website for it. It was just dumb enough and definitely fun enough to engage us. The Official March Sadness Selection Committee (Megan and Ander) selected 64 songs from the college rock era, and committed to writing 64 essays for 64 songs ourselves. We put it on Twitter. We put it on the website: Hey music lovers, hey essay lovers, come argue with us about music and experience some feels.

It was flawed from the start. Writing 64 essays was a lot but we did it for the first round. 32 songs got eliminated. We did it again. Down to 16, with some extremely difficult decisions. These difficult decisions—how do you pick between The Swans' "God Damn the Sun" and Pet Shop Boys' "Rent"? This Mortal Coil's "Song to the Siren" vs. Yaz's "Only You"? The Cure's "Pictures of You" vs. Radiohead's "Fake Plastic Trees"? It was hard to say. How we answered these questions told us something about ourselves, what kind of sadnesses we were drawn to and loved to endure, what kind of listener or reader we are, what kind of person we are.

When we got to the Sweet 16, we realized this was a lot of fun, and it would be more fun with other writers. We were friends with a bunch of music knowers and smart people and musicians and writers, so we asked some of them: do you want to write an essay advocating for the sadness of one of these 16 songs? They did, and thus we discovered the true format of the tournament: 64 writers enter, each writing an essay about one song on a yearly theme, and we play the tournament out until only one remains.

After that first year we had so many people who wanted to write essays for the next tournament (March Fadness, One Hit Wonders of the 1990s), that we had to establish a lottery for the 64 spots. Now each year 300 or so people, some writers, some musicians, some neither, all of whom love music and memory and arguing about music and songs and culture, put their names in for each year's lottery for one of the 64 essay-writing spots.

Each year has a new theme: **March Fadness** (One Hit Wonders of the '90s), **March Shredness** (Hair Metal), **March Vladness** (the Goth Bracket), **March Badness** (Bad Hits of the '70s and '80s), **March Plaidness** (The Grunge Bracket), **March Faxness** (Covers Edition), **March Fadness** ('80s Edition), **March Danceness** (Dance Hits of the '00s), and **March Second Chanceness** (Bringing Back Essays that Lost in the First Round).

At first we chose all of the 64 songs from which writers would choose for each tournament. This research, looking at charts and watching videos and reading lists and books and talking with friends, is exhaustive, social, and something we really enjoy. But we moved away from that a bit, and now we assemble a longlist of around 128 core songs from which the participants select. Writers may also argue for other songs, as long as they meet the selection criteria.

We tried different tournament structures, like in March Shredness, in our view so heavily weighted to the top seeds (Poison, Motley Crue, Guns N' Roses, Bon Jovi, Def Leppard, Cinderella) that we thought we should allow two songs from each band to play off in the first round and let the people decide. This turned out to be a poor idea: immediately half the fans of each band were mad at the outcome and lost interest from that point forward. Sorry not sorry, "Welcome to the Jungle": "Paradise City" really is the superior song. Come at us. It has TWO solos, just to start. As it turned out a band very few people had ever heard of, Loudness ("Crazy Nights") upset everyone else to take the crown.

The chaos is part of the game. There are a lot of ways to play March Xness: make a bracket (the bracket winner—the person who makes the most correct predictions—gets a prize), write an essay for the tournament and play as a participant, or read, listen, and vote. Social media and doing this publicly invites hidden fanbases of bands and musicians to participate, and regularly a band or musician gets involved and sends us a bunch of puzzled or flattered tweets or skeets or notes, and in a few cases, decides they want to win this tournament.

Arguing about criteria and seeding is part of the fun of the tournament. We love suggestions and we love conversations. Trash talk is encouraged, but the tournament is conducted in a spirit of friendliness and, if it's not too much to say, love. Twitter was a big part of the experience until it began to suck, and we still miss you, old Twitter, but we are not on there anymore.

So each tournament has a theme, a longlist (a playlist: shout out to our peeps who assemble playlists each year), a set of 64 essays, and prizes for the winner (at first trophies but now a championship ring). If you didn't know about March Xness, you can read all the essays, all 64 of each year's essays plus what we call extracurriculars, essays that don't fit in the tournament proper but are on related subjects. All of this, the essays, the songs, the videos, the playlists are archived on marchxness.com.

But sometimes you want a book, not a website. Even us. We like both things: books and websites. So, with thanks to Split/Lip Press, we present here for you some of our favorite essays, the ones that work in book form anyway, including each year's tournament-winning essay. The writers and the listeners and the readers and the arguers and the voters, all of us who care about music and memory and culture and meaning and make the tournament what it is each year: this book is for you.

—Ander and Megan

MARCH FADNESS '90s

Aaron Smith on "Torn" by Natalie Imbruglia

I was supposed to be writing an essay about Natalie Imbruglia's song "Torn" when my mother was diagnosed with kidney cancer. It was in the back of my head that I had a deadline approaching. Over the course of three weeks, I sat in rooms waiting to see what each doctor would say about my mother: urologist ("You have a big mass in your kidney"); oncology urologist ("Your lungs are clear"); oncology urologist again ("You've had this tumor for at least fifteen years"); and the post-surgery room where they take you and you worry the news is bad because they've isolated you. Thankfully, my mother's prognosis is good. After the doctor cut her in half, pulled out her kidney, he said: "Good news" and "She did great." He even drew us a picture with a pencil (kidney mass as a big scribbly circle and a "thrombus" (a new word we learned) moving toward her liver). My whole family listened, rapt and confused and relieved. I kept thinking: those hands have been inside my mother.

Every day after the diagnosis I told myself I'd work on the essay at night before bed. I'd hum the beginning of the chorus: "I'm all out of faith. / This is how I feel." And then I'd get distracted or too tired or someone in my family would need something or I'd think: *What if her cancer is as bad as we are afraid to imagine?* I'd say to myself on the back porch: "I don't think I can leave her body in the ground and drive the fourteen hours back home to Boston."

I first encountered "Torn" on MTV when I was in graduate school. I mostly wanted to fuck the guy in the video, who I found out is gay in real life when I bought an expensive British magazine in a gay bookstore on Pittsburgh's South Side that put everything a person bought into a brown paper bag. The bag told everyone you had a secret and it was sexy. This was right as the internet was beginning: bare-bones email and picture-less gay chat rooms, but nothing elaborate, and porn was still a tangible thing on VHS that my friends and I passed to one another, a kind of intimacy knowing which scene a friend liked and exactly what they were into. But it wasn't just sex I hid. It was anything that marked me as a fag. My shame then was a tumor as big and sick as my mother's.

Like I imagine many guys who grew up gay in the late '70s or early '80s, I got used to imagining myself in the place of women in movies, television and videos. Every shirtless stud was on top of me. That man was bringing me flowers. The guy, Jeremy Sheffield, in the "Torn" video might actually love me if I had glossy lips, a pixie haircut and tugged my sleeves like Natalie singing about being "naked on the floor." I didn't know then that guys like Jeremy—muscled, gorgeous, floppy-haired—don't usually date chubby, balding guys like me who wear glasses; they usually date guys who look like them: Narcissus pinching his own nipples, staring into the stream. I hadn't had sex with a man at that point, but I'd been every woman fucked by every sweaty man in every movie: Sharon Stone in *Sliver*, Melanie Griffith in *Working Girl* kissing Harrison Ford out of his dress shirt, Kim Basinger in *9 ½ Weeks*.

Everyone kept praying for my mother. Each text from her friends: *Praise God! We have everyone praying! Wait and see what god can do!* And I kept thinking: Why did god let her get cancer and carry it around in her body for over fifteen years? Why did she have to have cancer while her mother was dying? Why did she have cancer when she scrubbed the kitchen cabinets on Saturdays? Why did she have cancer at my parents' fortieth anniversary party my sister and I threw when she looked so pretty and happy and cancerless? "I'm all out of faith. This is how I feel."

Natalie Imbruglia's "Torn," written by American alternative-rock band Ednaswap, survives because of the melody, the springy guitar at the beginning, the catchy spin-around-your-room-in-a-circle push of it, the chorus and the electric guitar leading us out of the song while Natalie thrashes in her blue hoodie (the blond homo in the baby-blue sweater and nineties corduroys who, for obvious reasons, can't seem to get the kiss right).

The lyrics really don't make sense: "I thought I saw a man brought to life. / He was warm, he came around like he was dignified. / He showed me what it was to cry." It's as if the writers needed a rhyme, something to fit the established structure. What does dignity have to do with crying in this scenario? "Illusion never changed / into something real" leads us eventually to "You're a little late. / I'm already torn." Wasn't he, like my mother's cancer, already there?

I look at these lyrics and feel like I can make sense out of them sometimes, but then I feel like my writing students who try and try to understand a poem that makes no sense, that only the writer (barely) understands, and then try to convince me with Republican-spin that it's obvious, common sense, not confusing at all. I always say: "Sounds like you're writing a poem instead of reading one." I guess wanting to believe in anything requires a bit of spin (like Natalie twirling on that set), more work than we should be asked to do and still not quite making sense.

"So I guess the fortune teller's right. / I should have seen just what was there /and not some holy light." Now that things are looking good for my mother, everyone keeps saying that God had a hand in the result. I keep thinking about the doctor's hand opening her torso. I asked a lover once which finger he put inside me, and he flipped me off across the bed: *Fuck you* and *This is how I fucked you*. How to make sense of what's inside us? How to make meaning? Do we need it?

Maybe some songs just feel good. Maybe it's okay not to understand, not to pick at the threads. Maybe it's not necessary to point out whether a thing is poorly constructed or not. Maybe songs like "Torn" let us fuck a British guy in a video and imagine a life, even briefly, where we can have everything we want just the way we want it. Maybe the point is to belt out with passion silly words that sound good together because we don't have the right words for things we don't even know are inside us?

Perhaps songs like "Torn" are aptly titled "one-hit wonders." There's no need to really think about them, but year after year they come back to us because it just feels good to sing, because it just feels good to get fucked. They help us deal with the fact that there isn't a God who gives a shit about us. We don't need to waste our time hiding the things we want in brown bags.

Just because "the perfect sky is torn" doesn't mean we have to look.

ON THE ESSAY:

This essay is for Beverly Smith, 1948-2019.

Dan Chaon on "Natural One" by Folk Implosion

I'm driving down Carnegie Road in Cleveland past all these orange construction barrels and big open pits in the asphalt and this worker guy flags me down. He's wearing a Day-Glo vest and a hard hat, jeans, heavy work boots, and when I roll down my window he leans in and gives me a big smile.

"Hey, man," he says. "I hate to bother you. But listen. Can you give me a ride to my car? It's just down the street a couple of blocks? I'd walk, but it's fuckin cold as a bitch!"

It is, in fact, cold as a bitch. Not snowing exactly, but silvery bits of sleet glint in the air and melt on the windshield. The guy is shivering, doesn't have a coat on. He has a thin jacket with an IBEW patch on the chest. IBEW: International Brotherhood of Electrical Workers. That was the union that my dad belonged to.

I'm a college professor, but I haven't forgotten my roots!

"Sure," I say, "Get in."

*

"Natural One" by Folk Implosion doesn't really belong on a list of one-hit wonders of the 1990's. It cracked the Top 40, but only peaked at #29 on the Billboard Chart in March of 1996.

That was the same month that my dad died. It was the time of "1979" by the Smashing Pumpkins, also "Wonderwall," by Oasis, and "One of Us" by Joan Osborne. I listened to the radio a lot as I travelled to my dad's funeral. I didn't really hear Folk Implosion that often.

But I was in favor of the song!!! I dug it! I bought the soundtrack from the movie *Kids*, which contained the hit "Natural One," and I grooved on the songs that Lou Barlow curated for the film, which also included some Daniel Johnston and Slint!

It felt vaguely literary. *Kids*, of course, was an important art film produced by Gus Van Sant and directed by the famous photographer Larry Clark, and written by the 22-year-old wunderkind Harmony Korine, who is nine years younger than me, and who seemed like he might be the Voice of His Generation.

I thought that I would enjoy being the Voice of My Generation, so I kept a careful eye on Korine. I was closing in on 31.

*

The construction guy gets in my car and thanks me profusely. He's very charming and makes me feel good about myself for doing a good deed. He asks my name and introduces himself as "Robert."

The traffic is slow because of the construction. I say, "Shit, it probably would have been quicker for you to walk!"

"Yeah," he says. "Ha ha!"

The defroster blows dry hot air in our faces, and we pass the place where the workers' cars are parked.

I go, "Is it in that lot?"

"No, it's further down," he says.

*

1996 is the year that grunge wins! I was reading Denis Johnson's book *Jesus' Son*. I was reading *Fight Club* and Mary Gaitskill. I was not doing drugs or punching people or having sex on begrimed mattresses because I was a married dude with two toddler children, an adjunct instructor of composition and rhetoric whose father had just died, but I felt solidarity with the druggies and revolutionaries and all the sad of the world and one of the ways I expressed my kinship with other sufferers was by listening to "Natural One," by The Folk Implosion.

It's such a filthy song. It pushes your face into the mud. That's exactly what I wanted.

*

The construction worker says, "Dan? Do you think I could borrow some money? Just a couple of bucks. For gas."

Which is disappointing. I was hoping he wasn't a scammer.

"I don't have any cash," I say.

"There's an ATM at the corner," he says. "You could withdraw some."

"I don't think so," I say, and he shrugs agreeably.

*

My dad was 56 when he died. He was killed by a botched hernia operation. Peritonitis.

I drove to the airport, and I got on a plane and then I got off the plane and rented a car and drove three hours from Denver to Sidney, Nebraska and I don't think "Natural One" ever played on the radio. There were still local DJs then. In Cleveland, in Denver. The DJs had various personalities. There was patter as I drove.

*

The construction guy—at least he's wearing a construction guy outfit, IBEW and everything!—he says, "Turn here at this next right," and so I turn even though it's been a lot further than a couple of blocks. I'm wondering if I should ask him to get out, but don't want to be a jerk. An uneasy thought passes by.

Oh. Maybe he's not a construction guy?

*

"Natural One" doesn't actually appear in the movie *Kids*. It's only a part of the soundtrack.

The opening of the movie is ambient: two kids making out, and it's the most uncomfortable kissing to have to watch. It's really tactile. There are a lot of ugly smacking and slurping sounds. It's beautifully photographed but not beautiful. Isn't that what real life is like?

Most of the actors in the film were not, at the time, professionals. They were "discovered" by Clark and Korine, skateboarding in Washington Square Park, or hanging out on their front step, or modelling for *Sassy*. Some of them, like Chloe Sevigny, Leo Fitzpatrick, and Rosario Dawson, went on to significant acting careers.

There is something mesmerizing about these performances, a strange mix of the wooden and the feral, a kind of menacing, driven blankness. The song has the same tone. Even though "Natural One" never plays in the film, it's always playing, unheard, in the background.

*

"I guess I parked farther away than I thought," says the guy dressed as a construction worker, and I'm thinking of a way to politely but firmly drop him off at, like, a mini-mart or something.

"Listen," I say. "I really need to…"

He looks shocked and apologetic. "No, no, it's just up here a little ways more. Honest to God!"

*

There are certain songs—particularly in the world of alternative rock and rap—that place you in the perspective of the bad guy. They exude menace, and give you a slinky, wolfish feeling when you listen. "Natural One" is a song like that. You can picture yourself moving stealthily but confidently through the darkness, predatory and malevolent, and it feels really nice.

When I was little, I was so terrified of the dark that I couldn't go to sleep. Then my dad came up with a trick that helped me. "You don't have to be afraid of monsters," he said. "They're your friends."

*

I have no idea where I am. We've been driving for about fifteen minutes, and we're in a part of the city that I don't recognize. Over my shoulder, I can see the tip of the Cleveland downtown skyline. The guy who is dressed as a construction worker fiddles with my radio. Then, abruptly, he lifts his head and points. "Pull in here," he says.

He gestures toward an abandoned gas station. The windows of the building have been papered over, and the pumps under the awning have been removed, but there is still a large sign that advertises the price per gallon. The numbers have fallen off it.

I slow to a stop and he sits there in the passenger seat, considering. The air feels full of whatever he's thinking about.

"Okay, then," I say at last. "Well. Good luck. You take care."

But he doesn't move to open the side door and get out. He cocks his head and squints an eye at me and then at last chuckles.

"You're a nice guy, Dan," he says. "But someday you're going to end up on the back of a milk carton."

Then he gets out. Pulls his hood up. Starts walking away.

DO YOU WANT TO DIE?

Porochista Khakpour on "Possum Kingdom" by the Toadies

In the Nineties, I had a thing for dangerous white boys, but who didn't? It must have been the golden age of raw white boy pain and it was hard to escape it. The screeches and groans and growls and whines were on every radio station. Kurt Cobain, Elliott Smith, Scott Weiland—they all had it, and their pain still feels so alive to me that it's hard to remember they're gone. Sure, there were the girls too—Riot Grrrl culture was so important to me, but I found my ultimate shelter in it mainly because I was doing so much time with those angry, angsty white boys who refused to let you quit them.

While my Eighties were a glorious mess of hip hop and hair metal obsession, my Nineties were devoted to grunge with some dips into punk. There were the big popular bands, of course—Soundgarden, Alice in Chains, Pearl Jam, etc.—but there were also the one-hit wonders. They were often the most special to me because they mattered the least—what can I say, being a loser was cool in this era.

I couldn't tell you if The Toadies had only one hit, but "Possum Kingdom"—the only song of theirs I know—was one of my favorite songs of the era. You'd have to imagine me in 1995—seventeen, painfully skinny, mustached, perpetually in ripped jeans and some Gap V-neck T-shirt, with baby bangs and a bob, hoping for less Iranian-refugee-foreign as I was pining for the look of those androgynous white girls. I never made the cut—hair metal aesthetic recognized my fluffy hair and curves-in-training and brownness with more reverence, because exoticized sexualization was built into the scene's (misguided) politics of chivalry. The grunge guys weren't into that. You barely ever saw "hot girls" in their videos; they weren't from the world of grown adult women of all shapes and sizes. But they'd still claim them in their ballads and odes, always wronged by some woman or another. They were complicated, these dangerous white boys. Even with their skirts and nail polish, their dances with genderfluidity, you could never quite figure them out, and just maybe they knew this.

Like most music I came to love, I first heard "Possum Kingdom" on KROQ, LA's great alternative rock station. Immediately I thought there was something in the neo-thrash grunge aesthetic—the mid-tempo riffs, twangy guitar, and heavy bass—that reminded me of Pantera. I didn't know then that I was hearing what was also a Texas band in full Texas sound: groove metal essentially repackaged in grunge (I had just discovered Pantera and I'd play it on my Walkman at the lowest volume because I was certain if anything was that Satan's music that everyone was so upset about back then, this had to be it!).

And "Possum Kingdom" passed my first test: so damn natural to head-bang to.

Back then, they'd play the same hit song on the radio way too many times, and you could also request it—I'd call up and request songs every day—and so I got a good chance to study the thrillingly chilling lyrics of "Possum Kingdom" closely. "Make up your mind/decide to walk with me/ around the lake tonight," the song begins, with lead singer Vaden Todd Lewis commanding creepily like a sedated lunatic Roy Orbison (another beloved Texan of mine) after too many drugs and video games. Soon enough the song has broken down into its darker side, "I'm not gonna lie/I'll not be a gentleman/Behind the boathouse/I'll show you my dark secret." I was only a year or two into calling myself a feminist (or *feminazi*, just to irk my dad who had adopted the Rush-Limbaughism of that era)—and yet, I lived for these pretty-unfeminist-sounding darkest lines: "Give it up to me/do you wanna be/my angel?/ So help me Jesus." I mean, I was definitely a virgin—I'd only closed-lip-kissed a few guys during Spin the Bottle in my preteens—but I got it. I knew what the dark secret was, I knew what you were supposed to give up, I heard it loud and clear.

Or did I?! The song takes a turn, about four minutes in (yes, it's just over five minutes), and erupts into the full-scream refrain, "Do you wanna die?" Over and over. I remember waiting for my family to go to some outing I was too antisocial and angsty to go to—"I have a school project," I'd always automatically call to my parents when they'd knock on my door—and then I'd be myself: Walkman on, screaming at the top of my lungs into the roof, hoping the neighbors up above could hear, "DO YOU WANNA DIE?!"

It was the Nineties—you can bet I did. And oh, how I was the most dangerous white boy brown girl in all the land! After all, I never questioned what the hell that meant or why I was screaming it.

It took some time until I saw the video and, well, it was mostly like every video of that era. Skinny white guy with plaid shirt, shaved head (those boys always had long hair or no hair basically), angrily twitching and bobbing up down and around a microphone like it was *the* thing to manhandle if it weren't for some allegiance to something else. The tiny crowd they were performing for looked to be all men—in fact the only woman in the video was the bassist, Lisa Umbarger, the sort of tough tomboy I wanted badly to be, the one you could imagine had no trouble hanging with those angry white boys. But this is only one part of the video. Then there's these many disturbing scenes of a body bag being dragged out of a lake in one of those marshy yet dead, green and gray, defiantly gloomy Northwesternscapes of grunge. In the video, during the DO YOU WANNA DIE refrains, we have the climax: the body bag is hacked into pieces, just to reveal an ice sculpture underneath. That's it! No body, just some ice sculpture of a girl with eyelashes, and a drip of water, or perhaps a tear.

There was something disappointing in the violence of the song being just a tease, I remember feeling guiltily—file under one of my many *what is wrong with me* moments of that era. I also remember learning that Possum Kingdom Lake was a real lake near Fort Worth and that was disappointing to me too. And that there was a narrative that I learned about years later when I finally broke down and popped the song onto my iPod—that hit was part of another song I've never heard by The Toadies called "I Burn" about, well, setting people on fire to achieve some higher state. Somehow I felt let down knowing "Possum Kingdom" was a persona poem like the ones I read and loved in that era (especially Ai's). I just couldn't stand the fact that the song wasn't Satanic and that the band members were not homicidal and that the girl was just ice.

I wanted to understand my dangerous white boys as dangerous maybe.

I think a lot these days about the thrill of the dark side in the Nineties: how angst was almost a comfort, how anger was a swagger, how deep clinical depression made up the core of grunge counterculture. Evil was something to fetishize, the villains always our people. Maybe we didn't have real problems, maybe we didn't know about them. Maybe back then we slept thinking our world was still largely on the side of the good. Losers and slackers, what could we do? Everything was okay maybe, we thought. What could these dangerous white boys possibly do to that? Everything was okay. Maybe.

HOW ONE SEXY CAN PERPLEX ME: ME & "MR. VAIN"

Karyna McGlynn on "Mr. Vain" by Culture Beat

Whenever I hear "Mr. Vain," my soul takes on the sickly green effervescence of a Zima spiked with sour apple Jolly Ranchers. I can taste the cocaine residue along my gum line. I feel the ghosts of white thigh-highs like phantom limbs. Sure, the song is an adrenaline shot of youth, but I think I age a fortnight with each listen.

"Mr. Vain" was Culture Beat's first big U.S. hit. It was 1993. River Phoenix was still alive. So was Kurt Cobain. Bill Clinton had just become president. Donald Trump, in an interview that year, said: "I think certain women are more beautiful than others, to be perfectly honest. And it's fortunate I don't have to run for political office."

I was sixteen, living in Austin, Texas, still stinging from my failed audition for Richard Linklater's *Dazed & Confused*, which came out that year. I wasn't yet impressed by the on-screen debuts of Parker Posey, Ben Affleck, or Matthew McConaughey—because who the hell were they? I couldn't have imagined that twenty-two years later, McConaughey would give the commencement speech at my PhD graduation, using his "alright, alright, alright" as a life lesson.

But in 1993, I wasn't obsessed with McConaughey. I was more consumed by the fact that my erstwhile quasi-boyfriend, Mark, had landed a minor speaking role in *Dazed & Confused* as one of Wiley Wiggins' freshman friends. Whatever. I was a sophomore. I had my full-fledged driver's license, had defiantly quit Youth Group, and had discovered gay dance clubs.

I often went out in weird homemade outfits that literally disintegrated on the dance floor—like a halter top I made by gluing together half my stepdad's neckties, or a Warhol soup can skirt stitched from actual Campbell's soup can labels. Songs like "Mr. Vain" weren't just ubiquitous—they were lifeblood. I was burning the candle at both ends: sneaking out to clubs four or five nights a week, dancing and drugging with drag queens until 3 a.m. on weeknights, and getting up at 5:30 for drill team practice, followed by a full slate of AP classes.

Eurodance and Hi-NRG tracks by Crystal Waters, Haddaway, La Bouche, 2Unlimited, and Real McCoy were everywhere. They were my getting-ready music, my driving-downtown music. They pulsed through the clubs and laced the drugs. I dragged them drunkenly home down I-35, back to my bedroom where I'd peel off sweaty stockings, vinyl boots, and bustier tops—shedding fake ID, dollar bills, lip-gloss, a few Capri cigarettes—and crawl into bed only to *dream* these songs. It never quite felt like sleep. I'd shut my eyes and suddenly the alarm would go off—and not today's pleasant arpeggio of windchimes, but the brash electronic yawp of a clock radio playing those same songs: "Call him Mr. Raider, call him Mr. Wrong, call him insane…insane…insane!"

Out of bed. Back into yesterday's toast tights, geometric leotard, wind pants, Capezios. I had Mini Thins for breakfast. It sounds like cereal but was basically trucker speed. They sold it at the counters of every gas station. Did I mention I was bulimic? I was dizzy all the time. Most of the girls I knew were dizzy all the time. For lunch, we chewed cinnamon twists from Taco Bell and moaned theatrically before spitting them into paper cups.

Drill team is Serious Business in Texas high schools—but I didn't realize how *regional* that business was until much later. Not everyone grows up in the shadow of the Kilgore Rangerettes and Dallas Cowboy Cheerleaders, or under the glare of real-life *Friday Night Lights*. Not everyone hauls around the physical and social weight of Texas-sized homecoming mums.

For the uninitiated: homecoming mums are fake chrysanthemums covered in glitter glue and adorned with floor-length ribbons and lace in school colors. They dangle a whole menagerie of faux school spirit in the form of tiny teddy bears, tinsel, kazoos, cow bells, and plastic megaphones. Some mums light up, spin, or play little songs. You give them to your friends/boyfriends/girlfriends to wear during the week of the homecoming game, and the popular girls are simply dripping with them—jangling heavily, but triumphantly down the halls. Mums are only supposed to be *gifted*. Making your own is anathema. Nevertheless, I made about eighteen of my own over the years, and I still have glue gun scars on my hands to prove it.

A lot of outsiders confuse drill team with ROTC or flag corps, but it's more like the Rockettes competing in a hickish mash-up of *Battle Royale* and *So You Think You Can Dance*. Our team was called the Sundancers, and we lived in a state of constant competition—not just against other schools, but against one another, and against the limits of our own overtaxed bodies. We were always fighting: to get on and stay on the team, to be cast in routines, to rise through militaristic ranks, to join elite squads like "First Kick Line" or "Honor Jazz Line," to earn a coveted solo in our annual Escapade showcase, and to stay underweight for our monthly check-ins with the Director (who made us call her "Sir"). We lined up in a narrow hallway outside her office. She brought us in one at a time and closed the door. She asked us how we were doing academically and what our diets were like. If we had demerits, she asked about those. "Mm-hm," she'd say, pencil in mouth, dancing deftly around us, looping her measuring tape round our upper thighs and arms, our waists, wrists, neck. She scribbled everything down in a little green notebook.

We spent years leaping and high-kicking across the rubbery gym floor every weekday—6 a.m. to 8:30 a.m., 1 p.m. to 2:30 p.m., and 4:30 p.m. to 6 p.m.—plus pep rallies, football games, basketball games, rain or shine. Songs like "Mr. Vain" pulsed through it all. To make First Kick Line, we needed freakish endurance and the ability to literally *kick off* our own sequined cowboy hats (!) and to be able to do it with either leg, without bent knees, and without hunching forward. We also had to perform the "Texas Taint"—a move that involved executing a Texas-T jump before freefalling into the splits with a big Vaseline smile and a fun little bounce as our pussies hit the turf. We were a shiny, blue-eyeshadowed battalion of shin splints and self-starvation.

As long as I stayed on First Kick Line, I felt unassailable. So I *made sure* I stayed on: trucker speed, youth, the heartbeat of those manic Eurodance anthems. Songs as lyrically blurry and nutritionally void as those spat-out cinnamon twists. Songs that somehow kept me alive.

It was two days after my sixteenth birthday and I was late for practice. I tore through the wet street of the still-dark neighborhood in my seafoam green Ford Probe that looked like a shark. I jumped the curb and plowed into a mailbox, then a tree. The next thing I remember, a French man was yelling at me through a window. I didn't know where I was, why a French man was yelling at me, or what he was saying. Suddenly—because I had an A in French III—I understood: *Are you okay? Do you need help? What's your name?*

I waited for my mom and the tow truck in the French man's kitchen. His wife gave me an actual croissant that emerged warm and golden from her oven. I had destroyed these people's yard. Yet someone slid sliced strawberries onto my plate, then sliced bananas.

Around the same time, Culture Beat's founder, Torsten Fenslau, lost control of his Mercedes-Benz. It rolled several times and landed in a field. He wasn't wearing a seatbelt. He was thrown from the vehicle and killed. He was 29.

I didn't know any of this then. The internet barely existed. MTV was in Peak Grunge mode—definitely not reporting Eurodance traumas. I doubt I could've even told you who sang "Mr. Vain." They were a one-hit wonder from Germany with a terrible name: Culture Beat—an unimaginative Frankenstein stitched together from better bands like Culture Club and Bronski Beat.

Also, the song's lyrics are substantively, syntactically, and sexually perplexing (despite the song's claim that "one sexy can't perplex me"), featuring hilarious head-scratchers and contorted rhymes like:

> *Feel the presence of the aura of the man none to compare*
> *Loveless dying for a chance just to touch a hand or a moment to share*

And:

> *Just another fish to fit the worm on the hook of my line, yeah I keep many*
> *Females longing for a chance to win my heart with S-E-X and plenty*

The chorus, sung by the formidable Tania Evans—"I know what I want and I want it now. I want you, 'cause I'm Mr. Vain"—was equally confusing. I remember vaguely wondering, "Wait...*you're* Mr. Vain? Like, *you*, the woman singing this song??" This confusion is easily cleared up by a peek at the lyrics. Turns out, there's a barely noticeable "he'd say" dialogue tag that precedes the chorus, so the chorus is basically Evans quoting what Mr. Vain *would* say... like, if he were here? Where is he? Who *is* Mr. Vain??

The music video tries to explain. It features Evans and a solemn rapper named Jay Supreme in a baroque mansion party full of powdered dandies in puffy shirts and silver-vested ravers in oversized hats. Some of the women look downright Pre-Raphaelite. One dude wears a tricorn hat. Another, a doublet. Jay Supreme, it seems, is the titular and single-minded Mr. Vain in pursuit of Evans—following her up dark staircases and skulking after her down empty hallways. He wants nothing to do with the festivities down below—presumably because he "know[s] what [he] wants and [he] want[s] it now." Meanwhile, an epic arrangement of fruit has been served and the motley crew gorges on it. The whole dance party devolves into an orgy of juice.

But there's something more ominous going on. We keep cutting to these black and white shots of Jay Supreme sitting alone at a mirrored vanity. Easy symbolism there. Most of the time he looks like himself, but occasionally his reflection shows him in a state of decay, like his skin is starting to zombify and peel off. In any case, it's hard to tell exactly what's going on because the makeup job is bad—think middle school drama club's first experiment with spirit gum.

In the final shots—somewhere in the gothic upper floors of this pleasure palace—Tania Evans grabs a hand mirror and marches defiantly up to a glassy-eyed Supreme, confronting him with his own disintegrating reflection. Cut to a shot of a white rocking horse rocking eerily alone in a white room littered with leaves, as if it's being ridden by a Victorian ghost child.

And that's *it*. We're left wondering whether "Mr. Vain" is a Eurodance homage to the *Picture of Dorian Gray*. And whether this has anything to do with the fact that Torsten Fenslau was working at a club called Dorian Gray right up until his death. And whether it might be that easy to destroy the image of other vain sexual predators wandering myopically through their own pleasure palaces, thinking that "Girls all over the world...hope and pray and die for men like me...the male epitome."

Calling Ms. Tania Evans: 2025 needs you. Bring your magic mirror. I'll make you a homecoming mum. Or at least buy you a Zima. I hear they're coming back.

ON THE ESSAY:

When I wrote this essay in 2017, I was trying to reckon with the weird permanence of a throwaway pop song—and what it meant that I still carried it, and the self it soundtracked, inside me. I didn't know then that the world was about to tilt again, this time more violently. Or that the chorus—"I know what I want and I want it now"—would soon echo with new layers of dread and recognition.

Revisiting "Mr. Vain" now feels like opening a time capsule in platform boots. The glitter is still there, but so is the damage. And the music? Still catchy, still trash, still a little bit of life support.

Call it camp, call it cringe, call it canon. This song still perplexes me, but not as much as it used to.

DON'T TELL MY HEART:

Laura C. J. Owen on "Achy Breaky Heart" by Billy Ray Cyrus

In this brave new world, under the order of a President obsessed with winners and losers, it's comforting to know that there's one contest I'll always, always win: the who-has-the-worst-one game of *What was your first concert?*

While the rules are never laid out explicitly, this first-concert conversation always becomes a game of oneupmanship about whose first concert was more embarrassing. It depends on the generation, of course, but within my more-or-less-contemporaries a lot of boy bands are usually represented: New Kids on the Block, the Backstreet Boys.

Sometimes, it's an embarrassing admission baked into a humblebrag: *I went to an Eagles concert with my mom 'cause we didn't listen to anything recorded after 1980 in my house.* Translation: *I was uncool but not, like,* trendy.

I wait until everyone's finished chuckling at their younger selves, and then I win, number one with a mullet: my first concert was to see Billy Ray Cyrus.

"Achy Breaky Heart" is a great fucking song. It's catchy as hell, fueled by electric guitar, and shot through a wry melancholy, a broken-hearted persona ironically distancing themselves from their own heartbreak. Slow it down, make it more self-consciously ironic, give it a queer twist, and it's a Magnetic Fields song.

I just liked the stupid song. When I was ten years old, it seemed like a safe place to land: popular, recognizable, no SEX REFERENCES that I didn't understand that would later turn out to be minefields if brought up on the playground ("you *do* know what that means, don't you?").

"What music do you like?" is in and of itself a minefield of a question, and at around age ten I began to appreciate this. I could no longer slide along on the music my parents liked—it wasn't enough, anymore, to claim to like The Rolling Stones or The Beatles because my dad liked them: Adults would be impressed, sure, but other kids didn't give a shit. "The Beatles and The

Rolling Stones aren't really bands anyone cares about anymore," my fifth-grade teacher said. Even the adults were on to me.

So you had to say you liked something new, something popular, and something uncontroversial—no Madonna, for instance, because of SEX REFERENCES.

In 1993, in fifth grade, in Tucson, Arizona, "Achy Breaky Heart" fit the bill. That was what I liked. That was the song I liked. That would do. Everyone liked something, and so that was what I liked. Okay? I liked "Achy Breaky Heart." That was the song that I liked. Billy Ray Cyrus sang the song, so I liked him, too. Probably.

Yet it wasn't enough, I began to realize, to like "Achy Breaky Heart" because it was catchy and about self-pity (two qualities I'd later learn to identify as selling points in music for me). For starters, "Achy Breaky Heart" was on a cassette tape of other Billy Ray Cyrus songs and it became expected of me that if I liked Billy Ray Cyrus, that I own the cassette tape.

The cassette tape wasn't great. It was covered by Billy Ray, serious-faced in a denim jacket, head turned just enough so you can see that he doesn't actually have close-cropped hair—the long hair of a mullet peeks out over his shoulder, suggesting there might be a party in the back. But the album was no party. Aside from "Achy Breaky Heart," the only other okay song was "Some Gave All," a song that made use of the literary device of antimetabole to make a Statement about the Vietnam War. "Some gave All," sang Billy Ray, "but All gave Some."

Then there was a Billy Ray Cyrus television concert special on TV, which, when it was brought to my attention, I had to watch because now Billy Ray Cyrus was the music I liked. So I watched Billy Ray Cyrus' television special, live, on our living room TV, flanked by my parents. *They* didn't like the music, that was clear, but somehow it was important to them anyway, to let me watch it—because now I was my own person, with my own music, that I liked.

"I bet if Billy Ray Cyrus comes to town, you'll *make* us take you to see him," said my mom.

I once opened a fortune cookie that read "If it seems like the fates are aligned against you, they probably are." So it was that day, when mere moments after my mother spoke, an ad appeared on our TV, announcing Billy Ray Cyrus's tour stop to Tucson.

We were trapped. I didn't really want to see Billy Ray Cyrus in concert. My mom didn't really want to take me. I was sick of Billy Ray. I'd heard

"Achy Breaky Heart" a million fucking times at this point. I didn't give a shit about "Some Gave All" or Billy Ray's mullet or his concerts. But if you liked music, you liked concerts, right? That's what liking music meant, right?

So I pretended. And my mom was trapped because she'd *just* made a whole thing about it.

So it was just me and my mom that went to go see Billy Ray, just us two—because if you've been paying attention to context clues, you've realized that I didn't have any friends, and this was, I think, the real source of my parents' anxious anxiety around indulging my interest in Billy Ray Cyrus. They wanted to be reassured that I liked normal kid stuff and was being a normal kid and that's what you did with your normal kid, indulge their interest in music you didn't necessarily like because *oh, kids!*

But I didn't really have my own friends or my own interests, even though I pretended that I did. A neighbor kid next door was obsessed with New Kids on the Block, and I nodded and smiled and said, *Oh cool!* To her New Kids on the Block bed sheets. Clearly, that was what you did to be a normal kid: you liked a band, and so that meant you wanted to go to their concerts and sleep on their faces. It was a whole thing. So I needed to like a band, and there were no Billy Ray Cyrus bedsheets, and so my mom and I went to a Billy Ray Cyrus concert.

The video for "Achy Breaky Heart" gives you a good sense of what a Billy Ray Cryus concert was like. The main theme of the video is Billy Ray, pursued by terrifying women. Watching it now, I had a vivid flashback: oh god, the line dancing. They all did the line dancing.

My mom and I watched from our nosebleed seats, from which we could observe the bulk of the crowd. In addition to the line dancing, the whole concert was based around a singular narrative line: would Billy Ray Cyrus take his shirt off?

The crowd begged and pleaded. They yelled and howled. Briefly, they were distracted by line dancing. But it always came back to the same imperative: *the shirt, the shirt, take off your shirt!*

He obliged, eventually, although a thin wife-beater remained underneath, a clear cheat of the system, registered in the crowd's restive mutterings.

After the climatic shirt-taking-off moment, he solemnly sang "Some Gave All," and the crowd was shamed into briefly shutting up about the shirt situation.

The whole thing was orchestrated down to the moment. Years later, his daughter Miley Cyrus was both celebrated and shamed for her willingness to get skimpy publicly—memes emerged online of Billy Ray Cyrus, gazing down at her from above, wise-ancestor-style, as if to register his disapproval. To which I say: the Cyrus family does not owe its fame to *Miley* getting topless, and we would do well to remember that.

It became clear to me, up in that auditorium, ten years old, up way past my bedtime and longing for death, that liking music was complicated. It entailed albums, and album cover art, and concerts, and mullets, and stripteases, and earnest positions on the Vietnam War. You couldn't just like one song, one song that was impressively both catchy *and* sad, and so that's why you liked it. *What kind of music do you like?* Meant *Who are you as a person, economically, spiritually, sexually, and socially?* And I had no idea. Cleary I wasn't a line-dancing, woo-wooing, *take off your shiiiiiirrrrrrrt!*-type Billy Ray Cyrus fan, though I was jealous of them, because they were having a great time at this concert, while I was miserable. I had misjudged everything, everything, that liking a Billy Ray Cyrus song *meant*.

When people ask, *What kind of music do you like?* They are not just asking what you think is catchy, what you hum along to in the car, what you heard at age ten, what's *fun* to you, what your parents liked, that one song that was kinda good. It means *What are your values? What do you think beauty is? What economic and cultural groups do you identify with? What is your stance on mullets?* This is why *What music do you listen to?* Is such a dangerous question on first dates.

"What bands have you been listening to lately?" I overheard a man ask his date at a coffee shop recently.

"I haven't really been listening to any bands lately," she answered, deflecting the question in a wary way that was itself telling, like, *I'm spiritual but not religious* or *I'm just too busy to follow politics*.

Still, I felt some sympathy with her non-answer. We're not all ready to get so intimate on the first date. And there's no way *What bands have you been listening to?* Isn't a test, to which there are definite, definitively right and wrong answers. As it was in fifth grade, so it is forever.

What music do you like? Is so fraught because humans are contradictory creatures. This is captured pretty well within the lyrics of "Achy Breaky Heart" (originally titled "Don't Tell My Heart") in which different parts of the body are personified, each with their own distinct personality, with an unreliable umbrella narrator trying desperately to corral them all together:

Or you can tell my eyes
To watch out for my mind
It might be walking out on me today…

Parts of me can be trusted, the song suggests: my eyes, my lips, my arms, my legs. But then, some parts of me just can't bear to hear the truth: my brain, my ol' achy breaky heart. Most of me is okay: parts of me aren't. *Do I contradict myself?* Sings Billy Ray Cyrus: *I contradict myself. I am large, I contain multitudes. MULLET-itudes if you will.*

This kind of humor—personifying different parts of the body or mind—is a popular style online; it's easy to watch endless TikToks in which the creator acts out their Stomach, dismayed by the entrance of last night's Fast Food, or captions over two bugs fighting to the death: My last two brain cells. Pixar's *Inside Out* movies have made a billion dollars dramatizing the emotions inside one pre-teen girl's head (a key scene in *Inside Out 2* involves embarrassment over the music she likes—it's a boy band).

"Achy Breaky Heart" always made me think of the online Awkward Yeti cartoons in which the sensible-but-neurotic Brain is in constant odd-couple conflict with the whimsical, vulnerable Heart. *I love this song*, Heart instructs Brain, *play it until I hate music.*

Heart never envisions a world when it might get sick of a catchy number, where the passions of today quickly turn into the cringe of tomorrow. Don't tell Heart you'll one day get sick of that song, be embarrassed you ever went to that concert. To Heart, liking music isn't an identity contract, a social position, a commitment to an artist's touring schedule, or a reasoned presentation of self. It's the push of a pleasure button.

Billy Ray's career has taken some strange turns since "Achy Breaky Heart." He was in a David Lynch movie. This led to him playing a version of his real-life daughter's dad on a TV show. He was on a remix of country-rap song "Old Town Road," which was extremely popular with children. The Cyrus family has had some disturbing public drama. But what follows the "best known for…" in online biographies is still "Achy Breaky Heart."

I think that's glorious: "Achy Breaky Heart" now belongs to everyone and to no one. The beauty of fads and one-hit wonders is that they don't commit you to any musical philosophy, to any particular point of view, to any ride-or-die fandom.

"Achy Breaky Heart" is now freed from the 1993 baggage of being a Billy Ray Cyrus Fan, trademark (members must learn the line dance, buy the cassette, practice the sexual harassment). "Achy Breaky Heart" can now and always be what it is: a sad and surreal little number, as catchy as it is complicated, somehow corny *and* tongue-in-cheek, danceable and blue, full of twang and snap, a song I want to listen to until I hate music.

ON THE ESSAY:

I originally opened this essay about Billy Ray Cyrus' "Achy Breaky Heart" with a reference to the inauguration of President Trump, and, somehow, eight later, it remains still true: President Trump was just inaugurated. This time, Billy Ray Cyrus played at his inauguration! I wish I were making this up. Billy Ray's performance was considered a disaster, a shit-show acknowledged across the political spectrum. His son Trace begged him, in a moving public plea, to get help, a gesture Billy Ray apparently responded to by threatening his son with legal action. Everything is dumb!

One-hit wonders are the losers of the musical world, and I've always been the loser of March Xness, an essay-song contest in which my essays always go out in the first round, always staking an unpopular opinion: "Achy Breaky Heart" is a great song, I cry into the internet! No one ever agrees with me. Once again, I lose. But here I am, revising this essay about "Achy Breaky Heart." I got to make some more mullet puns! I am embarrassed to ache for Billy Ray, who does not want to be a loser, who does not feel he needs any help. Don't tell my heart what happened to Billy Ray, or rather, I suppose, what Billy Ray has done to himself. I'm just grateful to still be here, grateful to be asked to write about my little loser heart; I still like the stupid song.

MARCH SHREDNESS

YOU ARE THE HERO:

W. Todd Kaneko on "Crazy Nights" by Loudness

It's the first day of tenth grade in 1984. You're in traffic safety class, where you'll spend the next ten weeks watching driving simulation movies with a fake steering wheel on your desk. A long-haired dude sits down in front of you, a drummer who wants to start a band, and asks if you know anyone who plays bass guitar. You have never touched a musical instrument outside of that clarinet you spent a month pretending to play in fourth grade—you never practiced, so your mother took the clarinet back to the rental shop and said there would be no more music for you. But guys who are in bands have cool friends and go to parties. You have never been cool in your life, so you look that drummer square in the eye and nod your head. "Yeah," you hear yourself say. "I play bass."

*

You buy a cheap bass and some gear at a neighborhood garage sale. You're thankful the amplifier is so cheap that your new drummer friend can't hear you play over the sound of his drums because—well, you can't play. You spend the next year in your room learning songs by ear, playing along with Mötley Crüe, Black Sabbath, Iron Maiden and whatever other tapes you have shoplifted. You spend many hours practicing those songs over and over and over again.

Then one year later: Loudness, the first heavy metal band from Japan to score a major record deal in the United States releases their album *Thunder in the East*—you're captured by the opening guitar of "Crazy Nights," which is weirdly hollow and full at the same time, a powerful jam that washes over you like cold fire and 80-grit sandpaper. Akira Takasaki's guitar cranks out a riff that claws insidious at the air before the rest of the animal surges forth with drums and bass to swallow you whole.

And you would be swallowed gladly, if that was possible, because the chorus makes you a promise: "Rock and roll crazy nights / you are the hero, tonight." You have heard similar things from other songs. Mötley Crüe implores you to rise up and shout at the devil. Quiet Riot tells you to bang your head for your metal health. Scorpions offer to rock you like a hurricane, and you'll be all like *okay*, but the dudes in Loudness look like you. When singer Minoru Niihara says you can be the hero, it's like he knows your life story.

*

There are only a few Asian American kids at your high school. Most of your friends are white but they've never made you feel like you're less than them because of your race; however, you know you are different. You look in the mirror at the color of your skin and the shapes of your eyes. Notice the way other kids refuse to acknowledge you. Compare the hue of your hands against your homework in class, brown against the lightness of the paper—then jam your math test in your backpack instead of turning it in.

And there is no one who looks like you playing heavy metal, no one in any of those posters you have plastered on your bedroom walls. Bruce Dickinson, sweat-soaked and snarling under stage lights. Nikki Sixx posing sinister with his spidery hair and weird mascara. Randy Rhoads and Ozzy Osbourne, the saint of the six-string sling hoisted mid-guitar solo into the air by the Prince of Darkness. After Loudness, this heavy metal whiteness will go undisrupted until Living Colour hits in 1988, an African American band that your friends won't acknowledge as legitimate rock until they learn that their album *Vivid* was produced by Mick Jagger. You still hate that a nonwhite band has to be endorsed by a white rock star to be accepted as legit.

Whatever—in your love of all things heavy metal, you feel united with your fellow metalheads, banging skulls and stomping feet with hands raised to the sky in that devil-salute that proclaims your rebellion against everything your parents represent, against the principles your school upholds, against society because it's important to reject society before it rejects you.

*

After playing in a handful of garage bands in high school, you graduate to playing on the rock circuit in Seattle. When people find out you play in a band, they often look at you and say something like, *Asian bass player, huh? That's a good gimmick.* This makes you angrier than you'll ever admit, and you don't have an answer for them because all your metal heroes are white people—you'll feel like a gimmick until you learn in the late eighties that Soundgarden's bassist is Hiro Yamamoto, and while you won't ever meet him, knowing he is out there somehow feels reassuring.

In your mid-twenties, you have an opportunity to meet James Iha of Smashing Pumpkins. Your band opens for the Pumpkins on a weeknight in Seattle, but you are too filled with faux-punk rock anger and pride to knock on the door to their private backstage area and talk to him. Later, when you are much older and less proud, you think about how you wanted to ask Iha the same thing you wanted to ask Yamamoto: *what do you think about Loudness?*

And they would both have instinctively understood that you aren't trying to group the three of you into some weird Asian rock and roll trio. They would understand your real question: *is this all a gimmick?*

*

It was never lost on you, how Loudness named themselves after the stereo volume knob, that symbol of heavy metal's sway over its fans. In her book *Heavy Metal: The Music and its Culture*, Deena Weinstein defines heavy metal by its sonic dimension. She says "The essential sonic element in heavy metal is power, expressed as sheer volume. Loudness is meant to overwhelm, to sweep the listener into the sound, and then to lend the listener the sense of power that the sound provides" (23).

KISS sings "I Love It Loud." AC/DC sings "Rock and Roll Ain't Noise Pollution." Quiet Riot sings "Cum On Feel the Noize." And Loudness, by virtue of their name, just says *yes—we are all of that.* It's loudness that sweeps you up and inhabits your body. Other people dance in lines or squares to country twang or shake their hips to Motown, but heavy metal grabs your head and moves it back and forth in a frenzy. And when you strap a bass guitar over your shoulder and wear it slung low across the stage, you can't help but whip your head along with the audience in front of you, that sea of devil horns and middle fingers aimed at you in a vulgar rock and roll salute. It's this loudness—your loudness—that has brought you to heavy metal. Because when you were fifteen and alone in the suburbs, you enveloped yourself in loudness, hoping that one day you could harness this power too.

*

Your friends had so many explanations for the refrain in "Crazy Nights." M-Z-A is the name of a comet that passes close to the Earth making people go crazier than they do under a full moon. M-Z-A is a drug like XTC, but Asian. M-Z-A is a Japanese word for the devil. Minoru Niihara used to tell people M-Z-A stands for "My Zebra's Ass."

Nowadays, Niihara freely says that M-Z-A has no meaning. Like many foreign born rock vocalists in the '80s, Niihara sang phonetically and ended up singing a nonsense track for a pre-production demo of the song. They never came up with anything better for that section, so they just kept M-Z-A. Niihara says it's "like shouting 'hey hey hey' or 'wow wow wow' or whatever"—but these phrases have meaning in English. M-Z-A is just three syllables. Three punches thrown at the ceiling. Three beats for emphatic head banging. Fans of Loudness, fans of heavy metal, understand the meaning of M-Z-A, even if it has no meaning. Perhaps, you understand it because without meaning, that lyric "M-Z-A" is just pure loudness.

*

You don't speak Japanese, so Japanese metal songs from the '80s are stripped of lyrical content for you. Bands like Earthshaker and Bow Wow and Anthem clearly understood the genre as you understand it, the idiom of raspy guitars and high-pitched vocals, guitar solos that warble dissonant against the against the rest of the song, but propel it to greatness before driving the chorus into a trainwreck. Loudness's pre-American albums are no different. The chorus of the self-titled track that opens their first Japanese album *The Birthday Eve* goes, "We are the Loudness / come on now!" The rest of the song is in Japanese, so you have no idea what the words mean, but that doesn't matter because without lyrical meaning, you hear their music more clearly. It's obvious to you that before they came to America, Loudness's songs sounded like heavy metal in its purest form: aggression, power, and volume, all fine-tuned into a hook that earworms itself into your head for days. So once Loudness started writing songs in English, they should have been unstoppable, right? Right?

*

The video for "Crazy Nights" received relatively heavy play on MTV In 1985. When you watch that video now, you still can't help but notice how different the band looks from every other metal band that found mainstream success. They snarl and preen as well as the dudes in Mötley Crüe, but for all the makeup and Aqua Net, their faces are still markedly Asian. They are handsome, not in the way that Tommy Lee or Vince Neil are handsome because Loudness can't ever be that. You can't ever be that. And you wonder if this is how people saw your younger self (not handsome, just different), or even if it's how they see your middle-aged self. You moved away from the suburbs almost thirty years ago and now live in Michigan where you can go a week or more without seeing another face that looks like yours.

The other people In the video are also different. There Is a weird shot of a bunch of white kids headbanging, the fast-motion camera transposing them to a different time signature than everyone else in the video. Then those Japanese people in front of that glitzy Delish Curry billboard, those schoolchildren waving in a low-angle shot, that smiling woman in the kimono gesturing with delicate fists, those policemen brandishing their nightsticks, all of them chanting with the song: "M-Z-A! M-Z-A!" These are Japanese faces in place of the white faces that permeate most other heavy metal music videos. They are awkward, yet completely into the song. They are Japanese faces that could be your own face looking back at you.

*

When you load "Crazy Nights" on YouTube, the next song in the playlist is always David Lee Roth's "Yankee Rose." You hate this video for mocking so many stereotypes: the immigrant convenience store owner, the sassy black woman, the loud fat woman, and even the two party blondes (The lounge lizard says, "If there's a conversation, I don't have to be involved"). And then just before the song begins, Roth appears wearing face paint and wielding a spear. You get it. Sure, it's a joke, but you can't help but notice those people the video excludes from metal: black people, fat women, immigrants—it's painful to watch because you know you're in there somewhere too.

Meanwhile, in "Crazy Nights" Minoru Niihara sings, "we're gonna rock and roll you / come get on your feet," promising the loudness that is at the heart of heavy metal. And America, for the most part, says, "Okay! And hey—you're Japanese!"

*

In her book, Deena Weinstein describes the visual dimension of heavy metal, the ways that metal bands use logos, album covers and wardrobes to further convey their sonic messages. Judas Priest is hell bent for leather and chrome. Guns N' Roses is half gutter and half glam. Iron Maiden decks all their merch with Eddie, their undead mascot. Twisted Sister, Mötley Crüe, and Poison plaster their faces all in different shades of ghastly. It's no wonder you can't help but dig a band with a good gimmick.

Yet it's difficult for you to dig Loudness's visual dimension because under the usual heavy metal accoutrements (hairspray, leather), their gimmick becomes their racial markers: they are Japanese and play rock and roll. Loudness broadcasts this overtly with the sharp angles of their band logo and the rising sun image that appears on their T-shirts and album covers. Their stage costumes don't transform them in the way that most metal bands are normal young men and women who appear onstage as glamorous rock deities. On the contrary, for Loudness, the leather and spandex serve to standardize a band that looks otherwise non-standard for the genre. Loudness is Japanese, and in the midst of the otherwise homogeneous white landscape of American heavy metal in the '80s, that does the trick. Essentially, Loudness's gimmick is that they are simply Loudness. Pure loudness. Pure heavy metal. It's a gimmick you wish you could more fully embrace for yourself.

*

You have always played guitar by ear, but then you discovered YouTube guitar lessons. You found one channel where a dude teaches you how to play "1000 Eyes," "We Could Be Together," and so many of the songs on Loudness's first American album, including the intro to "Crazy Nights," which has never sounded right when you've tried to play it in your living room. The teacher has such reverence for Akira Takasaki, such admiration and respect for Takasaki's guitar prowess as he calls him the Japanese Eddie Van Halen and compares him to other metal guitar heroes. He shows you the secret to playing that opening lick of "Crazy Nights," the pinch harmonics on the power chords, muffling the strings with the thumb of your picking hand to create that strange overtone. He might be the best guitar teacher you've ever seen on the Internet.

And yet, in many of his Loudness lessons, he calls the band "Roudness" with a mock Japanese accent, even explaining to make sure you understand his joke: "I should pronounce it a-Roudness," he says. "Roudness. With an R." There is no malice behind it, probably, but it's ugly nonetheless. It hurts you, not in its political incorrectness or offensiveness, but in that this is how the world has been talking to you your whole life in one way or another. Heavy metal is beautiful and angry and awesome, yet it likes to remind you that you are always on the outside, even though you can bang your head like a motherfucker.

*

Ultimately, "Crazy Nights" comes down to everything you and every metalhead wants out of a song. You are still a child of the beast, rock and roller, lightning rider—or maybe you are still that Asian American teenager filled with disquiet and desire, with anxiety about where you belong in the world. If you will ever belong in the world. And heavy metal tells you that there is a story out there where you can be at the center of everything, a story in which you belong—not because you are the right kind of handsome or display the right kind of charm or go to the coolest parties, but because you feel loud. You are white or not white—it shouldn't have to matter. "Crazy Nights" says you are the hero, tonight. Sure, you might not be the hero tomorrow night, or ever again, for that matter.

But tonight, you're it

Tonight, that's enough to keep you going until tomorrow

ON THE ESSAY:

I love so many songs from this tournament. A teenage metalhead raised on Mötley Crüe's *Shout at the Devil* and Iron Maiden's *The Number of the Beast*, I lived through the '80s with the music of March Shredness in my headphones and blaring in my room until my mother couldn't take it anymore. However, no song on the list lives with me like "Crazy Nights" by Loudness. Once I got into writing, I found myself deeper in the feels than I had really expected. The song embodies so much of how it felt to live in the world back then—how it still feels to live in the world now, if I'm honest. I didn't write this one to win as much as I wrote it for me, so having this song win the tournament means a ton. MZA, y'all.

DOKKEN IN THE DREAM WORLD

Steven Church on "Dream Warriors" by Dokken

He had the gloves with the blades on and we were doing cocaine. So, he's using his blade fingers to serve up coke to everybody. With the knife hand thing. It was kind of surreal.
—George Lynch, former lead guitarist of Dokken

Mostly she just sits there quietly, occasionally sipping on a mug of coffee. She doesn't really talk all that much. My therapist also doesn't keep records or notes. Not unless I start telling her about my dreams. That's when she pulls out her notebook and pen and starts scribbling things down. I don't really know what she's writing but she clearly enjoys it. And I have to admit that there is something about the subconscious that *is* kind of fun to talk about and puzzle over.

My therapist practices what she calls "depth analysis," and has never "diagnosed" me or really given me what I'd call "advice." She just asks questions. A lot of questions. And I mostly ramble along in response, following whatever digression presents itself to me in the moment. Each session is a bit like its own essay and, at times, she seems a little lost or reluctant to admit that we've probably traveled the territory before. But when I talk about my dreams, about the 3 a.m. hauntings, the spinning brain, her face brightens, she sits up in her chair, talks more and offers me interpretations from a "clinical perspective," as she calls it. Our sessions become more lively and, inevitably, more bizarre.

There was the dream I'd had where my daughter and I visit a food court inside a huge renovated gas station or truck stop of some kind. I tried to order from one counter but couldn't understand the menu or anything the people were saying. Then we ran into my mom while waiting in a line for food at different restaurant, but we never actually ordered any food. And then there were the long picnic tables, rectangular and filled with people seated family-style around enormous deep-fried frogs, each one the size of a piglet, splayed out in the center like a sacrificial offering.

That one was pretty weird.

I've realized that I need a therapist now, as I've rounded the corner into midlife, to help me with things like generalized anxiety, bouts of depression, and deep-fried frogs—you know, to process the everyday strangeness of the subconscious—and I appreciate the help. But it *was* a little hard for me not to laugh when, during that session, she asked me if I have any conscious connection to frogs or to other amphibians, any memories I could tap into. It felt like a reach, like one of those leaps you take in a story, and nobody is sure where you're going to land. So I talked about the giant bullfrogs you can find in Kansas, some of them as big as a small dog, their throats bulging out like a birthday balloon when they made their deep-bass calls at dusk. Huge and grotesque, these frogs have been rumored to eat birds and fish and I can distinctly recall their croaking echoing off a pond like a chorus of ghostly didgeridoos.

My therapist kept nodding her head and taking notes as I talked about frogs.

"Have you ever eaten these frogs?" she asked, pen poised above the page.

"No," I said. "You don't eat these frogs."

I wished I could dredge up some deep trauma or serious weirdness connected to frogs, but there just wasn't much I could find, much she could use or make sense of that day. Maybe I was missing something. Maybe we'll find it together at some point, buried deep inside me or this essay. Instead I rambled on about bullfrogs for a while, talked about how, in my dream, at first the restaurant appeared to be a Kentucky Fried Chicken but, on the inside, was actually this food court of restaurants; and I talked about how my Grandpa Doc used to like to eat at the Kentucky Fried Chicken near his house.

"He liked the waitresses," I told her. "He'd just walk in, sit down, and wait for one of the 'waitresses' to come out from behind the counter and take his order."

It was kind of fun to retell these stories that my mom tells over-and-over, to re-forge these connections with memories in the therapy setting. And my therapist encourages my explorations, no matter how far they seem to pull us away from the initial thread. But none of these digressions gave us any real clarity on the original dream and the deep-fried frogs. The whole session was all so confusing and weird, but still oddly and essayistically enjoyable, as we tumbled over the oddity of my own brain.

This was not really the hard work of unpacking nightmares, which I mostly try to forget and rarely want to revisit in our therapy sessions, in part because what makes my nightmares terrifying is that they never seem to end, as if they're this continuous reality that exists independently of my agency, a *subconscious* reality that I'm forced to visit if the right collection of elements in my *conscious* life unlocks the door to its house of horrors. Let's just say it's a reality that I'm glad to know is just a dream and one I don't want to recreate in my waking life, not even in a "safe space" with a therapist to help. And I suppose one point we can take away from all of these digressive ramblings initially, one certainty, is that giant deep-fried frogs served family style in a renovated gas station food court isn't nearly as troubling or terrifying as entering a multi-leveled subconscious dream-state where you're being stalked and tortured by a vengeful, homicidal, child-molesting burn victim who wears a glove full of finger-knives.

The third Installment of *Nightmare on Elm Street, Part 3: Dream Warriors*, widely considered to be the second best in the *NOES* series (after the original), premiered on February 27, 1987, when I was just 15 years old, and marked the return to the horror franchise of Wes Craven, the writer and director of the first movie. It also featured Patricia Arquette in her first starring role and Freddy Krueger's return to haunting dominance of both the conscious and the subconscious world of contemporary American teen life in the 1980s.

The plot of *Nightmare on Elm Street, Part 3* is clearly tapping into a burgeoning cultural awareness at the time of teen mental health, addiction, suicide, and other forms of self-harm, combined with a focus on group therapy and lucid dreaming. In this iteration of the *Nightmare on Elm Street*, Freddy goes after the last living descendants of the parents who'd killed him years ago, each of whom happens to be confined to a behavioral health facility for a different reason. In this hospital, Dr. Nancy Thompson, an old foe of Freddy, is teaching the teens to control their dreams. Freddy, for his part, appears as some manifestation of their own demons and hunts down the teenagers, who fight back through group therapy and what might be called "collective lucid dreaming."

But more significantly, perhaps, the movie was also teased and promoted with a MTV music video tie-in featuring hair-metal legends Dokken and their hit single, "Dream Warriors," which was released later on their 1987 album, *Back for the Attack*.

The single was written specifically for the movie, and the accompanying music video became a kind of extended sneak-preview or "trailer." Released on February 10, 1987, roughly two weeks before the movie's premiere, the video offered us our first glimpse of the coming attraction while simultaneously displaying the awe-inspiring power of Dokken's brand of Rock.[1]

"Dream Warriors," reached as high as #22 on the Billboard charts and cemented itself in my consciousness when my best friend's six-year-old sister belted out the lyrics as she pummeled the underside of the hide-a-bed where I was sleeping one morning. Her feet pounded my back from below like Wild Mick Brown beats on the drums.

"Are you singing Dream Warriors," I asked her as I stirred from sleep, wondering if I was still stuck in some horrible nightmare.

"Duh," she said and kicked me in my right kidney.

Then she informed me that I was a dummy and a turdface and that she knew all the lyrics and she'd seen the video hundreds of times.

I told her I doubted she'd seen the video *hundreds* of times.

"That's impossible," I said. "It was just released."

Then she kicked me square in the spine.

To very briefly summarize the plot of the video, Patricia Arquette's character, Kristen Parker, who does double duty in both the video and the movie, is being stalked through a bizarre dream house by Freddy Krueger. There is drama and weirdness. But ultimately it is the undeniable and ineffable power of Dokken's song, "Dream Warriors," that defeats Freddy Krueger and saves the girl.

It's a classic Rock-Gods-Defeat-Evil-Demon story; and Dokken wasn't

---

[1] Of course it's entirely possible that Dokken's uniquely awe-inspiring brand of Rock, not to mention their rise and fall as a band, was fueled at least in part by a steady diet of the most '80s and most metal of mind-altering substances—cocaine. George Lynch talks here about the part it played in filming the music video:

> *They built this elaborate horror set for us for the video. And we were in the trailers, you know they had production trailers. We're supposed to be getting ready, and Freddy was all in make-up. So he looks like he looks in Nightmare on Elm Street. Which was kind of bizarre to be sitting there talking to a guy that looks like that, you know. He had the gloves with the blades on and we were doing coke (cocaine). So, he's using his blade fingers, to serve up coke to everybody. With the knife hand thing. It was kind of surreal. I mean hey, that is a long time ago, that is what everyone was doing back in the day sorry, but it's a true story.*

the first or the only band to wield the power of rock[2] against the forces of evil and emerge victorious, but they were one of the most commercially successful illustrations of this archetypal tale and a trendsetter for future multi-platform movie/music/video marketing tie-ins.

The song itself, "Dream Warriors," appears to be told from Kristen's point-of-view. The lyrics are mostly an expression of her desire not to dream anymore, to avoid the shadows that haunt her subconscious, combined with the somewhat vague hope that one day "maybe you'll be gone." Given the context of the movie, "you" here becomes Freddy Krueger, but also perhaps the speaker's "other" dream self, her vulnerable troubled self that is tormented by Freddy, and also, weirdly, the band, Dokken. Though she claims to be "standing in the night alone," she also admits to being there, "with the Dream Warriors," referring most likely to her friends and co-stars in the movie, who join her in fighting Freddy with their dream-state superpowers.

It is the music video, however, that truly affirms the band's unique ability to transcend the bonds of your everyday conscious life, enter your dreams and fight on your behalf against the forces of Evil, more specifically against a psychotic mass-murdering demon with a handful of finger-knives.

Show me another band that can do that.

Yeah, that's what I thought.

Anyway, in the film, Kristen is confined to a mental hospital with other troubled and disabled teens who've refused to sleep for fear of their nightmares and, specifically, of Freddy Krueger; but Kristen has the unique ability to pull other sleeping teens into her dreams and, once there, assembles them into a kind of (forgive me) Dream Team where everyone not only mysteriously regains their abilities (i.e. the wheelchair-bound boy can walk again) but also super powers that they use, largely unsuccessfully, to fight Freddy. Kristen, it turns out, is really good at gymnastics. And hysterical screaming.

The video's narrative is a bit difficult to follow and is conveyed through

---

[2] In the battle of Rock v. Evil, Rock basically has two devastating weapons at its disposal: 1) Sound warfare, wherein the evil demon/antagonist is subdued through sheer amplified volume of rock and typically responds by clutching their hands to their ears and wailing in pain. 2) Face melting, wherein #1 is wielded through the specific vehicle of the bombastic virtuosic screaming guitar solo that either literally melts the demon's face like the Nazis in *Raiders of the Lost Ark* (which, let's be honest, is a little redundant in the case of Freddy Krueger since he's already a crispy critter), or metaphorically "blows the mind" of the demon and tames him with the sublime hypnotic power of their Rock—sort of like rubbing the belly of an alligator until it falls asleep and you can make it into a wallet and a pair of boots.

a weird and clumsy pastiche of recycled scenes from the movie mashed together with new footage in a kind of hodge-podge story. Scenes of the band playing seem to be spliced together with film footage like one of those collages you made by cutting pictures out of teen magazines and gluing them to a piece of poster-board.

Our story begins with teenage Kristen up late, doing what so many troubled teens found themselves doing late at night in the '80s—building an elaborate Dokken-themed "Doll House."

She finishes her work and leaves the house on her desk before she curls up in bed. It is from this present action that we launch into the first dream-level. The video alternates between shots of Kristen sleeping and of Dokken playing, giving us close-ups of Don Dokken with his fountain of brown hair and George Lynch with his thick aura of black hair, his skull guitar, and those perpetual pouty lips. Jeff Pilson and Wild Mick Brown are there, too, driving the music. Lynch's acoustic-sounding guitar riffs rise slowly, quietly at first, and a pulsing drum beat from Brown provides some dramatic tension.

As we dive into the first verses of the song, Kristen wakes up in her dream standing outside a life-size version of the dollhouse (or is it a different house?) and, in the front yard, blurry children swing a jump-rope and sing songs. She approaches the porch and a little girl in a yellow dress rides a tricycle in circles, staring at her. It's all super creepy and any sane awake person would obviously hightail it in the opposite direction. But that's not how these things work.

Suddenly Freddy appears and beckons Kristen into the house, and like any good viewer of horror movies, some small part of you is screaming, "Don't go in the house, you idiot!!" But she doesn't listen. They never do in this genre.

Meanwhile, we jump to scenes of Dokken playing in some kind of underground industrial lair that looks vaguely familiar. Then we're back with Kristen and the Yellow Girl as the unlikely duo ventures down into Freddy's Boiler Room because, you know, that seems like a sensible thing to do. You don't ask why an old house has an industrial-sized boiler room or even if boiler rooms existed in the 1980s, or how the Yellow Girl got her trike down the stairs. You're not even sure why they're there until you hear the siren call of a gut-pounding drum solo. Kristen peers inside the boiler and you suddenly realize why the underground lair seemed so familiar.

Inside the boiler, behind a fence of human bones, a tiny Wild Mick

Brown drums for his life as the flames dance around him. Kristen screams, scoops up the Yellow Girl off her tricycle, and they dash upstairs.

But once there, she encounters Don Dokken and bassist Jeff Pilson, who begin stalking Kristen down a long hallway as she carries the Yellow Girl in her arms, a craft choice which seems designed mostly to provide up-shots of Dokken stomping down the hallway, lip-synching and making dramatic hand gestures[3] at Kristen while singing the lyrics. At this point, near the top of the list of things that are confusing here, Dokken seems to be the bad guy and kind of teaming up with Freddy to scare the crap out of a teenage girl.

That's when we get a shot of Freddy that seems to be recycled footage from the film, and Dokken actually chases our protagonist into Freddy's grasp. Kristen sees Freddy and then looks down at her arms, realizing she's no longer holding the Yellow Girl but instead a charred baby skeleton... yeah, I don't understand that part either, but it IS a dream, after all.

Kristen screams. Again. And then she wakes up...or does she?

It's at this point that we enter the second dream level.

Kristen falls back to sleep and the camera lingers for a second on the Dokken doll house as it lights up, glowing with artificial life. We are suddenly thrown into a dream within a dream as we jump to a scene of Kristen in the old house again. And inside the house, the lights flare and the carpet bulges and roils as something moves beneath it and up into the walls. Kristen screams. Plaster flies off the walls as the thing moves like a sea monster in shallow water. Here the music sort of competes with the film footage, as if the band is playing in another room in the house and all you have to do is open the right door to find them.

Kristen screams. Again. And you know Freddy is coming for her.

Then it's not Freddy Krueger but George Lynch, grinning like a school boy, who unexpectedly crashes through the wall[4] and launches into

[3] In the video, Don Dokken employs a couple of signature choreographed hand gestures: First, there's the index-finger-point-double-fist clutch-to-his-chest move that I call the "Rock Star Chin-up"; and then there's the index-finger-point-hand-opening beckoning move that I call the "Wizard's Spell" because it looks like Don is casting a spell or releasing a dove or something. Most of what he does with his hands is some variation on these two moves.

[4] I cede the floor here to the inimitable George Lynch who shall illuminate us on the filming of this scene:

> *I was so high (on cocaine) during the making of that video. I couldn't bust through the wall. There is a point in my guitar solo where I am supposed to come crashing through this wall. The wall is called a breakaway wall. It's made so that it looks like a real wall, but a fly could break through it, an infant could break through it. But I was so high and*

a face-melting[5] guitar solo that makes Kristen smile. Suddenly we're in a happy place, carried there by the *force of sentiment*. But just as quickly as it arrives, this lighter moment disappears.

Freddy reaches out from the wall, grabs George and pulls him into the wall, or into the weird industrial cave/temple/boiler room where we saw Wild Mick Brown playing earlier.

Kristen follows and finds herself in the cave/temple/boiler with Freddy, who has apparently unwittingly reunited the band. Foolish demon, what were you thinking? Dokken, no longer stalking Kristen through the house, are instead part of Team Kristen now. Mick Brown materializes mid-jam, perched above everyone on a cliff. Then an explosion! And the rest of the band appears. Like magic. Or some elaborate dreamy illusion. And we now realize that Freddy is the only bad guy in this story and Dokken are the *real* Dream Warriors, a united front of Rock fortified against Evil.[6]

This is the dramatic climax of the story, the final confrontation between Kristen, Dokken, and Freddy Krueger. As the band rocks and Don belts out the lyrics, they all stare menacingly at Freddy. Don does the Rock Star Chin-up move and Freddy cowers in the wash of their sonic power, covering his

---

so weak I couldn't even break through it. And they had to keep re-setting up the wall, and re-shooting it because I couldn't fucking get through it. They thought, 'Oh Lynch is buff, he'll get through that thing no problem' – which is why in the video, you watch it, I am laughing.

[5] The origins of the phrase "face melt" or "face melting" is of some debate. Many people connect the phrase to either LSD use or to *Raiders of the Lost Ark* and the melting Nazis. Most folks I've talked to seem to agree that the general character of "face melting" requires a virtuosic and bombastic guitar solo that has a profound emotional, mental, and physical effect on the listener. According to Research Guru Extraordinaire, Christian Exoo, the earliest use of the phrase is actually credited to the totally Shredworthy British essayist, William Hazlitt, who used it in "On Beauty" in the February 4, 1816 issue of *The Examiner*: "We sometimes see a face melting into beauty by the force of sentiment—an eye that, in its liquid mazes, for ever expanding and for ever retiring within itself, draws the soul after it, and tempts the rash beholder to his fate."

[6] I hesitate here to point out that, according to the rules and metaphysics of this reality, in order to enter Kristen's dream, Dokken would have to be pulled into her dream and, thus, they'd all have to be sleeping somewhere nearby, like in the same house. So I'm assuming that Kristen then lives in the House of Dokken, which I imagine must be some kind of home for wayward troubled children run by the band. Furthermore, it's interesting to note that, if we're sticking to the metaphysics of the movie reality, the band's transcendent power would be an alternate ability, a kind of superpower they have in the dream world but which is most likely missing in the waking world. In other words, the only place Dokken would be a truly great band, capable of defeating the forces of Evil, is in their collective dreams.

ears in pain. That's when Don throws out the Wizard's Spell hand move to defeat Freddy, who just sort of falls down, clearly cowed by the irrepressible power of Dokken's Rock, and it is over.

Kristen smiles, appearing happy, and for another brief moment, all seems right and good.

That's when we enter the third dream level and everything changes. Again.

We cut away from the scene, to a darkened room with a twin bed. Now we are in a dream within a dream within a dream, and things have turned. Suddenly, Freddy jolts up screaming and holding a yellow-haired doll. He throws the doll to the ground and says, "What a nightmare! Who were those guys?"

Damnit. We know who they were. Or we thought we did. They were Dokken, the Dream Warriors, mercenaries of the subconscious sent to ward off your demons and tame your tormentors with their Rock. They were more than just a dream to us! Weren't they? We believed, and now there's this whole other layer. Now we couldn't even be sure if Dokken actually existed or if they were some self-flagellating construct spawned from the tortured consciousness of Freddy Krueger. Were we now expected to believe that Freddy had a nightmare about a teenage girl having a dream wherein she has a dream in which the Heavy Metal Band, Dokken defeats Freddy. We're supposed to buy that his tortured subconscious created a world where he loses everything to the power of Rock. My therapist could have a field day with that one.

I like to imagine how I'd tell her about this video or even this essay.

"Well see," I'd say, "Freddy Krueger is like this horrifically burned child molester in a hipster sweater and a fedora and he wears this glove that has knives on all the fingers."

"Go on," my therapist would say.

"Yeah, and he's like this demon or ghost who haunts your subconscious but if he kills you in your dreams then you actually die."

"Hmmmmm," she says and her pen stops moving for a second. "So he can transcend the boundaries between the conscious and subconscious?"

"Yes!" I say, "And so can this metal band, Dokken! They enter the dream world, save the girl and defeat Freddy with their face-melting rock."

She looks up at me as if I'm speaking in tongues...which, of course, I am because that is sooooo metal.

I want to go on and on about the House of Dokken and how I like to imagine that the music video is an outtake from a short-lived '80s TV series featuring Dokken as a hair metal version of the A-Team, a group of misfits traveling in search of troubled teens, entering their dreams and saving them from real-life pain and suffering with nothing more than Rock and a whole lot of hair product.

"The A-Team?" she'd say, raising her eyebrows.

"Yeah," I'd say, "And Dokken would drive around in a sky blue van with some kind of airbrushed painting of a wizard, and it would be amazing."[7]

One of the mistakes student writers are often disabused of first is the tendency to rely on cliché tropes of storytelling and, in particular, what is often called the error of deus ex machina, which is Latin for "shitty Hollywood ending."

Ok, not really. What it *actually* means is "God from the machine," and

---

[7] This TV series, as amazing as it sounds, would never have lasted if only because of a long-running feud between Don Dokken and George Lynch, a feud which continues to this day, despite (or perhaps because of) several public reunions and subsequent break-ups. There are many stories, interviews, reports, gossip items, and rumors about this seemingly intractable conflict and, running through it all, an odd pervasive feeling of hope that somehow the band will reform and achieve a small measure of their previous glory. America loves its hair metal reunion story. But this one will likely never be told. The beginning of the end, by many accounts, was a fistfight in a limousine between Dokken and Lynch on April 13, 1988 in London, a little over a year after the release of "Dream Warriors," followed soon after by a disastrous Monsters of Rock tour where Don Dokken, self-medicating with Valium and booze, grew increasingly frustrated with his coked-up and hungover bandmates and their sloppy playing. In turn, his bandmates grew increasingly frustrated with Dokken's controlling rock diva ways. It didn't help that for the Monsters of Rock Tour the band was forced to follow the high-energy heavy metal storm that is Metallica, a band that seemed hell-bent on pounding the final nails into the coffin of power-ballad hair metal...with their faces. Don would admit later in an interview that, "After Metallica went out and played *Master of Puppets*, we sounded like the fucking Partridge Family." The stress was too much to take and Dokken the band just kind of imploded. The feud, by the way, continues in earnest even today, some 30 years later, with each adult man fairly regularly giving interviews in which they trash the other adult man. It's just sort of sad to see, honestly. It's possible, back in 1987-88, if given the right script writers and co-stars, they could've channeled all that angst and bitterness into some simmering on-screen tension that pushed them into the realm of superstardom. They could've had that van with the wizard and a lasting place in our hearts. It's also possible they would've killed each other. It's also true that this TV series exists entirely in my imagination. Maybe I *should* talk to my therapist about it.

is used now to refer to exactly the kind of storytelling move that the Dream Warriors video pulls at the very end—the surprise ending you never saw coming. If you've spent any time at all studying writing or thinking about how a story should end, you've encountered this mistake before. Perhaps you've even made it. We've probably all read these stories or seen these movies—long, intricately detailed, vividly rendered, filled with real-live action and suspense, risk and occasional rewards—only to find out at the end that "it was all a dream." Such endings are also what is known as a predictable "cliché," which is French for "shitty Hollywood ending." Basically, such endings are too easy, too deterministic without being believable.

It has often been said that the best ending to a story is both inevitable and unpredictable. The best ending is somehow predetermined, patterned, and designed by the existing logic and architecture of the story itself. The best ending is the only ending the story could have, *but* it is also an unpredictable ending that you can't quite see coming. It emerges from the fog of uncertainty into something resembling clarity without beating you over the head with it. It is not a twist, necessarily, or even a knot tying all the threads together but instead, perhaps, a kind of gathering of the threads, pulling them closer, and where you can feel the author's hand, ever so slightly, tugging on the braids of narrative. In other words, the best ending typically does not come when the author tells you that it was *all a dream*.

The heavy hand of *deus ex machina* forces an exterior logic or agency acting upon the narrative to "resolve" something or change the course of events and the reader's relationship to those events; and it typically feels forced, the stuff of amateur storytelling and easy answers, the kinds of endings we expect from ham-fisted Hollywood screenwriters and not from literature. However, these are also the kind of endings that, perhaps paradoxically, we often want precisely *because* of their authoritarian optimism. We want to believe in happy endings.

Isn't that why such endings are so commercially successful? We want to know that an omniscient narrative force is propelling us through a deterministic, predictable sort of journey that is tinged with the glow of facile resolution and happiness. We want to be immersed in a continuous dream and then be plucked from that dream and dusted off by the protective hand of an all-knowing storyteller who makes everything right. Perhaps we like to be fooled and forgiven. Is that so wrong?

Maybe it's also true that such popular narrative desires aren't also so antithetical to the more high-minded pursuits of literary work to which many of us reading these essays probably adhere. We can love schlocky '80s Hair Metal, cheesy videos, AND literature. Sometimes we can even love them for oddly similar reasons and risks. For example, I might offer up an essay I teach regularly, Bernard Cooper's "Capiche" from his book, *Maps to Anywhere*, wherein we as readers are seduced by the real, yet also surreal, scene of Cooper dining at an outdoor café in Venice when he is approached by a handsome man, Sandro. There are sensory details, action, dialogue, emotion and vivid imagery. Cooper's language is musical and luxuriant, patient but sharply evocative. He immerses you in the reality of the moment; and this essay is one of my favorites to teach in part because of how it breaks the rules. Near the end, as Cooper admits that everything he's just told you, everything you believe, is a lie, or at least a fabrication, an imagined reality inspired by the simple sound of a rooster crowing outside his window one morning as he woke up; he is basically saying, "It was all a dream."

It is true that this particular moment in the essay is often a fulcrum upon which the class opinion will tip one way or the other. Most people don't have a problem with it. Cooper somehow makes it work. But for other readers it feels like a bit of a betrayal, feels wrong and this feeling, at times, is fueled by some long-held fundamentalist ideas about what nonfiction can or should do. Some readers think he's broken the contract, they feel tricked, and thus find it hard to believe anything else he says in the book. Other readers, I think, get that same uneasy feeling you get when you feel the specter of *deus ex machina* haunting the page or the screen, when you not only see the magician's hand but also how the trick was performed. Cooper pulls the curtain back and reminds you of the artifice behind the realness of the dream; and I think this is deeply unsettling for some but, also, deeply satisfying for others.

I have a confession: that's all I ever wanted, and I think it's part of what I love about the nonfiction narrator at times and about the essay form. The essayist has that unique ability and responsibility to show their hand while still tricking you into believing in the continuous dream. The essayist must be both character on the page and in the scene, but also the narrator who is guiding you to see or think about the world in a different way, both magician and skeptical debunker. The essayist creates a narrative of thought, luring you into a unique reality while often also reminding you, sometimes more subtly than others, that it is a reality that has been constructed and crafted for your benefit. The essayist is the creator and critic of artifice. For me, Bernard Cooper's artful slight-of-hand in "Capiche," is exciting and seductive, like a warm embrace, as comfortable as any great ending, because it feels both inevitable and unpredictable, but also completely crafted and pre-determined. It enacts its own meaning as it becomes an essay about thought, associative logic, and the power of language to take us places, to transcend the present moment and offer us the gift of belief.

I'd like to tell you a story now about the origins of my appreciation for Dokken and how my Grandpa Doc died the same week that the "Dream Warriors" music video premiered in February 1987, and about how my brother and I drove with my cousin, Chip, to Springfield, Missouri in his Chevy Cutlass Supreme for a funeral held down the street from the Kentucky Fried Chicken where Doc used to eat every Friday because he liked the waitresses. I'd also tell you how, just outside of town, on a two-lane back road tented with trees, my cousin had let me drive and, a half-hour later, I'd stopped the car in terror and climbed out, waking the others.

"Oh, my God. Look at them!" my brother yelled as he sat up in his seat.

All around us, littering the blacktop, were the squished bodies of bullfrogs. More of them, the alive ones, croaked and hopped slow, pausing amidst the carnage, as I tried futilely to herd them off the road.

"They won't move," I yelled back at the car while my cousin, just rising from the back seat, barked at me to get back in or we'd be late for the funeral.

The frogs had come for the heat, for the warmth of the blacktop; and I'd like you to believe me when I tell you about the sun and the smell and the noise of cicadas thrumming in the brush. Or how, after the funeral, that night in the hotel room, as I tried to chase the image of the dead and doomed frogs out of my head, we ate Kentucky Fried Chicken from a bucket and watched Dokken's "Dream Warriors" video on MTV, talking about how excited we were to see the new *Nightmare on Elm Street* movie. I'd like to tell you this is the story I finally told my therapist that day when she asked about the deep-fried frogs.

But that would be too easy, too predictable. And none of it would be true.

Instead, as a way to end this essay, I'll confess that my Grandpa Doc's funeral was actually held a year later on April 4, 1988, about a week before Don Dokken and George Lynch had their infamous limousine fistfight en route to backing up AC/DC at Wembley Stadium. I'll admit that there were no frogs and no fried chicken, and that night after the services, back in our hotel room in Springfield, Missouri, we'd gathered around the television not to watch the "Dream Warriors" video, but to bear witness to our hometown basketball team, the underdog "Cinderella" Kansas Jayhawks, led by Danny Manning, defeat the Oklahoma Sooners for the NCAA National Championship. It was a thrilling, unforgettable, and unpredictable ending to three weeks of March Madness. It had, by all accounts, been a dream tournament for a team known forever as "Danny and the Miracles," which, come to think of it, sort of sounds like a band name.

ON THE ESSAY:

You're never supposed to pick a favorite child. You always say, "You're all my favorite." Because if you pick one, the rest of them could die in a bus crash tomorrow and that's all you'd have left. Just that one sad lonely creation. But this is my favorite essay. Or one of my favorites, I guess. I don't want to get carried away and be stuck with Dokken forever haunting my dreams because, you know, they can do that. But this essay was just fun to write and perhaps a good lesson or reminder for me of why I love essays in general. Many writers have said over the years that nonfiction writing is essentially telling a story of consciousness and I believe it was Solnit who said (when I was listening) that ideas are like characters; they grow and change and surprise you on the page. This happened for me with this essay. I was excited to tackle the '80s era in writing since it was so foundational to my identity in many ways, but the possibilities were nearly endless. So, I don't really know why I landed on the song, "Dream Warriors" except that it spoke to me as an underdog, a forgotten gem that had a natural overlap with two other foundational pop-culture institutions, MTV music videos and '80s horror movies. Truthfully, I wasn't even that big of a Dokken fan, leaning much more heavily toward bands like Cinderella, Ratt, Quiet Riot, AC/DC, or even Bon Jovi. But I remembered the video and knew it was something I wanted to revisit in part because it was trafficking in so many tropes of music video storytelling. And I remember my friend's six-year-old sister claiming to know all the lyrics. I didn't really expect the essay to drift into areas like dream analysis and meta-nonfiction, where I'm writing about nonfiction storytelling, but I also kind of enjoyed those surprise side-trips–so much so that similar digressions started to show up in other "Xness" essays that I've written since. I also kind of enjoyed the challenge here of making writing about dreams less like telling someone about that one acid trip you had in college and, instead, making the dreams central to the thinking on the page. I trust my intuitions, initially, letting myself roam and ramble for a while before I begin to try and craft it into something I could share. Much of the work was what I might call "stitching" or picking up threads and creating echoes so that there is at least some semblance of intention in the way a reader moves through the (admittedly long) essay. So, in the end, this big messy baby ends up being one of my all-time favorites; and I think it represents one of the things I love about the annual March Xness tournament. It's just fun, man. Even when it is deeply serious.

LUST FOR METAL:

Ryan Grandick on "Rock You to Hell" by Grim Reaper

Probably the best parts of the video for "Rock You to Hell" by Grim Reaper are the Toxic Avenger cameos. The rest of the video is a mixture of Grim Reaper playing in a vaguely post-apocalyptic women's prison and clips from a women in prison film co-financed by Troma named *Lust for Freedom*, also the name of a Grim Reaper track from the same record that features heavily in the film, though whether the movie inspired the song or the song inspired the movie's title is unclear. But the Toxic Avenger cameos serve to put the whole thing into context.

The vast majority of metal bands can be split into two groups: genuine or disingenuous. These are malleable definitions but they can be used, in retrospect, to understand why some metal movements succeed and some fail. Genuine in metal is not like genuine in punk or hip hop or pop or R&B, where the term represents a sort of realism. To be genuine in punk is to be plugged in, to be able to present a sort of authenticity. Metal doesn't work like that because metal is, at its core, about passion. Its version of ideology is different from other forms of ideology because metal isn't inherently political or even personal. It *can* be, of course. Lamb of God probably still hates Bush more than anyone on the planet. Metallica's best early tracks were largely leftist anti-war and anti-government songs. Judas Priest sought to position Rob Halford's, in retrospect, incredibly obvious queerness as an aggressive, rebellious act. Iron Maiden are *very* excited about these books about history that they've read.

But that type of ideological passion, in the grand scheme of things, is not all that different from Slayer's explorations of the nature of evil or Megadeth's apocalyptic nihilism or Cannibal Corpse's collection of books of rare diseases and medical photos. It's not that different from Amon Amarth's genuine love of weird Viking bullshit or Pantera's obsession with tough guy posturing. Even bands like Slipknot and White Zombie whose lyrics are goofy horseshit are so invested in creating a unique aesthetic, whether it is slippery ooze-filled bondage or pop art retro futurism that the aesthetic becomes the ideology. There's a vibration that you can feel off of truly genuine metal, a kind of unique keystone that either tunes into your own frequencies or doesn't but it can't be denied that it exists. This sort of genuineness, this passion, is why metal scares people who don't key into it. Because it's bad and it's good. It's why Nordic teenagers spent the '80s burning churches and murdering each other and getting really into white supremacy, but it's also why anti-authoritarian metal bands have been springing up in the Middle East protesting political and religious oppression. Metal aspires towards a kind of primal obsession and that has its positive and negative influences. But the key there is passion.

It's why Poison and Ratt and Warrant and White Lion and Staind and Limp Bizkit and about a thousand bad hair metal bands and a thousand bad '90s alt-rock bands and a thousand early '00s nu-metal bands died on the vine or couldn't survive the boom period. It's why most people forty years later know fucking Cinderella from a compilation of '80s power ballads. It's why nobody remembers hed(PE) outside of late-night stoned conversations about embarrassing bands they used to like. These bands could be doing *anything*. There's a palpable sense that Kip fucking Winger would be in a Color Me Badd tribute act if he hadn't gotten into a metal band first. Fred Durst always seemed like he'd rather be a rapper. There's a sort of shallow mockery with acts like this. Dudes who hung out on the sunset strip or grew up in the rich Detroit suburbs and will take the first opportunity to do literally anything else. Dudes whose whole ideology was that they wanted to bang underage girls and do bad '80s party drugs. And unlike Motley Crue or Guns N' Roses, whose records ring true because these are collections of the worst human beings on the planet writing about being the worst human beings on the planet, Poison just seem like a bunch of scam artists and hacks playing tourist in a drug and music scene where they were just good enough to find mainstream success but not good enough to be respected.

But then there's Troma and there's Grim Reaper and there's a weird, incredibly specific third category. These are genuine, yes, and they have that passion, but their passion is for the form itself. Grim Reaper is a metal band because Grim Reaper loves metal, but once they find themselves in position to say anything, they freeze up. They're the sort of person who's obsessed with the vase as opposed to what they can put into it. They are a metal band whose ideology is metal. Whose goal is to make metal. Whose belief systems are structured around metal. And they're passionate. But they are only passionate about context.

That's the story of Troma too. Within the exploitation world, they sort of exist between the hacks (Golan Globus, Canon) and the ideological auteurs (Roger Corman). Their movies positively ring with a love for the work they do, but the work they do is, more often than not, unwatchable. There's a purity in a group that just loves doing things for the sake of doing them, but when you're forced to question where you stand in relation to them, you find yourself looking for something to hold onto.

It's one of those weird existential artistic problems. Can we find worth in pure love of the form? Is a band like Grim Reaper creating metal for its own sake perhaps the most honest version of the genre, even if it isn't very good? Is that something to cling on to? Perhaps we have a tendency to appreciate music like this from a distance, with some layer of irony or superiority, because to make something, to create something just because we want to create it, is the most human shit imaginable.

"Rock You to Hell" isn't a very good song. It's got these overly simplistic "we are the youth and we hate being pushed around" lyrics performed by a group of men that have to be in their mid-thirties at least. The title and chorus are incomprehensible word salad. Troma movies tend to be almost impossible to get through. *Lust for Freedom* is a title more than a film. It's somehow both absolutely disgusting and poorly paced and boring. The video for "Rock You to Hell" is disjointed, with images seemingly taken directly from earlier Quiet Riot videos (lead singer Steve Grimmett begins the video in a padded room which is never referenced again), and shots from *Lust for Freedom* of women with machine guns and wrestling rings inserted almost without any sense of continuity or cohesiveness. The film stock changes regularly. Even the Toxic Avenger looks like shit.

But here's the thing. Lloyd Kaufman has produced and/or directed almost 200 films, shorts, and documentaries over the course of fifty years. All the lowest budget. All catering to the nichest of niche audiences. He's still making movies now. He'll probably find a way to make bad movies for the sake of making movies long after he's dead. Steve Grimmett lost his leg in January of 2017 and was on stage in July, playing shows with Steve Grimmett's Grim Reaper. Steve Grimmett will be playing "Rock You to Hell" in clubs in front of homemade banners and at nostalgic metal shows, propped up with a cane, standing on an artificial leg, looking a lot like Greg "The

Hammer" Valentine, just *nailing* "Rock You to Hell" until the day they put him in the ground.

That's what makes Steve Grimmett so compelling. Maybe the music you listen to isn't about you. Maybe our opinions have never mattered. Maybe there is a state above criticism and connection and ideology. Or maybe some people are just too stubborn and too passionate and too in love to die.

ON THE ESSAY:

In the seven years since this piece's publication, Steve Grimmett unfortunately passed, though he was planning a tour for 2022 when it happened, and Lloyd Kaufman directed the *Tempest* adaptation, *Shakespeare's Shitstorm*, which is also somehow about the opioid epidemic. It's hard to overstate how inspirational I find these men. Part of why I've always loved March Xness is that, in my better work at least, it gives me an opportunity to truly consider people I otherwise probably wouldn't. Why do people burdened by drive instead of genius, people more like me, keep forging ahead? For most of us, there is no good reason to make art other than an all-encompassing need to connect and create. There's no money, opportunities, or future in it. And if I told that to Kaufman or Grimmett, they'd probably rightfully laugh at me because what's any of that got to do with it?

Camellia-Berry Grass on "10,000 Lovers (in One)" by TNT

It sounds idyllic, right? You'd think, I don't know, merely one dozen lovers would suffice for paradise, but this is hair metal—despite all of the feminized aesthetics, it's a subgenre whose lyrics were so often meant for teenage boys and their hormonal fever dreams. Ten thousand lovers, then! Crucially though, the speaker of TNT's most notable song yearns for ten thousand lovers in one. A single woman whose passion is legion. Hyperbole is the way pubescence stretches desire, slows time, makes everything there is to want in life both almost within reach (one person to love!) but somehow so far away (who is as good as ten thousand people). But I wouldn't really know much about how young men desire beyond what they tried to force me into desiring.

*

This is an essay about how hair metal aesthetics affected me—a trans woman—as a teenager. But like my own coming out, I need to work myself up to it here. I grew up with the music and imagery of hair metal, and I knew enough then to see that the way these bands wore women's clothing & moved their bodies in such sexual ways was pointing to other possibilities than the normative rural masculinity that was already attempting to enlist me & subsume me. But the only vocabulary I had for this dynamic was that of drag. Biological essentialism constrains the imagination of children. Children in the Midwest aren't taught about expressing a genuine self or about not conforming to binary gender roles. They're taught that boys are one way & girls another. Anything that blurs the lines is just drag. Cross-dressing. Fake.

*

TNT is not like most hair metal bands. They began as a derivative power metal band only to take a turn towards pop, towards the feminine, on their third album, *Tell No Tales*. Lead vocalist Tony Harnell's voice is breathtaking in its range & control of pitch and vibrato. He reached Geoff Tate-level high register, but his band's music & look is far girlier, not so much Queensrÿche as just some queens.

The cover for *Tell No Tales* features the band draped in a lived-in femininity. Some bands of the era performed in bustiers and fishnets and heavy foundation and blush and eyeshadow and eyeliner and false lashes and setting powder and lip liner and lipstick—full drag. That's not quite TNT's look in 1987. Long, voluminous feathered hair? Yes, of course. But also oversized blazers worn with floral leggings or black denim cutoffs over black stockings or bohemian ruffled garments and Stevie Nicks headbands. But also light makeup. But also practical heels. By virtue of its exaggerated performativity, drag takes the feminine (or the masculine, in the case of drag kings) and *adorns* it onto bodies that are routinely & systemically denied access to it. Most hair metal bands revel in the adornment and performance (though the bodies of most hair metal band members are rarely denied access to anything, save perhaps each other's bodies). TNT's look by comparison is more relaxed, less theatrical, and thus more fully realized. Not so much dressing and draping oneself with femininity as much as simply *being* feminine. Less acting, more actualization. Which is overstating the case to be sure, but, well, perhaps the video will let you see what I mean.

*

There are two music videos for "10,000 Lovers." The original video is conventional for the genre: footage of the band is interspersed with a comic narrative about a teenage boy working a menial fast food job, daydreaming about sticking it to his boss & running away with a couple of hotties. The band enters the narrative's physical space at the end in order to perform some slapstick (in this case, serve an exploding chili dog to the grumpy boss figure). It was made to play on *Headbanger's Ball*. But I am much more taken with the band's more obscure, minimalist second attempt at a video.

Each of the members of TNT are standing on a tall black platform, their personal obelisks close enough to each other to perform as a band, but far enough apart to rule out touching each other. Between and around these lonely stages? Darkness. It'd be entirely black if not for the stage lights attached to lighting rigs aloft in the air. Gaps of nothing between each platform, a plummet into certain doom. The video contains just this single scene. The impact of such staging is immediate and obvious: the speaker of the song feels isolated by their desire.

*

This is the gut punch of "male socialization" for trans girls: that your entire adolescent and young adult life is about other people telling you what your desire "really" is and what your desire is supposed to be. For someone who is coercively seen as a boy, to desire the feminine is an act only understood by normative society in the capacity of sexual conquest, of healthy heterosexual drives. Desiring closeness to the feminine is seen as a misdirected form of those impulses. "You don't want to be a woman, no, you just love women so much that you want keep 'em all for yourself! You'd love to have 10,000 women around wouldn't you, you dog!" To be plain: if there's any substantive form of male socialization experienced by trans girls who are closeted, or who haven't quite figured out the extent of their gender nonconformity just yet, it's one that isn't felt or internalized or understood the same way as it is in cisgender, heterosexual boys. Normative boys are socialized to delight in sexual conquest. A young trans kid like me? I knew what was expected of me but instead of delighting in it I found it repulsive. And more to the point, I found that the gendered expectations just didn't understand *me*. I didn't want to take a lover, let alone a bunch of lovers. I wanted to be a lover, yearned for. I wanted to pursue my ambitions as a woman amongst my peers, not pursue women. I wanted to *be* feminine, not control the feminine.

*

Alone on his dark tower on the soundstage, wearing a velvet jacket and light foundation, Tony Harnell sings a song about desiring this woman who contains multitudes. This woman who is fractional by thousands and thousands but who is also whole. But I'd like you to think as best you can how a young trans girl might feel about these lyrics. Placing herself into the role of the speaker, how the song hits a young trans girl who is herself isolated by what she desires.

She desires herself. Not possession of herself but actualization of herself. She *is* the multitudinous woman. "Seems like I've known her a thousand years./ We've been together all through our lives." Great chasms & pitfalls between the boy she's seen as and the girl she is. To reconcile the two would be to fall, fall. But the two are always together, just out of reach. Stuck, alone, in a body and a social role that doesn't work, the spotlight of it all leaving your skin singed. "Just a kid on a highway to nowhere./ Wishin' for my girl to be real,/ she would satisfy my soul." The knowledge that your desire can save you but the suspicion that you could never make it real. That desire was first for you not about sexuality but about self-actualization. That you *are* the locus of your own desire, that you are what you desire, even, and that you are to blame for not attaining your desire.

*

Let me tell you how a single web search set me back a decade. I grew up in a modest rural town in Missouri. My mom was raising me & my little brother by herself on a teacher's salary. We were too poor to have a computer in our home until the early 2000s, when I was in high school. But without access to the internet, a rural trans kid like me is not going to have any information about what they are experiencing. There's no book in the library system that explains what gender dysphoria is. There's no resources at school on feminist thought. Sex education at a Midwest high school was the heteronormative cage that you'd expect. There's no community of queer elders in town. The only information on trans people is what you get from popular media. In the 1990s & early 2000s, all depictions of trans women on TV were ribald stereotypes of sex-crazed men in dresses getting into verbal spats on "Jerry Springer" and being asked about "the surgery." Trans women were the plot twist in movies; mostly they were killers, & even when they were depicted with femininity they were always outed as the fakes that the camera's lens (which is to say, society's normative gaze) saw them as, occasioning grossed-out faces & lots of pantomimed vomiting.

To be clear: trans womanhood is not that, and those bigoted depictions are harmful, have harmed me. Trans womanhood is a deep relational connection with other people oppressed under patriarchy. Trans womanhood is a relational desire to make shared culture and lifeways with women, as women. Trans womanhood is many things, but it is foremost that. And following that, it only makes sense that we have a desire to live our intimate relations as women.

The first time that I worked up the nerve to do a web search for "how do I know if I'm transgender?," I didn't find any info on gender dysphoria. I didn't find the narratives and experiences of trans people that would give me the vocabulary I desperately needed to make sense of myself. Instead, I got information on the scientific-sounding pathology called "autogynephilia"—love of one's self as a woman. This concept was theorized by sexologist Ray Blanchard, and developed further by J. Michael Bailey in his well-read pop science book, *The Man Who Would Be Queen*. That book came out in 2003, which was coincidentally the year I was 17 years old & realizing (not for the first time) that something felt very very wrong about my body & the expectations placed upon it. Which is to say that autogynephilia was in the news & was being championed as a legitimate diagnosis.

I will try to quickly break down Blanchard's absurd theory of autogynephilia. His thinking is that trans women are certainly not women. They are instead either 1) very homosexual men, who want to be with normative straight men so they feel more comfortable being seen as a woman in order to fit into that normativity, or 2) they are perverted heterosexual men who fetishize the idea of looking like or being seen as a woman. Seventeen-year-old me, inclined toward science, read all of this & deeply internalized it. I had to reckon with myself: was there sexual fantasy involved in my emotional experience? Well despite being largely asexual, then & now, the honest answer was yes. All the fantasies that I would masturbate to, all of the images of desire playing in my mind, involved me as a woman. Literally all of them. Instead of trying to find counterpoints to the autogynephilia theory, I just accepted that it was hard science & therefore correct (it is neither hard nor correct, as biologist Julia Serano demonstratively proves in her writing on the subject over the years). I didn't have the maturity or the resources then to realize that, duh, it's completely normal for women to think of themselves AS women when it comes to sex. Just open up any issue of *Cosmo*. I lacked the ability to see that I wasn't the perverted man that I was scared of being or growing into, but rather my subconscious was giving myself a glimpse of the freedom that I needed to pursue. Autogynephilia is bunk science that medical & psychological fields have come to nearly universally reject, and yet the cultural stigma of it still exists (and now in 2025, the theory has been revived among the anti-LGBTQ think tanks and podcast networks). I wouldn't let myself search for other information or experiences for many years. I wouldn't come out as transgender until ten years from that first web search.

*

So I did not want to consider the exploding chili dog. I did not want to think about the comic triviality of TNT's initial video for "10,000 Lovers" (though, even within its generic normativity, I spot a bit of eyeliner on our central figure of the all-American boy). I wanted to think about that stark second video, which captures for me the perilous feeling of being trans and mixed up by everyone else's confusion about trans people. To be told that I wasn't a woman at all, just a man who was turned on by the thought of being one & to see on TV the performative feminized aesthetic of hair metal musicians—whose lyrics and swagger scream masculinity in spite of the lace and the hairspray and the smoky eyes—reinforce that message & to have those same rock stars in drag be the closest thing to trans people I'd see for years. How [ ] alone I felt. Surrounded by great chasms, finally, ill-fatedly, I was told that I did not desire to be feminine. Really, says Blanchard and Bailey, I just wanted to possess the feminine to satisfy my urges. I was a sex pervert. A seventeen-year-old freak. A kid on a highway to nowhere. But through that pseudoscientific shame, part of me still knew the way life could be. Part of me still burned endlessly.

ON THE ESSAY:

While some see March Xness as a celebration of the music first & foremost, I approach it as a celebration of the essay. I've written four essays for March Xness and my favorite thing about it is taking a song that I have little personal connection to and letting my essaying take me wherever it takes me. I hadn't been familiar with TNT before picking this song from the Play-In Game possibilities for 2018's March Shredness, but that unfamiliarity allowed me to find the song's surprising depth. I did not know as I began to write that I'd be talking so directly about the sensitive reasons why I hated hair metal, that'd I'd write into such discomfort, but that's the magic of March Xness to me.

WRITE THE MARCH SHREDNESS ESSAY YOU WERE BORN TO WRITE IN TWO EASY STEPS

Jennifer Gravley on "18 and Life" by Skid Row

1. Harden your heart.

Hello, I am a cold person. My therapist assures me I did not come out of the womb this way, but I think back to childhood, not wanting the hugs and kisses of my elderly relatives, rejecting the advances of dogs who wanted to be petted. All my grandma's friends knew that my sister was the nice one.

When I was a kid, I thought I was scared of people, that I preferred being inside to outside, that I didn't like animals. But when I was a little older, I learned that what I was was cold. I remember the church matriarch, distant kin through some number of convolutions, tugging at my arm when yet again I didn't go up for prayer, trying to move me physically if she couldn't emotionally. Arms crossed, head down, I rooted myself to the bench. She told me my heart was cold. She told me I had a heart of ice.

For nearly three decades, "18 and Life" has chiseled through that iciness. There's a particular sadness to the songs of adolescence, a particular urgency to the nostalgia that has everything to do with those isolated moments that told us who we were, that turned us into who we are.

2. Watch the video.

I watch the video I didn't watch in 1989 in the mountains of North Georgia. I was fourteen years old and listened to the radio on an otherwise despised alarm clock. I had seen MTV only in the houses of friends whose families mine considered rich.

The men smoke in their cells, the opening chords setting the camera's pace. Black-polished nails on a guitar briefly overlay the bars, but soon Ricky comes into view, his arms folded. He looks blankly up and to the left, as if he might be in social studies, bored and angry. His brown mullet is the hairdo of every boy I knew and every older boy that I didn't. He is, even now, nondescript. The camera turns to him and overlays his face with that of Sebastian Bach.

1. Harden your heart.

I am good at this. I have hardened my heart before.

When I heard the word *cold*, the words *heart of ice*, I thought, *That's the way to do it.* For years I had been practicing, steeling myself against these good people who used my body against me. I couldn't instruct my face not to burn, my heart not to pound, my skin not to sweat. But I could tell my mind to ignore it. I could tell my heart not to feel it. I could separate myself—that trembling, snotting girl could not be me because I did not have feelings. I could bear being in that holy space.

2. Watch the video.

The video says: *You're looking at Ricky, but that's not who you are. You're on the outside. You're Sebastian Bach. Look how pretty you are! Your hair is blond and long and straight. Your voice—you have one!—it's the voice of an angel.*

1. Harden your heart.

One thing I didn't have the language for and wouldn't for years: I was, of course, already depressed. I spent my best weekends never changing out of my pajamas after Friday night. I cried. I knew had a lot more living to get through before I could get out.

2. Watch the video.

Before I know anything, I know that Ricky has a heart of stone. I watch his father push him through a door.

1. Harden your goddamn heart.

Does he feel anything?

2. Watch the video.

The video says: *He isn't good enough on the inside.*

The video says: *You've never gotten out in any meaningful way.*

1. Harden your heart.

I once made a mistake and tried not to be cold. After year after year of revival after revival, chance after chance to believe, to fall in line, to be who everyone who loved me thought I was born to become—I thought it might be easier to try.

I had no idea what to do, what I was supposed to do, what I was even supposed to be asking for. Everything was an uncomfortable charade. I didn't feel an urge that told me when to run up the aisle so I tried to gauge the social clues for an appropriate time—when the altar call had started but not gone on so long that it would end. I did the same when it was time to get up and leave the altar. There was never a moment when I had given up because I had never been trying. I had been waiting it out, head down on crossed arms on the mourner's bench. There wasn't anything I was struggling against except myself and the people around me.

2. Watch the video.

Sebastian Bach closes his eyes and wails. Ricky tears away part of a building. The video says: *Shake your beautiful blond hair*. The fatal shot is fired. The child blows a child away. The video says: *You're on stage! Shake your beautiful blond hair for the audience.*

1. Harden your heart.

I am cold. The video says: *Tell yourself.* I know fourteen-year-old me isn't some separate self contained within me, some iteration I can follow decision, circumstance, and lucky or unlucky break back to. Still, I am nostalgic for her. How can I not long for that feeling of shame and despair and defiance? Sometimes I want to attend church again, just for my heart crushing itself—

The video says: *Everyone who loved you as a child thinks that there's a hell and that it's for people like you.*

—but the only version of that past I can get back to is the version that lives in my hard cold heart, the version that is me, living.

2. Watch the video.

Ricky's further into his cell, his back against the wall. The door is open. My heart says: *He is telling himself he doesn't have feelings.*

Watch the video end with Sebastian Bach. Like all the best lovers, the video made me see myself as something I'm not, the instrument of emotion instead of the emotion itself, made me feel like I have control—the very best story—but I don't. I'm not Sebastian Bach. I'm in that cell, and so are you.

ON THE ESSAY:

It used to be true that I cried every time I heard "18 and Life," but watching the video 10,000 times for March Shredness eventually hardened my heart to Ricky's story enough that I no longer weep when it pops up in my playlist. As with slowly (very slowly, still) losing my aversion to violence on screen–this may not have made me into a better person. I didn't mind being the softie, the one who tears up or cringes or closes her eyes, probably because despite all evidence, I had always believed myself to be cold. Thanks to some psychiatric intervention, I know that that was a false narrative. I have walked out of the cell.

MARCH VLADNESS

ABSORB THIS AGONY:

Jim Ruland on "Marilyn, My Bitterness" by The Crüxshadows

You're 15 or 18 or 21 and it's your first time in the club.

It's dark and loud and a lot more crowded than you'd imagined.

You're with a friend or friends. No one goes to the club alone.

You stick close to one another until you find a spot where all this chaos won't seem so confusing.

You're not old enough to drink. Or you can't afford to. Or it's not really important to you. Or you got hammered in the parking lot before you came inside. Or the substance you got from a friend starts to kick in.

You're 15 or 18 or 21 and you came here to cut loose.

A new song comes on. Maybe you've never heard it before. Maybe you listen to it every day. But you've never heard anything this loud before.

Hearing isn't the right word for it. Hearing happens above the neck. This you can feel with your whole body, a feeling that sends you out onto the dance floor, into the loud shadows, and throbbing smoke, bodies seething all around you.

Do you remember that feeling?

Do you remember the first time you were summoned to the dance floor? Do you remember navigating that vertiginous strobing space? Do you remember the urgency of it all?

Of course you do.

You danced your fool ass off.

*

For me it happened at an all-ages Goth club.

I was a sailor in the Navy and my ship was stationed in San Diego. One of my shipmates had found a flyer for the club. Although he was 21, I was not. I wasn't old enough to get into bars and clubs, so he decided we should go.

This shipmate, let's call him Neal, turned me on to a lot of great music from Bauhaus to Bad Religion, Tones on Tail to T.S.O.L.

These were songs that I wouldn't have heard on the radio. Or, if they were on the radio, I wouldn't have known where to look for them.

I was a teenager from Virginia. My childhood was 1% Ramones, 1% Devo, way too much MTV, and 10,000 hours of classic rock.

I wasn't cool, not even close, but I was smart and hungry for new experiences. Neal obliged.

He made me tapes and gave me books. He encouraged me to buy a pair of Doc Martens and keep a journal.

We went to see Hunter S. Thompson and Love and Rockets and Crash Worship and Peter Murphy and Lords of the New Church. I took LSD for the first time and Neal made sure to play "Bela Lugosi's Dead" as the sun went down. (Years later, a friend in college described Daniel Ash's guitar work on that song as "frozen bat wings," which I think is a good description of the music, but even better when applied to the onset of an acid trip.)

I was 18 years old. I didn't know anything about anything. So when Neal said, "Let's go to the Goth club," we went to the Goth club.

"What's Goth?" I asked.

"Punk music you can dance to," Neal replied.

*

I wasn't much of a dancer—at least not anymore. For most of my childhood I was an Irish dancer. My brother, two sisters, and I took lessons every Monday night. In March, we performed all over northern Virginia, southern Maryland, and Washington D.C., and marched in the St. Patrick's Day Parade. During the summer, we competed in dance competitions up and down the eastern seaboard. The older of my two sisters was really good and nearly won a championship one year, but by then my brother and my other sister had dropped out. I was a decent dancer, good but not great, but it didn't translate into confidence in myself. This was way before *Riverdance*, and I had to wear a kilt, a fucking gold kilt, which I hated. Eventually the charm of being constantly teased and taunted wore off, and I hung up my dancing shoes for good.

*

Neal wore all black to the Goth club. He might have been wearing eyeliner but I was too weirded out to ask. I put on jeans, a sweater I'd picked up at Goodwill, and my new Docs. Neal's hair was too long for Navy regs. Mine was too short. I looked like a skinhead from the sticks. That was as Goth as I could get.

The club was packed with beautiful freaks. I felt awkward and nervous and super self-conscious, as I usually did around attractive women my own age. For the first time, I experienced the thrill of hearing "my" music at a gathering of strangers. I'd been to punk shows and rock concerts, but this felt different, more intimate.

Then it happened. The music overrode my inhibitions and I flung myself onto the dance floor. My crippling shyness slipped away. I stopped thinking about my body and its desirability or lack thereof. I ceased to be a person at all. I was just another body on the dance floor, a body orbiting other bodies that occasionally collided, each of us in our own cosmos, dancing, dancing, dancing by ourselves together.

*

This was years before "Marilyn, My Bitterness" by The Crüxshadows dominated Goth-industrial-fetish friendly dance clubs around the world.

Although "Marilyn, My Bitterness" came out in 1996 on the band's second album, *Telemetry of an Angel*, it blended in seamlessly with songs from at least a decade older.

Its surging synthesizers, relentless beats, melodramatic lyrics, and hushed vocals owe something to New Order's "True Faith." The Crüxshadows weren't a mega popular super group with major label backing, but a scrappy darkwave synth pop outfit out of Jacksonville, Florida, led by their charismatic frontman Rogue, who has kept the project going since 1992.

No consideration of The Crüxshadows is complete without discussing Rogue's white boy dreads. Shaved on the sides and gathered at the top like a carrot, the strands shoot up and fall forward. The effect is part Perry Farrell, part Sideshow Bob. If Iggy Pop moved to Florida in the '90s to become an ecstasy dealer, he'd probably look a lot like Rogue.

"Marilyn, My Bitterness" sounds both soothingly familiar and eerily timeless. From its riveting syncopation to its vaguely English-sounding intonations, it's one of those songs that seems as if it's always been in the playlist of your imagination, those drum machines endlessly churning in the back of your mind.

More than anything, "Marilyn, My Bitterness" is exceptionally danceable. The beat beckons, the beat beguiles. It's difficult to imagine listening to "Marilyn, My Bitterness" and not dancing.

*

Neal and I never went back to that Goth club, but the genie had been let out of the bottle. Neal and I started hanging out at dance clubs in Tijuana. The liquor was cheaper and danger lurked around every corner. We got to know a pair of Goth girls who thoroughly took advantage of us. We paid their way in and bought them drinks, but the only time they ever danced with us was when they were trying to get away from boys they were even less interested in than us.

We shipped out for a six-month cruise and sought out dance clubs all over the Western Pacific. Yokosuka, Hong Kong, Darwin. But the nights at California Jam on the infamous Magsaysay in Olongapo in the Philippine Islands were the best. The sound system was like nothing I'd never heard before and the cover band was truly spectacular. We combined San Miguel beer with Robitussin cough syrup and stayed up all night dancing at Cal Jam.

My Goth phase was short lived, but my affinity for the music endures. Bauhaus' "Bela Lugosi's Dead," the Cure's "A Forest," and Siouxsie and the Banshees' "Wheel on Fire" still do it for me. The Crüxshadows are still making new music, and while I'm hard-pressed to call it Goth, they are big in Germany and still have devoted fans.

I don't go to dance clubs anymore because I'm not 15 or 18 or 21, and before too long I'll be all of those numbers put together. I am an enthusiastic dancer at weddings, quinceañeras, and holiday parties. I don't drink or do drugs anymore, but my feet still know what to do when the beat becomes impossible to resist. They know what my heart knows and my brain sometimes manages to forget: all music is dance music.

ON THE ESSAY:

I always look forward to March Xness, but in 2019 life made other plans for me. My friend Jeremy Richman took his own life. This impossibly sad event was made even sadder by the fact that his daughter had been murdered at Sandy Hook Elementary on December 14, 2012. When the March Vladness competition got underway, I was at Jeremy's celebration of life ceremony in Newtown, Connecticut, feeling like I was under a dark cloud where history kept repeating.

Then an incredible thing happened. Crüxshadows' army of fans rallied around "Marilyn, My Bitterness" and the song kept winning, taking down all challengers. Each time my essay advanced, I'd show my wife the results on my phone and we'd laugh at how strange it all was. As improbable as it might seem, this tortured love song brought me a great deal of joy in a particularly dark time.

YOU WERE RUNNING OUT OF TIME:

Danielle Cadena Deulen and J. Max Stinson
on "Cities in Dust" by Siouxsie and the Banshees

It had been almost a year since I was last hospitalized when Kristin began making overtures. It might have been sooner, but I have always been frustratingly obtuse regarding signals from women. My natural gift for uncomprehending feminine attentions was certainly made worse by the torch I held for a girl I met in the hospital. Oh, Hospital Girl. I white-knuckle gripped that torch. Beyond the clear romance of meeting in a psychiatric ward and sharing some childhood trauma, Hospital Girl was a brunette, dark-eyed punk. Hardcore punk. Where I meekly suffered the aftereffects of my damage, she donned it like rusty spiked armor and threw her weaponized self at the world. In the radiance of her glorious self-destruction, all other girls were peripheral shades. So, I had to blink and look sideways at Kristin when she plopped down next to me on a smoke break between classes and asked me to prom.

"Prom? Us?" It was not just the "us" part, but I had never given prom serious thought. I was not able to properly imagine it.

She was visibly nervous and brought the bravado on heavy. Backhanding my chest, she said, "Hell yes, us. We would tear that place down, dude. We can storm the thing, and when we get bored just pull a fire alarm or something. Say yes."

"How much will it cost?" My weekend job at the car wash only covered gas, music purchases, and the exorbitant rates teens usually pay for their drugs and booze— which Kristin had been supplying me with during our lunchtime valium-and-vodka talks off campus. "And I have to buy a tux, too. Don't I?"

"I already bought the tickets."

"Really? Why?"

She shrugged. "I think it is going to be fun. I plan to blow the minds of some preppies. Come on. Say yes. And you rent a tux, not buy one. Be sure the cummerbund is red. I'm wearing a red sash. You don't have to go. I'm gonna go. If you don't want, it's no big deal. I want you to, but it's no big deal. I could sell the tickets."

I regarded her for the first time as a possible date. She was pretty. Slender and pale with reddish-brown hair and sharp features. She wore skinny black pants and a green flight jacket with her hair spiked up in all the right ways. She was a traditional punk, first and second wave. I was a mix of maudlin Brit synth pop and death rock. I wore red eyeliner to look especially unhealthy, a whip of blue hair across my face, and a general disposition of gloom. Kristin had an older sister who was living large in the LA scene and was a conduit for her tastes. For weeks, she'd been making me mixed tapes and loaned me VHS cassette collections of some damn obscure music videos. She introduced me to bands she enjoyed like Killing Joke and The Buzzcocks, and to music she rightly thought I would like, such as "Cities in Dust" by Siouxsie & the Banshees. In a nearby parking lot, we'd had the deep talks all teens think they are having while we ate our food, took our pills, and drank our booze. Looking away from me, waiting for an answer, her jaw tensed.

I held my hand up to calm her. "No-no. Sure. Yeah. It's gonna be cool. Let's do it."

She hugged me—a first—and headed back to campus. If she looked back, I didn't see it. I stared at my cigarette and tried to understand how I was feeling.

*

A banshee is a creature you hear before you die. Nasty hag, beautiful woman, singing soothsayer, omen embodied, she flies around the houses of the ill and injured, divining their deaths with a piercing wail. She screeched her hymns through famines and plagues. She wailed with storms, mudslides, floods, and when Mount Vesuvius opened its maw above the ancient city of Pompeii, it was her howl that erupted over the crowds of people just before they were covered in ash.

Nearly two millennia later, that banshee would return as Siouxsie Sioux, releasing "Cities in Dust" to a throng of devotees, making her own legend. An anachronistic diva. The future is the past:

Water was running children were running
You were running out of time
Under the mountain, a golden fountain
Were you praying at the Lares shrine?

The destruction of Pompeii has drawn imaginative attention from people in the Western world since it was unearthed in 1748. Some are drawn to the site because of its preservation of the past—the way it provides insight into everyday historical experience. Some are drawn to the narratives made from the remains of the human forms, some to how swiftly and completely an entire city was removed from existence—a terrible reminder of mortality. *You think you've got big plans, huh? Remember Pompeii.* But there's something about the particular moment in which Siouxsie composed the song that harmonized with the youth of America. The single came out in 1986, smack dab in the Age of Reagan—ultra-conservative, middle class, Christian values reigning everywhere, or at least the veneer of them—everything bleached and shining like the laminate kitchen counters in suburban homes.

There's a mocking tone of the opening verse that places itself in direct combat with domestic complacency: the children running, the fountain fashioned from gold, and the Lares Shrine—a guardian deity of the household often placed near the hearth—all gone in one fell swoop. Also, the "you." As in "you people." As in, *not me*—and maybe even *I ran away from your bullshit town a long time ago. You thought that trinket shrine would protect you...*

But oh your city lies in dust, my friend
Oh, oh your city lies in dust, my friend

But it gets worse. How, you might wonder, does it get worse than all the inhabitants of a city crushed or suffocated by molten rock and ash? Well, centuries later, the people who found their unmarked graves would be so fascinated by their horrible death that their bodies would be displayed, photographed, and fetishized, in the way capitalist values make nothing sacred:

We found you hiding we found you lying
Choking on the dirt and sand
Your former glories and all the stories
Dragged and washed with eager hands

*

The night was what it was. When this off-campus event called prom adhered to the school rules on smoking and everything else, I wanted to leave. I was a dud date, I am certain, preoccupied and angry. I can't remember if she even got a dance out of me. Most likely not. What a treat for Kristin.

"Let's go. Let's just take off and drink or something," I sulked. She was gracious enough to leave with me. I drove us to the elementary school near her house and parked where we drank more vodka and ate more valium. She put on a mixed tape she made for me, straddled my lap and kissed me so deeply that her braces began to draw blood. She whispered confessions of affection as we kissed and dry humped, the shadows from the street dimming her face, her spiky hair. When "Cities in Dust" came on, she climbed off me and sat in the passenger seat. She eased it down and pulled me over on top of her. Siouxsie Sioux sang out over the speakers:

Hot and burning in your nostrils
Pouring down your gaping mouth
Your molten bodies, blanket of cinders
Caught in the throes...

Kristin held my face, kissed my cheek. "I want this. I'm ready." She laid back, brought balled fists to her chest, and nodded. I realized she was a virgin.

I decided the night was over. I had had an unsettling amount of sex by the time I found myself in that car with Kristin, but I had never been a person's first, and had a big hang-up about that—maybe a hangover from my Southern Baptist past. I viewed the act of deflowering a person as evil. When the opportunity presented itself and she to me, I literally ran away. I rolled off Kristin and started the car.

"I should get you home."

"Wait—what? What did I do wrong?"

"Nothing. I just have to get home." I was starting to hyperventilate.

"Now?"

"Yes! Now!"

We were in front of her home in less than five mute minutes. The lights were on.

"I don't understand what just happened. What did I do wrong? Tell me. Can we leave before my parents see us? Let's go back, and you can tell me what I am supposed to do. I'll do it."

"This is me being weird. This just is not right. You are fine. I am the one messing up." This went on for a couple of minutes until her driveway light came on.

"Your parents are waiting. Go."

She climbed out of my car, bewildered. I was careful to not let the tires spin out as I pulled away.

*

Goth is a histrionic art. At the center of the arguments that deride the music, the style, is a distaste for the theatrics of it, which I suspect is disguised discomfort with the emotional, the feminine. The dramatic externalizing of pain through fashion and music might strike some as inauthentic—a commodifying of pain in the way capitalism commodifies everything. Pain, as Western people understand it, is a thing yoked to shame, and you don't parade shame around on stage, or sing about it. You let it burn in your pockets, on your tongue. You let it bury you. There's a distrust of anyone dangling their darkness out in front of them. *If she is drawing our attention to pain*—the civilized mind imagines—*she must not have actually lived it. She must be a liar, or deranged—hysterical.*

Hysterical. Histrionic. History. I think of the Salpêtrière asylum of Paris in the late 1800s—a place for vagabonds, epileptics, women with venereal diseases, old maids, malformed infants, and mad women. Upon arrival, they were whipped, interned once their "punishment certificate" was complete. The head physician of the hysterical wing was Jean-Martin Charcot, now known as the "Father of Neurology." Charcot was an exhaustive taxonomist of hysteria: drawings, photographs, observation, description, classification. He wanted to discover, claim, name, categorize—not *cure*. In his observational sessions, his patients were stripped naked and ordered to keep silent while he drew them, supposedly to focus on the symptoms that neurology might explain: motor paralyses, sensory losses, convulsions, and amnesia.

His theory was that hysteria was caused by lesions in the brain, so he waited patiently for his patients to die to crack open their skulls. He never found lesions, which frustrated him. Instead, he found how his philanthropic work with these women—*who would interact with such creatures except a saint?*—fascinated the people of high society. Hysterical symptoms were so tawdry, consumable: hypersexuality, imaginative to the point of hallucination, self-centered, emotionally demonstrative, given to violent outbursts when their stories of sexual trauma weren't taken as true. The lurid fascination for these frail and dangerous women reached fever pitch in Charcot's Tuesday lectures, attended by scientists and aristocracy alike, during which he paraded his patients under hypnosis, triggering them into outbursts, flashbacks or seizures—all for the approval of his audience.

What made these women so strange and wicked that they were kept away from the innocent public? First, they were haunted by their painful pasts, and second, they displayed their pain. In other words, *good girls don't cry*—and neither did good boys, for that matter. For decades, men suffering from similar symptoms, usually upon returning from combat, were treated for "male hysteria," then "shell shock" and now PTSD—a disorder that forms when a person has difficulty recovering from the shock of a traumatic event. By the time I was sent to the psychiatric hospital, the men and women suffering from what would have historically been called hysteria were treated together, in talking circles, with coffee and cigarettes. We could listen to each other's stories without flinching, recognize that we freaks could form a community.

I'm not saying that it's genius—the Goth way of making drama of darkness. In fact, most of the bands that have been credited with creating or riding the first wave of that post-punk genre give sour lips to the label "goth." Siouxsie despises being labeled "goth." So does Andrew Eldritch of Sisters of Mercy and Robert Smith of The Cure, and Peter Murphy of Bau-fucking-haus. They are fine with their fans calling themselves that, but they will also explain how their commercial successes cannot be laid on the shoulders of such a relatively small, niche purchasing group. This upsets the fans. Siouxsie does not care. This delights the fans.

More than that, goth fans delight in the genre's particular mode of defamiliarization. Siouxsie showed a different aesthetic, a different perspective. At the black heart of goth style is the subversion of the conventional ideals that trap people in a façade of nice. The theatricality surrounding pain, darkness, and death, is meant as a mirror to the theatricality of The Normal. To make art of confusion, the clothes remix contemporary and historical fashions in an anachronistic display. The make-up is clown-like both in image and aim—to unsettle its audience with exaggerated features, distorted mouths. You can see why this might appeal to those who felt sequestered inside the standardization of 1980s America: the madwomen, the queer boys, the totally reasonably depressed. Instead of hiding their strange backstage to protect the sensibilities of convention, they could strut out into the spotlight, into a bright applause. That is, we could applaud each other. As pearl-clutching mundanes and normies looked on with their own theatrics of outrage and unself-reflective chagrin, we could fall in love with each other's pain.

*

It was before midnight, and I got on the freeway to kill some hours before sunrise. I headed to Hospital Girl's neighborhood and drank coffee at a beachside doughnut shop, romantically dour until the sun came up. It was a school day, and I planned to catch Hospital Girl on the way out her front door. She would understand me leaving the prom. She would approve of me leaving Kristin without ruining her. She would, perhaps, be cool with my confessions of affection for her. I pulled up in front of her house and, too eager, I walked to the door and gently knocked.

Her mother answered. She looked burned out, exhausted, confused:

"What's going on? What's happened?"

"Is she here? I just left a prom date to come here. I need to tell her something. That I'm ready?"

"For what? What is happening? Have you heard from her?"

I learned Hospital Girl had run away months ago. Her mother had no idea where she was or if she was alive. I'd been harboring these feelings, this story about us, and she had a completely different story. I wasn't even in her story. I stood there stupidly for a moment, said something like "sorry to bother you, sorry she's missing" and went back to my car.

When I returned to school, I gave Kristin a wide berth and minimal acknowledgement. Everyone assumed we had sex, and I corrected them, I thought, to save her honor—though deep down I knew I was just covering up my freak out. Of course, I said nothing about how she was game or how I derailed the evening. Instead, I told people that her braces shredded my mouth and that there was no way I was going to have sex with her. I thought this was respectful of her and the best way. Kristin and I never really spoke to one another again. I dropped out of high school not long after.

Three decades later, and still that moment in my car with Kristin rising up every time I hear "Cities in Dust," I decided to find her on social media sites to see if I might apologize and explain my behavior. I didn't expect that it would change her life—maybe she didn't think of me at all—but I still felt like I owed her that much. It didn't take long for me to find friends of friends, who told me that she was dead.

She went in her sleep in her early twenties. They offered no further details and I didn't push.

*

A banshee cannot harm or heal. She can only give warning. Her voice points into a time, into a place, into a moment of illness, injury, disaster. She's not a reaper, but a seer, not a teacher, but a singer—her song a sonic crash between the living and the dead. In her arrival, she strikes the living into fearful contemplation. In her departure, she leaves contrails of questions.

ON THE ESSAY:

When March Xness announced its Goth theme that year, it was immediately clear that Max and I should collaborate on this essay. We'd been following March Xness tourneys in previous years with great enthusiasm, voting on our favorites and finding ourselves in long convos about aesthetics—exploring the origins of what we liked and didn't like, and how closely tied our tastes were to early-life influences. Those were rich conversations. We hoped our different perspectives on this song might give the essay interesting rhetorical texture. Max engaged the song with his personal story of a Goth-style teenage romance—clearly the heart of this work, complete with a necessary intensity. I came at it as a novice observer of the genre, but with all the analytical chops I could muster. Our hope was to build something we (and maybe Siouxsie?) could be proud of: a heart-brain meld of an essay.

For more discussion of "Cities in Dust" by our contestants, dial up episode 31 of their podcast, *Lit from the Basement.*

COME TO KILL YOUR SONS

Melissa Faliveno on "Exterminating Angel" by The Creatures

"Women just aren't good musicians," my cousin said. I was fifteen and she was sixteen. She, like me, lived in rural Wisconsin, our towns an hour apart, with populations of only a couple thousand, most of whom were working-class, God-fearing, and white, who drove pickup trucks with their radios tuned to the country station.

She, like me, was a black sheep. But while I tried to fit in, she reveled in her outsider status. She cut off all her hair, dyed it bright orange, and wore it in short gelled spikes. She painted her nails black and drew charcoal circles around her eyes, wore oversized black t-shirts with band names spattered across them like blood, and maybe, if memory serves, a wallet chain—those signifiers, sacred and profane, that we of the small-town sectors could only obtain from a weekend trip to Hot Topic. It was a look that, back then, and in that place, was sometimes referred to as *goth*. But usually it was just called *freak*.

It was a look I coveted. I experimented with eyeliner, chokers, and, briefly—one of many missteps in a failed understanding of goth aesthetics—JNCOs, but never went much further. I admired my cousin for having the courage and irreverence I lacked, for so fully embracing her weird. And so I followed her like a disciple into other obsessions, taking in the words she taught me: that women didn't make good music, that men were better actors and athletes and writers. And for a while, I believed them.

*

Here it comes again
Taste of jagged glass and rusty can

*

The Creatures started out as a side project. Formed in 1981 by Siouxsie Sioux and Budgie, the Banshees' drummer and Siouxsie's future husband, the drums-and-voice duo released their first full-length album, *Feast*, in 1983, the year I was born, followed by *Boomerang* in 1989. Their third record, *Anima Animus*, was released ten years later, when the Banshees had disbanded and Siouxsie and Budgie, by then married, had turned full-time to the Creatures.

Inspired by Carl Jung's concept of the woman inside the man, the man inside the woman, *Anima Animus* came out in 1999. I was sixteen. I didn't know who the Creatures were then. I didn't know who Siouxsie and the Banshees were, either. I had no concept of punk, post-punk, or goth. What I did know was goth's nebulous '90s progeny: industrial music.

My cousin got me into it. We played *The Downward Spiral* on repeat. We watched MTV2 in her basement, marveling at Marilyn Manson's vampiric sexlessness, both horrified and strangely turned on. As was the regrettable fate of so many teenagers at the turn of the century, we would soon move on to the angry-man titans of nu-metal: Limp Bizkit, Linkin Park, and Korn. But for a while, our truest love was a band called Orgy. Posters on my bedroom walls of androgynous boys like Leonardo DiCaprio and Jonathan Taylor Thomas were replaced by Jay Gordon's industrial quintet of androgynous men, with their asymmetrical haircuts, glam outfits, black eyeliner and lipstick and painted nails. Alone in my bedroom, I ran my finger along Jay's jawline and memorized the angles of his spiky black hair as he screamed New Order's "Blue Monday" through the speakers of my Sony three-disc stereo. It's embarrassing now, my infatuation with a neo-goth dude like Jay Gordon, who, when I look back, seemed so clearly to be playing with an idea he didn't really own, pretending to be something he wasn't. But back then, where my cousin and I came from, landlocked and limited to Top 40, before either of our households had an internet connection, bands like Orgy were about as transgressive as it got. And with his penciled-in eyebrows and high cheekbones, a swivel in his hips as he sang, Jay's was one of the queerest bodies I'd ever seen—even if he wasn't actually queer at all—long before I had the word for it. Like my cousin, he existed in a strange new space between the masculine and feminine, and I looked to them both with wonder: this boyish girl and this girlish boy, so far beyond the frontiers of normal, each possessing something I wanted and wanted to be.

*

Plumes of dirt
Caress a urine-coloured sun
Swarms of angels
Come to kill your sons

*

There are two ways, linguistically, to interpret the words "Exterminating Angel." First, as entity: The Angel Who Exterminates. (See also: the Angel of Death.) Second, as action: Killing the Angel. In both cases, in my mind, the Angel is a woman.

*

In her essay "Professions for Women," originally delivered as a talk to the Women's Service League in 1931, Virginia Woolf wrote, now famously, of killing the Angel in the House. From a poem of the same name by Victorian poet Coventry Patmore, the "Angel in the House" is the ideal woman: a devoted housewife who cooks and cleans and cares, whose purpose is to serve her husband and children and God. She is passive and powerless. She is charming, graceful, and meek; she is submissive, sympathetic, and self-sacrificing—"If there was chicken," Woolf writes, "she took the leg; if there was a draught she sat in it." She is pious and pure. And she should not dwell in the mind, but rather the heart; for it is the heart, and not the mind, that makes a woman.

It is the woman writer's job, Woolf says, to kill the Angel in the House.

"I should need to do battle with a certain phantom," she writes, "and the phantom was a woman. It was she who used to come between me and my paper when I was writing.... It was she who bothered me and wasted my time and so tormented me that at last I killed her."

"My excuse," she says, "if I were to be had up in a court of law, would be that I acted in self-defence. Had I not killed her she would have killed me. She would have plucked the heart out of my writing."

*

Oh those strange Argonauts
Digging again in your pit
Cover them in menstrual stream

*

The Exterminating Angel has made several appearances throughout history and across cultures. It's the name of a 1962 Mexican surrealist film (and a 2015 opera adaptation) and the nickname of a sixteenth-century French pirate. The Society of the Exterminating Angel, meanwhile, was a nineteenth-century Spanish Catholic group that killed liberals. But the iteration I like best, and the one I would wager inspired the Creatures' song, is a 1981 painting by Salvador Dalí.

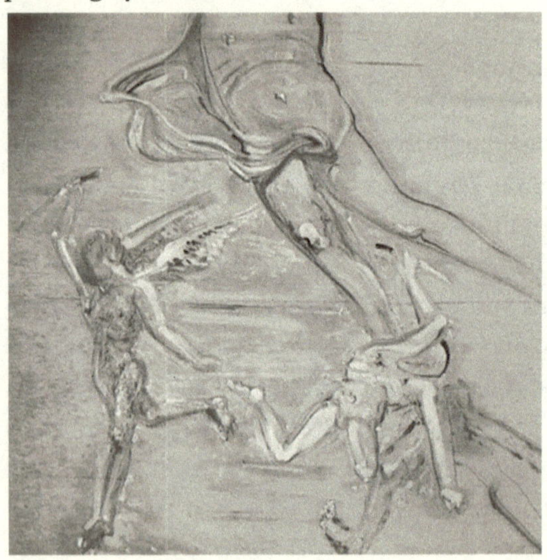

In the painting "The Exterminating Angels," an angel bearing a dagger appears to pour forth from the body of a woman—more specifically, from a gaping hole below her belly, in a stream of something that could be interpreted as menstrual blood. The angel, who has no discernable sex organs, raises one arm high above its head, clutching a dagger. Its wings fan out behind it. It is both flying and lunging forward—toward what? Another kill? We don't know for sure. What we do know is that in the angel's wake, beneath the woman from which it was borne, two bodies—one that might also be an angel (for it too clutches a dagger)—fall dead.

*

Cover them in black gold
Ripping through your menstrual stream

*

Anima Animus is a weird album. It's industrial, kind of, marked by lots of synths, metallic-sounding drums, and plenty of studio fuckery. But it's also techno, electronica, alternative, and art rock. It's a little bit of everything, and a thing entirely its own, uncategorizable and genre-defying. Whatever it is, it's dark, atmospheric, strange, and erotic. It's disturbing. It's haunting. It's undeniably goth.

The labels rejected it. It wasn't commercial enough, they said; it was too avant-garde. So Siouxsie and Budgie made it themselves, and created their own label, Sioux Records, on which to release it. The *Times* of London gave it eight out of ten stars, calling it "entrancing, hypnotic, and inventive." The *Sunday Times* wrote, "Siouxsie's voice has lost none of its ability to seduce and unsettle." They called the eighth track, "Exterminating Angel," "exquisitely menacing."

"Exterminating Angel" is a song about the end of the world. More specifically, it's about destruction borne from the body of a woman who's sick of it all. Let me be even more specific: it's about a giant, man-killing, universe-ending menstrual stream, and the woman who unleashes it. The apocalypse progresses like so: There have been some dudes—let's call them Argonauts—digging around in our hero's pit for far too long. And so, like the women of Lemnos, she decides to kill them. All of them. First: *Plumes of dirt caress a urine-colored sun.* And then: *Swarms of angels come to kill your sons.* These angels of death march forth in the great tide of our woman-god's menses, washing away the sun and the stars, covering the land in death and darkness. Oh, and there are also locusts: hordes of them, blotting out the sun, *raining down, rain on everyone.* It's chaos. It's biblical. It's a big, bloody war, and this omnipotent woman in the sky is waging it. After all the sons are dead, she's going after the bourgeoisie (*poor little rich thing, poor little misunderstood*), and then I'm pretty sure she's going to kill the angels, too. Because why not? She's had it, and this is Armageddon. And we the listeners: We're left somewhere out in space, in the aftermath. *There are just black holes where the stars would be watching. Just black holes where the stars should have been.*

Show me a song more goth than that.

*

Out of sync, out of phase
Out of sight, out of spite

*

I first heard Siouxsie in the early 2000s at a dance club in Madison, Wisconsin, called the Inferno. Like so many businesses in the Midwest, the Inferno was housed in a strip mall—a squat gray building next to a liquor store, a body shop, and a Chinese restaurant, out near the airport and the Oscar Mayer plant, where for many years my father worked. The club is closed now, but back then it was a haven for misfits in a city that afforded few such spaces. The Inferno hosted a monthly theme night called Leather & Lace, at which goth music and the city's kink scene converged. For a few years, in my early twenties, I went nearly every month. And it was on one of those nights—the Cure and Joy Division and the Banshees droning through the speakers, pale bodies disaffectedly bopping in the strobe lights, their fishnetted skin flashing in the dark—that I first *saw* Siouxsie, too. Projected onto a screen, which in my memory is massive, videos in black and white: Siouxsie in a black shirt and tie, Siouxsie in fishnets and leather. Siouxsie in short, spiky black hair, Siouxsie in painted black lips and eyes. She was everything I had once loved about Jay Gordon but so much better. Jay but so much more real. Jay but a woman, wearing a look that—like the cover song that made him famous—he had only co-opted, and she had created.

As for me, I wore PVC pants and knee-high leather boots. I wore a studded leather belt, a dog collar and cuffs, a tie or a corset or a zip-front Dickies dress, depending on the day. I cut off all my hair and wore it in short black spikes. For a while I ran in the kink scene, got tied up and tortured, and did plenty of the torturing too. I was top and bottom; I was neither and both. I went to houses in the suburbs, where men called Sir built dungeons in their basements and hosted BDSM play parties that doubled as potlucks—casseroles and crudité after a round of flogging; Midwestern bodies, mottled and red, eating Swedish meatballs from paper plates. And though I eventually decided the scene wasn't for me, I discovered some important things there, tied to a crucifix in a suburban dungeon, dancing at the Inferno, falling in love with women and men. I asked questions of myself—about my body, about desire—that I'd never been able to ask.

*

Siouxsie Sioux was born Susan Janet Ballion in 1957 and raised in a suburb of southeast London. Her mother was a secretary and her father was an alcoholic bacteriologist who extracted venom from snakes. Siouxsie was sexually assaulted when she was nine, an event that inspired both her music and her rejection of suburbia. She dropped out of school at seventeen, left home, and joined the punk scene in London, following the Sex Pistols and cultivating what would become her signature style: a combination of punk, glam, and bondage fashion—stopping in at least a few times to Vivienne Westwood and Malcolm McLaren's SEX boutique—her look would become an iconic part of the goth aesthetic.

"I was isolated," she said in a 2005 interview. "So I invented my own world, my own reality. The only way I could deal with how to survive was to get some strong armor."

Susan became Siouxsie and formed the Banshees in 1976. Two years later, the band's first single, "Hong Kong Garden," reached No. 7 on the U.K. charts. "Siouxsie just appeared fully made, fully in control, utterly confident," said Viv Albertine of the Slits. An impressive number of musicians have named Siouxsie an influence, from PJ Harvey, Shirley Manson, Sinéad O'Connor, and Santigold to Kim Deal, Ana Matronic, and Rachel Goswell of Slowdive (whose name derives from a Banshees song). Siouxsie Sioux was not just a pioneer of goth; she also changed the landscape for women in music.

Siouxsie Sioux is also a problem. Her name is an appropriation of a tribe of people to which she doesn't belong, a name she gave herself nonetheless. Much of Siouxsie's music has taken inspiration from other cultures, and the Creatures were no different: the drums on their final studio album, *Hái!*, were recorded in Japan. *Boomerang* was recorded in Andalusia, Spain, and incorporates brass arrangements popular to the region. The band's first album, *Feast*, was recorded in Hawaii, and features the Lamalani Hula Academy Hawaiian Chanters on several tracks. Like such influences, Siouxsie has said her name was chosen in honor of a people she respected. And some of her music, like "Hong Kong Garden," was written as a critical response to the racism she encountered in the punk scene. But even so, I can't help but see a white artist taking what isn't hers.

And how do we reckon with this? Where do we go with white, feminist icons who have given us something radical, something revolutionary, who have raged against various systems of power but who also take part in similar systems? The question is not a new one, but I still don't know the answer. What I know is that, much like loving misogynistic music as a teenage girl—singing along to the Prodigy's "Smack My Bitch Up" or Eminem's

Marshall Mathers LP—as a listener, I'm complicit. I know that, even though the song was written as a send-up of skinheads, I can't hear "Hong Kong Garden" without feeling uncomfortable. I also know that when I first saw that image of Siouxsie—dark, androgynous, slicing open the idea of femininity, of *woman*—something inside me broke open. That when I first heard her sing, projected on that screen in that dark Midwestern club, I was transfixed. I know that each time I write Siouxsie's name on this page, I feel the problem in my fingers. I know that when I listen to "Exterminating Angel," I hold that problem in my fist as I throw it into the air.

*

I grew up in a family that appreciated music. I was raised on oldies, folk, and classic rock, and my parents started taking me to shows when I was young. Of all the musicians we saw together, and there were many, none of them were women.

I grew up playing music, too. I sang in the church choir and was trained on the trumpet. I played classical and jazz, and I was good. I summoned solos more than I played them, the silver instrument an extension of my body. I was the grace of Handel, the guts of an improv over twelve-bar blues. I was the growl of a rolled tongue in the mouthpiece, the wail of a high D.

The trumpet was an instrument for boys. All the musicians we studied were men, and most girls in my school bands played the flute, clarinet, violin—those instruments more tender, softer and sweet. The trumpet was loud, and left no room for prettiness. You had to get ugly to play it. I knew this as I tightened my lips, as my face turned red, as the tendons in my neck stretched and the veins in my temples bulged. But I didn't care. All that mattered was the music.

It could have been the same for guitar. I got my first acoustic when I was eighteen, my first electric ten years later. Both guitars were gifts. I never bought one for myself, I think now, because I never thought I deserved one. I was living in New York when I got the electric, a pretty sunburst Ibanez given to me as a birthday present by my boyfriend, and by then had played in a handful of soul bands as a backup singer and horn player. Two of those bands were fronted by women vocalists, but it was always men who played the music. When I started playing guitar in a band of my own, I was terrified. Even though I'd been playing on my own for a decade, in a rock scene made almost entirely of men, I felt like a fraud. On stages throughout the city, I stood with my guitar in my hands and felt like an accessory to the real musicians—the men—who played lead guitar and bass and drums on those stages with me. Somewhere, in the darkest recesses of my brain (probably in the same corner of shame where I stored the Limp Bizkit phase) I heard my cousin's words. When I gripped the neck of my guitar, my fingers shook.

*

Piss on it
I'm sick of it
Enough is enough
I wanna fuck it up

*

I'm still learning to forgive myself for the misogyny of my youth. I'm still learning to destroy it. When girls are raised in working-class towns, where men are defined by their jobs and women are defined mostly as mother and wife; when most of what girls have access to is the work of men, the music and movies and writing of men; when they are told that men make the money, that men are the heroes; they internalize it. In places like where I grew up—even when one is raised in an open-minded family, where girls are told they can do anything they want—sexism is as indoctrinated as the importance of hard work and independence, as a love of guns and land, as the worship of God and beer and football and hamburger casserole. It builds up in us like a fortress, and it takes a very long time to dismantle.

"She died hard," Woolf writes of the Angel in her House. "Her fictitious nature was of great assistance to her. It is far harder to kill a phantom than a reality. She was always creeping back when I thought I had dispatched her."

I used to think of my own Angel only in terms of my life as a writer. It turns out I've had to kill her to make music, too. In both cases, it's a murder I'm committing every day.

*

I was bleeding when I started writing this essay, and I'm bleeding now, a month later, while I finish it. Maybe this is a coincidence, and maybe it isn't. But after spending so much time examining a song about an apocalyptic man-killing menstrual stream (and the woman who sang it), I'm struck by how hard it is to even mention my own.

*

The Creatures released their last record in 2003. A year later, Siouxsie toured for the first time as a solo act. Budgie was still on drums, but hers was the only name on the bill. The Creatures disbanded in 2005, and Siouxsie and Budgie announced their divorce in 2007.

In an interview that year, Siouxsie was asked about her sexuality—a question she dodged throughout her career. "I've never particularly said I'm hetero or I'm a lesbian," she said. "I know there are people who are definitely one way, but not really me. I suppose if I am attracted to men then they usually have more feminine qualities."

The same year, when Siouxsie turned fifty, she released her first solo record.

I wonder, sometimes, if Siouxsie ever felt like an imposter, a woman standing on a stage of men, pretending she belonged there. It's hard to imagine Siouxsie Sioux feeling anything but confident, so utterly herself. But I can't help but think of the Creatures as Siouxsie's real sojourn into selfhood. The band was both Siouxsie and Budgie, sure. But to me, it seems, the Creatures—and in particular "Exterminating Angel"—spoke of something that had lived inside Siouxsie for a long time and was finally making its way out: something darker, something stronger, something about to split open. Of all Siouxsie's work, "Exterminating Angel" is perhaps the most turbulent. It's fed up, and it's angry. It's a feminist battle cry, a call to arms. It's an incantation, a spell, a summoning of creatures brutal and dark. It might also be a proposal: to kill the Angels within us—that were born in us, that were instilled in us, that have lived inside us for so long—so that we might be free.

Maybe "Exterminating Angel" is Siouxsie's own breaking free, as a musician and a woman, after existing for so long in a band, in an industry, in a world made of men.

Or maybe I'm just seeing what I want to see. Like all art, we bring to it our own interpretations. Our experiences and desires and hopes become what we make of it.

*

About a year ago, I bought myself a new guitar. It's a Stratocaster, its body a glossy black. I replaced its colorful pick guard with a black one. It's a gorgeous machine, and so exquisitely goth. I'm still learning how to trust myself when I hold it, to walk onstage and play without thinking about how I'm being judged. I'm still learning to believe I belong there. Sometimes when I play I'm a kid again, unafraid, my body a part of the sound I create. It vibrates in my fingers and rises up in my spine and fills my chest like I'm made of it. And sometimes my cousin's words still ring in my ears. When that happens, I might channel Siouxsie Sioux. I might channel Neko Case or Karen O, Shirley Manson or Kathleen Hanna or Joan Jett or Sister Rosetta Tharpe—any number of women who I have loved, who came before me, who did this long before I did and in circumstances far less forgiving. Who raged against systems that were made by men, who killed whatever angels lived in their houses in order to do it. Who got onstage and said, *Enough is enough. I wanna fuck it up.*

ON THE ESSAY:

I still think this thing should have won the Vladness championship. I mean, a song about an apocalyptic man-killing menstrual stream? What's more goth than that? Cruxshadowed in the final (iykyk), it belongs in those hallowed Xness halls of fallen bangers, and there's a certain pride in that. But man, it was fun to write. It also shreds a lot harder than I do, currently, as my bandmates and I have since left New York, and I mostly play music for myself these days. I'm sure I'll be back onstage someday, with my sweet black Strat in hand. Until then, I still listen to nu-metal when I lift weights sometimes. I teach Virginia Woolf every semester. I'm still killing my own angel every day, when I sit down at my desk, and I'm helping my students—most of whom are women, many who are queer—learn to kill theirs. I'm stoked to see this essay, this strange creature (the first I wrote for Xness, which will forever be my favorite writing community and my favorite time of year) get a little new life here, alongside so many friends. Here's to all the angels in all the houses who might be killed in its wake.

I HEAR YOUR EMPIRE DOWN:

Ander Monson on "Lucretia My Reflection" by The Sisters of Mercy

I have a lot of things I want to tell you about the Sisters of Mercy—a band that I've been preparing to write about my whole life, it feels like—but the most important thing is that their entry in March Vladness, "Lucretia My Reflection," is as great a goth song as you'll find. Top tier. Number one all time. It's released right at the ideal point in the band's trajectory, midway, where Andrew Eldritch is most full of his own ideas and ambition and before he loses touch with whatever once fueled him or kept him tethered to reality and wanders off into the wilderness, where he still is (arguably) today. "Lucretia" is dramatic, grand but not grandiose (actually it's definitely also grandiose, but I love that its grandiosity is inclusive: it invites us to play). Full but not overstuffed, filled with actual goth content, and fun as hell, "Lucretia" captivates. It rules. It makes a great argument for what Goth is/was capable of and what it still can mean, even decades later.

"Lucretia" sums up the perfect balance between what's great about the Sisters of Mercy (and goth as a whole) and what some see as stupid about the Sisters of Mercy (and goth as a whole), which is the same thing: it's the commitment (overcommitment?) to an idea, and a willingness to follow it as far as it'll go, no matter how dumb others may believe you look while whistling "Black Planet" in the stairwell poorly. Never mind how *good* that idea is: *good* is for chumps, for things that never get made. Is it a *good* idea to name your band after a Leonard Cohen song? To call yourself not just Andrew William Harvey Taylor but Andrew Eldritch? To name-check your *own* band in an early single ("Adrenochrome")? To beef with the best iteration of your band just after dropping your first—and most excellent, first and last and always—album, then to get pissed and kick everyone else out of the band except your *drum machine*, which you name not just Doctor Avalanche but *Doktor* Avalanche? To then troll those former bandmates in an epic fashion by releasing an album as the Sisterhood that you recorded over the weekend in order to stop them from legally performing as the Sisterhood and claim a record company's bounty, and begin it by taunting them about the money you stopped them from getting, followed by yelling "JIHAD!!!" to kick off an epic if somewhat half-baked goth-dance track with the same name? To inexplicably record a solo piano number about the sadness of being alive in 1959? To title your third album *Vision Thing* after a George H W Bush talking point and in so doing yoke your star inexorably to his, and what's more to take this whole goth thing you'd basically solved in a BIG ROCK direction and try to out-Axl Axl Rose to the point where your guitarist in the "More" video even *looks* like Slash (but, let's face it, does not quite have the chops, nor are you quite Axl enough to be Axl, speaking of dudes who took it way too far)? To collaborate with *Jim Steinman* (of "Total Eclipse of the Heart" and Meat Loaf fame) on a series of what can only be termed "rock operas"? To write a song called "Doctor Jeep"? To write another called "Detonation Boulevard"? To get in a for-the-ages pissing match with your record label (the same record label that you once so assiduously courted) that poisons your ability to ever release new music (which you claim you've written but will only release for millions of dollars, which you will certainly not receive after having outkicked the coverage and the shadow of your own fame)? To henceforth live like a lonely wizard in the empty forest of your own making?

No, these are probably not *good* ideas, but yet Eldritch had them, and did them, and pulled most of them off (I'm a particular fan of the Steinmanization of Eldritch, or the Eldritchization of Steinman). As a result, the Sisters of Mercy end up being responsible for some of the most gloriously over-the-top songs in the most gloriously over-the-top genre (goth), and damn if their whole discography, best summed up in "Lucretia," doesn't make me feel filled with so much darkness that I can run through a wall or blow up a star with it, and that's why "Lucretia" ought to win music.

And if Eldritch won't accept the black crown at the end of this tournament, that doesn't mean we shouldn't give it to him anyway. We don't give it to him for *him*; we give it to him for *us*, because of how this song makes us feel, because of the spell it casts, and what it does to us.

Maybe I just mean what "Lucretia" does to *me*: I'm not ashamed of it. It still ensorcels me, even 32 years later. It gives me confidence to use the word *ensorcels* in an essay, even.

*

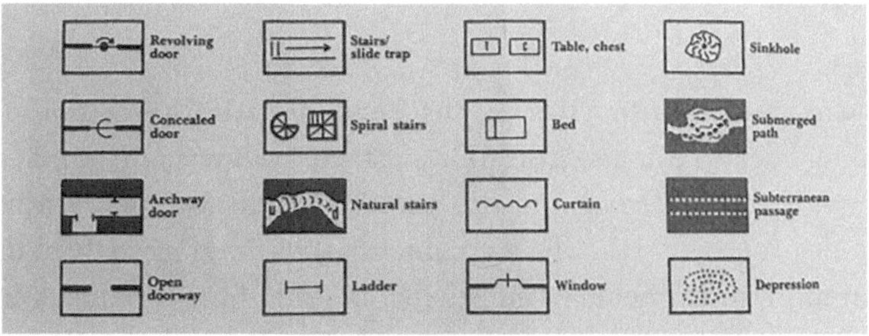

Like many of us, I was not as goth then as I would like to be able to claim now. Oh I more than flirted with it: I had my net.goth t-shirts; I discussed the particulars of goth furiously on the BBS forums; I had a lot of tapes; I listened to them constantly; I even had my dad monogram my black Lands' End bag *TGR* (for The Grim Reaper, my kool hacker handle), and if dad didn't know what that meant, all the better; I was keeping it real and by real I mean interior and very strange. I lived too far away from anything remotely approaching a goth show to *go* to a goth show until the whole scene had gone and went (along with Eldritch's acceptance of the moniker); and in the time before the internet and total availability I worked for it, my hard-won point of entry into darkness, and even if it was *Vision Thing* rather than the cooler *Floodland* and the even cooler *First and Last and Always*, not even to get into the hard early singles and EPs, I worked for it and I let it define me. I did some shit. I was some shit. I was a shit. I liked Eldritch a great deal: he was the shit and knew it, then he disappeared.

What I want to know now is: what's wrong with goth? I love my good goth feelings; I slip into them way too easily. So why do I have more anxiety about feeling them now? Why does it fill me with anxiety to betray my black heart to one of my students, let's call him James, when he asks me what kind of music do I listen to *really?* I mean, you seem like a *69 Love Songs* guy, he says, and that's right on, but beyond that—before that—well, I say, goth, *obviously*, and he says, wait, what? I say, you know, Sisters of Mercy, Siouxsie, Alien Sex Fiend, Christian Death. He's never heard of any of these bands; his mouth makes a little O. I say what do *you* think that means? He thinks it means Hot Topic and I guess, whatever, maybe Linkin Park? Evanescence? He can't picture me with eyeliner. And if I do harbor some love for Evanescence, even against my better judgment, I can still feel it rising in me, my purist fury, not that Sisters of Mercy were every particularly pure (*see also* Jim fucking Steinman). James, I want to say: I have a whole world to show you. Open up your Midwest heart. This essay is for you.

*

I discovered the Sisters in reverse order, beginning with *Vision Thing* (1990), then going back to *Floodland* (1987), and then to *First and Last and Always* (1985), with a brief detour into the Sisterhood's hilarious and surprisingly good troll-gift *Gift* (also in this tournament). And listening to them this way they get more instrumentally interesting as, aside from Doktor Avalanche and Eldritch, we see Andreas Bruhn and Adam Pearson join and leave the band, and Patricia Morrison joins and leaves, and then Wayne Hussey and Ben Gunn and Craig Adams are there for a while, and then eventually even Doktor Avalanche leaves the band, and it's just Eldritch and Gary Marx (also instrumental in Ghost Dance's entry in March Vladness), reportedly writing and recording songs because they wanted to hear themselves on the radio. (This is a pure origin story, and one that should speak to all of us.)

That the only continuity in the band is Eldritch, aside from the programmable and non-royalty-check-collecting Doktor Avalanche, tells you almost all you need to know about what makes the Sisters of Mercy great: that they *named* the fucking drum machine, and that Eldritch then kicked everyone else out of the band except for Avalanche's programmable ass is a testament to the power of Eldritch's own self-belief (also to his sense of humor, which one imagines must be extremely wicked, dry, and deep).

But then Goth is *about* self-belief. You have to have some self-witchery in you to reveal yourself as so obviously *other*, to deviate from the sunlit normy norm as Goths do. That is, if you revealed yourself at all (plenty of us did so only in secret) aside from literary tournaments.

What redeems this self-belief is that Eldritch actually is a genius. Or maybe "was": because he hasn't released anything new in decades aside from occasional songs in live shows and website screeds and forum screeds and bitchy interviews and threats to drop a new album if Americans did something so stupid as to elect Trump president (to which I and many others respond: yo, we did our part, fucking TWICE: now we need you, Eldritch). Because of all of this it's hard to really take the measure of where he's at. But one thing's clear to me: Dude had *ideas*. He had the ego to know he could pull them off, and the drive to do it. He knew what the sound would be like, and what the look would be like, and it was all driven by a desire to say something fucked about the fucked world he saw and felt. He was probably a total asshole to work with, much less to date, but as listeners we don't have to do either.

Unlike a lot of goth lyrics that rely on familiar tropes, in "Lucretia My Reflection" Eldritch is making *arguments*. He's into Subject Matter, too: American politics, the cold war, "the prostitution of Europe by the Americans," Shelley's "Ozymandias," and the Great Depression, and Lucretia Borgia, and Russia Russia Russia, among other things (and you'll note these subjects seem to have aged right back into relevance). He's also obviously having a hell of a time dungeonmastering this adventure for himself and for us.

In fact I got so obsessed at one point with the SoM that as Dungeon Master for my group of friends I insisted on soundtracking whole adventures —

(*The Sinister Secret of Saltmarsh*, just for instance)

—with *Floodland* on repeat, particularly the moodier numbers like "Neverland" (particularly the superior full version), "Driven Like the Snow," "Flood I," "Flood II," and "Torch."

I have no clue know how this came off to my friends but they were my friends so they let me get away with it (and thanks for that, y'all, a couple decades on, and to reward you, YOU ENCOUNTER:

*

(These are actually my miniatures; my daughter and I painted some rocks black to better get at the Vladness spirit as a background.)

Ahhhh. Breathe. One more dungeon map before we move on, because even looking at it plunges me into darkness once again.

*

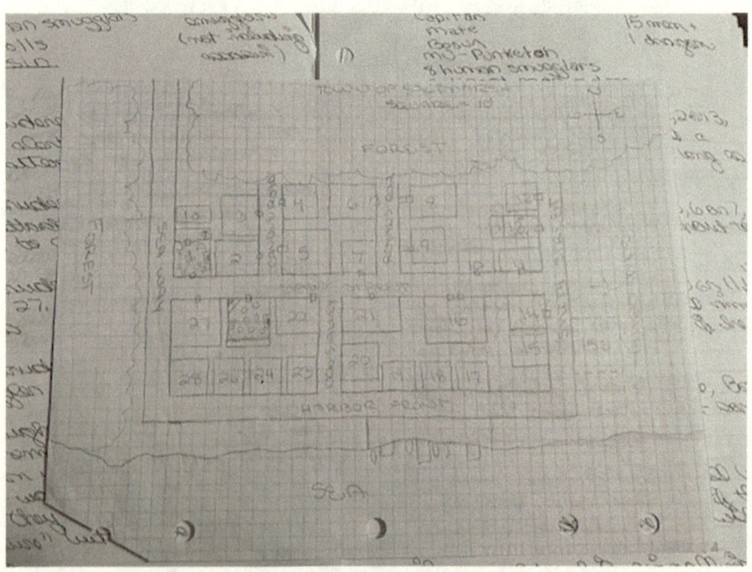

I know what listening to the Sisters of Mercy has felt like (darkness + energy), and how it's bent and sustained me, but listening to "Lucretia My Reflection" (and their whole discography, particularly *Floodland*) thirty-two years later, I can't stop wondering: Can *listening* to goth (which is a kind of *being* goth) —can listening to a song like "Lucretia My Reflection"—bring down or halt the progress of empire?

I have my doubts, because empire flourishes in spite of Goth, and in spite of the Sisters of Mercy, but...

and yet, when I turn the song on now, and it cuts in just a tiny fraction off the beat, and there's the bass and there's the voice and something happens to me. It's not the same thing that happened to me then, but it's related, and it folds those two moments over each other. It's a submerged path I'm following, a subterranean passage.

Goth songs are songs of dissent, of disconnection, of spectral self-involvement, of opting out from one culture and into another. Goth dance songs like "Lucretia" do something else: If they don't quite get us to collective action, they *can* get us to collectivity, if only on the dance floor.

That is what Goth is: a summoning, an opting out, a turning inward, and a performing outward, out there with other bodies, moving. That summoning / that turning doesn't have to be public, though it's dramatic when it is (the eyeliner and the white face paint sure signifies something—something terrifying, a reminder of our own mortality and the long game of time, which as the Silver Jews remind us, only children play well). It can be a private opting out too that we do when we listen to a song, when we let ourselves get caught up in a song. In doing so we choose to live in another's world, let it articulate emotions that we otherwise can't or won't or haven't thought of yet until we hear it, and we let it hold us as long as it will.

This kind of submission remains rare.

Thank god we have access to it—and at the click of a button or a needle on a record! Our lives flatten us, push down a little bit every day on who we used to be. We build ourselves by repetition, by performing and re-performing one of the many roles we play. But when I get caught unawares and hear a song like "Lucretia," something old and yawning, something outside of rationality opens in me.

Lucretia and these other songs are songs of opting out of big chunks of mainstream culture, or at least feeling like we are. At the extreme end of things, a good (goth) song casts a spell so powerful that it can take a person over. It can possess you, even if it just summons you (who never dances) for the first time to the floor (even if it's just your own) and gives you that moment of abandon, free among others, present or imagined.

We fear and covet and revere these spells and those who cast them because they are powerful. It is easy to make fun of those we do not understand, and even easier to mock those we do. These spellcasters push beyond the rational, the sensible, the predictable. We persecute them when we can.

So when Eldritch sings that he hears your empire down, I imagine he means to tell you that he witnesses your empire crashing down, to which also: 2025! He's singing to you from the ruins, but in listening and singing back, we're singing to *us* from the ruins (as many in this tournament have noted, the notes on general ruination that goth offers continue to age well as we descend further into environmental and political and human rights nightmares, and as the circumstances of "Lucretia My Reflection" do not seem to have changed all that much, except for the worse).

But I like to think, and every time I listen to this song I become more convinced, if just for the 4 minutes and 20 seconds on the 7" version or the 9 minutes and 51 seconds on the 12" / CD version, that it casts a spell so powerful *as to suspend time*. It *hears your empire down*.

While we're in the bubble of it, "Lucretia My Reflection" actually *halts* the progress of empire—on me at least it does, or maybe I just think it does (there is no way to know for sure). I mean that *hearing* the song itself is a bewitching, and that hearing takes me somewhere outside of empire, and not just that but that hearing is contra to empire.

What empire wants is for you—for me—to produce and to reproduce, and to not pay too much attention to the roar of the big machines.

To open up a hole in empire's desires, to point to the machinery, to reveal the spell you are—we all are—under, well, you need a powerful spell to break that other spell. "Lucretia" isn't the only one, but it's a big one, and it's good enough for me. It embiggens me when I listen to it, when it operates on me as it does. That's because it pairs pretty complex (at least by rock song standards) lyrics with an all-time-great bass line, a heck of a rhythmic strut, Eldritch's roar of a voice, and even Doktor Avalanche does its part (overly so on the later remastered versions that overemphasize the drums) to get us on the floor. And once we're on the floor (and maybe we haven't ever even *been* on the floor before) we find ourselves dancing there to the fall of empire, and I think that weakens empire, or the empire we've consumed by a nonzero amount.

And if Eldritch looks the part, and the witchy Patricia Morrison, ostensibly the bassist, does, all the better. Half the experience the Sisters offer is visual anyway, and the video sure delivers. I love the brief intercuts of the machinery that visually track Avalanche's digital snare. I love the empty buildings and then Eldritch gesticulating in a sweatshop and swinging what looks like a long thin pipe or maybe an extendable majorette's baton like the savior he means to be. He doesn't interact with the workers of the factory: they're here to illustrate (which maybe isn't great by today's standards but you can't have everything all of the time). It's all mood, and I'm its mode.

Either it's awesome or it sucks, and I'm all in for awesome.

Could Eldritch be doing more to dismantle the machinery of empire—maybe that same machinery that prints his tour merch cheaply? Sure. And could this song push a little harder against cultural norms (á la Christian Death or even "Exterminating Angel")? Definitely. But it knows its limitations too: "We got the empire, now as then / we don't doubt, we don't take reflection" (itself, I want to note, a reflection: oh Eldritch, you tricky mistress). We can acknowledge the contradictions we're dancing to and still enjoy the dance and all the electricity we generate doing it and be changed a tiny bit.

"Lucretia" also just kicks ass. It's propulsive. Collective, even, how it pulls us with it. The bigness of the song and its lack of anxiety about its bigness makes it easier for more of us to get carried away by it, if we're willing, and whether we wore black then and painted our faces or if we just listened to it in secret, or shared it with a select few, that's fine too. You're welcome here, Eldritch says, gesticulating, as long as you don't want royalties.

And listening to it now with you as you read this sentence, no longer 19 as you are probably also not, I want to do all these things. I'm old enough to know that one should take the invitation when it's offered. So I'm gonna hit the floor. You can too. Sing it with me now: Lucretia, my direction, dance the ghost with me.

I'M HARDCORE, BUT I'M NOT THAT HARDCORE

by Lela Scott MacNeil

I missed the whole goth thing by a few years but even if I hadn't, I would never have been a goth. It wasn't the aesthetic I had a problem with, and it wasn't the music. I write fiction some have called *painfully dark*. I'll watch anything with vampires. I love Gothic architecture and Gothic literature and black velvet and black lipstick and Joy Division and Nick Cave and Siouxsie. When I say I would never have been a goth, it's not something I'm proud of. It's a failure of courage.

If you were the natural outcast type growing up, the books-over-social-skills type, and I was, you had two choices. You could make it your singular ambition to *become cool*, or you could give up and let yourself love what you loved. I know I made the wrong choice. What I'm trying to understand is how people make the right one.

There's a way to read the Mountain Goats' album *Goths* as fanfiction about a fandom. I've heard fanfiction defined as loving something so much you want to make stuff about it. I don't think I've ever loved something that much. Except when I was twelve, I cut out every newsprint film still of Baz Luhrmann's *Romeo + Juliet* I could find and glued them into an ugly collage that hung proudly on my bedroom wall for years. In 1996, it was very cool to love Baz Luhrmann's *Romeo + Juliet*. I saw the movie in theaters with Sara and Josefine, who were the coolest girls in class because their jeans were the widest and their messy buns the messiest. I risked nothing loving that movie. It was required. Like when my friend Tim realized if he was going to be taken seriously in the business world, he would have to take out his piercings and become a sports fan. The dominant narrative depends on Tim rooting for the Eagles and twelve-year-old me wanting to dress up like an angel and kiss Leonardo DiCaprio, dressed in his suit of armor. And I did want to kiss him, hard, especially in the scene where we first meet Romeo, smoking a cigarette, floppy hair backlit by the sultry California sun, Radiohead's "Talk Show Host" in the background, Thom Yorke softly moaning, "You want me, fucking come and find me, I'll be waiting, with a gun and a pack of sandwiches," Romeo scribbling moodily in his journal, "Why then, O brawling love, O loving hate."

I wanted to kiss Claire Danes too, wanted to giggle with her under the sheets, but I didn't tell anyone about that. Recently, someone told me there's a whole thing about lesbians having their queer awakenings to '90s era Leonardo DiCaprio. It was strange to learn I wasn't the only one who took that movie and transformed it into something that made sense to me. I hadn't realized how reflexive this sort of internal rewriting is for those of us who have to squint to see ourselves in "all men are created equal."

The Mountain Goats' album *Goths* is not about the kind of fandom that gets you invited to Sara and Josefine's super cool joint birthday party. It's about the kind of fandom that inspires you to file your teeth into sharp points, the kind that sends you hurtling down the highway with a cooler full of Corona and Pineapple Crush, wearing a purple velvet waistcoat stained with Maalox and dried vomit, Siouxsie blasting from the stereo, as you watch the red and blue flashing lights grow closer in the rearview mirror. It's the *suffocated splendor of the once and future goth band*, as Mountain Goats songwriter John Darnielle puts it, played to a musty, mostly empty club, and the kindred lost souls in the audience who discover one another and *revel in the darkness like a pair of open graves*. It's the singer, having locked up his crusty black boots and taken on a mortgage, fondly remembering the time his band was paid in cocaine. It's the forgotten brothers of Gene Loves Jezebel, who had to get jobs, even though Billy Corgan brought them on stage that one time. It's a place like Leeds, where everyone, even Andrew Eldritch, comes home to eventually, a place Darnielle loves so much he wanted to make stuff about it.

Although he never identified as goth. "On the West Coast, the term 'death rock' was floating around in the ether. Nobody really used 'goth,'" he told VICE, "there weren't any bands saying, 'Oh yes, we play death rock.' But I liked that term a lot. I was 16 years old and I loved that the word 'death' was right there up front. Who has never been 16 and not thought that was cool stuff to be thinking about? To me, goth was Wuthering Heights, and I was more into gore. I wanted stuff that had death in it, not people that faint."

In an article titled, "Fandom is Broken," Devin Faraci offhandedly described the young fanfiction community as "a group that seems uninterested in conflict or personal difficulty in their narratives (look at the popularity of fan fics set in coffee shops or bakeries, which posit the characters of a comic or TV show or movie they love as co-workers having sub-sitcom level interactions. I had an argument with a younger fan on Twitter recently and she told me that what she wants out of a *Captain America* story is to see Steve Rogers be happy and get whatever he wants—i.e., the exact opposite of what you want from good drama)..."

Reading this, I think how the brilliant fiction writer Aurelie Sheehan taught me the power of showing your characters just getting coffee, how the mundane offers a way to unlock stubborn truths. There's a common understanding readers and writers of fanfiction are overwhelmingly women, and there's research to back it up. In one survey, more fanfictioners identified as genderqueer than male. Knowing this, it's hard for me not to read critiques like Faraci's as gendered.

When my writer friend Jess was in high school, she spent up to ten hours a day reading and writing *Harry Potter* fanfiction, sometimes staying up all night. Her focus was on stories that shipped Draco Malfoy and Ginny Weasley, and she ended up helping run one of the top Draco/Ginny sites. She won multiple awards, including a *Prisoner of Azkaban* movie poster signed by all the stars, which still hangs in her house.

I bought her a beer the other day because I wanted to find out how she balanced the intense adolescent pressure to be cool with a love as gloriously geeky as Draco/Ginny fanfiction. She told me being cool didn't feel like an option for her, and also the cool kids weren't interesting, so why would she try to be them? She's a few years younger than me, and this felt like progress. Although maybe there have always been people who think this way, and I was just too afraid of being seen as uncool by association to talk to them. Jess grew up in a house full of chaos, and fanfiction was a place she could express the full range of who she was without making her home life more complicated by coming home drunk or getting arrested for shoplifting. At an age where I was writing bad poetry in my journal about the *very deep* sadness of the *very cool* boys I was getting drunk with, she was spending every free waking hour in an intensive, craft-based writing course, learning how to give and receive constructive feedback, how to write within a consciously chosen framework of stylistic techniques, how, as she put it, "to use writing to focus on something outside yourself."

"What did the kids you went to school with say about your fanfiction?"

I ask her.

"I didn't really tell the kids at school."

She showed me her old LiveJournal, with its drabbles and ficlets, with story summaries like: *'There's this mirror,' she told him. 'And I need to use it.'*

I was intrigued. She was visibly cringing. I asked her why, but I knew the answer.

"I don't know," she said, "It just feels childish."

In *The Republic*, Plato wrote, "All the pursuits of men are the pursuits of women also, but in all of them a woman is inferior to a man." In 1837, Poet Laureate Robert Southey wrote to Charlotte Brontë to say, "Literature cannot be the business of a woman's life, and it ought not to be." In 1922, T.S. Eliot wrote to Ezra Pound to say, "There are only a half dozen men of letters (and no women) worth printing." "Leave the writing to me," Saul Bellow told one girlfriend, explaining to another, "Women are the rails on which men run." In 2010, Bret Easton Ellis said, "There's something about the medium of film itself that I think requires the male gaze." When I was in grad school for fiction writing, a male classmate refused to read Mary Gaitskill because her writing was "too woman-y" and a male professor called my writing "a waste of time." It's very possible that the last comment was personal and had nothing to do with my gender, but you start to see things in a context.

I don't include the above list to "feed the outrage machine," or to "femsplain," or because I'm "freaking out with hysterics," although I worry you'll think all those things about me. I'm trying to carve out a small space for what it means to write when the people in the books and the people writing the books and the people writing about the books and the people whose job it is to teach you to write and the people learning to write alongside you are saying your writing is a waste of time. Are saying don't take it personally, there's just something about the medium that requires the male gaze. And no, #notallmen, but enough men, saying the same words, echoing each other across the centuries.

"My preferred explanation is the idea that the vast majority of what we watch is from the male perspective—authored, directed, and filmed by men, and mostly straight white men at that," writes professional fangirl Elizabeth Minkel. "Fan fiction gives women and other marginalised groups the chance to subvert that perspective, to fracture a story and recast it in her own way...It often feels as if there isn't much space for difference in the dominant cultural narratives; in fandom, by design, there's space for all."

If I were to write fanfiction, I would write about John Darnielle of the Mountain Goats. In it, he and I would be close friends from way back, although because we're both so busy, we wouldn't get to see each other as often as we'd like. One summer, my wife and I would finally make it out to visit him and Lalitree in Durham. John and I would embrace, then settle onto the porch I imagine he has, looking out at his backyard, which would be lush and beautiful and a little wild. The air would be heavy with the smell of sunbaked wood and late summer leaves. We would drink local craft beer and catch up, while our wives, close friends themselves, drank wine and talked about poetry in the kitchen.

I'd tell John how *Goths* showed me how to reclaim a part of myself I thought I'd killed a long time ago. I'd tell him I think he does that for a lot of people. He would deflect and say something nice about my writing in that shy, charming way he has of responding to compliments. When I pushed him, he would open up about how it felt to record *Goths* without the driving guitar riffs that made him famous. He would tell me how good it felt to be out of his comfort zone. His eyes would brighten as he talked about working with Nashville pro Robert Bailey, a longtime singer in Garth Brooks' touring band who sings backup vocals on *Goths*. He'd tell me how Bailey worked with Wynonna Judd and sang on Jim and Tammy Faye Bakker's televangelist show in the '70s and '80s. The conversation would drift to the new novel he's working on, and he'd ask what I thought of the narrative structure. I'd play him some of the songs I'd been writing, something he'd encouraged me to try, and he'd offer kind and helpful feedback.

The conversation would take a turn for the deeper, like a flashlight dropped down a well. He'd say something like "Suffering is seldom joyful, but expressing one's capacity for survival almost always is." Pretty soon we'd both be crying about the deaths of our complicated father figures. Our wives would come out and laugh at us, tell us it was time to stop crying and start cooking because they were hungry. John and I would cook something simple, pasta with tomatoes and basil from the garden, a loaf of good crusty bread, the two of us side by side, slicing garlic, falling into an easy rhythm in the kitchen. The next morning, we would all go to a cafe, or maybe a bakery.

I haven't always loved the Mountain Goats. I didn't know about them back in the '90s, back when it was *really* cool to like them, back when Amanda Palmer liked them. I liked "This Year" and "No Children," and I think I had "Woke Up New" on a breakup playlist, but before last March, I would barely have considered myself a casual fan. And then last March I found myself driving solo across West Texas, and decided on a whim to use up the time on a new podcast called *I Only Listen to the Mountain Goats*. In it, Night Vale podcasting genius and Mountain Goats fanboy Joseph Fink goes song by song with Darnielle through the 2002 album *All Hail West Texas!*, their soaring, twisting, spiraling conversations exploring how important the experience of fandom is to those of us who make stuff.

As I drove through those big, empty West Texas hours, listening to Darnielle's nervous, vulnerable voice, something started to collapse in me, fast and slow, the way it does when you're falling in love. At the end of each episode, a fellow musician and fan would do a cover of the song being explored that episode. I listened, enchanted, as Dessa talked about transforming Darnielle's simple composition "Balance," sad and shouty, recorded on a boombox, into something symphonic and richly layered, like a melancholy Bond theme. By the time I got to Eliza Rickman and Jharek Bischoff's wistfully sublime "Riches and Wonders," the sky was black and full of stars and I was sobbing. The weeks that followed were dizzy and love sick as I made my way through the band's discography and read Darnielle's two novels, as I started quoting him like a missionary, telling friends things like "Well you know, John Darnielle says, *Life is hard, you're tired, and there's disease. The strategy that works for children is to be delighted by the things that delight you.*" When the Mountain Goats came through my town, I bought a ticket, and a poster, and I pushed my way towards the stage and I cried, right there, in front of and along with my people.

Studying the narrative structure of *All Hail West Texas!* helped me figure out what I needed to do to fix the novel I'd been avoiding for two years, but that isn't the point. The point is I don't love the Mountain Goats because it's cool, or productive, or rational. My love for them is hopeless and absurd and total. This feels good and also sad, because how much time have I wasted not loving this way?

The way the dominant narrative regards fanfiction shifted a little after the success of the (fanfiction based) *Fifty Shades* trilogy led to everyone at Random House getting bonuses. Minkel told this story at San Diego Comic Con in 2015: "I remember maybe five years ago, I told a coworker—I work for a fancy magazine that I probably shouldn't name, not to indict anyone—and I told her that I'd spent the weekend writing fanfiction (it was *Torchwood* fanfiction, but I didn't mention that part) and she said, 'Don't say that word in this office.' You know? And I was like, 'Oh God, I'm so sorry. Like,

I'm so embarrassed.' And now when I talk about fanfiction with these people in publishing and magazines, they, like, want to buy me lunch." This isn't the point, either, but it feels like the only success story we know how to tell. And if commercialized fanfiction helps displace the tide of realist novels about straight white boys looking back at their childhoods and having complicated feelings about that one time they found a dead animal in the woods, I guess that's something.

My friends who work with youths tell me that these days, it's all about K-Pop, so I reached out to Instagrammer @jdiminiee, whose account is devoted to the K-Pop band BTS, and who likes BTS enough to write fanfiction about them. Last year, the band made headlines by beating Justin Bieber, Selena Gomez, and Ariana Grande to win Billboard's Top Social Artist Award, after receiving more than 300 million votes on Twitter. I wanted to know what it means to be a part of ARMY, as BTS's mostly female fans call themselves. I wanted to know how the choices of fandom have changed.

"Being in ARMY changed my life a lot," said @jdiminiee. "I learned how to love myself and care for others. ARMY is like another family to me. BTS helps me through my anxiety and depression. They also make me a lot happier." Predictably, people are upset. K-Pop is "evil and should be eradicated from the planet," according to tharp42, and Antoast_cheese writes, "Kpop is really a horrible genre filled with autotune and a really rabid fabdom idolizing men looking like girls (no offense to LGBT there)."

But maybe it doesn't matter what people think about our *rabid fabdoms* anymore, because maybe the tyranny of cool is starting to loosen its cultural death grip. @jdiminiee also told me this: "Being cool is not something I care about. All I want is to just be myself and be kind to others."

In my Mountain Goats fanfiction, John and I would discuss K-Pop, and decide that even though we don't get it, we support it, because it's good for the world for people to love things in a way that is hopeless and absurd and total. And then bassist Peter Hughes would come over and he and John would let me watch while they made out a little.

ON THE ESSAY:

I wrote this at a time when I was waking up to the fact that the rules I'd clung to, the ones I'd let shape my life, were cruel and random. I was in the market for new prophets. John Darnielle and his Mountain Goats appeared to me as if in a fiery vision and I had no choice but to love them, hopelessly, in a way I hadn't loved before. As artists, we're fans first. Discovering my capacity for fandom, total, irrational, unlocked new pleasure in writing and also in living. This essay was my attempt to capture the sweet, sad tenderness of being fully alive for the first time while mourning all the years I spent half-dead.

MARCH BADNESS '70s/'80s

DO THAT TO ME NO MORE TIMES

Elena Passarello on "Muskrat Love" by Captain & Tennille

Muskrat mating season begins in March. I doubt songwriter Willis Alan Ramsey knew this when he composed his infamous ballad of Susie and Sam, two muskrats with bewilderingly WASP-y names. According to Ramsey's misguided (and possibly 'lude-induced) lyrics, the coital behaviors of muskrats include: eating bacon and cheese, the jitterbug, and a sort of ambiguous and whirling *frottage*, all of which takes place by candlelight. The song we all know as "Muskrat Love" was originally called "Muskrat Candlelight"—a dubious detail, since muskrats do most of their mating in the water.

If it's March when you're reading this, you can bet your ass that right now, in some nearby wetland, a real-life muskrat Sam is hunting for his Susie. Finding her isn't as mellow-gold as Ramsey imagines it, however, because there are often myriad Sams vying for the fittest Susie of a pond. They'll fight viciously throughout the month for the right to mount her. Males choose their queen based on the pungent scent she squirts from the oily glands encircling her anus. Maybe this biological fact appeared in Ramsey's earlier drafts of "Muskrat Candlelight" but then had to be cut for time.

The final lyrics aren't wrong about all the muzzle-nuzzling; many zoological texts list "kissing" and grooming as part of muskrat courtship. Things go off-script with the line about Sam sidling up to Susie and "rubbin' her toes." In reality, muskrats don't have toes, or fingers, either—they're more like half-webbed murder mitts covered in needle-sharp hairs and topped with claws. And since it's not uncommon for aggressive muskrats to use those claws against rivals, when a real-life muskrat Sam offers his paramour a foot rub, the claws he uses to massage her could still be sticky with the viscera of his enemies.

"How old are you?" skinny Sam might ask Susie while tickling her with his bloody digits.

"I just turned one, so I'm ready to breed!" she'd answer.

"You smell like a hot dumpster. Let's get it on."

The muskrat penis is wide and knob-tipped. It probably evolved these features to better maintain purchase inside the slippery muskrat vaginal canal while the breeding pair "whirl and twirl and tangle" in the water. My favorite thing about muskrat sex (a phrase I never thought I'd type; thanks, Ander and Megan!) is the fact that two muskrats *in flagrante delicto* will occasionally take the humping to the next level by throwing their bodies onto a passing plank of driftwood, so they can float while they do it. I'm no biologist, but this could be some sort of twisted *Titanic* role-play, and I imagine its finale involves Muskrat Susie pushing Muskrat Sam off the wooden plank, like Rose did to Jack in the movie. As she watches Sam sink to the muddy river bottom, Muskrat Susie climaxes.

Anyway. Sam and Susie's floating kink—their musk-*raft* love—is a risky addition to the mating dance, since bonking on a log exposes the pair to predators. Raccoons pose the biggest threat to muskrats, though humans have also been known to hunt the rodents for their fur and, occasionally, their flesh. Eighteenth-century missionaries along the Detroit River were permitted muskrat during the Lenten meat fasts, and certain sects of the Michigan diocese still honor this with "Muskrat Friday" dinners from Mardi Gras to Easter (apparently the meat tastes better if you drown it in sherry). Michigan's raccoons must be pissed that the Catholics keep poaching their food source every March. Unless, of course, said raccoons are Catholic, too.

The male half of The Captain and Tennille, who isn't a Captain and whose real name is Daryl, grew up Catholic, but he did so far away from any muskrat stew, in southern California. Both he and his wife/musical abettor Toni Tennille were vegetarians when they released their hit cover of "Muskrat Love" in 1976. And speaking of 1976—*and* of raccoons!—that same summer, Tennille went to a coke party at Gordon Lightfoot's house where everyone else was blasted out of their gourds and oblivious to the large family of raccoons that had taken over Lightfoot's kitchen!

I read this terrifying anecdote in Toni Tennille's memoir, which is stuffed with alarming '70s details like Lightfoot's trash panda kitchen crew, the risks of early hair transplant surgery, and the time Queen Elizabeth dozed off during a command performance of "Muskrat Love" at the White House (Henry Kissinger stayed awake, but was visibly disturbed). Tennille also devotes considerable page space to the merits of the sitcom *Big Bang Theory*, but only briefly mentions that she's never seen a muskrat in her life—even though the animal screws its way through her third most popular song.

She says she first heard "Muskrat Love" in the car on the way to a nightclub gig, about a year before she and Captain Daryl were discovered. Given the timeline, they probably heard the band America's 1973 cover of Willis Alan Ramsey's song. This was both the first recording re-named "Muskrat Love" and the first to receive any real radio airplay. Weirdly, singer Lani Hall recorded a soporific take on the song, renamed "Sun Down," the year before, at the label that eventually signed Captain and Tennille. "Sun Down" has the same tune as "Muskrat Love," but uses new lyrics that omit the Susie and Sam storyline, and I fully reject this heinous act of muskrat erasure.

Unlike Lani Hall, the band America weren't about to remove the titular muskrats; their version keeps all of Ramsey's rodent lyrics intact. This is unsurprising, since America's first two albums made notable contributions to the canon of animalian soft rock. Remember that one song about the "alligator lizards in the air" (how did they get up there? Did somebody toss them)? And that other song about the horse with no name, which features crackerjack naturalist observations like "there were plants and birds and rocks and things?"

America's "Muskrat Love" is borderline Yacht Rock—so smoothed-out, it's menacing. Their rendition sports both an acoustic bass guitar *and* bongos, plus a double-tracked, whispery voice that a creepy date might use to offer you a post-coital doobie on his bearskin rug right after he gives you crabs. The band ignored their label's pleas not to include the song on their third album and, perhaps as a middle finger, they made it the record's opening track. They also cockily titled the album *Hat Trick*—an act of hubris made even funnier when it flopped. Guess they should have stuck with alligator lizards.

And hey! Since we're on the subject of lizards, here's something else I learned from Tennille's book. Guess what Captain Daryl's last name is? Dragon! Meaning somebody once looked at a tiny little baby and decided to name it *Daryl Dragon*. Which leads me (and, I'm sure, all of us) to wonder why in the world these two didn't call their act the freaking Dragon and Tennille? That's infinitely cooler! And you know what would be even cooler than that? *KOMODO* DRAGON AND TENNILLE!!!!

Imagine an America (the country, not the shitty band) where the Billboard Hot 100 juggernaut of 1976 wasn't "Muskrat Love," but instead "Dragon Love," about the erotic thrill-seekers Komodo Dragon Sam and Komodo Dragon Susie. They tie the knot in a badass desert ceremony with live snakes flying about and a basilisk egg dowry. That night, Komodo Dragon Sam takes K.D. Susie to his lair so they can get busy atop a bunch of direwolf skins, and then she has to eat a raw horse heart in front of him while he makes hungry Aquaman eyes at her and pools of horseblood seep into her white-blond Khaleesi braids and yes, I *did* rip all those details from the Jason Momoa love scenes on *Game of Thrones* rather than look up the mating practices of Komodo dragons because I've already Google-image-searched "muskrat penis" like fifteen times to write this essay, so I'm probably pushing it with the NSA as it is.

OK fine, I just Googled "Komodo Dragons doing it" and to my surprise, their lovemaking actually seems quite gentle. But *my point here* is why in the actual muskrat fuck would Daryl Dragon rebrand himself with some bogus naval rank when his given surname evokes a fire-breathing hell lizard? The answer to this question, my friends, is the 1970s.

I was born at the end of the '70s, within months of Jason Momoa, which means we both could've been conceived while "Muskrat Love" played on the radio. Perhaps many of you reading this were born around then, too, and we, The Lost Children of "Muskrat Love," should start a support group. While the particular tune to which our parents got busy is difficult (and awkward) to confirm, we do have plenty of documentation proving that the '70s—the petri dish that grew Momoa, myself and countless other late GenXers—were absolutely insane. All those thick chintzy fabrics and disco boots with goldfish in the heels and Queen Elizabeth falling asleep while a president that nobody elected grooved in the chair next to her. People smoked about thirty cigarettes a day—forty if they were on an airplane—and brassieres were illegal. There was too much garbage and not enough gas and folks had basically stopped voting because it no longer seemed to work. Everyone was both alarmingly hairy and disturbingly horny and somebody gave a weekly TV show *to a pair of mimes*.

Captain and Tennille also had a show in the '70s, despite the fact that Captain Dragon was the opposite of camera-ready. He often went days without speaking (maybe he was a mime, too?) and reportedly hated: jokes, TV studios, dancing, people, and basically anything that wasn't a macrobiotic food product or a bulldog. Their show ran on ABC in the year of the Muskrat, 1976, and featured a skit about a bionic watermelon in which Toni portrayed her own arch nemesis, Queen Elizabeth II. They also staged a lip-synched performance of "Muskrat Love" for the show that now serves as the closest thing to the song's music video.

This fever dream of a number involves two actors in full-body chipmunk suits who have been shrunk by some analog camera trick. They bounce on Tennille's shoulders and on Cap'n Drag'n's famous hat. At one point, they jump off the hat and look like they're travelling downtown to fellate him, but it turns out they're just headed to the edge of his keyboard, where they groove with the terpsichorean skills of the guy who spins the Qwik Payday Loans sign in front of my Walgreens.

This video makes "The Bionic Watermelon" look like *Citizen Kane*, but underneath the terrible visuals you can hear the special brand of Badness that "Muskrat Love" offers. And I've been thinking about that Badness—delighting in it, honestly—all week. I needed something to distract me from, I dunno, every single piece of news I encountered. You don't Google rodent wangs for a straight hour unless you're seriously trying to forget the state of the world for a while.

The only indefensibly bad components of this "Muskrat Love," the aspects I would erase if I could teleport back fifty years, are the Captain's various electro-keyboard flourishes. With a few rare exceptions, any time a white dude discovers a new electronic musical toy, the results age poorly. Remember when the Monkees learned about synthesizers? Or when John Tesh bought a keytar?

Most of the Captain's sonic aggressions are MOOG-related: the rococo flips and gibbers and binary burps at the outro that, according to Tennille, were meant to approximate both the dance of the randy muskrats and their eventual *petites morts*. While it's true that courting muskrats chirp and babble while they posture for one another, no muskrat ever sounded like a broken Nintendo farting along to the *Deep Throat* soundtrack.

These noises do add the Captain to a long tradition of pop musicians misrepresenting sounds of the animal kingdom. A robin, be he rockin' or not, won't sing *tweedlydeedlydeet*; the flight of the bumblebee isn't nearly as modulated as Rimsky-Korsakov imagines it; and even though Prince sounds amazing while screaming it, no dove has ever cried "*Skype! Skype! Skype! Skype! Skyyyyyyyyyyyype!*" on the A below High C.

Pop music has never really been about accuracy, of course. I also think pop forms are designed to harbor Badness, and their doing so makes space for interesting work. Many of the entries in our tournament support this. Sure, it's a bracket of awful songs, but the tunes are rarely bad because they're tedious (save maybe "Disco Duck"). Our bracket features Badness that manages to cultivate energy, and I hope we all celebrate the Energetically Bad in our voting this muskrat month. A few hundred listens in, I think "Muskrat Love" retains its energy via the very components that make it so pungently odious: Ramsey's bestial lyrics, the Captain's electric wanking, and all the tawdry '70s vibes conjured by Tennille's vocals.

Context plays a part, too. This song represents a monoculture of Badness we'll never experience again: an age of only three channels and snail mail, when coke-addled cultural gatekeepers made unchecked decisions about what got injected into the living rooms and car speakers of almost everyone. "Muskrat Love" is a capsule from a time that managed to be simultaneously puritanical and overheated, family-friendly and gross. The song epitomizes not just what was wrong about the Seventies, but what was *spectacularly* wrong about them, and thanks to thirty years of Boomer nostalgia, it's this wrongness that I have been programmed to miss.

This nostalgia is aided by the overall production of this track, which is honestly pretty damn solid. Rather than the acoustic, lazy-hippie approach that America took, this "Muskrat Love" sports the mellowest Hammond B3 you've ever heard. The lilting chords smear Ramsey's melody around in soft, pastel drips. It's a pleasing accompaniment to Tennille's vocals, which are also on point. Toni Tennille isn't much of a memoirist, but mama knows her way around a ballad. She's got this wonderful, almost golden, mid-throat delivery that's raspy and chewy and not only intoxicating; it sounds *intoxicated.*

Though she claims to have just said no throughout the decade, Tennille sings "Muskrat Love" like she's orbiting the moons of Jupiter, like many great voices from that era. If you asked me to guess what drug yielded Tennille's "Muskrat" tone, I'd probably guess an eight-ball of physical love. Toni sounds absolutely *fucked* in this song. You can almost hear the glow in her cheeks as she pulls a satin sheet around her, sits up, and lights a Newport menthol.

Tennille's signature sound is also ironic, given what she describes as an icy-cold marriage with her musical partner. Despite how well they jibed professionally, he avoided showing her affection for over forty years. Can we stop for a second and take that in? This song that people have loved to hate for my entire life is the sound of a thirty-six-year-old woman with a Prince Valiant haircut singing like she's been shagged within an inch of her sanity, and she's singing right next to her husband, who "couldn't even give [her] a hug." We hear her use whatever that does to a person's psyche to croon about *two horny muskrats.* That, my friends, is an aesthetic Rubik's cube I'll never click into place.

Tennille's vocals are a teaser for what's to come in "Do That To Me One More Time," her 1979 hit that is so stanky with white-lady coital fervor, it makes "Muskrat Love" sound like "Old Shep." But I never want to hear "Do That To Me One More Time" again. That song is a different brand of bad. It's the kind that rarely interests me because its bad aspects are enough to flatten it: the self-indulgent tempo, the single-entendre verses, the Lyricon solo that's nothing short of a federal crime.

For another example of the irredeemably bad, look no further than America's flop album *Hat Trick*. A few tracks down from their lesser "Muskrat Love" is a song with a suspiciously similar title: "Molten Love" (not to be confused with "Molting Love," a song I just wrote about Muskrat Susie getting hot while watching Sam shed his winter fur). I just listened to "Molten Love" six times and immediately forgot everything about the experience other than 1) I hated it and 2) someone blows bong bubbles in the fadeout.

All this is to say that yes, "Muskrat Love" is rotten, and I hope you've all got it topping your brackets, but even if it wins this pantheon of Badness, I'd still take spectacularly bad—loaded vocal delivery bad, '70s doomsday bad—over *forgettably* bad any day. "Muskrat Love" beats "Molten Love" in my heart forever. Sure, this version has topped Worst Song Ever listicles for years, but it's managed to stay alive. It has rented space in the consciousness of three generations, like that family of raccoons in Gordon Lightfoot's kitchen.

And lord knows being a modern human can make you crave some ludicrous outlet—like, say, an ode to two insatiable semi-aquatic mammals, or a memoir about the troubled pair of bipedal mammals who sang said ode. Maybe "Muskrat Love" also sticks because it proves to us how truly bad life in America (the country, not the shitty band) can get. It reminds us that our citizenry often craves the ridiculous as some sort of national coping strategy. On both personal and public levels, we find ourselves aching to stop and smell the muskrats, which makes this song a stinky Badness life raft. Nimble, loaded, catchy, and gross, it's a last-ditch transportation device. We use it to float away from the parts of our world that make even less sense.

ON THE ESSAY:

The Xness tournament is like a skatepark–or what I assume a skatepark to be, as I have literally never been to one. I'm guessing that you get to hang out with your friends, show off a bit, and enjoy some healthy competition. All the other writers were in my mind when I made this little run of muskrat flips and ollies. Imagining them reading, and also anticipating what tricks they were going to pull once March came around, made the process so awesome. I remember sitting in my office chair, clacking away. The writing was coming so fast; it felt like I was playing the piano. I wanted to make the piece as yucky as possible, which turned out to be super entertaining. My husband came into the room and I shouted "THIS IS SO FUN! Why can't writing always be this FUN?!?" It was fun because I was imagining my friends there in the room with me–which I suppose is another way of saying that the Xness universe makes writing feel less lonely.

T Fleischmann on "Morning Train (9 to 5)" by Sheena Easton

How do men listen to music and what is bad?

I started caring about music when I was in the seventh grade, after I got a small CD player for Christmas. I went to a school dance, where I heard the song "Why Haven't I Heard from You" by Reba McEntire. It captivated me in the junior high gymnasium, and offered a perfect emotional landscape in which to cast myself as I pined over this butch girl in my class, a girl who did not call me on the phone anymore, like how the man Reba scolds in the song does not call her on the phone, either. The next chance I got, I bought three Reba CDs to complement my only other album, by Ace of Base.

That was 1997, and since, I have maintained just the worst taste in music. I listen to absolute trash, over and over, with little to no variation. Specifically, I tend toward the soft rock spectrum, with lots of lady singer-songwriters from the 1970s through the 1990s. It's what you hear on *Delilah*, the radio call-in show that premiered one year before I found Reba, in 1996. To this day, five nights a week, someone calls in like, Delilah, help, my kids have gone to college and my husband doesn't buy me flowers anymore. In response, Delilah asks, does your husband show you that he loves you in other ways? But she does not listen to the answer. Delilah just mouths a few platitudes and then plays a wildly inappropriate song, maybe in this instance "Pina Colada," an absolute banger about getting caught in the rain and infidelity.

In the evenings, all my adult life, I have listened to Delilah play my favorite songs. She plays my Hall and Oates. She plays my Jewel. She gives me my Lionel Richie and my Air Supply, and maybe, if I am lucky, a little pop country, just for the hell of it. Occasionally these songs are "good," but most often, and even when they are good, they are quite bad.

Hush, I say to my husband as I turn the radio back up after a commercial break. Delilah is back.

I don't think cishet men listen to Delilah. Not because they listen to good music (I've heard what they like!), but I think because they listen to music differently than everyone else. The gloss goes, in a shortage of media that parallels our own experiences of gender and sexuality, the associated gays and women project ourselves outside of our identities, into straight worlds and boy worlds. In a dominant culture in which only men and women sang, I, untethered, sang along to everything. I could become the vocalist or her object of affection, everything in endless gay variation forever. Wide open spaces, room to make a big mistake, where I fly some girl as high as I can into the wild blue. The island and the stream both, I've been waiting for a girl like me.

From what I understand, when they listen to music, men just pretend to be the men. This would make it difficult to immerse in most of the Delilah songs, which, even when sung by men, are most often about the emotional lives of women. By men here I mean like straight white dudes with jobs or whatever. Guys who would maybe get a song like Sheena Easton's ridiculously catchy hit "9 to 5" stuck in their heads, but even then, would never imagine themselves as the woman singing the song. Men, I assume, do not happily sing about how some guy takes another train home again to find me waiting for him. If anything, the song just offers straight men an opportunity to fantasize about going to work and treating a girlfriend properly.

Incidentally, I am confident that straight women do, in fact, imagine themselves all over the radio because straight women are desperate to be any kind of gay. I know this because when I was younger I spent a lot of my time with straight women, and they liked to confess their secrets to faggots, often with a cocktail or cigarette. This happened a lot in the early 2000s because of how the cable station Bravo rebranded itself. And constantly during those years, straight women told me that they wished they were either a gay woman or a gay man. Sometimes they would also confess to playing around at lesbian things. So based on this I'm sure that straight women love singing the boy parts, too.

None of these generalizations really apply to the youth, though. At a protest recently, my partner heard a bunch of kids chanting "Hear the youth calling, gender nonconforming." I thought this was a horribly embarrassing thing to chant and so I kept chanting it for weeks, around the house and when I was walking to the library. "Here the youth calling, gender nonconforming." It was catchy. Catchy like my baby takes the morning *train*, with that nice emphasis on public transport. Like he works from nine to five and *then!* But even though I think, personally, that "hear the youth calling, gender nonconforming" is not the kind of thing we need to be chanting at rallies right now, I can't really blame anyone who is chanting it, what with how men have been for so long stuck in their tacky genders, not imagining themselves into Bette Midler songs. The youth are just trying to help, my partner explained to me.

Gender, like music, persists long after it is outdated. Like 1981, when Easton's literally unforgettable smash hit competed on the charts with Joy Division's "Love Will Tear Us Apart" and Rick James's "Super Freak." Or how straight men still walk around thinking that they are straight in the year 2020.

"9 to 5" is weirdly anachronistic in this way, too—not timeless, but the qualities that make it perfect sitcom sequence music also make it sound more like a late '50s la-di-da than a theme for the early '80s girl of the world. On surface, it's hard to find a more regressive idea of gender from that year's pop culture, with everyone from Miss Piggy in the *Great Muppet Caper* to Joanie Cunningham in *Happy Days* displaying more liberating visions of heterosexuality than the singer in Easton's hit. The title even has a progressive predecessor from a year earlier, the Lily Tomlin / Dolly Parton / Jane Fonda movie *9 to 5*, where some bad bitches get drunk and kind of kill their boss, a lovely romp.

But the regressive romantic vision that two-hit wonder Easton offers is what is maybe good about the song, or if not good, then bad. Good and bad like the songs on an episode of *Delilah*. I do not want any of that noxious romance in my actual life, where I react allergically to displays of attachment and coupledom. Disgusting. Yet when it's Carly Simon's 1987 comeback hit "Coming Around Again," I love that shit. I sing it all day long to the husbands and wives in my mind.

"9 to 5," like this, does heterosexuality, making what is outdated about it catchy (man goes to work, lady doesn't). And the woman, yes, she is in love with this man. What makes Easton's song so brilliant, though, is that she only sings half of heterosexuality, the part where the man goes away. In fact, she devotes the lyrics to describing in specific detail what it is that this man's going-away should be about:

He goes to work every day, and takes public transit to do so.
When he comes home, he gives her sex if she wants it, sometimes all night without rest.

On occasion, he is allowed to take her to the movies, dinner, dancing, or alternatively, to "anything [she] wants."
She gets his money.

In contrast, the woman's responsibilities and time are left undefined. She says that she'll be around in the evening, which seems fine, considering that they sex each other all night long—a reasonable thing to stick around for. And during the day, she thinks fondly of her man, also fine considering the legendary dick he's apparently giving her, and which she brags about for much of the song. But outside of getting horny for the sex, no part of the singer's days goes to the man, these days that "seem to last forever," blank slates through which she can do anything she wants. She does not clean, she does not work, she does not brush her hair. Whatever she does, it's none of your business.

What a cool bitch.

The way we listen to songs has as much to do with what makes them good or bad as the song itself. Whoever you are, listen to "9 to 5" again, and allow yourself to become the singer. Revel in this glorious song about a man who leaves to earn money, then comes home to give you that money and, when you want it, sex. Imagine, as the chorus returns, all the things you might do if left alone with your days, and relieved of two of the constant struggles in which so many of us live, the labor hell of endless capitalism and the humiliation of tracking down dick to suck. Without these burdens, where else might your time go? Smoke joints and read novels, maybe, or carry on lesbian affairs with your neighbors. Perhaps you would organize your friends into a small group to wait outside of the local prison and help recently released people connect with resources and housing. Maybe you would burn down an oil line, or train yourself to be a very good spy.

Really, it can be anything, la-di-da and catchy like Easton's song. Don't worry, you won't have to tell your man about it, or acknowledge in any way that you have a private life. The man, who only sings along to the boy parts of songs anyway, does not ask. And with how broken the public transit system is in the United States, he might well be gone for ten, eleven hours a day, hours in which you might privately bloom.

This particular cultural, political, environmental moment is as good as any for the people of the mainstream United States to do what should have been done centuries ago, to disrupt the normal flow of events and dismantle the settler state. The consequence of the United States continuing as it has been seems quite clearly to be apocalypse. But still, the horrors of the world screaming, people go on. They go to corporate jobs, drive cars, watch shitty entertainment about straight people, marry, and so on. The men intuit that they should do something different, I think, but still, they are unwilling to stop, as unwilling to imagine themselves as someone else as I am unwilling to listen to music that came out later than 2005. This makes the men seem like pussies but whatever, that's just kind of how it is. I didn't ask to believe that Sheryl Crow's *Tuesday Night Music Club* is one of the best albums of all time but when I put the tape on, my ears don't lie.

Easton's sweet, celebratory, infectious song gives these aimless men something they can hold onto, which is again just to take public transit to work and then give their money to women, and also to satisfy their sexual partners properly.

By the logic of straight men, where the boy parts of songs are what matters, I think that this must feel pretty great. Easton really throws herself into the eroticization of the guy going away to work, and the lady being horny for him. She makes it so that, if you were a guy, presumably, you'd just really want to go along with what she's talking about. In the music video, she seductively rides her bicycle to the train station, sending you off with a moan, then humps the train itself. It's kind of silly, sure, but again, I like to pretend to be a femme singing about her lost dyke while I croon along to Vanessa Carlton (brilliant), so no one is trying to judge here.

And, perhaps most beautifully, men do not actually need a Sheena Easton of their own to do this, just like I did not need an actual Indigo Girl in my life, but in fact only needed myself to go to the doctor, mountain, and fountains. There are women all over the world who want money and who have been denied it by white supremacy, and men, single or partnered, can just give their money directly to these women. You simply go to Twitter and search "pay black trans women," cruise around for a minute with your social media literacy, and then get to it with your Venmo and your Paypal. And just as any person can listen to "9 to 5" and dance around the apartment and think of all the things you might do, unencumbered, while your man is at work, so too any person with a job can do the boy parts of the song. So too can white women, for instance, give their money to black and brown trans women.

Yes, as Easton shows, it feels good to give away the money. And when a man then listens to the radio, he can know that Easton is singing about how good he is, so long as he has given his money to women already. Because women love men who take public transit and then give all their money away so much, they write songs about it. And everyone, literally everyone, wants to be loved by women.

Sexuality and gender never fit comfortably into themselves anyway. I'm sure, for instance, that rat-faced Pete Buttigieg only sings the boy parts, and that Jeff Goldblum pretends to be the lady. And thank the goddess, we're not left with only the artifacts of the shitty culture these days. The straight lie is weaker, and the youth are chanting. We don't have to be anyone we don't want to be. And when we find ourselves burdened with our identities and our habits anyway, still, we can imagine new lives inside of them, as gloriously as I have imagined a transsexual fantasia through the hit singles of the band Chicago.

Because it's the culture itself that is bad. The state, the family, your job. But if you're going to listen to the music anyway, Sheena Easton's "9 to 5?" I fucking love that song. It's a god damn hit and you know it.

JACKET REQUIRED:

Elisa Gabbert on "Another Day in Paradise" and Phil Collins' Yuppie Rock

An aspect of research I do not enjoy is finding out that everything I thought I knew about a subject was wrong. For years I have carried a belief in my head that the term "yacht rock" derives from the cover of Crosby, Stills & Nash's 1977 album *CSN*, which features a photograph of David Crosby, Stephen Stills, and Graham Nash—in that order, no less—chillaxing on a sailboat. If I can believe the internet, this isn't the case—the term did not exist until 2005 and was coined by J. D. Ryznar, Hunter D. Stair, and Lane Farnham, the creators of a mockumentary web series about the musical genre which was known in its own time, the late 1970s and early '80s, as "the West Coast Sound" or "adult-oriented rock." According to these fellows, mockumentarists turned podcasters, and their acolytes, yacht rock—a derogatory category that, like "dad jokes," we've decided to embrace, because liking things we used to mock is bizarrely exhilarating—is not an umbrella term for any song "about a boat, or the ocean, or sailing."Timothy Malcolm, a food editor with strong feelings on this topic, writes that yacht rock "can be characterized as smooth and melodic, and typically combines elements of jazz, rhythm and blues, and rock," with "very little acoustic guitar" but lots of "Fender Rhodes electric piano." The "folkie songs" of Crosby, Stills & Nash, he adds, decidedly do not qualify.

This bums me out, because when I choose a Yacht Rock station on a streaming music service, the first song I want to hear is never the inevitable first song, "Sailing" by Christopher Cross, one of the available options in this tournament of badness. What I want to hear is "Southern Cross" by Crosby, Stills & Nash. There's a video on YouTube, which I've watched dozens of times, of the trio playing this song live at a concert in 1982. It was still pretty much their heyday—the album they were touring, *Daylight Again*, went platinum—but what I love about the video is that they already look washed up. I am inordinately fond of these dorks in their various stages of balding, overweight, and just unfashionable. Despite the acoustic guitars, the song displays many defining aspects of yacht rock: It's "bubbly" and melodic, "yet oddly complex and intellectual" to use Malcolm's words. The yacht has to bear a lot of metaphorical weight: "So I'm sailing for tomorrow, my dreams are a dyin' / And my love is an anchor tied to you, tied with a silver chain / I have my ship and all her flags are a flyin' / She is all I have left and music is her name." Stills wrote the lyrics, he explained in the liner notes to the CSN box set, "about a long boat trip I took after my divorce…it's about using the power of the universe to heal your wounds." The themes of "reassuring vague escapism" and "heartbroken, foolish men," sailing away from their problems, are also key features of the genre—the first episode of *Yacht Rock* is about the writing of the song "What a Fool Believes" by the Doobie Brothers.

There's a scene in the 1984 action/romance movie *Romancing the Stone* where Michael Douglas and Kathleen Turner take shelter in a wrecked cargo plane in the jungles of Colombia. The plane was transporting weed, a kilo of which he proceeds to throw into the campfire. Stoned, they get to chatting, while the Douglas character ("Jack T. Colton") idly flips through an old issue of *Rolling Stone* he finds in the plane. He sits up and cries out, "Aw, goddamn it man, the Doobie Brothers broke up." (I found this line *hilarious* as a child, though I could not possibly have understood almost anything about it—who the Doobie Brothers were, when they broke up, what "doobie" means or the effects of marijuana—I think we must appreciate the formal properties of jokes before we understand their content.) I bring this up because the movie ends with Jack buying a boat—paid for by selling the giant emerald that was eaten by an alligator they had confronted in Cartagena—so they can literally sail away together. The fantasy of boat life was fundamental to the yuppie dreams of the '80s, and at least as important as the fantasy of sailing itself was the fantasy of being able to afford a boat.

Yacht rock, at its tail end, aged into yuppie rock, alternatively known in my own mind as suit rock: think Huey Lewis, Robert Palmer, and of course Phil Collins. In the early days of Genesis, he was post-hippie prog rock, photographed in fleece-lined jackets or shirtless and in cutoffs, with long hair and a surprisingly lush beard, but at the time of my first exposure to Collins, when I was beginning to form memories and an identity, around '84/'85, he was always in a suit. He wears a suit—an abstract-print jacket over a white shirt, fully buttoned but without a tie—in the video for "Against All Odds (Take a Look at Me Now)," my sentimental favorite Phil Collins song. In his memoir, *Not Dead Yet*, he says he wrote most of the song back in 1979, around the same time as "In the Air Tonight," but he didn't finish it until the director Taylor Hackford asked him for a song for the soundtrack to his 1984 movie *Against All Odds* (which is kind of a good movie, worth watching if for no other reason than seeing Jeff Bridges at peak hotness—he plays an ex-pro football player). He wears a suit—a double-breasted tan suit, with a yellow tie—in the video for "Easy Lover," his duet with Philip Bailey from Earth, Wind & Fire, a song that in the past few years has begun to follow me everywhere; I seem to hear it on car radios or over the PA system in grocery stores about a once a week. (I'm not complaining.) He wears a suit—gray, double-breasted, yellow tie, white sneakers—in the video for "Sussudio," a nonsense word that Collins says came "out of nowhere." "I can't think of a better word that scans as well as 'sussudio,' so I keep it and work around it," he says in his (ghost-written) memoir. This makes no sense at all, since what he actually sings is "susussudio," with an extra syllable. "If I could have a pound for every time I've been asked what the word means," Collins says, "I'd have a lot of pounds" (doesn't he?). (The whole memoir, for some reason, is written in the present tense, so you get sentences like, "Things are bad at home—his wife Jill is having a difficult pregnancy, which is not something I'm aware of at the time.") He's wearing a suit in the video for "One More Night"—the video is black & white, so it's hard to say exactly what color the suit is, but even in grayscale it looks like his signature yellow tie. He's wearing a suit in the video for "Two Hearts"—actually several different suits, since he plays every player in his band in the video. He wears a suit—gray sleeves pushed up to the elbow—in a Michelob commercial from 1986 that is almost a video for the Genesis song "Tonight, Tonight, Tonight." This commercial, a montage of concert footage and steamy yuppie nightlife in what I took to be downtown Manhattan, informed my whole idea of adulthood. (I never noticed, but apparently the song is actually about drug addiction, so using it to sell beer is kind of like playing "Pink Houses" at the Republican National Convention.)

I honestly love this era of Phil Collins. George Bradt, a research analyst at MTV from 1983 to 1988, has said, "The best 'testing' artist of all was probably Phil Collins. Research showed that viewers never got tired of his videos, so they were played regularly, months or even years after they were hits." He was writing and recording both with Genesis and as a solo artist, doing production work or drumming for people like Eric Clapton and Robert Plant (whom he calls "Planty"), and appearing on benefit singles like "Do They Know It's Christmas?" and in benefit concerts like Live Aid. He was ubiquitous, and now he has a kind of sheepish defensiveness about his success, like *Could I help it if I couldn't stop writing gold hits?* At one point in *Not Dead Yet*, he says that *No Jacket Required* sold 25 million copies—"I only know this because I looked it up on Wikipedia"! "In the eye of the tornado" he couldn't be bothered to keep up with his sales. It was a baffling choice for the name of his '85 album, considering his penchant for jackets. The story is that he and Planty were trying to get a drink at a hotel bar in Chicago, but they wouldn't let him in without a jacket. "I am wearing a jacket," Collins said. "A proper jacket, sir...not leather," the bar man replied. "I've always hated stuffiness and snobbery," Collins writes, "so *No Jacket Required* becomes my album title and, yes, why not, ethos." Collins' album titles are uniquely terrible—why so many ellipses? He titled his first hits album ...*Hits*.

Phil Collins' discography fascinates me because his good songs are *so* good and his bad songs are *so* bad. I truly hate "A Groovy Kind of Love," a cover song from 1988—it is unlistenably bad, much more offensive than the original version, recorded by The Mindbenders, a beat rock group, in 1965. Collins slows it down to the syrupy tempo of a music box lullaby. "Another Day in Paradise" is down at the bottom with it. From his 1989 album ...*But Seriously*, the single was a No. 1 hit and won a Grammy for Record of the Year. It's odd because I think of it as a song that everyone always despised. (It stands to reason that the more popular something is, the more well-known it is, the more people have the opportunity to hate it: the *Eagles Greatest Hits* effect.) I remember reading an article in *Sassy* magazine in the early '90s in which a male, possibly British staffer made fun of Collins' worrying over the homeless problem, writing something very close to, "Maybe it's because you have all the money, ya bald bastard." Collins' yuppie era had given us tracks like "Take Me Home," one of the good ones, a song that fits right in with the exhaustion porn power ballads of hair metal (see Bon Jovi's "Wanted Dead or Alive" or Motley Crue's "Home Sweet Home"). "I've been a prisoner all my life," Collins sings, which makes me think of Lady Gaga tweeting, "Fame is prison." The video shows him traveling the world—lip syncing in front of international destinations from the Eiffel Tower to the Sydney Opera House to the Hollywood sign. But four years later, the '80s were almost over, and people were starting to tire of yuppie excess. Some of them, at least, were also starting to tire of Phil Collins. His management supposedly called MTV and asked them to play his videos less.

"I'm loath to use the dreaded eighties phrase 'conscience rock,'" Collins says, but he wasn't so loath to write conscience rock. He got the idea for

"Another Day in Paradise" during the tour for *Invisible Touch*. When the band landed in D.C., Collins asked their driver about "the cardboard boxes lined along the pavements in the shadow of the Capitol Building." He was "gobsmacked" to learn they were "the homes of the homeless"—"so many of them, so close to all this wealth and power." *Dude*, one can't help but think. The song was seen as exploitative by many, just clueless and cringey by others. I'm not entirely sure why the Genesis song "Land of Confusion," which also has a "message," feels less cheesy and detestable—maybe because it's more upbeat, with a sort of funny video (featuring life-size puppets of Ronald and Nancy Reagan). Its politics are also vaguer, a general less-war, more-peace vibe: "There's too many men, too many people / Making too many problems / And not much love to go round." It's a reminder for the youth that good politics are much more aligned with age cohorts than generations. Mike Rutherford, who wrote the lyrics, was born in 1950. "My generation will put it right," Collins sings, "We're not just making promises that we know we'll never keep." (OK, boomers.) The video is going for laughs, though—it ends with the Ronald puppet trying to call for his nurse and accidentally hitting the "Nuke" button instead.

"Another Day in Paradise" is comparatively maudlin, maudlin by any standards really. It takes itself utterly seriously. The video begins with a shot of Earth from space, a version of the "Blue Marble" image that famously inspired the environmental movement. (Many astronauts claim that seeing our planet from space completely changed their perspective on global relations, a phenomenon known as the "overview effect.") As we zoom into Earth, the color goes sepia tone: instant melancholy. In between clips of Collins singing with a highly furrowed brow, we see a bunch of still shots of homeless people sleeping in the street, a few stats about homelessness in all-caps text ("3 MILLION HOMELESS IN AMERICA") as if in a PowerPoint presentation. Some of these images are really harrowing—a shirtless child lying on newspaper, a flap of cardboard over his head. Watching the video again as I write this, for the first time in many years, I don't know quite how to feel about it. Because I'm me, of course I think of Sontag, who writes in *Regarding the Pain of Others* that for "antiwar polemicists," "war is generic" and images of war "are of anonymous, generic victims." As such a photo of a child killed in wartime might be used toward any end, to justify any position: "Alter the caption, and the children's deaths could be used and reused." You can look at all painful images as manipulative, in this light. In Collins' case, a slideshow of the homeless is being used to sell records. He did donate a bunch of money to homeless shelters during this time, though—his intentions weren't terrible. I think I hate the song in part because I can't entirely hate it; my distaste is too close to ambivalence. The piano part is undeniably catchy. It's a song I might catch myself humming along to before, with a jolt, I remember I don't like it and change the station.

Collins' appeals for sympathy in *Not Dead Yet* read as kind of pathetic, and he knows it. In a passage about his former bandmate Peter Gabriel (Gabriel left Genesis in 1975), Collins writes:

> I do envy Pete. There are some songs he's written that I wish I'd written—for one thing "Don't Give Up," his gorgeous duet with Kate Bush. But even here at the height of my success it seems that, for every achievement or great opportunity that comes my way, I'm starting to accrue bad press as a matter of course. Pete seems to get good press seemingly equally automatically. It seems a bit unfair, which I appreciate is a pathetic word to use in this context. A few years later, in 1996, when I release *Dance into the Light*, *Entertainment Weekly* will write: "Even Phil Collins must know that we all grew weary of Phil Collins."

For Phil Collins to whinge about unfairness is of course absurd—but he kind of has a point. Critical attention and favor are whimsical; some great artists are recognized in their time, while others are not; otherwise Herman Melville wouldn't have died in near poverty. This is not to say that Peter Gabriel isn't good, just that it can always be counted as luck—coincidence, even—when good art is appreciated in kind. (I too wish I wrote "Don't Give Up," because then I'd get to be in the video, hugging Kate Bush for six and a half minutes straight.) Pathetic or not, Collins is a somewhat sympathetic figure, to me. In late life, as he tells it in the memoir's penultimate chapter, he moved to Switzerland to be near two of his kids, though he had divorced their Swiss mother; he became a full-blown alcoholic out of sheer boredom. He eventually had to be put on Antabuse, which blocks the enzyme that allows your body to metabolize alcohol, so he could stop drinking and not die of pancreatitis. (Duff McKagan, the bassist from Guns N' Roses, almost died this way too—after years of drinking ten bottles of wine a day, an effort to cut back after years of drinking gallons of vodka, his pancreas burst and gave him third-degree burns on his internal organs. In the ER, the morphine they gave him had next to no effect. He begged the doctors to kill him.)

Nothing Collins says in his book is especially insightful. (When I was reading it, or skimming it anyway, I saw a conversation on Twitter about who qualifies as a "writer's writer." I joked that Phil Collins is definitely not that, and at least four or five people replied that he is, however, a "drummer's drummer.") I'm just *fond* of him, the way I'm fond of fat David Crosby, who sang backing vocals on "Another Day in Paradise." (They sang it together on the Arsenio Hall show! Collins wears a gray suit over a black shirt with an improbably large collar, almost forming its own bowtie; Crosby's mustache, the ideal mustache, maybe the only mustache in history I like, and his mutton chops are nearing full gray.) I'm fond of Collins' hairline, a deep male-pattern-baldness version of a widow's peak, like the grandpa from *The Munsters* but fluffier. I'm fond of his corny dance moves, the little toe taps and bounces. And I'm fond of his wardrobe, the bucket hats and Hawaiian shirts, the pleated pants, the sweater vests over polos and, yes, the suits. They remind me of a brief time when it seemed cool to be an adult, and to do adult signifier things like work on Wall Street and have an accountant. I may not have yearned for a yacht per se, but I couldn't wait to be old enough to wear shoulder pads and "pumps," to go to a franchise fern bar and order something like an Irish coffee. Adulthood meant freedom of choice, and that, to me, was glamour—not sailing but the ability, the option to sail.

I was six or whatever, so I didn't understand that by the time I was old enough to do those things, they wouldn't be cool anymore. I experience this as an actual loss: I never got to have that alternate life as an adult in the '80s. Nostalgia is a kind of pain.

ON THE ESSAY:

I only participated in the March Xness tournament once, because the competition aspect gave me anxiety. But I remember this piece as one of the easiest and most fun writing days I've had in the past five to ten years, confirming my theory that anything you've been thinking about for most of your life makes good material for an essay, no matter how trivial.

THE BRANCHING TREE OF BAD DECISIONS:

Kathleen Rooney on "Seasons in the Sun" by Terry Jacks

During the Renaissance there was a vogue for the "paradoxical encomium," a rhetorical jest typified by Erasmus' *In Praise of Folly*. This form of virtuosic display originated in adoxography, an ancient Greek practice of praising people, things, and conditions undeserving of praise, such as poverty, ugliness, stupidity, drunkenness, and so forth. Often semi-satirical, the paradoxical encomium was a playful transformation of negatives into positives, flaws into strengths. In other words, the paradoxical encomium could be an early formula for admiring something so bad it's good.

This essay, though, is not going to be one of those, because "Seasons in the Sun" by Terry Jacks flat-out sucks.

The saccharine dramatic monologue of a dying man bidding his beautiful world a tearful farewell, the ominous, aqueous, jangling riff that opens Jacks' take sounds promising, as though it might not be out of place in a Scott Walker song. Alas, then, Jacks' twerpy voice begins to mewl, followed closely by a needling organ, and within 15 seconds, the combination makes this listener think of the terminally ill narrator: *Just die already*. It's a melody you can imagine coming out of a slot machine. A carousel from Hell going endlessly up and down a little too fast, never stopping to let you off.

Somewhere between 11 million and 14 million people who have bought the single worldwide would disagree with me. Released in the United States in December of 1973, the song cracked the *Billboard* Hot 100 in January of 1974, ascending to the number one spot by March 2 and remaining there for three weeks, after which it stayed in the Top 40 until around Memorial Day. To put that achievement into perspective, "Seasons in the Sun" is still one of fewer than 40 singles ever to sell over 10 million copies globally.

Admittedly these are awe-inspiring—and, depending on how one feels about the song, dismaying—feats. Yet, because there's no such thing as absolute authority over aesthetic value, nor any way to establish objectively or universally whether something is bad or not, it would be futile to try to prove that Jacks' "Seasons in the Sun" ought to be heard by every listener as awful, or that millions of people are wrong for liking it.

It would be more fun instead to study Jacks' version's path into existence—to make ourselves the Lomaxes of soft rock for a sec and follow "Seasons'" lines of descent. Because whatever else it does, Jacks' take on "Seasons" provides an invaluable object lesson in how poor decision-making can diminish a particular work's quality in a way that's illuminating about art in general.

Before doing that, though, I confess that it's tempting to crap spectacularly all over Jacks' effort. Plenty of people have. The reference series *Contemporary Musicians* describes Jacks' version as a "schlock/pop classic." Schlock, of course, means *cheap or inferior goods*; *trash*, deriving from the Yiddish for *dregs, dross.*

In 2018, the blog *Cracked Rear Viewer*, dedicated "to fresh takes on retro pop culture," called the song a "schmaltzy little ditty" and shared it with the warning "ATTENTION DIABETICS: better take your shot of insulin before clicking on the next video!"

An August 2017 article in the Australian *Inquirer* entitled "The Nadir of Postwar Popular Music" reported that Jacks's version "often tops lists of the worst records of the 1970s or of all time. It was once left off such a list because it was judged to be in a category of awfulness unreachable by mere mortals."

But the same article also reminds readers that Jacks' offering went to Number One not only in the United States, Canada, and Britain, but also "most European countries, South Africa, New Zealand and Australia, where it stayed on the charts for 27 weeks."

And in 2015 the Canadian tabloid *The Province* pointed out that, "People loved it while others loathed it, usually for the same reason: Its blatant sentimentality."

Whenever something so polarizing achieves such enduring popular resonance one wonders: how did this happen? Was it produced to specific consumer tastes? Was it an accident? What the heck?

Maybe the key for Jacks' hit is that he originally intended it for the Beach Boys. One imagines that if Brian Wilson had not been out of commission, then perhaps he could have given it a hallucinatory fever dream feeling more innovative than Jacks' treacly haze.

In *The History of Canadian Rock 'N' Roll*, Bob Mersereau explains that after Jacks' band the Poppy Family—which, as its name suggests, cranked out a considerable number of pop hits—dissolved, his interests turned toward writing and production, and he began to seek out new studio gigs. He met the Beach Boys through touring, and with Brian Wilson's mental health crisis growing more severe, "Carl Wilson and Al Jardine both asked if I would produce them," Jacks said. "They knew I liked the Beach Boys and Brian was out of it then." He thought that his version of "Seasons in the Sun," could be "the smash hit the Beach Boys were looking for to revamp their stalled career."

Unfortunately, as Jacks recalls, "None of the Beach Boys were hanging together, you had to bring them in separately. It wasn't unified because Brian had gone crazy. It was an honor to produce them, but [...] I was just turning into a nervous wreck. I said, 'I can't do this anymore.' I just left." But he took the song with him, and his version found "markets most artists never heard of: Brazil, for instance, where it became the country's top-seller of all time."

In an interview preceding the Beach Boys' rough cut of "Seasons," Jacks' wife and former band mate Susan Jacks asserts that part of the problem, too, with getting the Beach Boys to finish their recording was the divisive nature of the song. Her interlocutor says, "The interesting thing about 'Seasons in the Sun' is that's one of those songs where you either love it or hate it. I have seen people vote that as their all-time-favorite song and I've seen other people say it's the worst song that was ever written. I don't know. That's true of a lot of tearjerkers..." She agrees, "Oh, I know, I know, and they're usually hits," before sharing her version of the experience during which the Beach Boys "went into the studio and they could never get it finished because some of the guys were really into it and some weren't."

So is the subsequent solo Terry Jacks version of "Seasons in the Sun" the worst song of all time? No, "My Ding-A-Ling" by Chuck Berry is. However, part of being bad has to do with missed opportunities and dubious choices, and by that metric, Jacks' "Seasons" is a serious contender.

How did this song get into Jacks' hands to try to hand it to the Beach Boys in the first place, and why does his version sound so sugary when compared to its spicier source material? Let's climb the branching tree of bad decisions and find out.

I. Brel, or, Avant Jacks, Jacques

The mawkish melt of gooey cheese that is "Seasons in the Sun" is an adaptation—or a degradation—of the Jacques Brel song "Le Moribond" with lyrics interpreted by Rod McKuen (about whom more later).

The Brel original absolutely slaps. Compelling in its lyrics, its arrangement, and its delivery by its composer, one can see why Brel was basically the Belgian Elvis. Little wonder that musicians from the aforementioned Scott Walker to David Bowie to Joan Baez to Marc Almond to Cyndi Lauper and on and on have covered his songs.

Sarcastic and bitter, Brel's first-person narrator is also dying and making his farewells. He says goodbye not to Jacks' "trusted friend," but to a specific "Emile"—"as good as white bread"—whom he knows "will take care of my wife," a lyric whose meaning becomes more unsettling the more Brel repeats it.

The chorus, too, has a frantic quality that seems sort of shocking the first time we hear it:

I want everyone to laugh,
I want everyone to dance,
I want everyone to have fun like crazy people
when they put me in the hole.

He bids adieu, too, to the curé, or parish priest, with whom he admits that he didn't always agree, but with whom he feels kinship because "we were seeking the same port." He knows, again, that because the priest was her confessor, he "will take care of my wife."

The source of the song's intriguing unease exposes itself fully at last when the narrator makes his goodbye to an Antoine. "It's killing me to die today while you are so alive / and even more solid than boredom" he sings in a truly sick burn. "Seeing that you were her lover," he adds, "I know that you will take care of my wife." The turn here reveals that this has been the nasty and impotent lament of a cuckolded husband the entire time.

At last, he says goodbye to his faithless spouse: "I go to the flowers with my eyes closed, my wife. / Seeing as I've closed them often, / I know you will take care of my soul."

With its blend of macabre content and an upbeat tempo, the song is *funny.* We are all fools, the chorus says, and the only remedies to our folly are laughter and death.

When Brel sings, the listener senses the complete sweep of the fictional world this narrative unfolds in—Brel knows more about the milieu and its characters than the surface can show. This implication of underlying fullness enacts a musical illustration of Hemingway's proverbial tip of the iceberg.

Jacks, as will be explored below, guts the song and leaves only the tip, a lonely floe with nothing beneath.

This lack of subtext is part of why getting the Jacks after you've been fond of the Brel is like ordering Aperol and receiving Fanta. It's drinkable; it's not Drano. But it disappoints with its insipidity. Like hearing a Beethoven sonata performed by a wind-up toy, you can tell that you're hearing a product of genius, but the mechanism delivering the song falls short of the challenge.

This listener finds Jacks' version to be quite bad, but kind of fascinatingly extra-bad because Brel's original is so powerful, but gets garbled almost to death in a transatlantic, international game of Telephone.

According to the best comment presently on this performance's YouTube page posted three years ago by kabiriazampano3: "Jacques Brel's version is about friends and priests that he knew were doing his wife, he accepted that and recommended all of them to take care of her after his death. Terry Jacks was a version that had nothing to do with the original, american chinnese food, american pizza, american capuccino. Brel was a sarcastic poet, he went for the blood."

II. McKuen, or, Don't Spare the Rod

Wait, though—Jacks is not American, but Canadian. So who is the American to blame for the inferior version? Rod McKuen. Kind of.

The young and largely self-taught Bay Area singer-songwriter and poet moved to France in the early 1960s where he and Brel became fast friends. An enormous fan of Brel's versatile and theatrical *oeuvre* in the genre of *chanson*, McKuen took it upon himself to introduce Brel's catalog to an Anglophone audience. His version of Brel's exemplary "Ne Me Quitte Pas"—Americanized though it is—turned that song into an international standard.

His version of "Le Moribond," while arguably not as great as the original, is still pretty good. Significantly, McKuen altered the title from "The Dying Man" to "Seasons in the Sun," not, obviously, because he didn't know what he was doing, but because he did. A mindless, word-for-word translation of Brel's lyrics would not sit well on the melody, nor would it retain the lyrical rhymes. McKuen knew that better than a translation would be an adaptation.

Looking closely at the aspects he adapts, one sees McKuen proceeding thoughtfully. One might disagree with his decisions, but would be hard-pressed to say that anything he does is mistaken or stupid: He does lose the priest, changing him to an actual father: "Good-bye, Papa, please pray for me. / I was the black sheep of the family."

But crucially, he keeps—and even improves upon—the cheating spouse, exhibiting that he understands the Brel song tonally; he gets the sarcasm. If anything, McKuen's version is less sexist because he chooses to give the wife a name, while retaining the irony. "Adieu, Françoise, my trusted wife / without you I'd have had a lonely life. / You cheated lots of times, but then / I forgave you in the end, / though your lover was my friend."

It's not that McKuen didn't properly appreciate Brel's sensibility. In a characteristic and touching McKuen-esque excess of sentiment, he said that when he heard that Brel had died at the relatively young age of 49 in 1978, "I stayed locked in my bedroom and drank for a week. That kind of self-pity was something he wouldn't have approved of, but all I could do was replay our songs (our children) and ruminate over our unfinished life together."

Because of his friendship with the man himself, McKuen understood that he could not do Brel as Brel. He's not a sardonic, smoldering, *jolie laide* Gallic icon, but an affable, sensitive, pansexual proto-hippie. Thus, McKuen's version—not a translation, but an interpretation—makes decisions that one might disagree with, but that are ultimately defensible. He's doing a take, not a cover, and he wants to head in a different direction.

The Brel version, though brilliant, is a bit of a mess—as can be the case with the literate genre of *chanson*, its lyrics are phenomenal, but the chorus hook is not that infectious of an earworm. The experience of listening feels disturbing—you get to the end and need to review what you just heard. As a composition, it's formally complete, but keeps pulling the listener back into the knowledge that the fucked-up situation the narrator leaves behind will continue after he's gone.

McKuen chooses to make the song smoother and more tied-up-with-a-bow, adding a much prettier chorus, both lyrically and melodically, plugging in lyrics with a variation of vowels and consonants that render it more euphonious and hookier. When you're done with McKuen's version, you're still slightly unsettled, but you're also reassured. Instead of manically telling his survivors to laugh and dance like a bunch of crazies when they stick him in the grave, McKuen's narrator possesses memories of "joy" and "fun" and "seasons in the sun." A bit sanitized, yes, but "the hills that we climbed / were just seasons out of time" is smartly sad, a death-tinged admission that even sunshine goes dark and rarely comprises the bulk of a life.

McKuen's version is not bad, just different—if anything, it reveals how flexible Brel's song is. It shows the same dramatic situation, but through a different lens. It's not a shot-for-shot remake, some CGI *Lion King*, but rather an homage. McKuen wants a side effect of his song to be to make the listener look back to the Brel, and if they like the original better, that's fine by him; it's part of his aim.

Brel's version is splenetic—contemptuous and comic and in no way wistful. But you can tell that because McKuen, too, plays the scenario as kind of a what-can-you-do joke, he at least gets the humor, even though he principally wants it to be a pretty song. Brel seems to be saying "I win because I'm dead"—a nihilistic, punk avant la lettre double bird extravagantly flipped. Even when he's saying some of the same stuff as McKuen retains, he says it with a shrug, a hairflip, a big old IDGAF to life and everyone who has to remain in it. Is his song spoken from the perspective of a suicide? A person dying of natural causes? Either way, the parting shot seems to be, *I'm glad I'm leaving and you're staying here because you all deserve each other.* Whereas McKuen's version seems to conclude, *Now that I'm facing death, I appreciate the time we had and I forgive you all. Mostly.*

That mostly is vital to McKuen's version's emotional complexity, best embodied by the narrator addressing his wife:

Adieu, Françoise, it's hard to die
when all the birds are singing in the sky.
When spring is so much in the air,
with your lovers everywhere
just be careful I'll be there.

Hold on, how? As a watchful spirit full of forgiving tristesse at the absurdity? Or as a vengeful ghost seeking to wreak punishment? This edgy ambiguity, along with his various other interpretive choices, cause this listener to maintain that McKuen's version is still pretty interesting. You can't deny that McKuen was onto something—Brel's song is a banger and deserved to be brought over to the States.

But his decision to excise the bitter tone of Brel's original does open the door to some weak misreadings.

III. Terry, or, All Jacksed Up

Enter Terry Jacks by way of that door.

At times the line between genius and foolishness seems to be a fine one. McKuen may tip this piece of Brel-ian brilliance toward foolery, but remains upright, whereas Jacks comes along and pushes it right over the edge. As biographer Alan Clayson explains in *Jacques Brel: La Vie Bohème*, McKuen's version is "anodyne," but Jacks' version is unforgivably "harmless." "With all further what's-the-use-of-it-all ugliness removed," he writes, it emerges "as a sentimental lay about some old idiot's happy memories—with ascending key changes to pep it up."

To listen to the Jacks version is to hear him chew a substantive song into pallid bubblegum. In the hands of Jacks, "Seasons in the Sun" has an almost polka rhythm ill-suited to the putatively sad content. Whereas the bouncy, hysterical pseudo-cheer of Brel's version creates a pleasing yet disturbing tension of opposites, Jacks' version grates. He permits no comedy, no bitterness, no irony, no resentment. Puritanically, there's no cheating wife and therefore no sex. Aesthetically unforgivably, there's no emotional complexity.

Jacks takes something that was pretty good—the McKuen version—which itself drew on something great—the Brel—and ends up with something awful. He faced two moves at his branch of this decision tree: 1) He could have climbed back in the direction of Brel, making it more complex, or 2) He could have done what he did, clambering in the opposite direction: rendering the heretofore individual speaker into a cardboard cutout.

Jacks' loses Emile in favor of the "trusted friend." In McKuen's telling, the labeling of Emile as "trusted" is caustic because we still learn that Emile has been cheating with the speaker's wife. But Jacks allows no layers; everything is exactly as it purports to be, and the friend is truly trusted. This makes his version feel brainstemmy, stupid, repugnant—one worries, if one likes it, that perhaps one likes it for fairly dumb reasons.

But, you might be saying, isn't Jacks doing what you said McKuen did—really, what any interpreter does? Emphasizing some aspects over others? Yes, but interpretations, like originals, can still be questionable. Jacks chooses to cut or conceal the most provocative aspects of the song, which make his version a frustrating experience, even if one is unfamiliar with its source.

McKuen drifts toward the sentimental, but Jacks crashes full-steam upon the shores of kitsch. In addition to his emblandening subtractions, the one addition he does make suggests that he doesn't trust the listener to find the deathbed scenario sad enough. No, he opts to throw in a soon-to-be-partially-orphaned daughter (with an awkward repetition of "sun" and a cliché to end the verse to boot):

Goodbye Michelle, my little one.
You gave me love and helped me find the sun,
and every time that I was down,
you would always come around,
and get my feet back on the ground.

For though aware of the Brel original, Jacks chooses to manipulate the song away from idiosyncrasy and complexity toward an empty and pandering Hallmark generality. According to a 2004 article in the *Vancouver Sun*, Jacks knew of the song's unsentimental origins. "Brel wrote it in a whorehouse in Tangiers," he said. But Jacks purposely sentimentalized it in response to "a good friend of mine" who died of "acute leukemia." Or as the Australian *Inquirer* put it, "Jacks returned to the song, wrangled a few more maudlin thoughts into the last verse and recorded the syrupy results."

Worth noting is that maybe Jacks knew exactly what he was doing from a commercial standpoint. There's always good money to be made in pandering—producing stuff that's ostensibly art, but that soothes and reinforces the most conservative values. Jacks' song does not confront death, not truly. His speaker has no regrets aside maybe from regretting dying, and what interesting person hasn't got some regrets? To the extent it has anything to say, Jacks' version says of its narrator and by extension its listener: *if you think death is sad, you are having the right feelings; the decisions you made in your life were good ones, and the values you held are the best values.* Cultural products that speak in such platitudes tend to fly off the shelves.

In this regard, "Seasons in the Sun" reminds me of the colossally popular Victorian sculpture "Motherless," which I happened to see last summer in the Kelvingrove Art Gallery in Glasgow. Formally known as "Statue of a Motherless Girl and Her Father," the late Victorian work by George Anderson Lawson has been phenomenally well-liked since its creation.

"It's proof that sadness can be popular," says the wall text explaining the piece and instructing viewers where they can purchase their copy—either in the gift shop, or online. "Also available in bronze!"

But it does not prove that sadness can be popular; it proves that sentimentality and kitsch can be popular. "Motherless," like Jacks' "Seasons in the Sun" gives the audience not messy, multifaceted, subtle emotion but the pure spectacle thereof; it's not sadness, it's SadnessTM depicted and sold, yet felt not at all.

Kitsch, of course, is something of tawdry design or content created to appeal to popular or undiscriminating taste. And sentimentality per Wikipedia is "a device used to induce a tender emotional response disproportionate to the situation at hand, and thus to substitute heightened and generally uncritical feeling for ethical and intellectual judgments." In this way, then, both "Motherless" and "Seasons in the Sun" induce their audiences to invest previously prepared emotions disproportionately to generic situations. Upon closer examination, Jacks' supposed sadness does not deserve the designation of sad. It's a simulation of sadness. A representation of sadness that's really a simulacrum that allows its susceptible listeners to believe falsely that they've dealt with a difficult emotion.

In the Reading and Writing Poetry class I teach at DePaul University in Chicago, we use the text *Western Wind: An Introduction to Poetry* by David Mason and Frederick Nims. An eccentric and engaging book full of unexpected charts, photographs, and diagrams, the chapter called "The Color of Thought: Emotions in Poetry" includes this image of the Emotional Color Wheel. "We can visualize the emotions as a color wheel like the ones we see in art-supply shops, a wheel in which selected colors are arranged, like spokes, according to their prismatic, or 'spectral,' order," write Mason and Nims. "If we start blending the colors themselves, there is no end to the number we can make, just as there is no end to the number or complexity of our emotions."

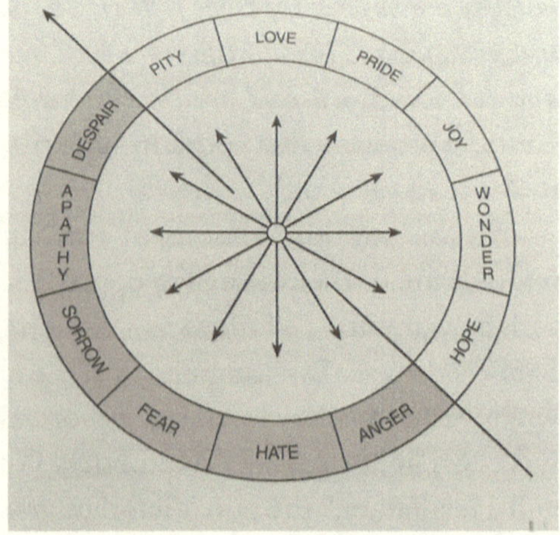

My students tend to find this visual metaphor particularly illuminating when it comes to improving their understanding of how a good poem operates. The idea of the Emotional Color Wheel becomes a shared term of class vocabulary—why, we ask, limit yourself to just one emotional color when you could potentially achieve a deeper effect through the use of two or many more? Or as Mason and Nims put the same concept in musical terms: "In most poems we get not one emotion in a solo, but rather duets or quartets or even symphonies of many emotions."

We can apply the Emotional Color Wheel here. Brel's "Le Moribond" is a rancorous rainbow of negative emotions cut through with bleak comedy. And McKuen's "Seasons," though less of a rainbow, still retains a pleasing balance of complementary emotional colors. But Jacks' version displays a single, soppy color—self-pitying and weepy, smugly drunk on its own tears. Climbing the decision tree from Brel to McKuen to Jacks, the listener experiences a reduction in emotional interest—a leaching of emotional color from the song.

If you're not yet convinced, I present two parting points as to why Jacks' version of "Seasons" is pretty damn bad. First, it's a full 30 seconds longer than the all-killer-no-filler 2 minutes and 56 seconds of the Brel original. Not only is it much worse, but there's also more of it.

Second, lest anyone remain in doubt as to Jacks' thoroughgoing immaturity and fatuous taste, the *Inquirer* reports this illuminating side-note: "Unlikely as it sounds, ["Seasons in the Sun's"] B side is worse. Jacks reckoned he set out to record something unremarkable so as not to distract disc jockeys from what he saw as the main attraction. Loaded with puerile sexual innuendo, 'Put the Bone In' is ostensibly about a woman ordering dog food from her butcher. 'I figured nobody's going to play that thing,' Jacks said later." If you hate yourself, you can listen to it on YouTube.

In the introduction to *Permanent Red*, John Berger writes:

> After we have responded to a work of art, we leave it, carrying away in our consciousness something which we didn't have before. This something amounts to more than our memory of the incident represented, and also more than our memory of the shapes and colors and spaces which the artist has used and arranged. What we take away with us—on the most profound level—is the memory of the artist's way of looking at the world.

The branching tree of bad decisions shows that Brel's way of looking at the world is incredibly colorful and interesting. McKuen's is still interesting, albeit slightly less so. Jacks' way is vacant and ridiculous. And yet, and yet…

Without Jacks' having sent his "Seasons" to such stratospheric fame, I doubt I'd be writing appreciatively about Brel's original. I might not be aware of it at all. Nor would we have the many post-Jacks covers of "Seasons" that prove that—with the Jacks factor removed—the song still has a certain something.

Take Bobby Wright's version, which hit the Billboard Hot Country singles chart in 1974, as well. Perhaps because the expectation of corn is priced into country, this version is, to this listener's ear, better. The steel guitar and strings, the slower chorus, and the slight churchiness make me wish dearly there were an Elvis cover. And the Hong Kong pop band the Wynners' version, also from 1974, sounds somehow superior to Jacks, with its slower tempo and more mellifluous, less whiny vocal.

On the other hand, there's the 1999 version by Irish boy band Westlife, a Christmas #1 in the UK that year. With its synthesized flute and extreme chime curtain, it may, in fact, be worse than Jacks'. Then again, there's the Daniel Johnston version, which doubles-down on the addition of Michelle, the little one, by having a child sing the chorus. The amateurish, out-of-phase quality feels worthy of a paradoxical encomium, so delightfully cracked it's charming. Moreover, Johnston's take possesses a beyond-the-pearly-gates cherubic vibe, like the narrator might already be dead—spooky and great.

So thanks, Jacques; thanks, Rod; and thanks, grudgingly, Terry, I guess, for all these sunny seasons.

ON THE ESSAY:

A rhetorical approach of which I am especially fond is to go super-deep in my analysis of something that could potentially be extremely shallow. It's easy to dispense a quick opinion about a piece of art: "I like it," or "I dislike it"; "that thing's good," or "that thing sucks." Far harder, but more rewarding, is to dig way down into how a given piece operates and the circumstances surrounding said piece's creation: the people, the time, and the place responsible for a work's existence. The more attention you pay to something, the more both it and you get enriched. I'm grateful year after year for the chance March Xness offers to get profound about music and what it does.

My participation in the tournament never fails to make me a better writer and thinker, and to help me pass those habits onto my students.

THOSE OF YOU WHO WILL NOT SING:

Martin Seay on "My Ding-a-Ling" by Chuck Berry

"My Ding-a-Ling" was Chuck Berry's only number-one hit.

I'm going to say that again. "My Ding-a-Ling" was the *only* song Chuck Berry ever recorded that hit number one on the Billboard pop charts.

Chuck Berry, y'all.

Like a confident litigator who calls no witnesses and simply states that the correct verdict is self-evident from the facts at hand, I am tempted to end my March Badness essay right here. By any metric you can think of—misguided conception, half-assed execution, unworthiness of its performer, unmerited popularity relative to the rest of the artist's oeuvre, the sweeping systemic out-of-jointness that its success represents—"My Ding-a-Ling" is obviously the worst song in the modern history of popular music. And it ain't close.

But bad things have much to teach us about where value resides, though their lessons can be painful. To that end, let's spend a moment with each of the three major elements of the catastrophe:

1) "My Ding-a-Ling" was
2) Chuck Berry's
3) only number-one hit.

1

In each of its recorded iterations, "My Ding-a-Ling" is a song about having a penis.

The version we're most directly concerned with is the one issued as a single by Chess Records in July of 1972, the one that held the top spot on the Billboard Hot 100 for two weeks in October of that year, thereby qualifying for the present contest while causing a couple of vastly superior songs—"Use Me" by Bill Withers and "Burning Love" by Elvis Presley—to peak at number two. In a narrow technical sense, this is the best "Ding-a-Ling" on record, in that it announces its aims most clearly and achieves them most successfully. (But should we at this point consider whether we ought to call it *the best* when those aims are deleterious? When a song is *fundamentally* bad, shouldn't we want it to be *less* effective? Wouldn't it be better if it were worse?)

The first important thing to note about "My Ding-a-Ling" is that many people are to blame. Sleeve notes always credit Berry as the song's only author, which he definitely was not; the original was written by Dave Bartholomew, a legendary New Orleans bandleader, producer, and arranger who—along with a small, scattered coterie of collaborators and rivals—determined in the years following World War Two what the next half-century of popular music was about to sound like. (In addition to being an architect of what became known as the New Orleans sound, Bartholomew wrote or co-wrote classics like "I'm Walkin'," "Blue Monday," "I Hear You Knocking," and "Ain't That a Shame"; suffice it to say that "My Ding-a-Ling" is not among his best work.) In 1952 Bartholomew and his band recorded it for both the Imperial and King labels, under two different titles; a couple of years later, Imperial released a new version—now called "Toy Bell," still crediting Bartholomew as the composer—by the Bees, a group mostly remembered for launching the solo career of singer Billy Bland.

Bartholomew's own renditions of the song are just straightforwardly dumb. In them the eponymous ding-a-ling is a euphemism more than a double entendre: very little attempt is made to suggest non-penile connotations. The Bees—maybe hoping to attract a larger, more respectable audience by imparting some semi-plausible deniability—were the first to introduce the ironic frame that defines Berry's hit: the opening declaration that the ding-a-ling is literally a toy bell, and not, y'know, whatever *you* filthy people might be thinking. This move allows the singer to address a double audience by adopting a childlike faux-naïf persona that matches the baby-talk register of the title phrase, a persona that's further bolstered by the addition of a new verse set in Sunday school and by the rearrangement of Bartholomew's original verses into roughly auxological/gerontological order, concluding as follows:

When you're young and on the go
Your ding-a-ling won't ever get sore.

When you are old and you've lost your sting
You won't need the doggone thing.

None of these records charted. Like an unexploded mustard-gas shell deep beneath a Flemish field, "My Ding-a-Ling" lurked in sinister obscurity for years. And then Chuck Berry came along.

It's hard to pinpoint exactly when this happened. In his deeply strange, often creepy, occasionally amazing 1987 autobiography, Berry writes that he "had been singing it for four years prior" to its ascendancy as a hit single; this curiously specific timeframe is probably an oblique reference to "My Tambourine," his first documented crack at adapting it, which appears on his 1968 album *From St. Louie to Frisco*. Although Berry began his recording career on the scrappy independent Chess, and to Chess he'd soon return, "My Tambourine" dates from his lackluster three-year stint on the much larger Mercury; one suspects that Mercury and its attorneys were somewhat less shrug-emoji about intellectual property rights than Chess was, because there's quite a bit of daylight between Berry's "Tambourine" and his "Ding-a-Ling": the central metaphor, obviously, is different, and so is the melody. The end product circumvented legal jeopardy mostly just by sucking in an uncommitted way, and thus not attracting much attention. The copious reverb, probably slathered on to make Berry seem relevant to kids accustomed to heavier rock, doesn't suit the song; meanwhile, the mambo-inflected rhythm is at least a decade out of fashion, and Berry's hipster phraseology—"she dug my music and my routine"—seems forced. By 1968 even the tambourine itself had largely passed its moment as a hippie signifier.

Also, the tambourine metaphor just doesn't work. Penises, while roundish, are not generally wider than they are long; nor, absent certain modifications, do they jingle. More to the point, "tambourine" wasn't an established code word for much of anything, whereas most speakers of American English would have understood Bartholomew's anatomical referent immediately. While the entry for "ding-a-ling" in the *Oxford English Dictionary* does not indicate its usage in print to mean "penis" prior to 1972, this is one of those areas where print lags common parlance. "Tinkle," somewhat relatedly, was in place prior to the midcentury as an onomatopoetic euphemism for urination; from there, the resemblance of a flaccid penis to the swinging clapper of a bell is a pretty easy leap. "My Tambourine" advantages itself of none of this, and without nailing the anatomical metaphor, the song never comes together. The last verse, in which the tambourine is "linked up" to a tenuously vaginal graduation ring, is a complete conceptual disaster.

But in this version we do find two elements that show a path forward. The first is the rhyme of "grammar school" with "vestibule," which is actually really good, a move that only a few other pre-hip hop lyricists of note—Lorenz Hart, Cole Porter, Bob Dylan, maybe Willie Nelson—could have come up with, and that any of them might have admired. The second is Berry's adjustment of the original lyrics to amplify themes of preadolescent sexuality and to remove references to senescent impotence, topics that are respectively extremely on- and extremely off-brand for him. "My Tambourine" was a misfire, a venting of steam that hinted at the churn of as-yet-unseen magma; "My Ding-a-Ling" was not done with Chuck Berry, nor he with it.

Flash forward to February 1972, the Lanchester Arts Festival, the Locarno Ballroom in Coventry, England. Early in his career—mostly to maximize revenues, and probably on some level to minimize his personal and professional entanglements—Berry had adopted the unusual practice of touring without a band: he'd tell each promoter to provide him with a Fender Twin Reverb amplifier and a competent local group, he'd show up with his guitar minutes before showtime, and the concert would begin, with no rehearsal, not even a setlist. (Early in his career Bruce Springsteen was in one of these local bands; in a 1987 concert documentary he recalled the extent of the guidance he got from Berry: "I said, 'What songs are we going to do?'" "And he said, 'Well, we're going to do some Chuck Berry songs.' That's all he said.") If the musicians were shaky, the shows could be awful; if they had good ears and were fast on their feet, they could be great. The show in Coventry went pretty well. Chess had had it recorded—allegedly without Berry's knowledge—and used much of it as the second side of *The London Chuck Berry Sessions*, an LP released later that year.

These unrehearsed gigs also went better when the audience was enthusiastic, and by all accounts the crowd in the Locarno Ballroom was nuts. Berry was known for playing short sets and doing no encores; he didn't encore in Coventry, but he did extend his set, feeding off the room's energy, and this created consternation for the festival organizers. By the time he finished up with a blazing "Johnny B. Goode" he'd run over his allotted time by fifteen minutes; the *Sessions* LP ends with the crowd chanting *We want Chuck!* as the emcee pleads with them to settle down so Pink Floyd can take the stage. If you listen closely enough you just *might* be able to hear the spark of UK punk in that moment.

Anyway, the main reason why Berry ran over his allotted time is that when the emcee signaled him to come off, he instead turned back to the crowd and played "My Ding-a-Ling."

For eleven and a half minutes.

Seriously. Berry's original recorded version of "My Ding-a-Ling"—under that title, at least—is ten seconds longer than "Sad Eyed Lady of the Lowlands." Now, to be fair, most of that runtime consists of Berry's instructions to the audience and his salacious patter between verses. Then again, to be fair, salacious patter between verses is a huge part of what his "Ding-a-Ling" is all about.

If the folks at Chess knew they had a hit on their hands, there's no real evidence of it. As Bruce Pegg recounts in his unauthorized Berry biography *Brown Eyed Handsome Man*, the trip to England didn't yield as much usable material as the label had hoped: Berry's microphone blew midway through the Coventry show, rendering most of the audio unusable (half of *The London Chuck Berry Sessions* consists of hastily-scheduled studio recordings that turned out surprisingly well, thanks in large part to the recruitment of three excellent players: keyboardist Ian McLagan and drummer Kenney Jones of the Faces, and bassist Ric Grech of Blind Faith and Traffic). Had that mic not blown, it's not clear that "My Ding-a-Ling" would have made the cut.

As the story goes, after the LP came out, Chess began to hear from a few radio deejays—all apparently unconcerned about their job security—who'd been playing "My Ding-a-Ling" on the air in its entirety, to an overwhelming response. In the early days, the Chess brothers had run their business with the understanding that every hit song is on some level a novelty song, and a certain measure of that spirit still remained in 1972; the label decided to take a scalpel to the full-length "Ding-a-Ling" with the hope of locating a coherent single therein. This daunting task fell to legendary producer Esmond Edwards—then Chess's vice president for artists and repertoire, one of the industry's first African-American executives—who had previously worked on recordings by Eric Dolphy, Coleman Hawkins, and John Coltrane, among many others, and one can't help but wonder whether he paused at his console for a moment to ponder the series of events that had brought him to this odd episode in his distinguished career. Edwards's efforts yielded the four-minute, eighteen-second edit that Chess released in July of '72, and that's the one that worked its way inexorably, virulently up the Billboard charts.

A number of technical factors made "My Ding-a-Ling" a hit after "My Tambourine" wasn't. The first, of course, is the restoration of Bartholomew's original metaphor. The second, I think, is the freedom that the restored metaphor provided Berry to imaginatively inhabit the song. While Bartholomew's and the Bells' renditions are wry, cool, and a little philosophical—describing events in an indefinite past tense, making general observations about sexual potency and the waning thereof—Berry deploys his prodigious storytelling skills to sketch vivid, inventive, particular scenes that emphasize the corporeality of the ding-a-ling, presenting it not as a sexy metonym but as an organ: susceptible to injury, a site of compulsive pleasure. In Edwards's edit this focus is even sharper, shorn of content that's slack or redundant. (Edwards had the wisdom, for instance, to cut the Sunday school / Golden Rule verse that Berry had lifted from the Bees' version, while retaining Berry's own similar but superior grammar school / vestibule addition.) The pared-down material that remains, while not *good*, per se, will for damn sure hold your attention: it's agitated, aroused, and anxious, live in more than one sense.

And that's the biggest reason why Berry's "Ding-a-Ling" hit: the fact that it was recorded live. The song's humor, such as it is, requires an impression of spontaneity that's antithetical to a studio recording. It also benefits from the presence of an audience, by way of the deeply-rooted human tendency to laugh when other people are laughing, a phenomenon to which innumerable mediocre improv troupes owe their subsistence.

Do we buy Berry's assertion that he didn't play "My Ding-a-Ling" live prior to 1968? We do not. Berry performs it like something he's lived with, thought about, and road-tested for years. His rap with the audience—which is no less rehearsed than the song itself, as the multiple performances available on YouTube that I watched so you don't have to (you're welcome) clearly attest—has the feel of material that he developed in the early Fifties, in the little East St. Louis clubs where he got his start. By 1972 this is a song that he *knows*, that he's been adding to, subtracting from, tweaking based on crowd responses, and generally making his own to such a great extent that he might have sincerely forgotten that he'd copped it from somebody else.

And, so, yeah, okay, a word about that.

2

"Leonard Chess had explained," Berry writes, describing his preparations for his first professional recording session, "that it would be better for me if

I had original songs. I was very glad to hear this because I had created many extra verses for other people's songs and I was eager to do an entire creation of my own."

Berry's autobiography abounds with statements like this. What seem at first like careless bits of self-incrimination are in fact rhetorical moves, gentle suggestions that those who'd accuse him of misbehavior might be using the wrong rulebook. From the outset Berry understood—quite correctly, and probably better than people on the business side of pop music cared to admit—that the distinction between original and borrowed material is not binary. For all his considerable sophistication, Berry thought of himself as participating in a folk tradition, one that includes blues and country and Cajun and calypso and every other music played by and for the working class, in fields and freight-yards and factories, brothels and barrooms and barrelhouses, a tradition that derives much of its vibrancy from being in unrestricted conversation with itself. He didn't seem to acknowledge a huge difference between inventing something entirely new and just doing something somebody else came up with better than they had done it.

But this formulation gets a bit sticky in the extremely frequent instances when the artist who does the borrowing is doing it from a position of elevated privilege, particularly when that privilege is white. Berry and/or his record labels may have neglected a few footnotes over the course of his career, but he unquestionably gave more than he took, having been ripped off—reverently or cynically, directly or indirectly, with credit or without—six ways from Sunday by a large percentage of literally everybody who picked up a guitar at some point during the past 65 years.

Not all of Berry's debtors were white, but the most successful certainly were. The story of the dawn of rock 'n' roll is often told, but worth reviewing: starting in about 1955, the cohort of artists who were achieving commercial success by adapting jump blues into something distinctly modern was multiracial, with Berry, Little Richard, and Fats Domino keeping pace with Bill Haley, Elvis Presley, and Jerry Lee Lewis. Berry's breakthrough single "Maybellene" was in fact the first pop hit by an African-American to outsell the cover versions of it released by white artists, an achievement that for a glittering moment suggested that interracial exchanges legally prohibited throughout much of the United States might yet be accomplished, in some small but significant way, through commerce in popular music. But as the days passed, white rock 'n' rollers continued to emerge and prosper, while black rock 'n' rollers generally did not, and within three or so years it was all pretty much over, with Elvis in the Army, Lewis in disgrace, Little Richard back in church, Buddy Holly, Ritchie Valens, and the Big Bopper dead in a plane crash, and Berry...well, we'll get to that in a minute. Fare such as "Stupid Cupid," "The Battle of New Orleans," and "The Purple People Eater" took over the charts, and for a time pop music went to shit again.

The significance of those rock 'n' roll pioneers didn't really become evident until the following decade, and even then you had to know what to listen for. The up-and-coming rock artists who repurposed this early material were generally honest, or at least frank, about citing their sources—to do so was proof of connoisseurship—but for the most part the audiences didn't care, and without getting demand letters from attorneys the music industry wasn't cutting anybody any checks. Of the first-generation rock 'n' roll innovators, no one was plundered more extensively or blatantly than Berry. I'm not talking about Pat Boone covers here, or any other unambiguously cringey instances of whitewashing; we're after bigger fish. Berry collected legal settlements from both the Beach Boys, whose "Surfin' U.S.A." uses the melody of "Sweet Little Sixteen" without attribution, and the Beatles, whose "Come Together" draws music and some lyrics from "You Can't Catch Me." While it's not close enough to land anybody in court, the similarity of Bob Dylan's "Subterranean Homesick Blues" to the comparably motormouthed "Too Much Monkey Business" is also pretty hard to miss.

As you may have noticed, I just named what are arguably the three most iconic white acts of the 1960s—the ones most often credited with Changing Music Forever—which leads me to a point that has gone unstated too long in this essay: Chuck Berry was a goddamn genius, securely numbered among the most consequential figures in the history of global popular culture. This cannot be overstated, and is not in dispute. In the concert documentary mentioned parenthetically above, Eric Clapton explains how "If you were going to play rock 'n' roll, or any upbeat number, and you wanted to take a guitar ride, then you would end up playing like Chuck, or what you learnt from Chuck." In 1961, on a train platform in Kent, a young man struck up a conversation with another whom he'd spotted carrying a copy of a Berry LP that was hard to get in the UK; the men's names were respectively Keith Richards and Mick Jagger. In 1976, when Ann Druyan and Carl Sagan were putting together musical selections for the golden record placed aboard the *Voyager* deep-space probes—a record designed to communicate the essence of humankind to any extraterrestrial beings who might one day encounter it—the only rock song they chose to include was Berry's "Johnny B. Goode."

Steve Martin joked about it on *Saturday Night Live*, predicting the first message that Earth will receive from beyond our solar system: *SEND MORE CHUCK BERRY.*

Chuck Berry was a goddamn genius. Were this not the case, the sordid stupidity of "My Ding-a-Ling" wouldn't be worth complaining about.

We should, however, try to be specific regarding of what exactly his genius consists. Strictly speaking there's no aspect of Berry's craft that hadn't been done before; his most-often-cited innovations—onstage showmanship, overdriven electric guitar, two-string leads, pushing the rolling boogie-woogie of jump blues toward the more urgent two-four of Western swing—could all be plausibly claimed by predecessors and contemporaries, from Ike Turner to Bill Haley to Louis Jordan to Sister Rosetta Tharpe. Berry's contribution lay in putting the pieces together better than anybody else, and demonstrating the breadth of what the new form could accomplish.

"Maybellene," the aforementioned breakthrough single, qualifies as a major compositional achievement even though it takes its rhythm and most of its melody from the Western swing tune "Ida Red." In addition to his fast, noisy, not-quite-under-control guitar work, Berry supplies a new chorus and verses that establish him right out of the gate as one of the two most innovative lyricists of the 1950s. (The other one, Willie Dixon, happens to be the bassist on the recording.) Berry's words glide along on the familiar melody, rushing with the music, dancing alliteratively among varying vowels, setting scenes and evoking action in a manner that any novelist might well envy. What's particularly striking is his confidence, which may be the most rock-'n'-roll aspect of the performance: when he can't find the right language to make a line work, he just coins his own and keeps going. "As I was motorvatin' over the hill," he sings; "motorvating" isn't a real word, doesn't mean anything, except suddenly it is and does: not only a word, but the *perfect* word.

Most importantly, Berry understood that true verbal mastery must always take account of the audience it addresses, and what that audience wants. In one form or another, "Ida Red" probably goes back to the Civil War; it had certainly been widely known for more than a decade when Berry first started playing it and similar material in the clubs where his career began. As he writes:

> The music played around St. Louis was country-western, which was usually called hillbilly music, and swing. Curiosity provoked me to lay a lot of the country stuff on our predominantly black audience

> and some of the clubgoers started whispering, "Who is that black hillbilly at the Cosmo?" After they laughed at me a few times, they began requesting the hillbilly stuff and trying to dance to it. If you ever want to see something that is far out, watch a crowd of colored folk, half high, wholeheartedly doing the hoedown barefooted.

Throughout his career Berry maintained an impressive unwillingness to stay in his lane. Whenever he encountered a pop genre or trend that seemed fun, interesting, or potentially lucrative—not just country, but blues, ballads, calypso, even Latin- and Italian-themed songs that were briefly in vogue—he'd take a swing at it, and an important aspect of his overall bequest to his successors is the modeling of this catholicity. He helped establish rock music as both a potent solvent of social and ethnic barriers and, not coincidentally, as the soundtrack of recuperative capitalism.

Of all the fence-hopping Berry did, the first instance remains the most notable: his discovery that African-American audiences—despite, or more likely because of, the towering legal and practical barriers that kept them separate from it—were utterly fascinated by the culture of their white working-class counterparts. That discovery made Berry a big draw in his native St. Louis, but it also hipped him to the flip side of that phenomenon: the fact that the fascination was no less intense in the other direction.

This was a realization that he needed the help of others to exploit. Here we should note that despite all the mythology surrounding its heroes, rock 'n' roll was almost entirely the result of economic and demographic factors—i.e. the post-Depression baby boomlet hitting puberty, with the postwar baby boom close on its heels—as well as the rise of technologies that expanded these kids' capacity to make consumer choices independently of their parents and other authorities: affordable cars, good highways to drive them on, portable transistor radios, and high-powered radio stations. The most important single figure in rock 'n' roll isn't a musician at all, but rather deejay Alan Freed, who popularized the term and helped define the sound by playing the records of both black and white acts in huge broadcast markets. (Freed is in fact credited as a writer on "Maybellene," to which he contributed neither a word nor a note; the credit was a way for Chess to funnel him royalties in exchange for spinning its records, one of the shady practices that would end Freed's brief career when the payola scandal broke in '59.)

Musicians, of course, had been listening to each other across racial lines since forever, but these post-war technological advances made it possible for *audiences*, principally teenage audiences, to effortlessly traverse such lines without leaving the privacy of their homes and vehicles. A big part of Berry's genius is the fact that he saw this shift coming, and understood what it meant. It's noteworthy that many of his early songs—"Roll Over Beethoven," "Rock and Roll Music," "Johnny B. Goode"—more or less announce themselves as cultural forces: they tell you what they're doing even as they're doing it.

Berry's canny analysis of his young audience's unspoken desires certainly helps explain why, starting in 1957 and continuing for several years thereafter, he wrote and recorded a series of singles that featured teenage protagonists, often set in schools. While never overtly unwholesome, songs like "School Day," "Sweet Little Sixteen," "Almost Grown," and "Little Queenie" were unmistakably intended to seduce teenagers, to affirm and encourage their agency, especially their sexual agency. This begins to seem a little creepy when we consider that Chuck Berry was thirty years old in 1957. Add a little more biographical context, and it begins to seem a lot creepy.

Because here's the thing: in addition to being a genius, Chuck Berry was also, by many credible accounts, quite an asshole. This is a point that *can* be easily overstated, because the most-often-cited complaints against him—that he was rude, stingy, cold, mercenary, embittered, distrustful, deceitful, ungrateful, prone to engaging in head games and power trips at the expense of effective performances, and generally just shitty to deal with—can be largely explained, if maybe not entirely excused, by the shoddy and exploitative treatment he got from every corner of the music industry throughout his career, treatment that was often explicitly and just about always implicitly racist.

Some complaints about his conduct, however, are harder to dismiss. Though the consequences were worse than they would have been for a white musician in comparable circumstances, much of Berry's trouble was at least somewhat earned, and of his own making.

In the early 1940s, if you had asked any resident of the Ville, a prosperous African-American neighborhood in St. Louis, to predict which of Henry and Martha Berry's six children would go on to have a successful career in music, that resident a) would have known who you were talking about, and b) would definitely have answered Lucy, the third of the six, who was an accomplished mezzo-soprano and a skilled pianist who'd benefitted from an excellent music education at Sumner High School. The Berrys were a bourgeois family in a bourgeois neighborhood: Henry was an independent home-repair contractor and a Baptist deacon, and Martha was a well-read schoolteacher; she named her youngest son after the poet Paul Laurence

Dunbar. The fourth child—Charles, later called Chuck—was known less as a musician than as a charismatic fuckup; he did give a memorable performance of a blues song at a school talent show once, but it was remembered less for its quality than for scandalizing the Sumner faculty, who maintained that such music was beneath the dignity of its pupils. Berry didn't like school, and got held back a couple of grades, but he was still officially enrolled in 1944, when he and some friends committed and were arrested for a series of armed robberies and the theft of a vehicle. He received a ten-year sentence for the offenses, of which he served three.

This was not to be his last stint in prison. In 1960, just off the height of his fame, Berry was indicted under the Mann Act for transporting women across state lines for "immoral purposes" in two separate incidents, respectively involving a white girl between sixteen and eighteen years old and a fourteen-year-old Apache girl. (It's safe to assume that Berry wasn't the only well-known musician having sex with teenagers, and therefore also safe to assume that race had some bearing on the prosecutor's decision to charge.) Although acquitted in the first case—the young woman testified that she was in love with Berry, which the jury apparently accepted as evidence that the couple's intent wasn't immoral enough to be illegal—he was convicted in the second, and sentenced to five years. Berry's attorney appealed based on energetically racist statements made by the judge; the Eighth Circuit agreed, and ordered a new trial, at which Berry was convicted again. This time the sentence was three years, of which he served twenty months at the federal lockup in Terre Haute, Indiana, beginning in early 1962.

As was noted in court and widely reported at the time of his sentencing, Berry was a thirty-three-year-old married man with three young daughters at home, and one imagines some concern around the Chess offices over whether his fans would desert him, just as many of Jerry Lee Lewis's fans had jumped ship following the revelation that he had married his thirteen-year-old cousin. These concerns turned out to be largely unfounded: Berry started recording singles again immediately after his parole, and some of them—including "No Particular Place to Go," a humorous song about driving a woman around in an automobile with carnal intent, released four years after Berry was convicted of driving a woman around in an automobile with carnal intent—charted impressively, which suggests either that public mores had suddenly changed, or that Berry's fans had already priced in his misbehavior, that it might even be part of his appeal.

In 1979 Berry pleaded guilty to evading federal income taxes and did four months in the federal correctional institution in Lompoc, California, a period that he seems to have almost enjoyed; according to his autobiography he treated it more or less like a writer's residency, taking a typing class during which he banged out much of that very book. It was to be his last sojourn behind bars, though not his last brush with the law. In 1987, under circumstances that remain unclear, he hit a woman in the face at a hotel in Manhattan and drew an arrest warrant for assault; he eventually pleaded guilty to a lesser charge and paid a fine to resolve the incident.

That's not all. In his later years, Berry concentrated on various real estate and other business ventures, one of which was the Southern Air restaurant in Wentzville, Missouri, a St. Louis suburb where he had long maintained a sprawling compound. Berry's first encounter with the Southern Air was a meal that he and his ne'er-do-well friends ate there in the days immediately prior to the crime spree that first landed him in prison; the restaurant was whites-only then, and they were served through a side window. His return years later to buy the place would have been a good basis for a heartwarming narrative of triumph but for subsequent events. In 1989 Berry was the target of a class-action lawsuit by group of women alleging that they had been videotaped without their knowledge or consent while using the restroom at the Southern Air; the prosecuting attorney of St. Charles County was also gearing up to charge Berry with multiple felonies—including child abuse, based on the fact that children had been among those videotaped—and probably would have done so had he not been defeated in his reelection bid. In *Brown Eyed Handsome Man*, Bruce Pegg argues persuasively that the nationally-publicized Southern Air affair was driven by the animosity and greed of a couple of disgruntled employees, the prosecutor's political aspirations, and the longstanding racist hatred that many residents of St. Charles County felt toward Berry. What Pegg cannot dispute, and all but confirms, is that Berry had indeed been shooting voyeuristic videos of the women's restroom. Eventually he paid out a settlement, and the issue slowly went away. Berry remained in Wentzville and continued to play regular gigs until 2017, when he died at the age of ninety.

What's most disturbing about Berry is the inescapable suggestion that these two major traits—virtuosic pied piper of America's youth, and sexually compulsive predator—cannot be disentangled: that his genius cannot be easily extricated from his bad behavior, that the latter infests the former to its core. Part of the dangerous, faintly illicit thrill of Berry's best music comes from the impression of these tendencies circling each other, sparks arcing through the gap between them, achieving an unstable equilibrium.

And part of what makes "My Ding-a-Ling" so awful comes from the impression of this equilibrium collapsing, just utterly showing its ass.

3

Near the end of his autobiography, Berry advances a rather peculiarly-worded vision of a future "when all races and nationalities in the United States will be merged":

> Now, wouldn't that be real nice? A one-race, normal-face, average-shade, medium-made, balanced-weight, open-fate society with no disturbing variants. [...] But there's no way people would be content with such monotony. It just wouldn't work.

Read in 2020, that sounds painfully like the sort of optimistic, daydreamy prediction that one might remember hearing expressed circa 2009; I suspect it fell similarly upon the ear when it was published in 1987, evoking a strain of facile, fatuous hippiedom that hadn't aged particularly well.

What strikes me as interesting is, first, that it's an unusual idea to see expressed by an African-American musician, given the history of such sentiments being used opportunistically by white people to avoid confronting persistent injustice and unacknowledged injury; black music post-James-Brown has tended to emphasize dignity and visibility, rather than aspiring toward some post-racial amalgamation. Berry's rise to fame, of course, had been closely associated with exactly this sort of ethnic boundary-blurring, but it manifested in other aspects of his life, too; Pegg, for instance, documents the light-skinned Berry's early efforts to pass himself off as American Indian or Polynesian, and Berry himself writes with amusement about his use of photographic tricks to appear white in publicity photos. When he wrote "Johnny B. Goode," Berry reports, he decided to make Johnny hail from Louisiana because New Orleans was "where most Africans were sorted through and sold"—but he also changed the original lyric from "colored boy" to "country boy," so as not to "seem biased to white fans." This move—simultaneously evoking and evading the topic of race—is extremely Chuck Berry.

The second (and more) interesting thing about this post-racial vision is the degree to which it's specifically bodily, and implicitly libidinal. The merging that it posits is presented as purely genetic, not social or cultural, and population-scale genetic merging requires a bunch of promiscuous, procreative sexual intercourse. I mean, it just does. This tendency to understand society in principally libidinal terms is also reflected in the summary of Berry's heritage that appears in one of his early chapters; it emphasizes his mixed African, Anglo, and indigenous American ancestry, and reads like a softcore adaptation of Genesis 5: genealogy as erotica.

If we step back and look at Berry's life as a whole—his crossing of racial lines in both music and sex, his disregard for the age of consent, his wantonness throughout his seventy years of marriage, his unapologetic criminality, his refusal of professionalism as a live performer, even his casualness about copyright—a pattern emerges, which is the willful obliteration of distinctions and limits. Given that bourgeois values are chiefly defined by the strict maintenance of distinctions, I would argue that Berry is probably best understood as an anti-bourgeois artist.

Bourgeois values are stuffy as hell, I get that. Berry smashed a lot of extremely tacky shit during his cartwheels through America's china closet, shit that needed smashing. But the problem with obliterating bourgeois strictures willy-nilly is that a more equitable means of organizing society doesn't automatically materialize to take their place; in practice, what emerges often ain't pretty, as any number of early-70s Laurel Canyon songwriters observed. When we cease to regard one another sentimentally, we usually end up regarding one another *instrumentally* instead, much as Berry seems to have regarded fellow musicians, concert promoters, and the young women with whom he had sex. Viewed from this standpoint, our very personhood recedes, becoming fictional, false.

I don't think it's too much of a stretch to suggest that Berry's attitudes were first manifested, and may have originated, in the dynamics of the prosperous household where he grew up: the strict religious parents, the large group of siblings, the praise and local renown accrued by a gifted older sister. Of all the telling anecdotes in Berry's autobiography, one that describes his rivalry with that sister—years before he had the self-possession to write "Roll Over Beethoven"—strikes me as particularly revelatory:

> Lucy, becoming more and more sophisticated in music at school and at home, was constantly gaining recognition for her singing accomplishments. Playing and singing her classical songs consequently gave her priority above any of us to play the piano at home [...]

> which greatly limited by growing enthusiasm for picking out my favorite boogie-woogie numbers. I got so mad at her one day that I broke wind in one of Mother's old fruit jars, put my hand over it, came back, and set it out on the piano in front of her to pollute her playing.

There you have it, my friends: "My Ding-a-Ling" is the jarred fart of modern popular music. Because, let's be honest, if it were merely a bad song by one of the great geniuses of the twentieth century, it *still* wouldn't be worth complaining about. (Few among us, by comparison, spend time and emotional energy bemoaning the existence of Bob Dylan's "Wiggle Wiggle.") What qualifies it as the absolute worst is its reach, its power, its demonstrated ability to infect and to spoil.

What's upsetting about "My Ding-a-Ling"—Chuck Berry's only number-one hit, you'll recall—is the fact that it was rewarded so abundantly. Not even that, it's the fact that it was rewarded so abundantly when it was the *worst thing Berry ever recorded*, while the *best* things Berry ever recorded are among the best things *anybody* ever recorded. It's almost Lovecraftian in its perfect wrongness: an aperture to a world in which our lofty ideals and principled aspirations are parodied and defiled...or, worse, *through* which that world has already permeated our own.

Listen to him one more time, cooing instructions like he's running icebreaker activities at an orgy. Berry repeatedly addresses the predominantly teenage audience as "children," putting himself in the role of tutor, which would be risqué coming from just about any performer given the nature of the material; coming from Berry, less than a decade out from his Mann Act incarceration, it's positively squirmy. And the kids love it. Listen to the singalong, the creeping participation, the compliant self-sorting by sex. *We want Chuck!* To what extent is their enthusiasm sincere, and to what extent sarcastic? Are they laughing with him? At him? Both? To what extent is Berry in on the joke? Does it matter? *Those of you who will not sing / you must be playing with your own ding-a-ling!* Ha ha ha! Onanism and fucking: there is nothing else.

When we hear a great song—"We're in the Money," "These Foolish Things," "Over the Rainbow," "Don't Get Around Much Anymore," "La Vie en rose," "Bésame Mucho," "Ich bin der Welt abhanden gekommen," "That's All Right," "I've Got You under My Skin," "Respect," "I Want You Back," "Inner City Blues," "Águas de Março," "Mannish Boy," "Heroes," "I

Will Survive," "Time After Time," "This Charming Man," "Raspberry Beret," "How Will I Know," "Check the Rhime," "You Oughta Know," "Single Ladies," "Dancing on My Own," go on, go listen to that shit, you owe it to yourself—our embodied experience of the world is enriched and expanded, and we're freshly amazed at what human beings in our best moments can create. These songs leave us more alive, more alert to the present moment and the possibilities that spill from it.

"My Ding-a-ling" does more or less the opposite, suggesting that despite any and all pretentions to the contrary, we amount to no more than genitals schlepped around by motile meat. We not only accepted this message but sought it out, insisted that it be dumped onto our airwaves, demanded through our sheer numbers that it be packaged for individual sale, the better to throw our money at it. We split ourselves in two; we laughed and we sang. We wanted this, and chose it. It is what we are.

ON THE ESSAY:

I have had six essays make it into March Xness brackets, but I usually play to lose. My inclination is always to drag my patient fellow Xnessers deep into rabbit-holes that are of limited interest to anyone but me, which is not a good victory strategy. Besides, competition is stressful!

For March Badness, however, I knew my cause was righteous, and I went uncharacteristically hard. I still sincerely believe that "My Ding-a-Ling" is the worst pop song of all time, but I was honored to be defeated in the Elite 8 by Elena Passarello and her extremely good essay about the Captain & Tennille's version of Willis Alan Ramsey's "Muskrat Love"—which, while quite bad, is, let's just be real here, not THAT bad, y'all.

Many thanks to the Selection Committee for their wisdom and labor! March Xness remains one of approximately five good things about the internet.

MARCH PLAIDNESS

IN AFTERNESS:

John Melillo on "Bound for the Floor" by Local H

"Bound for the Floor" was Local H's most commercially successful song. It was the first single from the album *As Good As Dead*, released in April 1996. At the time of the song's release, Local H was an interracial duo composed of singer-guitarist Scott Lucas and drummer Joe Daniels. The band—really Lucas's project—began in 1990 in Chicago, and it continues to make music today. Local H is the last grunge band.

What I mean by this is that while this is an essay about this particular Local H of 1996, of "Bound for the Floor," it is also about lasting beyond a particular moment, a particular bit of radio play, and a particular genre. Listening to this 1996 Local H again makes me wonder about what it means to persist in ruins, what it means to linger in the coming after. Listening to this song and this album again, I realize that this song asks me (and all of us) to reckon with debt and mourning and influence.

Local H in 1996 worked in a deeply Nirvana-esque style. I say this as a matter of course: the total internalization of quiet-loud-quiet; of textured guitar distortion; of melodic screamed sickness unto death. Local H kill their idols with the kindness of repetition. This is absolutely a compliment.

That's because for Local H in *As Good As Dead*, this mastery and retransmission of Nirvana's style produces a kind of newness, even in its fidelity to a previous model. Style as knowledge and homage is something I want to dwell in here: it's what makes the repetition a swerve, a slight difference. It's what composes Local H's afterness and lastness: their continuation.

"Bound for the Floor" and the other songs on this album take up grunge as an idiom in a way that is both totally inside of and removed from it. Mastering grunge (Nirvana's grunge) as a musical style—as a duo no less!—means opening up a gap between recognition and rehearsal, between the enraptured first listening and the task of taking apart and making sense of that listening. This gap shows a band giving in to the power of a style, doing it again not because it is an emotional territory to be misread and mined but because one can continue to work in its nuances and possibilities. Local H represents, for me, how the minor swerve works just enough to manifest a concrete feeling, rather than something tired, cliché, and embarrassing. There is a clear contrast between Local H and the insipid irony-free post-grunge masculinist tragicomedy that filled rock radio in the second half of the '90s.

On a purely technical level, they simply sounded better—better lyrics, more interesting sound textures, better drumming—than the many other Nirvana-esque bands. Their transformation of the power trio into a power duo was inspiring. They worked out an even more efficient system for reducing rock to rhythm and noise.

But the afterness and lastness of Local H—their ability to straddle the abyss between grunge's operative moment in rock and its cultural exhaustion in the mid-90s—goes beyond the technical details of their music. On this album—and in this song's style and delivery—they are aware of their belatedness. That belatedness neither silences nor alienates them. Rather, it grants them voice. "Bound for the Floor" emerges in the wake of a double death: a death that is actual—Kurt Cobain's—and another kind of dying: a loss and resolution of the vividness and ongoingness of the past into the concluded fact of the object—or, the photograph, the status update, the conclusion. The end of Nirvana froze grunge into a death mask. Alice Notley describes this feeling in an essay on Frank O'Hara: "I discovered a curious thing: ...Frank O'Hara's poetry had frozen into art for me. It, like my own past, wasn't my life, a vivid motion-filled thing; it had died into artifact."

All over *As Good As Dead* it is hard not to hear this process of grunge dying into artifact. But to be *in* that process, to demarcate it as it happens: that is the magic of Local H on this album. This happens in both sound and lyrics. Throughout the album, it's hard not to hear Cobain as the "you" addressed by Lucas. For instance, on "O.K." he sings:

Drawing a collective breath
I could cry myself to death
And wash this all away
In a flash, you were gone
Leaving me a couple of songs
That I listen to everyday
And I don't even care
That you were so unfair

Or on "Manifest Destiny (Part 1)" we hear:

You're on to something good
But I can't believe it's all
That matters to you
A fool
Who never seems happy
When things are great
It's too late...

Fidelity—to the call, to those other songs—grants the possibility of speaking to the dead. Your voice both is and is not their voice. The other popular single from *As Good As Dead*, "Eddie Vedder," expands on this attitude. It is an angry turn on the one who has left, the one rejecting the singer (and the world): "You go ahead / as good as dead / That's it / I quit / I don't give a shit." The one who is dead and gone was always "as good as dead." The pronounced semblance of death now precedes the actual loss of death.

Such a projection seems to be the power of afterness: the ability to warp time and remake causality.

I should say that this structural atemporality was also part of my lived experience of this music. At the time, *As Good As Dead* and *Nevermind* were co-emergent in my adolescent brain: my summer '96 awakening to grunge (brought on by a chance radio listen of Nirvana's "Drain You") manifested as a near constant desire to listen to and make these sounds. To hear Local H was to hear the possibility of the reproduction and continuation of not just grunge music but *music*. Even in the act of repatterning my brain by listening to *Nevermind* on a nightly basis, I was also hearing other "Nirvana" (i.e. Local H) songs that could distance and somewhat displace the Nirvana-idol-sound-image. That little bit of separation in the music—what at the time I heard (and still hear but less intensely) as distinctions in presentation, in voice, in texture, in attitude, in the sounds of the songs themselves—granted me futurity. The music seemed to be saying: "Can't go on, must go on."

All this time passed and passing. So much repetition and difference. "Bound for the Floor," with its intensely repeated lines—

You just don't get it
you keep it copacetic
and you learn to accept it
and oh it's so pathetic

—is on the surface a mantra of alienated self-hatred. But it's also difficult to ascertain the tone of the hatred here: does the singer hate himself as the one keeping it copacetic, hate others for keeping it copacetic, or hate a particular other for going too far? Is the "you" another way of saying "I"? Is the "you" the quiet seeker of a false normality? Is the "you" the potential suicide who holds back and sustains their dread, until the end?

The mantra becomes a magic spell, simultaneously undoing itself and reveling in its failure to undo a single goddamn thing, to change that "you" it calls to. The song seems to be telling us: "Don't keep cool! Get the fuck loud! Scream!" while also freezing in place, stuck in its own cycle. The song battles an affectlessness that I can't help but hear as a particularly Midwestern take on grunge. I flash to my sophomore year, to the commute with my father across the city of Wichita in the blue Chevy Astro van to the high school where he taught English and coached football. What were the effects of hearing this song nearly every morning on the radio? Was I hearing myself hate myself or hearing myself hate my dad? Or hearing myself hate the self that dad, school, football, world were making of me? "What good is confidence?" Or hearing myself hate the very emptiness of a self that would admit to such influence? Or hearing myself hate the afterness of adolescence, the irredeemable fall into desire, responsibility, compromise? "Bound for the floor." Or hearing myself already hate death, that single death which stands for death in general? "Born to be down."

All, none, others.

There is something about minor voices, the voices that are perhaps underrated or forgotten by the mass projections and delusions of immense popularity, that helps answer the question: how do you survive this shit? Debt, mourning, influence. To come after grants the possibility of survival, the grace of keeping things going. To call to Cobain and to recall Nirvana's sound both freezes and animates the object. It remains there as immovably movable as the stars. We pass into the afterness—which is, at least, still passing.

ON THE ESSAY:

From the beginning of March Xness, I had been looking forward to a March Plaidness. I started my musical/critical life with grunge as the model and the object. It was Nirvana's grunge, along with Local H's "just-in-time" version of it, that created some feeling of contemporaneity in my adolescence–even though it was already uncool, over. Local H led me backwards and forwards in powerful ways, and so I offered and then wrote about this song. Of course, I did not realize the band and their fans would carry the essay to the championship. It was so cool to share this work, talk to the band, and see them participate in the whole spectacle. In the midst of the pandemic that felt affirming: I see now how the essay's tone is suffused with the dread of 2020-2021. I feel lucky that it lives on to speak about an important aspect of grunge in general: it was always too late, and that's what made it new.

THE BEST CHRISTIAN IN THE WORLD

Matt Bell on "My Own Prison" by Creed

Let's get this out of the way first: there's a good chance you don't think Creed is a good band, or that Scott Stapp is a good singer, or that "My Own Prison" is a good song. If so, you wouldn't be alone. Despite selling millions of copies of their first few albums, despite achieving near-ubiquitous radio and music television presence for years, despite selling out constant live tours for a similar amount of time, Creed has from the very first had more critical detractors than champions. In an infamous cover story for *SPIN* in 2000, writer Gavin Edwards summed up the band's critical response in a devastating paragraph that, two decades later, my wife and I both still remember:

> *To wit, some of the phrases critics have used to describe Creed's music: "white-bread, bloated, and monotonous"; "bland and bombastic"; "aimless, formless, charmless bluster"; "Pearl Jam knockoffs." [Apparently tired of the comparisons, [bassist Brian] Marshall recently said that Eddie Vedder "wishes he could write like Scott Stapp." Stapp subsequently apologized on behalf of the band, calling Marshall's comments an example of "arrogance and stupidity."] An Ohio paper called Stapp a "Prince Valiant-Jesus-Jim Morrison cartoon rocker." Shawn Crahan of Slipknot complained to a Canadian newspaper, "If I gotta listen to bands like Creed anymore, I might as well shoot myself, dude."*

Similarly, in a brutal 1998 review titled "Grunge Gets Religion, and It's Not Pretty," a *New York Times* reviewer mocked Creed's lyrics, Stapp's stagecraft, and the band's religion, before finally concluding: "Convictions aside, Creed's weakness is its music."

If Creed wasn't for any of these critics or fellow musicians—and it decidedly was not—then who was Creed for?

Maybe Creed was grunge for people born a little late for grunge, as well as Christian rock for Christians ashamed to admit that's why they liked it, made by a Christian band equally reluctant to admit what it was, if doing so would cost its members their one best shot at fame.

*

I was 13 when Kurt Cobain committed suicide in April 1994, a date I personally count as the end of the grunge era, whether or not that's exactly right. I was a fan of Nirvana and the other grunge bands—at least the most radio-friendly ones I could hear in rural Michigan, the usual suspects like Pearl Jam and Soundgarden and so on—but I was young enough I came to their first albums late, only to find much of the music a little over my head, especially given the inscrutability of much of the genre's songwriting. Instead, my favorite CDs in the first half of the nineties were albums like *New Miserable Experience* by the Gin Blossoms, *August And Everything After* by Counting Crows, or *Throwing Copper* by Live—all albums by bands who, like Creed, were frequently mocked then and still are now, even as each had its own rabid fanbases and big hits.

What was it that I responded to so strongly in these albums? Perhaps it was only that, in the famously ironic nineties, Doug Hopkins and Adam Duritz and Ed Kowalczyk were deadly earnest songwriters—just like I was a deadly earnest teenager.

When Creed's post-grunge/grunge-derivative *My Own Prison* released in 1997, at the start of my senior year of high school, I discovered an album even more perfectly fit to my own particular expression of earnestness, an album whose music was for once immensely popular but also somehow full of secrets, special messages for anyone who understood its references and symbols, anyone *special enough* to be a Christian like me, like the members of the band.

Maybe you too were a youth group kid like me, or at least recognize the type: from the start, I was compelled to point out every biblical or spiritual reference in their lyrics to anyone who would listen, starting with "My Own Prison" and its opening Judgment Day court convening to consider Stapp's impossible-to-appeal sin, its spiritual warfare-referencing "demons cluttering around" and the beatitudinal nod of "we the meek," plus what I still think is the song's best line, "should have been there on a Sunday morning, banging my head," the rare Creed line that has enough ambiguity to suggest a double meaning. Most notably, the third verse sees Stapp imagining himself witnessing Christ's crucifixion—"I hear a thunder in the distance / See a vision of a cross / I feel the pain that was given / On that sad day of loss"—while the bridge, perhaps the most famous part of the song, repeats: "I cry out to God / seeking only His decision / Gabriel stands and confirms / I've created my own prison."

There's really no way to deny that the song isn't composed almost entirely of Christian reference points, both in symbols and allusions employed in its lyrics and in Stapp's personal expressions of doubt and longing for redemption. But does writing and performing Christianity-influenced songs like "My Own Prison" mean Creed was a *Christian band*, like groups like DC Talk or Jars of Clay, as so many people like me wanted them to be?

*

In his aforementioned *SPIN* article, Gavin Edwards pursued this same line of inquiry, one I remember pondering with friends first in my high school cafeteria and then later in college dorm rooms: "One question follows Creed wherever they go: Are you a Christian band? No, no, no! they insist, though they do realize they have a significant number of Christian fans." Guitarist Mark Tremonti, who grew up in Michigan among Roman Catholics like I did, tried to dodge the question in *SPIN*, saying, "I think there are a lot of kids in strict families who are allowed to listen to us because we don't have any negative messages in our music," while Stapp objected in his own way on the now-defunct (but very era-appropriately named) creednet.com: "We are not a Christian band. A Christian band has an agenda to lead others to believe in their specific religious beliefs. We have no agenda!"

Fair enough. But what did *no agenda* and *no negative messages* mean, to a band whose debut album included a song with righteous pro-life/anti-abortion lines like "we kill the unborn to make ends meet" and Stapp snarling the seemingly homophobic complaint, "only in America, sexuality is democracy," before proudly declaring "my soul sings a different song"?

No negative messages is absolutely a subjective judgment here, and if the band had no agenda of its own, then the viewpoint represented by lyrics like those in "Only America" was still a decidedly Christian one, rooted in a specific era of evangelical religion and politics.

Believing I recognized these evasions for what they were, I felt frustrated by Stapp and Tremont's objections, even as I understood them completely: like the members of Creed, I wouldn't have wanted anyone to make too much of my being a Christian, at least not outside of church. But like the band's members, I was one, and earnestly, fervently so: I'd been raised Roman Catholic, went weekly to a small rural Michigan church with my mother who frequented bible studies and prayer groups, who believed in a personal relationship with God, who I believe thought of angels and other miraculous beings in literal, physical ways. By the time I was seventeen—the year *My Own Prison* released—I also saw myself as a firm believer and participant in church, having completed my sacraments and progressed from altar boy to lector, frequently reading the liturgies during mass, something I took pride in even as I felt embarrassed if anyone acknowledged it. On my own, I read the Bible cover to cover—unsurprisingly, I especially enjoyed Genesis and Exodus and Revelations, plus all the parts of the Old Testament most like the fantasy novels I loved—and prayed frequently, alone, with my mother, and at church.

I also tried my best to study my faith on my own, in catechism and youth group, in bible studies, and by reading novels written by other Christians. I especially liked unpacking the religious references in the Narnia books and *The Lord of the Rings*, and I was briefly obsessed with Frank Peretti's *This Present Darkness* and its sequels, Christian horror novels whose villains were demon-influenced New Age spiritualists and artists, college professors and ACLU lawyers, all people I now recognize as reliable boogeymen of certain kinds of evangelicals (and whose broad types now make up most of my friends). I went to youth conferences, where my church's Catholic doctrine mixed with other non-denominational faiths in ways I didn't realize weren't part of mainstream Catholicism, introducing me to spiritual warfare, speaking in tongues, and being slain by the spirit. This was also where I first heard that rock music was nothing more than coded Satanism, something I didn't take particularly seriously, although I vividly remember having the sinful sexual content in the lyrics of AC/DC's "You Shook Me All Night Long" passionately decoded by what must have been someone else in the group's mother.

Scott Stapp famously grew up in a strict Pentecostal household, one where rock music was forbidden and all extracurricular activities except sports were prohibited, a situation that Stapp says caused him to attempt to prove his worth to his stepfather and to God through academics and sports. Despite his best attempts, by 2000, Stapp said he didn't feel the same spiritual connection his fellow churchgoers seemed to feel as they spoke in tongues and were otherwise overcome with the Spirit: "I thought something was wrong with me," he said. "I constantly found myself asking God to prove himself to me...I'd lie in bed and say, 'God, if you're real, just make my light go off so I won't doubt it. I promise I'll be the best Christian in the world.'"

I mentioned above that my wife and I both remember reading the 2000 *SPIN* article, which is why I keep returning to it: I know this last quote is something that resonated with me at the time, because I was in the exact same place Stapp was describing. In my eyes, I'd done my best to be a good Catholic—which isn't to say I wasn't brutally, guiltily aware of my every failing—and to seek the kind of personal relationship with God that my mother and others described. But I never felt that, not once that I can recall. I know all the usual objections to this complaint, because so many other people of faith have pointed them out to me: in his own narrative of this desire for *SPIN*, Stapp calls the wanting for God's reciprocity "a sin," and anyone I expressed this fear to in my teenage years would have told me it isn't up to God to prove himself to me. I understood all that, but the fact remained that I felt I was doing everything could to earn God's love, a love I never once felt, not in the ways other people around me described it.

There are other, smarter reasons I eventually stopped believing in God, but it's also true that my feelings were hurt. Other people were worthy, and I was not, and whatever was wrong with me wasn't something I could seem to fix.

And so one day I stopped trying.

No more God for me.

*

In R.O. Kwon's fantastic novel *The Incendiaries*, the protagonist Will abandons his faith, then struggles with the loss, in one of the only literary depictions that matches my own experience of the same. Early in the novel, Will says:

> In time, they'd all want me to explain how I lost my faith...Scripture indicates there's no hope for the apostates, like me: having known His love, then repudiated Him, I'm believed to be past saving. I exist beyond His grace. But I tried: will that count for anything, Lord? In the final lists You won't compile, allotting a life that You can't give because, in failing to exist, You've left us behind.

But I tried: will that count for anything, Lord? That was how I felt, exactly as

Will does—beseeching a God you no longer believe in, by the end—in the years when I was trying to fulfill my faith, and in the first years when I lost it, a time that corresponds almost exactly to the years in which Creed was a major part of my life. The end of my faith was a long and messy affair, some of it emotional, some of it intellectual: studying in an attempt to bolster my faith, I accidentally read my way out of it. After Catholicism, I went through a series of experiments in replacement religions—a little self-taught Buddhism, some suburban Ann Arbor sweat lodges, a dabbling in psychedelics and so much New Age-inflected environmentalism—before finally coming out the other side entirely, into what was for many years an angry atheism, logically sure, emotionally furious.

Mostly that anger and hurt has faded now, thankfully. (After all, how long was I supposed to stay mad at someone I didn't believe was real?) If religion comes up at all these days, I might jokingly refer to myself as an "expatriate Catholic," because even though I haven't been a believer in two decades, it's obvious I've been permanently altered by my early fervent religious earnestness. I still have the potential to be just as zealot-like as I once was—I like to think of it as *obsessiveness*, but sometimes it's better to call it what it is—and the stories, symbols, and mysteries of the Catholicism I was brought up in have settled deep in my imagination and my thinking. My novels are, for better or worse, obviously written by someone who spent a lot of time with biblical imagery and with Catholic modes of thought: in them are retellings of the Garden of Eden, debates about sin (which I wish I could call anything else) and about guilt and redemption, as well as a continuing thinking through of the Genesis ideas of stewardship and dominion.

Even now, twenty years later, I rarely give a reading from my books without someone in the audience asking me if I'm a Catholic.

I was, I answer. I'm not anymore, I demur. I will be forever, I often admit.

*

It may not be obvious from the way I'm writing about Scott Stapp, but I really am trying my best not to project my issues onto him, or to map too much of my psychology onto his. I can't know for sure where Scott Stapp was in his spiritual journey when he wrote the lyrics to "My Own Prison," can't know if I'm right that in those days his faith was present in everything he wrote even as he was afraid to let anyone see its full power over him, especially if it might let others mock him for it or somehow cost him the popularity his band was seeking. After my own uber-fandom, after the general ambivalence that followed and the decades of his ambient celebrity, where the only time I thought about Stapp was when the news covered his arrests, his drug addictions, a sex tape, and his felony domestic violence arrest, how can I avoid making up my own myths about who he is and why he did and said the things he did?

I won't make any excuses for any of Stapp's well-documented personal problems or alleged criminal behaviors. But I will say that I wonder what it cost him to live those early years of his explosive music career in opposition to his upbringing's strictures (here *no rock music* is a rule broken, not bent), especially when the saving grace of his music's earnest spirituality—its deep roots in Christianity, its sincere wrestling with doubt and sin and judgment, its detectable values broadly in line with the mainstream Christianity of its time—could be seen as diminished by the band's constant denial of their music as Christian music, which always felt less like the honest truth and more like a public relations calculation.

The members of Creed didn't believe they could be megastars if they were defined as a Christian rock band, so they never admitted that's what they were, even if all the evidence suggested it was so. But what does it cost you to deny what is you've made and who it is you are, even if by doing so you reap all the worldly rewards anyone could want?

Twenty-plus years after "My Own Prison," Scott Stapp seems to have come to terms with whatever the cost was of his dueling faith and his personal demons, embracing his own imaginative and emotional landscape to make new music outside the scrutiny of the early Creed years. His last solo album came out in 2019, and even a cursory listen finds Stapp openly embracing themes he once denied, with clearly spiritual songs like "Purpose for Pain," "Heaven in Me," "Mary's Crying," and "Last Hallelujah," the last of which is full of direct biblical imagery, desert temptations and walking on water and crowns of thorns.

Through most of the intervening years between "My Own Prison" and now, the person I thought Scott Stapp was and the music he made felt increasingly far away, buried in both our pasts. But I sense there's still two sides of him—a 2019 *Billboard* interview doesn't mention Christianity, Pentecostalism, or faith, while another recent interview in the evangelical magazine *Charisma* mentions almost nothing else—but also that there's more harmony between the two halves than in the past. As he told *Charisma*:

I've finally gotten to a place where there's resolution... There aren't

> any conflicts anymore… No longer having to deal with those things brought me to a place of clarity where I could finally turn that into the content of the songs… The depth of the music that I was creating reflected the new inner peace that was going on inside of me. It set the table for the melodies and lyrics to come out and actually deliver exactly what I feel I was supposed to do, my purpose in life.

Good for him, I think, as I read this—but isn't there some part of me that resents his newfound peace, his bringing together of his disparate selves?

Of course there is. There always will be resentment in me, aimed at anyone whose faith passes through doubt and comes out intact.

*

I saw Creed play live only once, in the spring of 2000, at the Saginaw Civic Center with Sevendust and Three Doors Down opening. I went with other employees of the restaurant where I bartended in the years after I dropped out of college, and now, twenty years later, I remember just two things about that show: first, how a woman I worked with bragged about her ability to get backstage returned to our group with a member of one of the opening bands on her arm; and second, that after Creed finally took the stage, Scott Stapp's performance so quickly became such an over-the-top attention-seeking parody of a rock star that it burst the last spiritual mystique he still held for me. He was just a normal guy in an ordinary rock band, I decided, not worth the amount of importance I'd given him, his story, the myth I'd made of how our struggles with faith were alike. In an instant, whatever connection I'd once felt was broken. I'd still listen to Creed after that night, but it was never the same, and it wasn't long before I stopped.

A third thing about that concert, not a memory but something I didn't know at the time: my future wife was in the audience that night too.

Maybe it's a cheat to try to leave this essay here, to flee through this escape hatch I'm about to make without explaining the intervening steps between that night and my meeting my wife. So be it. Because here's the truth: once I thought God would save me, that my faith would set me free from all that was wrong with me. Later I thought it might be music or books, drugs or alcohol or meditation. But what finally let me rescue me from myself wasn't faith or art or inebriation; it was my one person, a fellow Creed fan I wouldn't meet for another two years but who was there with me in that crowd, in the biggest arena in our small city.

That night, at my one and only Creed concert, I had two more years of being lost ahead of me, two more years of being lost ahead of me, two more years alone with the doubts and hurt feelings my faith had become.

They were, as I recall, hard hard years.

But they did not last an eternity. Nothing does.

If those years were a prison at all—my own or someone else's—I did at last escape.

ON THE ESSAY:

I'm thankful for how essays that blend criticism and memoir like this one allow me to write about my life in a way that might be impossible if I tried it straight. The essay is about "My Own Prison," of course, but talking about Creed and Scott Stapp helped me finally revisit my journey with faith (and the later lack of it). I thought then that this was one of the most personal essays I'd written, and it feels even more so now, when the conditions of my life have changed again. Without knowing it at the time, I partly became a fiction writer so I could access my emotions in a safely defamiliarized space. For a long time, I didn't know how to do the same in nonfiction—but a few years of March Xness got more of this kind of writing from me than almost anything else.

Danielle Evans on "Seether" by Veruca Salt

I have seen *Charlie and the Chocolate Factory* in its entirety exactly once, in elementary school, and I am using "seen" loosely here, because I was a squeamish and sensitive child and once I gathered that our class was being shown a horror movie for children, I cradled my head on my desk and peered up only occasionally to see what fresh hell was happening on screen. As best I could follow the plot, we were meant to root for Charlie, a sycophantic boy who passively and complicitly watched his competitors, also children, be systematically tortured by a wealthy factory owner and was then rewarded by becoming the new factory owner. In the moral world of the movie, the other children deserved their fates because they committed the respective crimes of being fat, unproductive, boastful, and a spoiled girl who demands what she wants.

In the version of the film we watched, after a rather delightful musical number, in which she screams, among other things, "I want the world I want the whole world" and "I want it now," Veruca Salt is sorted into the trash by a machine designed to collect chocolate eggs from magical geese. The internet informs me that in the book and the 2005 film, Veruca is torn limb from limb by squirrels who deem her rotten. I was horrified enough by the version in which a child disappears into the trash chute.

I was predisposed, then, to love a band called Veruca Salt for their name alone, for embracing a feminine lack of restraint, a willingness to be loud, spoiled, rotten even, if the alternatives were punished or deprived. Their debut album, American Thighs, took its name from an AC/DC lyric, "She had the sightless eyes, telling me no lies/ Knocking me out with those American thighs." The band introduced themselves by invoking a particular cocktail of aggression and desire and girlhood and honest rage. "Seether," Veruca Salt's first single, was part boast, part apology, part warning, a love letter to the kind of anger that breaks out when you try to hold it back. "I can't see her til I'm foaming at the mouth," sang Nina Gordon and Louise Post, the band's frontwomen. Portions of the music video are footage of the band in a Chicago animal shelter, surrounded by cats who are uninterested in the production, but somehow make the song's tone both more vulnerable and more ominous. "I try to keep her on a short leash," the lyrics say, while on screen a tabby cat yowls into the camera, as if to say "Yeah, OK, good luck with that leash."

For a song with fairly straightforward lyrics—the seether is a personification of explosive anger—it generated enough secondary interpretations (the seether was an illness, the seether was a vagina...) that in the song "Volcano Girls" on their second album, the band offered a footnote: "here's another clue if you please/the seether's Louise." Though "Seether" is a song about anger, the title locates it in the before of anger. What's most interesting about the seether is not the specific quality of her rage, which is somewhat abstract, but about how long the seether can go dormant, and how hard the fight to keep her in her place is. The seether is rocked in her cradle, the seether is knocked out, the seether is boiled, the seether is swallowed, the seether is subjected to all manner of violence and domesticity, but the seether survives, and there's some triumph in it. Also, perhaps some prescience— the positive reception to Veruca Salt's debut thrust the band into the spotlight, and then a cocktail of industry struggles, among them grueling tours, personal crises, rejection by some in the indie music community that had helped form them, the difficulty of sustaining an intense friendship under even the best of circumstances, and perhaps Louise's famously immortalized temper, led to the band's breakup after their second album. For years, Gordon and Post weren't on speaking terms.

Here's where I confess that I squeaked into the grunge essay tournament despite missing the heyday of grunge. I was a few years too young for Generation X, and I was a Black kid growing up in the late '80s and early '90s, when music and radio were much more firmly segregated. In our car the radio presets were two R&B stations, two hip hop stations, one oldies station, and one generic pop station. When a friend of mine had a '90s themed 30th birthday party in the mid-2010s, most of the guests showed up in plaid flannel; I showed up in glitter makeup and the bright blue wig I'd coveted since Lil Kim's appearance in "Crush on You." Up through my years in middle school, if a white person had made music after 1970 and hadn't made it to the Top 40, odds were high I hadn't heard of them. I had heard of grunge, and understood the word well enough to tell people some of my classmates were into it, but not well enough to answer my mother's question when she asked "Why would they call it something that sounds dirty?"

Not knowing much about what my classmates were into had become something of a badge of honor for me. In the third grade I'd tested out of my neighborhood school and been moved to a gifted classroom in which I was not just the only Black person, but one of only a few kids without blue eyes. It hadn't been welcoming. When my mother looked for a neighborhood school where the gifted class might be more diverse, she discovered I was the only Black child in my grade in the gifted program in the whole county (I was also in the minority in having been placed in the program by the school's own tests—most of the gifted students had gotten their placements through tests administered by paid private psychologists, something Black parents in the county weren't regularly told was an option). We did move, to a school where I was still the only Black student in my class, but no longer the only person of color, but I clung tight to my sense of identity being in part about what I wasn't. I didn't want to become *that* kind of Black girl, one people worried didn't understand she was Black. I assumed I wouldn't like whatever pop culture my white classmates were into in part because it made the ongoing rejection feel mutual, and in part because I didn't want to wonder who I'd be if it turned out I loved it.

By the late '90s, MTV and the radio were better integrated, and I, in high school and in possession of a more fully-formed identity, was less defensive about my own tastes. Plus, it was the birth of streaming music services, and for a few brief years before it all got shut down as the widespread theft system that of course it was, through the magic of Napster and Limewire I could hear all the music I'd heard of but never actually heard. The aesthetics were different, but I recognized in grunge feminism a bravado, a willingness to lack decorum and shun respectability, that reminded me of the most interesting women in the hip hop and R&B I'd grown up with, women who also had to navigate a scene run by men, women who developed a way of talking about sex without being reduced to it, women who didn't have the privilege or grow up spoiled or expect to be met with delicate treatment, but had still found a language for telling the world what they wanted, had found the boldness to make demands, had found, in music, a kind of freedom even if it required relentless performance to maintain. Some of the music of the alternative early '90s bewildered me, some it took me years to come around on, but I loved "Seether" from the first time I heard it. I understood "Seether" because it understood how much effort goes into performance, how hard it is to keep yourself in a mold.

Anger—who can express it, who gets punished for it, who gets called hostile and who gets praised for being firm or direct—is of course always political. I was raised alongside a generation of women who were fed slogans like *girl power* and *lean in* and *you can have it all*, words meant to inspire but which sometimes feel in retrospect like the words that built a generation of girls who were told it was our fault if we didn't ask for enough but failed to build a world prepared to give us much of anything we asked for. I was born into the first full generation of Black Americans raised in a post-Civil Rights Act country, a generation of kids sent into schools people threw rocks at their parents to keep them out of, raised by a generation of Black parents who understood that entering formerly segregated spaces and seats of power was the beginning of the work, just as the country was patting itself on the back for having reached the end; by 40 I had already watched some of those legal gains dismantled. I was raised in a generation that was fed a story of endless growth and possibility and a bright tech-led future while we watched the wealth gap explode and the social safety net stripped apart and whole industries that had once been the source of stable jobs and communities vanish altogether or shift into gig work.

There are costs—physical and mental—to constantly advising people to ask more of a world that keeps telling them no and judging them greedy for wanting it. No wonder all these years later so many people still love a song about seething.

But I had a harder time explaining why I loved "Seether" in the deeply personal way that I love songs that have given me a vocabulary for a part of myself I didn't know I needed to name. I don't generally seethe at people. I rarely yell. I am almost never angry when people think that I am. I am a Black woman with an expressive face, a person raised by New Yorkers who spent nearly a decade of her adult life in the upper Midwest, and I eventually learned to anticipate that people would often interpret all manner of emotions— hurt, mild dissatisfaction, indifference, confusion, enthusiasm about an opportunity for change, directness when making a neutral statement of fact — as anger, and that it wouldn't do me any good to protest. But if I am talking to you, I am almost never angry. I am at best, tired or exasperated or very sad. Well before I'm angry enough to scream, I've usually decided the person I'm angry at isn't worth the effort.

I have two modes of truly angry: I am never going to acknowledge someone again unless it will cost me money not to, and I am never going to acknowledge someone again, but first I am going to tell them why, calmly but at great length and in specific detail, so that I know the bridge is burnt thoroughly enough that I never have to say a word to or hear a word from them in the future. My purest rage is not an explosive anger as a cold one, a calculation. You win a fight with someone who is screaming at you or trying to hurt you by being indifferent or refusing to hear them out or failing to register pain. You win a fight with a person who is careless by caring even less about them than they do about you. You win a fight with a narcissist by ignoring them.

Of course, this strategy only works when you have the power to walk away. It costs something to build a life where you almost always have the power to walk away. It costs something to understand that most of the time when someone is cruel or careless, it's not because you misunderstood them or are lacking a secret exculpatory piece of information known perhaps only to them, or because you did something to deserve it and can still undo whatever the thing was. It costs something to understand that a person who treated you badly probably did so because they believe you're a person with whom they can afford to be cruel and uncareful, either because they don't value you much or they didn't expect you to value yourself enough to object. It costs something to object. It costs something to know that you can, in your heart, forgive people for *how* they let you know they didn't value you, but you cannot in your heart unknow it, you cannot, in your life, hold space for people who don't value you, or pretend that you'll be open to them again. It costs something to believe that you deserve more than people you care about often believe they should give you.

After I have walked away from someone or someplace that treated me badly, I still remember what it cost, even when I'm not sorry, even once I'm as close to forgiveness as I'll come. If forgiveness means I've stopped saying a hex for you at night before I go to bed, well then sure, I've forgiven a lot of people. If forgiveness means I have to be friendly...well then. I don't seethe before I've reached a breaking point, but I often seethe after, when the cord has been cut and there's nowhere for the anger to go. It can't be directed at a person or institution I've already cut off. When I rock and soothe and fight and swallow and boil my anger, I'm not trying to keep it away from someone else before it hurts them. I'm trying to get rid of it before it hurts me to hold onto it. It's hard though, to let go of something you know has saved your life more than once.

But letting go of anger apparently has its virtues. It would have been a depressing end for one of the best known grunge bands fronted by women to emerge from the era as another cautionary tale about the cost of feminist rage and desire, another story with the message that you can want the whole world and want it now if you must, but the machine will eat you alive or the world will tear you to pieces, and no one will blame it: you were a bad egg, a nut. But that's not, after all, how the story ends. After years of open hostility, Gordon and Post met up to sit down and talk things out. The full original band got back together. In 2015, they released a long-awaited new Veruca Salt album, appropriately titled *Ghost Notes*. It's moody and playful and sharp and delightful and sounds both like the third album they might have made together in the '90s and also like an album that needed another decade of adult life to get made. NPR's review says "A group of friends and musicians who have overcome internal turmoil and external pressures that caused them to part ways in the '90s would sound this invincible. Embracing a throwback sound isn't stagnation for Veruca Salt. It's celebration." "I wanted to live so I pretended to die," opens the first song on the album "The Gospel According to Saint Me," a tongue-in-cheek song about resurrection and coming back from the dead. The song concludes "Surprise surprise it's gonna be bright."

ON THE ESSAY:

Time passes and I only grow seethier. I remain full of rage about the suppression of justified anger and desire, the unraveling of the already limited promises of progress the '90s made us, the way women are vilified for having a piece of something we had to claw to get, and the fact the *Charlie and The Chocolate Factory* is billed as a fun children's movie. I have not yet forgiven anyone but I am frequently full of joy anyway.

YOU'LL GET THE MESSAGE BY THE TIME I'M THROUGH:

Kristine Langley Mahler on "Only Happy When It Rains" by Garbage

Fuck grunge right into the ground, like the freshman girls who sat at my art table in 2000, hornily bragging about how they were going to drive to Seattle and dig up Kurt's corpse so they could have sex with it. A world-weary senior, I side-eyed them and internally scoffed *what were they, like EIGHT YEARS OLD when Kurt died? I mean, I was at least ELEVEN, so.* I could have been crueler if I'd been able to bolster my disdain by noting, "You know Courtney had Kurt cremated, right?" But like most grunge facts, that was one I didn't know either.

All "grunge" ever meant to me was those dark phone calls from a "friend," commanding me to recite the lyrics to "my favorite" Nirvana song, then messing up the line in "All Apologies" by saying "choking on the ashes of heredity" instead of "choking on the ashes of her enemy."

Grunge was the flannel shirts I didn't have, the second-hand Ralph Lauren corduroy pants I bought from Goodwill—like I was supposed to—but never wore to middle school because my mom told me corduroys were dressy pants and I didn't know how to contradict her. I didn't know what I *was* supposed to wear with them, but I knew it wasn't a "nice sweater." Grunge was Ben and Tate using Kool-Aid to turn their blond hair faintly pink, cool Amanda with low pigtails and dark lipstick in her 8th grade school picture, Jessie dubbing the classroom praying mantis Green Day when she won the naming lottery and me thinking her choice was super poetic until my "friend" scornfully informed me that Green Day was a *band.*

Grunge was a code word for all the things I didn't know. Grunge was the perpetual feeling of never being cool enough, never knowing enough. Was every adolescent generation as plagued by insecurity as mine in the mid-90s? Was there ever a worse time to witness the collision of a cultural movement—where secret knowledge was the passcode—smashing into the age where a girl realizes everything she doesn't know?

What a horrible time to be twelve: before the internet, when the only way to source information seemed to be through an older sister or brother who somehow, organically, had found it out and passed it down. A horrible time to be that older sister to two siblings. I didn't know I was supposed to read *SPIN*. I didn't even know *SPIN* existed. I didn't know how to distinguish between the CDs in the racks at Camelot, to delineate between which bands were "over" and which ones were cool. I was too young to go to local shows, if there'd even been any (we still drove an hour to go shopping in the state capital). Grunge was defined by passwords that were constantly shifting, and when I think about grunge now, it only makes me angry. I suppose the anger is to mask the insecurity that never went away.

Grunge was nothing but sneering, and I swear it was worse than the disdain from indie band fans in the late '90s/early 2000s. Half the music I always thought of as "grunge" was rejected from this dang tournament's bracket. WHERE WAS OASIS, I ASK YOU? Distortion and anger. That's what grunge meant to me.

The only place I was ever able to enter grunge was through Shirley Manson.

*

band du jour
Garbage

You're flipping through cable, past MTV. Wha? You go back, pause. Who the heck? Cool chick singing the bejesus out of a song you've never heard. You do the clueless and wait for the video's postscript. Song: "Vow." Band: Garbage. You laugh. You immediately go buy the CD, also called *Garbage* (Almo Sound/Geffen). You play it, thinking the Scottish lead singer, Shirley Manson, sounds like a cross between Chrissie Hynde of The Pretenders and Deborah Harry. You decide the catchy pop-a-delic music is like the four elements: earthy, watery, airy and fiery (or in rock terms, gritty, fluid, ethereal and hot) all at once. You play it some more. You play it until your mom threatens to have you committed. You think, If I had a guitar, I'd learn to play every song on the CD.

—Claire Connors

Shirley Manson, the lead singer of Garbage, is wearing a satin black short-sleeve shirt in the November 1995 issue of *Seventeen* magazine, arms crossed behind her head, standing in an old-time elevator with the rest of the blurry band. *Seventeen* called Garbage the "band du jour," and I can still recite the entire article, right down to the "Wha?" reaction, because I reread it so many times. *Cool chick singing the bejesus out of a song you've never heard. You do the clueless and wait for the video's postscript.* But I didn't learn about songs through music videos, I learned about them on the radio. If I wanted to watch MTV, which was forbidden in my house, I had to go to my friends' houses. Which I did.

You decide the catchy pop-a-delic music is like the four elements.

I was intrigued by the idea that this perfectly-turned-out grunge girl with her dark black eye makeup and dark lipstick, posing like a prisoner, could control nature, harnessing all four elements—earth, air, fire, water—to bend to her will. In the photo, she was surrounded by three men—Butch Vig, Steve Marker, and Duke Erikson, her fellow band members in Garbage—but it looked to me like she clearly knew how to make those men fade out.

I know what you're thinking. "How the hell are you gonna take BUTCH VIG, who produced Nirvana's *Nevermind*—a credential which, since we didn't hand the March Plaidness championship over directly to Nirvana and "Smells Like Teen Spirit," should have arguably meant we handed the championship to the man who produced the song that was the true champion of the Plaidness era—and relegate Butch to the role of a background boy? Garbage was Butch's PROJECT! Butch, Steve, and Duke had a whole thing going long before they called in Shirley!"

Maybe because, in a *SPIN* interview for the 25th anniversary of Garbage's self-titled debut, Shirley spoke about her early days with Garbage, saying "I was shocked when I got to Madison and realized what a hot mess they were. I had come from bands that were very self-disciplined. But when I got to Madison, these dudes were so laid-back, drinking beer in their Green Bay Packers baseball hats. I'd never spent time with people like that before in my life."

Shirley met the dude-bros in her new band where they were, but my Queen of Discipline and Control didn't change herself to fit in with their lax-AF, just-keep-it-chill approach. I saw Shirley as a girl who had learned the things I wanted to know.

*

I saw Shirley in *Seventeen* magazine in 1995, but it wasn't until the following spring when I finally saw Shirley in action, kinetic on the television at my friend's grandma's house in Buffalo, New York, where my friend and I had been dropped off for spring break.

Spring Break in Buffalo was about as popular as you might imagine—no one travels to Great Lakes New York in March, especially not when your actual home was only an hour from the Outer Banks of North Carolina, but there we were, nevertheless. I was thirteen years old in March 1996, and my mom had allowed me to use a 7-10 day Clairol kit to dye my hair for the first time. With my freshly-red hair, I sat in the backseat as my friend's dad drove us up the inner Atlantic seaboard, away from my cooler peers who'd headed out to their families' beach houses, and deposited us in the elderly, icicle-laden home of my friend's grandma.

My friend and I slept in a small basement room, furnished with two blow-up mattresses which barely fit inside. The walls were whitewashed, and so we chalked it with messages like "Who's the bomb? We're the bomb!" We played Yahtzee. Walked to the neighborhood library and checked out books on temporary library cards. Took the train downtown to go shopping at DEB, where I bought a baby-doll ringer tee with yellow smiley faces pooling at the hem. Went to bingo with my friend's grandma. Talked about *Gone with the Wind*, which I was obsessed with—a fact that tickled my friend's grandma, who thought it was charming that a teen girl knew the same embarrassingly vast quantity of facts about the 1930s movie and book as she did.

In that TV room where we watched *Gone with the Wind* with her grandma, my friend and I also watched MTV. It was there, in Buffalo, that I saw the music video for Garbage's "Only Happy When It Rains" for the first time.

It surely was moody, gray, and rainy that spring break in Buffalo, but I don't remember that—what I remember was how the brilliance of Shirley Manson, in her bright blue dress and blue eyeshadow, her pink dress, her knee-high black boots, outshone it all.

"Captivated" isn't the right word. Do you remember what it felt like as an early teen to see someone and realize *that is who I have been waiting for*? The way your mouth went dry and your heart rate sped up and you weren't sure if you had a crush or a complex? Where your aspirations crystallized into a projection: *if I were as cool as her,* _____ *would happen* (_____ *would never happen*)?

I am here to defend a song—and as a Garbage devotee of nearly 25 years now, able to quote from all but the most recent album, I can crack the whip at my waist and harness plenty of textual/musical praise—but my love of Garbage's actual music came way, way later.

I know I have to stay on topic.

Here: I never thought the lyrics to "Only Happy When It Rains" were making fun of grunge, the way some people have interpreted them. I thought they were a directive, a lesson plan. *This is the method to belong, Kristine: only smile in the dark. Your only comfort is the night gone black. Now remember to make sure people know YOU DIDN'T ACCIDENTALLY TELL THEM THAT.*

Everything was intentional.

*

Come on now, go ahead and tell me how you saw Garbage perform at a local show in 1995 just after they cut their debut album, before anyone had even seen the video for "Vow," not a year-and-a-half later on an antennaed TV in Buffalo in a music video for their second damn single. I'm not surprised. Everyone has always had cooler grunge stories than me. The first time I saw Garbage live, I paid $22 to see them perform with Lit on the 1999 MTV Campus Invasion Tour. Yes I said 1999.

In an interview before Garbage's 2017 tour, Shirley said "We're exploring the idea of pulling out our Bond song because we haven't played it in a long time and very few people have ever gotten to hear us perform it."

And yet I *had* gotten to hear it live, eighteen years earlier. Trying to sound cool later, listing my concert attendances to my college friends, I mocked MTV's poor choice of "campuses to invade"—they invaded Indiana State University? In TERRE HAUTE? But at the time I was grateful to MTV's inept concert bookers, because I was only seventeen and even though it was a school night, my parents had allowed me to drive down to our basketball

arena—the one where Larry Bird had famously played twenty years earlier—to see my dream girl. The arena was set up much like it had been when I'd gone two Octobers previous, in 1997, to attend the Harvest Moon dance (unfortunately escorted by my best friend's brother, not my actual crush, Ryan): the fabric wall was up at half court, because Hulman Center wasn't going to fill up that night.

Garbage opened with "#1 Crush"—a dreamscape of orgasmic sighs—and then tore through the entire first half of *Version 2.0*, layering in the radio hits from their first album, before devastating with the last song of the set, "You Look So Fine."

It still sticks with me, all these years later, the way Shirley left the stage first during the outro for "You Look So Fine," followed by all of the band members slowly leaving, one by one, as their parts ended. Shirley said what she'd wanted to say before leaving us all there, breathless, waiting. In October 1999, my boyfriend had recently broken up with me and I could hardly bear it. My best friend and I were seated pretty high in the bleachers, but there were a few filled rows behind us, where Ryan (my '97 crush) and Ben were seated, but I was too focused on watching Shirley emote my pain for my ex-boyfriend to care; Ryan's presence was, momentarily, negligible.

After Garbage played the encore, including their Bond song, "The World is Not Enough" (it never is) and, of course, closing with "Only Happy When It Rains," my best friend and I stayed in our seats, unwilling to leave. Ryan and Ben came down the stairs and stopped beside us, saying something about my dancing during the show. As I turned to face them, so surprised they had noticed me that my heart was still in my teeth, I didn't have time to disaffect—*tell me you aren't going to make fun of me and that, instead, you thought I was beautiful.* And the thing was that they did tease me anyway, but I think Ben saw something in my face that must have made him soften because the teasing was gentle, gentler than he'd been in school.

My best friend and I stopped at Taco Bell on the way home and Ryan and Ben were, surprisingly, there too. We would have never hung out together in the daytime at South—Ben was cool, Ryan wanted to be—but we had shared an experience together. So we shyly waved, and the boys motioned us over to their table, and we ate our post-concert bean burritos while making small talk. Ryan mentioned my dancing one more time, kindly, and as my best friend and I drove home, it occurred to me that I'd made an impression. I had been someone he hadn't expected me to be, and he was still stunned by it.

That was power.

*

Garbage gave me the language for a tormented kind of longing, the sort of crushing desire that makes you crawl on your hands and knees across the carpet to a ghost. As a teen, I was frightened and exhilarated by the intensity of my emotions. I was confused by how badly I wanted to fit in and, simultaneously, how badly I wanted to be seen. Those years were a fluorescent-lit smear, every mistake highlighted and yet indistinguishable, at the time, to anyone other than myself. I was only happy when it was complicated. I carefully listened to the lyrics of Garbage songs, deciding that I could actually brandish power by basking in my obsessions, as the bittersweet pleasure of unfulfillment became an obsession.

Shirley was a give-me-what-I-want-or-I-will-take-it revelation, the Dark Princess from *Rainbow Brite and the Star Stealers* brought to life, a flame-haired, black leather siren. I didn't even realize how much I'd idolized the Dark Princess until I saw Shirley.

I dyed my hair red for decades, starting in summer 1998 (right before *Version 2.0*), trying to mimic the prominence Shirley innately carried with her presence and I wanted to believe I could still grow into. At Prom 1999, I wore a gunmetal gray dress, and for years afterward, when I would describe how I looked that night, I wrote "flame-haired and ready to fuck someone up, just like Shirley." If I'd owned the black Doc Martens I would buy that summer (I have always arrived at the party too late), I would have worn them that night as well. There is beauty, and there is power. I wanted both.

*

When Kurt died in 1994, I was eleven years old, listening to R&B like SWV, although when pressed by a waiting circle of kids at a middle school church lock-in that fall, I would claim my favorite song was "Tomorrow" by Silverchair. Later that night, as the other girls who already knew each other pulled their sleeping bags closer and loudly whispered and giggled about things I could never know, I slid across the cement floor of the social hall to lie near my mother, a chaperone, because I was homesick for someone who knew me. Within the week, after the sort of pre-teen fight that loses its reasoning over the years but felt *so important* at the time, what I remembered most was my mother throwing my lie back in my face, telling me she didn't even know me anymore, didn't even know the song I'd claimed was my favorite. But my mother did know me—the me I was, not the me I wanted to be—because my true favorite song was "Something in the Way She Moves" by James Taylor, the first song on the first side of the white cassette we listened to in the minivan after church, driving the rural highways of Pitt County, my mother and sister harmonizing as I tried to stay on key.

I was only happy when it rained, but not for the dramatic reasons you might expect from an adolescent. I was still homesick for Oregon, where I had lived before moving to North Carolina, and where the rain was a constant moody drizzle. When I grew into moodiness as a teen, it felt like a return to the person I had meant to be. No, that is not true. I was not morose when I lived in Oregon. The weather was morose, but I didn't know any different. I was happy when it rained in North Carolina because it reminded me of something I actually knew.

*

I am sitting in a yurt in rural Nebraska now, cows in the fields surrounding me, wind battering and pattering rain against the canvas walls. I packed a Shirley-like outfit to write in, a cropped mauve furry sweater and pleather leggings. I brought the red lipstick I seldom wear, black eyeliner, and the pot of *jane eyeshadow I have had since high school. I didn't use a brush to apply it, because I didn't have a brush in high school. I didn't know I needed a brush, because no one ever told me or showed me. I always used my ring finger on my right hand, so when I applied it to my eyelids this morning, it was a sense memory, knowing how much to pat, how to smear, remembering the residue that I always tried to wipe off against the inner palm of my left hand instead of a tissue.

I am as Shirleyfied as I can be, at 38. She was 29 when "Only Happy When It Rains" came out, which means that 25 years later, she must be 54. Duke Erikson (Garbage's bassist) is from Lyons, Nebraska, a tiny little town up in the northeast corner of my state. He is 69 years old this year; will be 70 by the time this essay comes out. Butch (drums) is 65, Steve Marker (guitar) is nearly 62. We have all grown past who we were in 1995; our cells have regenerated through at least three selves by now.

I tried to co-opt Shirley's style for years, listing her as my icon in countless email questionnaires. In that viral 2010 commercial for a glasses brand, where Shirley and Elijah Wood are bored on Sundays, it felt like validation, because for many years, I had been told that my husband looked like Elijah

Wood. In 2013, I chopped off my hair (very "Androgyny"-era Shirley) to take control over what I admired in men, realizing I could actually embody it in myself.

After all, Shirley modeled the power in growing beyond who others thought we were meant to be, saying in a 2020 *SPIN* interview "I think of how different I was as a person, compared to who I am now. I was so young and so afraid."

*

Garbage is not the grungiest band in the Plaidness tournament. And "Only Happy When It Rains" isn't nearly grungy enough to define the era; it's a pop song with grunge sensibilities and grunge cred, thanks to Butch. I think it's pretty remarkable that Shirley was able to call out all the tropes of grungedom in that song—*you fucking sell-outs, you're "only happy when it's complicated"? Fine: here's your song*—while simultaneously embodying them. I'm telling you that Shirley was the representation of grunge that brought me in, showed me the girl I could become: a girl who didn't give a fuck whether or not she belonged. So fuck the best grunge song, fuck the way grunge made me feel. The only thing that matters is how Garbage and Shirley made me feel. Like I could finally say FUCK GRUNGE.

*

MAHA Music Festival, August 11th, 2012. Shirley has a high ponytail, ripped black tights, black shorts, short sleeved black shirt, black wristbands. Rain starts to fall just as Garbage begins to close their set with "Only Happy When It Rains." Shirley smiles and calls it a "precious moment," says this has never happened before.

I was at that concert, four months pregnant with my third daughter, and when Butch pounded the drums, my daughter pounded on my stomach. I took my Elijah Wood-alike husband's hand and made him feel how our daughter moved only when the beat thumped. I am reporting a fact: when Shirley demanded "pour your misery down on me," God himself responded. Shirley said, "I'm only happy when it rains," and the air thickened, condensed into water to put out a flame on earth, all four elements wanting to please her. Power.

ON THE ESSAY:

Since 2016, the month of March has been Essayist Christmas in my house: 64 essays on 64 songs from 64 writers who really care about making us care—they want to win the championship. I constantly break my own brackets after reading an essay that changes my mind, that elucidates something I hadn't appreciated about a song/artist, or sometimes, just because the essay is so good. I've contributed four tournament essays and three extracurriculars because Xness is a community of gentle shit-talk, but also rapt quote-tweets of admiration and support. It's a month of unexpected delights!

This essay went up on the first day of March Plaidness '21, and that afternoon, I stared at my screen: the official Twitter account for Garbage had responded with praise from my queen, Shirley Manson, who'd tweeted "Thank you for your loving essay. It moved me deeply." That's the magic of March Xness.

"I DON'T FEEL LIKE NOTHING BUT A GOOD TIME": HOW GRUNGE DIDN'T KILL GLAM

by Amy Rossi

Most rock docs or essays with a retrospective bent on 1980s glam metal offer the same clean narrative: Quiet Riot's number one album, the rise of Motley Crue then Poison, the music videos, the copycat bands, and Guns N' Roses blowing onto the scene with something new and raw, "Cherry Pie" as emblematic of everything wrong, and then grunge ending it all.

It's a tidy story. And it's not true.

Quiet Riot's *Metal Health* reached number one on the Billboard charts in November 1983, the first heavy metal album to do so. Nirvana's *Nevermind*, the album credited with ending glam metal's reign, took the top spot in January 1992.

In between? A pretty solid run, aided immensely—and then cut down—by MTV.

Ever since white people stole rock music, television has helped make rock stars, selling an image and experience, packaging cool. Variety shows like Ed Sullivan's helped create a rock n' roll image long before MTV was an idea. What MTV did was make music constantly, pervasively visual. And glam metal bands who cut their teeth trying to stand out by any possible measure—confetti cannons, strippers on stage, silly string, searing neon flyers—in a 1.5-mile stretch of the Sunset Strip, where you could choose between seeing a show at the Roxy, the Whisky, or Gazzari's, were ready to be pervasively visual.

Just not forever.

There's a binary created by the grunge-killing-glam narrative, a kind of musical purity test. Glam metal was oversaturated with copycat bands pushing a tired formula of anthems and power ballads; grunge bands were doing something new and different, speaking to the time. Nevermind that the versions of the same argument followed grunge-era bands as well. One was artifice. The other was real.

*

The basic facts are true enough, to a point, but somehow it ends up implicating only the glam metal bands and not the executives who were trying to cash in—the ones who were actually pushing the formula, paying for hair extensions, repackaging bands who had failed to attract an audience before, signing new groups because they were similar enough to a successful act rather than looking for something different.

It's not insignificant that "Cherry Pie" is the song and video that's used as a stand-in for the tired excess of glam metal. Jani Lane had planned for the album's title track to be "Uncle Tom's Cabin," a song he was truly proud of. The president of his record label wanted something else, something catchier. Lane cranked out "Cherry Pie," and apparently the pizza box on which he scrawled the lyrics in less than an hour could, at one point, be viewed at a Hard Rock Cafe in Florida.

In the book *I Want My MTV: The Uncensored Story of the Music Video Revolution*, Adam Levine of Maroon 5 announces that "even at 12 years old, I thought, 'wow, how tacky," when he first saw the video for "Cherry Pie." Of Montreal's Kevin Barnes writes in Pitchfork that being a hair metal fan as a teen is a "skeleton in his closet," and even if it's tongue-in-cheek, we're supposed to get what he means—the confession is inherently embarrassing.

It's the purity test in action: the line of thinking assumes glam metal as lesser. Even a kid could find it tacky (or an adult could claim that they found it tacky at the time). It's just a production. It's inauthentic—all style, no substance.

But a lot of art is authentic before money gets involved.

It happened with glam metal, and it happened after Nirvana hit number one. *Billboard* editor Steve Knopper called it the "grunge gold rush:" every label was looking for their Nirvana—just like every label had looked for their Poison, Guns N' Roses, or Motley Crue a few years before. The genre that was supposed to save us from videos and bands that looked and sounded the same was quickly going to be packaged and replicated and commercialized by record labels who were prepared to treat another scene as a monolith in order to cash in.

In the 1996 documentary *Hype!*, about the early-90s rise of what outsiders would call the Seattle scene, Megan Jasper of Sub Pop Records described the frenzy as "Christmas Eve at a shopping mall when the mall closes at 6 o'clock, when it's too crazy and it's loaded with sub-moronic idiots prancing around buying anything they can their hands on." And Nirvana's former publicist Susie Tennant recalls bands who'd never played live receiving huge advances.

By 1995, *Spokane's Spokesman-Review* was lamenting the *second* wave of copycat grunge bands, placing Stone Temple Pilots firmly in the first wave. STP were the poseurs, cogs in the corporate machine and fodder for B*eavis and Butthead*, for no reason that seems to hold almost 30 years later. Sure, early singles may have included Scott Weiland making use of Eddie Vedder's rigid-jawed yarl, but the band's only real transgression was having the misfortune of releasing an album after Soundgarden, Nirvana, Alice in Chains, and Pearl Jam did. Swap out a few adjectives and band names, and you could probably find something similar in LA Weekly ten years before.

"It's so profitable, and they'll keep taking and taking and they can't restrain themselves," Vedder said in *Hype!*

This is 100% accurate, and also Pearl Jam themselves signed to a major label, as did Nirvana.

To be clear, I'm not questioning the authenticity of either of these bands. You can participate in the commercial music industry and also push it to be better. The more interesting thing to me is how it opens up questions about accepted definitions for the visual signifiers of authenticity versus artifice, as videos made image important for the consumption of each genre.

While watching both *Hype!* and a 1996 MTV program called "It Came from the Eighties," I was struck by Selene Vigil of 7 Year Bitch and Tom Keifer of Cinderella having the same dispirited response, almost word-for-word, to reading their reviews: all anyone wrote about was what they looked like, not about the music. Even the name of each genre is based on image—both grunge and glam (or hair metal) became shorthands for appearance as much as, if not more than, sound.

So why is the image projected by Pearl Jam viewed as more authentic than that of Poison? After all, there are some pretty impressive coifs in early Pearl Jam videos. Both images are consumed and commodified; both are styles that are intended to define the person embodying them. A stripped-down anti-style, even one based on weather, is still a style. It's entirely possible to feel like your most authentic self in leather and eyeliner, regardless of your gender. It doesn't feel like a coincidence that the bands brushed off as shallow are the ones who appropriated traditionally feminine—read: obvious—styles.

For me, the narrative of grunge killing glam persists because in its neatness, it gives hair metal a comeuppance that hindsight has suggested is necessary. It was too excessive, too decadent, too much—something had to give. The unspoken part of "grunge killed glam metal" is that the latter deserved it.

*

One of the problems with the narrative is that it assumes glam metal *intended* to stay static and that grunge ignored an entire decade of popular music. It avoids the overlapping period of commercial success—at the end of 1991, both Nirvana and Firehouse were occupying the upper quadrant of the Billboard Top 200. It skips over the fact that Alice in Chains opened up for Van Halen and Poison in 1991, the latter at Bret Michaels' request, as he tells it, right in the Pacific Northwest. (The openers were even invited back on stage to join the headliners for a cover of "Rock and Roll Nite.") It ignores the fact that Alice in Chains first played as both Diamond Lie and Alice N' Chains as a glam metal band in their own right. It overlooks glam rock's clear influence on Stone Temple Pilots, the elements of the genre that were in full force on 1997's *Tiny Music...* and in the band Scott Weiland would later form with members of the Cult and Guns N' Roses.

And, despite the visual evidence, it ignores the very simple fact that fashion and style were changing by the late '80s, and plenty of glam bands changed along with it.

You can only push excess so far before it loses its thrill, its originality. Cinderella is remembered for how they appeared in the "Nobody's Fool" video but the lace and corset tops were gone with the second album. By the time we get to the "Don't Go Away Mad" video, Tommy Lee and Nikki Sixx have traded big hair and platforms for undercuts and Docs. Once Poison caught everyone's eye with their heavy makeup for the *Look What the Cat Dragged In* cover, they toned it down significantly, embracing a more biker aesthetic, and Bon Jovi wasn't too glam for Pearl Jam's Mike McCready to basically crib Richie Sambora's entire vest and flat-top hat look in Pearl Jam's "Alive" video.

Or take the much-maligned Trixter, a New Jersey band that gets casually thrown into conversation as synonymous with an oversaturated, copycat glam metal market. But if you watch the video for "Give It to Me Good," it's just as much jeans and flannel as it is hair, almost like it's two different bands. The action takes place primarily in a garage and in a park—no fireworks or spandex or glitz. There's even a young woman wearing Umbros. Maybe Trixter was a copycat band, but looking at them in 1989, straddling the aesthetic of the past and the future, they don't appear to be too concerned about copying style.

Which is to say they didn't look all *that* different than Alice in Chains did around the time "We Die Young" was released.

*

These signifiers persist in telling us who to take seriously and who to brush off. Grunge looks more unaffected, more accessible, and that makes it easier to take songs with a serious message seriously. The big hair glam look appears to nullify what's in the music; power ballads are dismissed as chick bait (as though that's automatically a negative) without any acknowledgment for how hard both Poison and Skid Row went in "Something to Believe In" and "18 and Life," respectively. Jon Bon Jovi has said trickle-down economics policies influenced Tommy and Gina's story in "Livin' on a Prayer," and if that sounds like a joke, well, sometimes the least threatening person carries the message best. Warrant's "Uncle Tom's Cabin" is, at its heart, a song about corrupt law enforcement, and the video is *truly weird* in its attempt to do something different.

But that's not the video that lasted. And one of the ways the narrative persists is through the very same means glam metal gained and lost commercial success. In the aforementioned "It Came from the Eighties" episode, glam metal artists are basically invited by MTV to distance themselves from the era.

There's a deep pathos to Jani Lane saying, "Alright, it's our fault. We were the band who brought down the '80s," knowing how his story ends. Bret Michaels tries to answer a question about the demise of glam metal, a question that again ignores the fact that he'd enjoyed playing with one of the bands credited with bringing about his own group's end. He rambles on about how in every genre of music there are the A-list performers who raise the bar and then the B and the C, before finally getting exasperated and saying, "I don't know what the fuck I'm saying. I don't know. MTV stopped playing the videos." Like Jani Lane, he's laughing, but there's a genuine pain in that moment.

And the fact that this aired on MTV, without the MTV interviewer's response, shows how the narrative took root—even though an article published in *Variety* had the answer by November 1992. Both columnist Lonn Friend and marketing executive Bob Chiappardi pointed to MTV's abrupt pivot to grunge videos, not the existence of grunge itself. "The big thing that's killing it, though, is MTV, because they've basically turned their backs on a lot of these bands. I don't know if it's fair or not because they made it the monster that it was," Chiappardi said.

It continues now: a recent A&E *Biography* special about the early years of MTV recounts how its staff became tastemakers—for a certain kind of music, anyhow. Executives look back on their decision to exclude Rick James and cite the sexual content of the "Super Freak" video, noting that it didn't get past the approval board. Gale Sparrow, who was part of talent relations, makes her disgust clear: "That video should have been shown in a strip club. He was a pimp with a bunch of women."

No one has much better things to say about the hair metal videos—distilling them all into basically the worst parts of "Looks That Kill" (1983) and "Cherry Pie" (1990) despite the time gap that exists between the two. Whatever made Rick James inappropriate in 1981 didn't seem to apply any longer.

Misogyny is often cited as a reason hair metal needed to die. And grunge undoubtedly took rock music in a much stronger direction there, with more women artists receiving attention, men artists taking vocal feminist stances, and songs and videos that weren't seeking sex.

But from this vantage point, it looks like the people programming the videos are comfortable dismissing glam now without taking any culpability. It's one thing to evolve your position, like some metal artists who've taken to using their platform for social issues. It's another to act like these videos spanning *nearly a decade* came out of a vacuum and that MTV had no role in creating and promoting this as a sellable image for others to replicate and no role in dumping it.

"I just held my breath and thought, 'This has to be over soon.' It was demoralizing," says Judy McGrath of the glam metal video era in the A&E special. McGrath rose from MTV promo writer to eventual CEO, and her concerns are reiterated in *I Want My MTV*—and brushed off by a male colleague as an "internal controversy."

Glam metal's misogyny is worthy of critique. It's curious when people only seem to invoke misogyny when it relates to something they don't like, but not when, say, it comes to ignoring concerns voiced by a colleague like McGrath.

And think about the language employed to talk about glam as opposed to grunge: in 2009, Chuck Eddy referred to certain musicians as "glam poodles" in *SPIN* magazine; Kevin Barnes did the same while also describing Ratt's look as the "gayest biker gang ever." Music critic Dawn Anderson puts the bands who came from Seattle in context against "this big poodle metal scene, just tons and tons of hairspray, eyeliner..."

In 1990, Jani Lane talked about Warrant being stereotyped as a young girl's band, and Susan Orlean's profile of Bon Jovi explains how the release of "Wanted, Dead or Alive" as a single was rushed because the band was drawing too many female fans and needed to delay the next ballad. Not only did the feminized image hurt glam's credibility, so did the legions of women who found the genre more accessible.

It becomes an ouroboros of sorts. In perpetuating the idea that glam needed to die, it becomes all too easy to slip into speech that degrades or dismisses women: the very thing glam is (fairly) critiqued for.

Of course, in all the commodified nostalgia VH1 and MTV spent the early parts of the 2000s peddling, artists aren't asked about sexism in lyrics or videos—or even about their decision to appropriate style. Those angles aren't really pushed. It's kept as surface-level as the bands are accused of being, limited to the rise and fall and advent of grunge without much context for the world the music was created in.

Distinct time periods launched glam and grunge, the things that inform the kind of music people want to make and hear: coming out of a recession and entering one, the beginning of the Reagan era and the repercussions of it, AIDS as ignored and misunderstood and AIDS as a part of public health. It makes sense that rock fans needed something more or at least different—the world itself was both more and different.

Instead of it being another moment when music evolved in response to its surroundings, this time, audiences were saturated with 24 hours' worth of visual markers of that change.

Grunge didn't give Tom Keifer vocal cord paralysis. Grunge didn't create conflict between George Lynch and Don Dokken. Grunge wasn't responsible for the addictions that fractured bands like Guns N' Roses, Motley Crue, Ratt, and Poison. And grunge didn't program the video schedule.

The music you want to make when you're 22 isn't necessarily the music you want to make at 28. And the music you make when you're wanting is different from the music you make when you're having, which is likely where the real authenticity versus artifice argument lies. What Kurt Cobain said of the grunge label applies across the board: "You have to take a chance and hope that either a totally different audience accepts you or the same audience grows with you."

Every era has its expiration date, for whatever reason. We should continue pressing the issue of misogyny in glam metal because being honest about music's past helps build a more equitable path forward—as we should press the predation and abuses of the so-called "baby groupie" era in the early '70s and the culture that gives credence to speculation that Courtney Love had anything to do with her husband's death (and that persists in defining her artistry in relation to his). And, while the stakes are not the same, it's also reasonable to question why big fun songs that attract a lot of women and bands who adopt an over-the-top feminine style are dismissed as lacking substance. Big fun isn't the most important thing, but it's part of rock.

To position glam metal as having failed or grunge as a killer because one didn't last forever and the other happened to be next is to ignore everything that came before and everything that came after. The conclusion grunge met looked different, and was more tragic, but it came all the same.

In the end, grunge couldn't have killed "the hair bands" because neither of those things exist. Those particular labels were useful primarily for record companies, for scouts, for the people who choose which videos to play or to stop playing. It's marketing, and if anything helped MTV end the glam metal era, it was the choice to try to make bands fit in a box of what had been successful before rather than play to individual strengths, the choice to create a formula rather than highlight what made a band popular in the club scene, the choice to focus on a quick buck now and developing talent later. While glam metal bands indulged in excess, so did the corporate machine.

And instead of learning from these missteps, when *Nevermind* hit #1, it was time to do it all again.

SOURCES:

Augusto, Troy J. "'Seattle Sound' Melts Down Pop Metal." *Variety*, Variety, 2 Nov. 1992, variety.com/1992/music/news/seattle-sound-melts-down-pop-metal-100719/.

"Biography: I Want My MTV." A&E, 8 Sept. 2020.

"Body English." *Chicago Tribune*, Chicago Tribune, 6 Dec. 1990, www.chicagotribune.com/news/ct-xpm-1990-12-06-9004110785-story.html.

Du Lac, J. Freedom. "Grunge II: It Looks Like Pearl Jam/Nirvana; It Sounds Like Pearl Jam/Nirvana; But It's Really Something Completely Different (Sort Of)." *Spokesman.Com*, The Spokesman-Review, 4 Oct. 1995, www.spokesman.com/stories/1995/oct/04/grunge-ii-it-looks-like-pearl-jamnirvana-it/.

Eddy, Chuck. "Myth No. 2: Nirvana Killed Hair Metal." *SPIN*, 31 Mar. 2015, www.spin.com/2009/11/myth-no-2-nirvana-killed-hair-metal/.

Fricke, David. "Kurt Cobain, the Rolling Stone Interview: Success Doesn't Suck." *Rolling Stone*, Rolling Stone, 27 Jan. 1994, www.rollingstone.com/music/music-news/kurt-cobain-the-rolling-stone-interview-success-doesnt-suck-97194/.

"It Came From the Eighties II: Metal Goes Pop." MTV, 1996.

Knopper, Steve. "The Grunge Gold Rush." *NPR*, NPR, 12 Jan. 2018, www.npr.org/sections/therecord/2018/01/12/577063077/the-grunge-gold-rush.

Marks, Craig, and Rob Tannenbaum. *I Want My MTV: The Uncensored Story of the Music Video Revolution*. Plume, 2014.

"Of Montreal: Best and Worst Hair Metal Bands." *Pitchfork*, Pitchfork, 21 Mar. 2005, pitchfork.com/features/article/5996-of-montreal-best-and-worst-hair-metal-bands/.

Orlean, Susan. "Bon Jovi: The Kids Are Alright." *Rolling Stone*, Rolling Stone, 25 June 2018, www.rollingstone.com/music/music-news/bon-jovi-the-kids-are-alright-105022/.

Pray, Doug, director. *Hype!* Cinepix Film Properties, 1996.

Yarm, Mark. *Everybody Loves Our Town: A History of Grunge*. Faber & Faber, 2017.

ON THE ESSAY:

I started writing this essay in the fall of 2020. My first novel was on submission and I had just gotten dumped. All of my anxiety about these situations and also the state of the world went into these words. Each night, I retreated into my research, which could have gone forever.

As isolated as I was then, because of March Xness, I was still part of something. And that's why I love Xness—the connections it forges through time and distance and memory.

This subject is my Roman Empire, and I relished having the chance to upend a tired narrative. It was a joy, a reprieve, my solace, and it was community. But when I think about this piece, I think about having something to hold on to when I needed it most. That's what music does. That's what essays do. And that's what Xness is. Thanks, Megan and Ander.

MARCH FAXNESS

NOT THE LONELIEST COVER YOU COULD EVER DO

Brooke Champagne on "One" by Aimee Mann

Two can be as bad as one, it's the loneliest number since the number one.

She first made herself known not through sight, but sound. What did she sound like? Like a cartoon bubble bursting over my head. Like the bright *pop* sound Andy Williams makes in the chorus of The Chordettes' 1958 song "Lollipop," sticking his forefinger into his cheek and uncorking the champagne bottle of his mouth. Half-believing I dreamed the *pop*, I stood up from bed at 2 a.m. and felt a slow leaking, as if my body had forgotten how to hold itself together. At first I thought I was pissing myself. Suddenly, about a gallon of bloody water emptied from my vagina.

My daughter was due in almost a month, but she'd be arriving today. Still, I had reasons to remain calm. The hospital was only one backroad mile from our house. My husband slept soundly next to my wet spot, but there was no need to wake him yet to pack a bag. I'd read that we wouldn't need to leave till contractions were four minutes apart, and that was likely hours away. All I needed was my phone timer and something to do. And I knew just what that was. "Okay, this is good," I thought. "I have papers to grade."

It was the middle of the fall semester and I had subs to cover my classes, but I didn't want to leave them with a full set of ungraded memoirs. Besides, I like reading student memoirs. What's a "bad" one look like? Too self-centered? Too incomplete a narrative arc? Screw all that. My students share their lives with me. They may not completely plumb the depths of why things happen the way they do or what it all means, but they're getting there. They open up to me in ways they may not with their parents, in ways that—holy shit—my daughter might also close off to me someday. Yes, I was already this far afield while timing contractions and commenting on my students' uses of reflection and scene, entering grades ranging from A-minus to A-plus. Then, I was somewhere twenty years in the future: who would this early girl be, and what would she mean to me. I couldn't imagine the answer; the question itself was terrifying.

In fact, the question required further distraction, so I scrolled through my DirecTV guide to where I usually find it: HBO. Paul Thomas Anderson's *Magnolia* had just started—a perfect movie for the desperation I was masking. Then, I was nearly twenty years in the past, first watching the movie and hearing the dial tone as the song "One" begins, *beep beep beep beep.* The singer leaned on the word "one" so deeply, so coolly, "*One is the loneliest number that you'll ever do...*" The opening film credits revealed a magnolia blossoming at hyper-speed, followed by the slow unraveling of sad, lonely characters I would spend the next three hours only half paying attention to. Like I said, I'd seen them all before.

Now I spend my time just making thoughts of yesterday.

She first made herself known not through sound, but sight. In my second year of college, my mom's best friend Gloria burned me a CD with a homemade cover design. She often made me gifts like this, introduced me to R.E.M. and Radiohead and all the Gen X coolness I'd always been slightly too young for. On this CD, a long, lanky woman, blonde and cool-looking, like Gloria herself, wore a tankini and her name written in script across her body: Aimee Mann. Oh boy, I thought, another beautiful, blonde singer. But I trusted Gloria. She'd never married or had kids, and so from my purview her life comprised of great-art consumption, astute political commentary, and believing in me. She cheered my amorphous writing ambitions, even masochistically asked to read early drafts.

Gloria wasn't an artist, but loved art in all its forms. She could name all the architects who designed her favorite buildings in our hometown of New Orleans, and she was fun; she knew every rooftop bar in town. Because my mother spent much of her adult life raising three daughters, three stepdaughters, and cycling through three husbands, she didn't have as much time to slow down, pay attention. Whether or not a piece of art or music or film was beautiful didn't much matter. My mother rarely analyzed or let a thought or feeling linger. She accepted a breadth or dearth of beauty and moved on. At that time, in college, I saw in these two women two discrete paths for womanhood. The Gloria path was glorious. Freedom, one-ness, living life mostly for yourself. Though my mother is no martyr, I feared choosing her path would mean my own martyrdom. To be encumbered, constantly needed and tired, having little time to contemplate art and the self in the one life I was living. I needed time. I wanted to write, to make art, like this childless, beautiful Aimee Mann.

Because I wanted to impress Gloria, I didn't just listen to Aimee Mann, I studied her. I read somewhere that Anderson wrote the screenplay with Mann in mind, that he wanted his movie to be the equivalent of an Aimee Mann album. In that sense, the film was a cover of Mann's musical oeuvre established in the early-mid '90s. The soundtrack's first song, "One," opens the film, and it wasn't immediately my favorite. The song contains no images. It's pure argumentative lament. When I first heard the album from start to finish, I was most gripped by the track "Save Me." It begins with the lines, "You look like a perfect fit / For a girl in need of a tourniquet." If you've ever really loved someone who's damaged, or been that damaged person, it's a perfect simile.

Anyway, "One" is an ostensibly simple song with simple lyrics. The relationship referenced is one where a presumed lover, or loved one, is gone. That's all we know. When I first heard it, the English major in me found it fascinating to hear that one was a number you could "do." As in: enact, or perform. The rest of the song felt pointless to deconstruct. "One" is lonely, "no is the saddest experience...," yes, I get it. I remember sometime after Gloria burned the CD for me, I asked her what she thought of the song, to confirm if I was correct about it. She laughed and said, "Well, yeah, it's sad, but 'one' isn't *always* the loneliest number." Given that I planned to take her solitary path, I was glad to hear it.

Over the years, as I dug further into Mann's oeuvre, I learned "One" was a cover with interesting tweaks to the 1968 Harry Nilsson original. Mann's version includes an electric guitar, and her tone makes the song's argument more starkly than Nilsson. He sings "one is the loneliest number" like it's a suggestion; when Mann sings it, "one's" loneliness is fact. But what I love most about the cover is how much Mann relies on Nilsson's voice, both at the opening and closing of the song. In the opening, just after the *beep beep* of the dial tone, we hear a male voice shout, "Okay, Mr. Mix!" Which feels totally weird and nonsensical. Turns out it's Nilsson, from another of his tracks called "Cuddly Toy." And as "One's" final cryptic line concludes—*one is a number divided by two*—Mann's voice recedes, and Nilsson's enters again.

He sings the following lines, which are not lyrics from "One," but from another of his songs called "Together":

And one has decided to bring down the curtain
And one thing's for certain
There's nothing to keep them together.

I knew none of this when I obsessively listened to the soundtrack, but hearing a song titled "Together" superimposed over "One" is a bit ironic, and something that two decades ago, I could've written an A-plus paper about. Now, thinking about my relationship with Gloria, the song, and my daughter, who six years ago was in the process of being born as I listened to "One" while timing contractions, I'm considering the nature of covers. What makes a good cover? What should a cover song *do*? As in: enact, or perform. According to Ray Padgett's book on cover songs called *Cover Me*, musicians worried for years that if their song was covered successfully, that meant an erasure of their original. Padgett vehemently disagrees with that conclusion. For him, a cover expands the original, adds new textures and contexts, invites a new audience to enjoy the update and revisit the old. In other words, a successful cover only makes the original stronger.

It's just no good anymore since you went away.

She made herself known that balmy January day of 2022 not through sight, or sound, but smell. Warm jambalaya and cold, olive-stuffed muffulettas waited upstairs at Schoen & Son Funeral Home on Canal Street in New Orleans, where my mother and I would eat after we'd said goodbye to Gloria.

Though I didn't speak at the memorial, I thought a lot about what I'd say. One of the things that made Gloria the best was that she was legitimately interested in what I thought, which stroked my ego in a way my busy mother couldn't always do. But she was also interested in everyone else, too. There was some artistry, I suppose, in how she plumbed the depths of why people were the way they were. This is why she had so many conservative friends despite being one of the most politically liberal people I knew. Proof was all around me in the hundreds at the memorial, a great gathering of both the masked and unmasked.

The first to eulogize her was a young attorney, one of many for whom

Gloria worked at the downtown law firm where she and my mother were legal secretaries for almost four decades. The attorney made a joke about the great unmasked, saying it was a testament to Gloria's patience and grace that there were so many Trump supporters in the room. It reminded me that when Trump first came down that godforsaken escalator, right around the time Gloria was diagnosed with breast cancer (proof that if there's a god, he's a bastard), I raged and scoffed at the stupidity of anyone who could consider this monstrous moron as anything but a joke. Gloria reminded me that listening to others' wrong-headed ideas only strengthens our positions, because we're empathizing where they won't.

Over a dozen people spoke beautifully at the memorial, including members of the great unmasked, but it was her college-aged niece whose impromptu speech most touched me. "I didn't plan to say anything, but, my Aunt Gloria, there's probably no other person as responsible for making me who I am as she was. She shared with me what was good, what was cool. Every piece of music I listen to or television I watch and love is because of her. I can't imagine not being able to talk to her about any of it anymore."

But silence touched me as well. During the parade of memorial speakers, I asked my mother if she wanted to say something, said I'd hold her hand and walk up there with her, if she liked. She just gently shook her head, and later, in the privacy of plating our jambalaya and muffulettas, said it'd been enough for her to tell Gloria's family everything she felt, what losing her meant—losing the best friend she'd ever had, losing a piece of herself. In Gloria's final days under home hospice care, Mom had been with her. She held her hand, watched her slowly go. She didn't need to enact or perform her love.

One is a number divided by two.

It's sad, embarrassing really, how much I learned about Gloria from her obituary and memorial, simple facts I'd never bothered asking her about. Like me, she attended Nicholls State in Thibodaux, LA (a.k.a. Harvard on the Bayou), and graduated from LSU. How had we never discussed that? She was born earlier than I'd thought, in 1958, the same year, in fact, that Andy Williams swiped inside his cheek in the chorus of The Chordettes' "Lollipop," the very first sound I conjured when my water broke. The song "Lollipop" itself is a cover, first recorded by a long-forgotten duo named Ronald & Ruby. The oddly, wonderfully comparable sound would've never entered my mind upon my daughter's arrival had it not been for The Chordettes and Andy Williams' famous *pop*.

Covers are so ubiquitous now that we take for granted the term itself—why they're called covers at all—and as stated in Padgett's *Cover Me*, there are three theories for its derivation. The first is that a music label would "cover its bets" by releasing a recording of a popular song; in the second, the idea was that the new version would literally "cover up" the old on record store shelves; and the third, most capitalistic theory was how music label execs would answer, when asked if they had any copycat versions of a popular song to release: "we've got it covered!"

I can't help but find a metaphor in these theories, and how they apply to the relationships I've held most dearly. Having a child is a way to cover your bets: if you can't get everything you want out of this life, maybe your child can. Maybe they can cover up your shittiness, your aging, your (hopefully) slow bodily unraveling. If you choose to have children, a secret, sacred hope is that when you get old, they'll care for you; they'll have you covered.

Before deciding to have children, and still, I've been both afraid to be covered, and afraid not to be. I've feared motherhood would mean half-measures in artistry, and vice versa. And I've feared the obverse: that without motherhood, I'd have no excuse, no cover, for my mediocre art. But in listening to "One" again to write this essay, perhaps more obsessively than I did twenty years ago, after re-hearing the lament and singularity of being *one*, I see that although I planned to take Gloria's path, and instead took my mother's, the two paths weren't discrete at all. The overlap lives in their love for each other. "One" can be sad, but "two" can be, too, and children won't always cover our loneliness, or any other parts of us that need covering. This essay is an inadequate cover for the originality, the oneness, of Gloria. And of Aimee Mann. And of being a mother to my daughter and a daughter to my mother. But I'm making this cover, anyway. I'm still singing the song I've heard before, only singing it differently.

I've learned, too, that just the concept of covers is relatively modern. Before the advent of rock n' roll, it was the song that was paramount, not the singer. The quality of the song mattered more than the person performing it. So to extend that cover-as-relationship metaphor, if my daughter is my cover, the question isn't what she makes of me, or I of her; the singular song she makes of her life is what counts. My daughter, my cover, who first made herself known, truly, not through sight or sound or smell, but touch. After twelve hours of labor, when she crowned, then blinked, then screamed,

I brought her to my breast, and tasted what it was for me to be born into someone irrevocably different, both alone and not alone, not joined together anymore, but not two, either, and never quite *one* again.

ON THE ESSAY:

I knew little about music writing, less about how to play March Xness, but I knew the essay form. I knew I loved Aimee Mann and the glorious Gloria who'd introduced me to her music. Shortly before the tournament, Gloria passed away, so I imagined the large community grieving her—much of New Orleans, it felt like—as my audience. For two weeks I frantically wrote this essay to them, and for her. My husband is my first reader and best editor, and when I sent him my final draft he replied with three words: *you're gonna win.* Tournament time came, and I squeaked through the first round by a handful of votes. Winning somehow became possible; now, I wanted it. Over the next few rounds, I tapped into every friend group I'd gathered over decades—former students, gym buddies, peers from every school and job I've ever had. Once they had buy-in on one round, I didn't have to remind them; we were all part of the "One" team, for Gloria. We won the whole thing for her, together.

KICKING THE DOOR IN

Erin Belieu on "Satisfaction" by Devo

It's October 14th, 1978, Omaha, Nebraska, and I've been a teenager just shy of three weeks.

It's the year I begin creeping down to the TV room once my parents are in bed, sitting in my dad's surpassingly ugly recliner, smoking the leftover ends of the four cigarettes that framed his after-supper ritual: four Larks, four Triscuits, each topped with a sweaty square of Colby cheese, and four Manhattans.

By 10 p.m., I knew he and my mom (with her own best time in this nightly liquid marathon) couldn't clock an oom-pah band marching through the house. I've come down this evening to watch *Saturday Night Live*. For a girl living in the *Brigadoon*-like mists of Nebraska, my weekly illicit viewings of *SNL* are proof of life.

Because it is a truth universally acknowledged that being thirteen sucks. Or it should be. I still recall the intensity of how terrible it feels to be that age. The enraging in-betweenness of it—too young for the older kids to bother with, but a galaxy beyond the babies you're stuck "watching" at the card table end of Thanksgiving.

I'll make the further case that being thirteen in 1978 was above-average terrible: economy tanked, oil prices stratospheric, the Cold War still slouching on, a machine whose reason or purpose no one seemed to remember, Son of Sam's trial on the nightly news, and that terrible picture on the cover of *Time* magazine, countless bodies splayed where they'd dropped after drinking the purple Kool Aid.

1978 also wins for peak divorce rate in America. Whatever spackle held the grown-ups together had rotted away over the course of the decade, as more and more of my friends were contractually obligated to spend weekends sleeping at their fathers' divorce-sad one-bedroom apartments. Moms now had boyfriends, sketchy guys with receding hairlines named Denny and

Cliff. Two of the kids in my neighborhood had uncles living in their basements, soldiers come home but not quite returned from Vietnam.

And the music. Uff. It was bleak from my position—that is, as a white girl from a suburban family barely clinging to the middle class, raised in an aggressively segregated midwestern city. I caught flashes on the periphery (from *American Bandstand* and *Soul Train* on Saturday mornings) that something musically vital was happening somewhere, but it wasn't music to which I had real access back in the informational Before Times.

I had the soporifically wholesome stylings of "the Ol' Redhead" Don Cole on KFAB AM radio announcing the treacly ballads that defined that year in pop music, a slough of already overplayed rock "classics," the Gibb brothers' Hydra-headed disco juggernaut, and the "Desperado" singer-songwriters whose stale "You know I gotta ramble, girl" machismo hit me as up its own ass even at that tender age. A perfume capturing the mainstream musical essence of 1978 in America would contain notes of ditch weed, Velveeta casserole, and polyester slacks (worn commando).

So I'm sitting in my dad's chair smoking butts and regretting my nascent life when *SNL*'s host Fred Willard announces that week's musical guest, some unknown band called Devo that in the next couple minutes will permanently alter how I perceive...well, everything.

As is true of any wildly original art that kicks the door open for much of what follows, the event of Devo's appearance that night (back when we had three channels to choose from, and maybe PBS if you got the TV antenna pointed just right), this happening live on nationwide TV—it's hard to capture the super-size audacity of their performance in our present time when you can experience everything anywhere always.

The danger-yellow biohazard suits, the evil-toy choreography—they looked like animatronic aliens who'd landed their spaceship in the uncanny valley. With unfashionably lean and punchy drums (especially compared to the era's prog rock behemoths) and rhythm guitars laying out a tweaky, industrial through line, the song's opening bars have more in common with Antheil's score for *Ballet Mécanique* than anything the American public identified as a pop music at that point in history.

It's not until Mark Mothersbaugh rips into his sugar-cereal amped version of the iconic hook of "Satisfaction" that you recognize this controlled demolition as a cover of one of the world's most famous songs. The glitching robot vocals (Mothersbaugh spitting his famous "babybabybabybabybabybabybabybabybaby" line like a possessed gumball machine), Gerald Casale's boingy, *Looney Tunes* bass putting the party in the proceedings—they were the exact musical definition of "WTF??"; a weirdo bolt of lightning that shook the audience to their boogie (oogie oogie) shoes. It took Devo a little over two ferociously tight and catchy minutes that night to plant their harpoon in the bloated, boring, and twee nonsense clogging the airwaves at the time.

*

While our subject is cover songs, I'll admit I have a hard time calling Devo's version of "Satisfaction" a cover. That's a toothless word for the Derridean surgery they perform on The Stones' charismatic, seductive but ultimately backward-facing original. As T.S. Eliot said—who knew from demolishing traditions—"Immature poets imitate, mature poets steal."

By this standard, Devo's futuristic deconstruction of "Satisfaction" works as a crime-of-the-decade heist, hijacking the Stones' song into something indelibly and completely their own. Respect to Mick Jagger for approving their use of the song, but what Devo does to "Satisfaction" has no basis in homage. The bluesy, roadhouse sex appeal that defines the Stones' music is ruptured unto death by Devo's mordantly playful amalgamation of Dadaism, Nihilistic philosophy, postmodern satire, and sci-fi kitsch, pressurized into the ear wiggy-ness of the corporate jingle structures they origamied into scathingly political pop music. And beneath the performance art drag, Devo had the added virtue of looking completely ordinary to their audience, genetic "spuds" as they called themselves—nothing like the sex panthers, renaissance fair troubadours and Valhalla cosplayers folks were used to. For all their obvious smarts and art house surreality, Devo was appealingly DIY for the kids who discovered them that night, both musically and visually; non-descript dudes indistinguishable from the college guys sacking groceries at my local Hinky Dinky.

Of course, I didn't have any of this language or context at thirteen, only a freshly minted teenager's heat seeking radar for music so fresh and exciting—SO FUCKING NEW—that it left me slightly alarmed, disturbingly aroused and usefully confused. And I wasn't alone.

Soon after their appearance on *SNL*, some of the certifiably coolest boys at the neighborhood high school covered Devo's "Satisfaction" at the annual talent show causing a joyous riot that became an immediate legend every kid in town heard about. A friend of mine, a well-known novelist (name redacted for the sake of personal dignity), told me after seeing their *SNL* performance he immediately dismantled his shower curtain and wore it around his tiny, conservative hometown to feel "Devo-esque," despite the serious abuse he took from the normie kids (and proving once again being in the vanguard isn't for the weak). My response was to start regularly pedaling my bike the four miles (uphill! Without permission!) to the closest record store, using my chore money to raid the bins for music I learned was called "New Wave": Elvis Costello, B-52s, Talking Heads, The Pretenders, Blondie (and bless you, Chrissie & Debbie, for showing me women were damn well included too).

Seemingly overnight, it was a glorious time to be thirteen.

It's a mystery to me and no small shame that on a recent stroll through the Internet I found surprisingly few "10 Greatest Covers of All-Time" lists that include Devo's "Satisfaction." I don't even understand how that's possible.

For many music nerds and budding musicians, Devo's cover of "Satisfaction" was a seminal moment in their early lives, a Schedule 1 introduction leading directly to the dive clubs and rumpus rooms of punk and new wave that would quickly infiltrate and reshape music worldwide.

Maybe Devo is considered more "performance art" than music to your more parochial sorts? Too equally committed to the satiric videos (MTV soon made ubiquitous) for the crankier purists to approve? Perhaps some simply take a pass on their music's avant-garde complexities and experimentation?

Or maybe Devo is ultimately too Cassandra-like for some list makers with their upsettingly unsentimental "Jocko Homo" critique of post human devolution, zombie consumerism, and cannibalistic capitalism? I mean, nobody's gonna vote Devo's music Most Likely to Get You Laid.

I suppose this last reason makes the most sense to me. Little more than a year after Devo's performance of "Satisfaction" on *SNL*, Ronald Reagan (*shudder*) won the presidency, ejaculating a backlash of fifties nostalgia porn as cultural "corrective" to the "dangerous" ideas unleashed by the Civil Rights, LGBTQIA+ and Women's Liberation movements. During Reagan's first administration, it remains in memory the only time I ever openly swore at my father—a public school administrator—paradoxically dedicated to working in lower income schools for 40 years—who ended up voting for Reagan not once, but *twice*. "WHY DON'T YOU JUST SHOOT YOURSELF IN THE FUCKING HEAD, DAD? IT'D BE A LOT QUICKER."

So the great and greedy sleep of white America recommenced in the '80s with a revenant's vengeance. In his second term, Ol' Purplehead openly trolled the nation, using Bruce Springsteen's obviously and indisputably brutal "Born In The USA" as his feel good campaign song while Alex P. Keaton clones were more than satisfied to dance along mindlessly in their whale print turtlenecks and Topsiders.

It's hard not to think the human devolution Devo informed us, of starting in the late '70s, is all but complete in the apocalypse-adjacent aftermath of another racist, bigoted, and corrupt D-List actor's presidency. That night on *SNL*, Devo delivered a message to the nation—a musical harbinger of the future soon to come--but hasn't this always been America's most singularly defining feature—not hearing what we don't want to hear?

("Freedom from choice, *it's what we want.*")

ON "SWEET DREAMS" (& UNEASE):

Danielle Geller on Marilyn Manson & the Spooky Kids

The week of the March Faxness draft, Kanye West staged a listening party for his new album *Donda*. His team built a replica of his childhood home and plopped it down on a mound of dirt in Chicago's Soldier Field. During the opening performance, ye, DaBaby, and Marilyn Manson congregated on the front porch, where Manson leaned heavily on the black metal railing and looked more bored than menacing.

As the internet lit up with familiar outrage, condemnation, and faux disbelief, Evan Rachel Wood posted a video to Instagram with a simple dedication: "For my fellow survivors who got slapped in the face this week. I love you. Don't give up." Fittingly, in the video, she stands on the blue-lit stage of the Bourbon Room and delivers a sweet and slow rendition of New Radicals' "You Get What You Give." And as the song patters into the lyrics that label Manson a fake and offer him a light ass-kicking, Wood drags a middle finger toward her heart.

That could be it for us. A survivor in a white dress reclaiming a moment. A small nod to a cover that didn't meet the tournament's criteria. You could walk away from this essay, cast your vote for the other song in this bracket, and move on. Or we could hang out a little longer and talk about sweet dreams.

*

When I first fell in love with Eurythmics' original, I was a girl living in a trailer park in South Florida with my sister and grandmother and step-grandpa Don. I attended Catholic school. I took swimming lessons and ballet. I liked to read and climb trees and crush aluminum cans in the duck-billed can crusher nailed to the front porch. I collected toy horses called Grand Champions. I poured salt on my nightly bowl of ice cream and stirred it into a lukewarm soup.

There was an unease to my childhood, of course. We lived at or below the poverty line. My parents were alcoholics, which was how I came to live with my grandmother. My father was often in jail. I was taught to be distrustful, especially of my friends' fathers and stepfathers, though more generally of men.

Unease is an emotion that clings to memory. It's a particular shade of orange. The sound and shape of the word "birthday" in my mouth. The tension in Annie Lennox's voice, accompanied by an optimistic, synthetic beat. It's South Florida, wood-paneled living rooms, and the hydrogen sulfide that contaminated the water in our well. Unease is a soggy boardwalk over a marsh. Empty peanut shells. It's a young Brian Warner in his grandfather's basement: the opening pages of Marilyn Manson's memoir, *The Long Hard Road Out of Hell.*

*

As a high school freshman, I tried to convince my Honors English teacher to let me write a book report on his memoir. It was part provocation, part laziness; I had already read the book. She said no and then took it a step farther, calling a meeting with my grandmother to stage an intervention. But it had already been a few years since my grandmother lost sway over us girls.

After our step-grandpa died and we moved from Florida to central Pennsylvania, I quit ballet and toy horses and God. I started wearing oversized shirts from Hot Topic and jangly bondage pants. In the break-up letter I mailed to my Catholic school best friend, I claimed I worshipped Satan and that she wouldn't understand.

In an interview Manson gave for *The Observer* in 2015, Carole Cadwalladr asked him, "Do you think that you created a monster as a way of externalising the difficult feelings you couldn't cope with? You, Brian, gave them all to Marilyn Manson?" To which he responded, "Are you trying to mindfuck me?" He didn't answer her question—no confirmation or denial. Instead he shifted gears, suggesting they move on to "more cheerful things."

I can't lie and say his character's memoir didn't resonate with me. My problems were more serious than my minor rebellions let on. Alone in my room after school, I met with much older men online. What began as role-playing wolves and vampires in fantasy chatrooms transitioned to playing a different kind of girl in back alleys and slave markets. One of these men liked that I was the same age as his son, though I lied, and he knew it—they all knew it—when I told them how old I was. Alone in my room, I walked an uneasy line between the girl I was and the girl these men told me to be over text, then on camera. As Marilyn Manson writes in his memoir, "...I had begun to feel removed from the world of morality. Guilt had become more a fear of getting caught than any sense of right or wrong."

I knew how to be quiet, and I too had found a way of externalizing the guilt I once felt.

*

When Evan Rachel Wood refers to her abuser on social media, she calls him "Brian." No room to conflate the reality of abuse with a character's make-believe.

*

In Fort Lauderdale, Florida in 1989, Brian Warner and Scott Putesky met at a club. Brian was a journalism student who liked writing sad and bad poetry, and Scott was a guy from Jersey who liked to play guitar. Scott thought it would be fun to form a band with a writer, and shortly after, Marilyn Manson & the Spooky Kids was born. Brian created the spectacle; Scott created the sound.

When I began working on this essay, I went back to Manson's memoir (I discreetly repurchased a used copy on the web). Retelling those early years of the band, Brian fluctuates between dismissive ("...no one was particularly impressed by his guitar playing...") and resentful of his cofounder Scott ("He just kept bragging about the musical shit he could do"). After the band collected a few new members and signed to Trent Reznor's label, Nothing Records, Brian began to push Scott out. His absence from the new album's demo concerned Reznor, who warned Brian that Scott's guitar style was the backbone of Marilyn Manson.

Initially, I was surprised this conversation made it into the book. It gives Scott more credit than one might expect. In the world of music, isn't it *music* that lends a band its credibility? Instead, Brian told Reznor, "...nobody even talks about the songs."

*

In an interview with *The Guardian* about the origin of "Sweet Dreams," Annie Lennox dispels its associations with sex or sadomasochism. Instead, she explains the lyrics came from a sense of hopelessness and nihilism about the music industry. "I felt like we were in a dream world, that whatever we were chasing was never going to happen," she says. Her partner Dave Stewart (high on speed and thus slightly more optimistic) found her lyrics "mind-blowing, but depressing." He suggested the addition of the lines "hold your head up, moving on" to make it "more uplifting."

They set the music video in a record company's boardroom. Annie Lennox sported a black business suit and cropped orange hair. They added a cow to the video meant to signify "reality." The cow pissed everywhere.

*

Brian conceived of the "Sweet Dreams" cover during an acid trip in South Florida when the band still had its Spooky Kids. "I need to get away from this surreal scene," he writes, "away from all these people who are treating me like I'm some sort of star they can suck a little brightness out of." He imagines the song slower, darker, meaner, which might have been closer to Annie Lennox's version if not for the influence of her partner. It's so often the people we love—who love us—that help us see outside ourselves.

As credited on the album, Marilyn Manson's cover of "Sweet Dreams" is brought to life by Scott's "Electric Twangdoodles." "The track is slow and grimy, filthy, sleazy, teeming with decay," The Cubist writes in a review on Nerd Bacon. "The guitar solo midway is the very antithesis of what it means to dream…"

Scott's guitar is meant to be destroyed in the song's video shoot—at around the 1:00 minute mark you can see him half-heartedly knocking it against a wall—but is saved ("So what if it keeps feeding back," Brian recalls him saying). As Scott's place in the band became more uncertain, and to fill the time he wasn't given to work on the new album, he began recording new songs with the "Sweet Dreams" guitar and his four-track recorder. Then Trent Reznor, seemingly frustrated with the band's lack of progress on their new album, smashed it to pieces over an amp.

Scott opens his resignation letter to the band like a divorced father saying goodbye to his estranged kids. He absolves everyone—the Kids, Brian, and "Uncle Trent"—of any blame. "I do not want to say anything negative about your mom but we have agreed to see other people," he writes. "We both love you all very much and we hope you understand." The resignation shifts from personal to business abruptly, from heartfelt to a bullet-pointed list of grievances that include damage and destruction of personal instruments; creative, interpersonal, and business frustrations; exclusion from recordings; lack of compensation; and "blah, blah and blah..."

His resignation letter, along with sheet music, guitars, and Spooky Kids memorabilia, is put up for auction to cover medical expenses. In 2017, he died of colon cancer at the age of forty-nine.

After Scott's passing, Brian posted a short tribute on Instagram: "Scott Putesky and I made great music together. We had our differences over the years, but I will always remember the good times more." He told his fans to listen to "Man That You Fear" in his honor. It was their favorite, he said.

Brian's tribute to Scott has since disappeared from his page.

*

In 2007, Marilyn Manson released "Heart-Shaped Glasses," an objectively *terrible* song. Its music video features Evan Rachel Wood, his then-girlfriend. Wood was nineteen; Brian, thirty-eight. Watching the video now is uneasy, as if I am made witness to her abuse.[1] In the publicity surrounding the song's release, Brian drew allusions to *Lolita*, which he claimed to be reading at the time, though the song's title is a reference to the red plastic glasses made popular in Stanley Kubrick's adaptation of *Lolita* in 1962.

In an interview with BBC Radio One, he described a revelation he made while writing "Heart-Shaped Glasses," saying song-writing "should be the part of your personality that you might feel guarded or too secret...." The thing is, Brian has never been guarded or secretive about abuse, and there are many more timely articles that have been written about the red flags we collectively ignored. His issues with women are both common and predictable, stemming from low self-esteem and fear of rejection. His ghost-writer described him as a man who "does everything he can to trick people into liking him" because he is so consumed with contempt for the world and himself.

[1] Shortly after I finished this essay, articles about Evan Rachel Wood's documentary *Phoenix Rising* included new abuse allegations surrounding the "Heart-Shaped Glasses" music video. "I was essentially raped on-camera," she says. And, "No one was looking after me." *Rolling Stone* reported a crew member at the video shoot corroborated her account, but Warner's lawyer once again denied all allegations.

After the allegations against him became public, Brian posted a statement in self-defense. Because his posts have a habit of disappearing, here is his statement transcribed:

> Obviously, my art and life have long been magnets for controversy, but these recent claims against me are horrible distortions of reality. My intimate relationships have always been entirely consensual with like-minded partners. Regardless of how—and why—others are now choosing to misrepresent the past, that is the truth.

Brian doesn't spend much time on the "how—and why" his accusers are returning to the past, but context is important.

The first time Evan Rachel Wood came forward with her story was in 2018, when she testified before a House Judiciary Subcommittee in support of implementing the Survivors' Bill of Rights Act at the state level. She did not name Brian Warner at that time.

In 2019, she testified in front of the California Senate Public Safety Committee in support of the Phoenix Act, which would extend the statute of limitations on domestic violence felonies from three years to five and require police officers to complete additional training on intimate partner violence. Her evidence, which included both photographs and video, could not be viewed by the state because the statute of limitations on her case had run out. She did not name Brian Warner at that time.

She named her abuser a year ago, in February 2021, saying, among other things, that she was done living in fear.

*

A few weeks ago, Evan Rachel Wood donned a suit and ruffled blouse in homage of David Bowie's Jareth, the Goblin King. *Labyrinth* was *the* movie my sister and I rented every week at Blockbuster, so often my grandmother complained we never picked anything else (she probably should have just bought us a copy). We memorized every line, every song. Jareth was my second childhood crush; the first was Tim Curry's Darkness, a red-toned devil with three-foot black horns, which could explain how I ended up here.

Evan Rachel Wood captions one of her "Goblin Queen" photos with the title of a song, "As the World Falls Down," a Geller household favorite. The song comes at a turning point in the movie. Jareth traps Sarah, the object of his affection, inside one of the crystal balls he has been twirling between his fingers all movie long. Within, he stages a masquerade ball; he dresses her in a white gown that glitters with silver embroidery; surrounds her with cackling revelers in elaborate, devilish masks.[2] As he stalks her through the room, he sings about the pain of obsession masquerading as love. Sarah shatters the illusion when she grabs an unassuming chair and hurls it through the glass walls.

In their final scene together, he procures a clear crystal and begs her to reconsider. "Look, Sarah," he pleads. "Look what I'm offering you. Your dreams."

As he talks, she walks toward him–face blank, voice monotone–and recites the lines of a play that hold the key to her freedom.

"I ask for so little," he insists, backing away. "Just fear me, love me, do as I say, and I will be your *slave*."

The final line comes to her like a revelation: *You have no power over me.* Jareth's face twists in disappointment, and he tosses the crystal into the air. When Sarah catches it, the ball winks out of existence like a mere soap bubble. It's meant to be a moment of triumph, a moment I couldn't comprehend as a girl. Jareth was so completely devoted to her, so sexy in his tight gray pants. I knew Sarah was just dumb to turn down a guy like him.

*

In interviews with Brian after his relationship with Evan Rachel Wood ended, he claimed to have called her 158 times. "I wanted to show her the pain she put me through," he said. He told reporters he fantasized about killing her with a sledgehammer. His team later backtracked, attributing the comments to a theatrical rock star generating publicity for a new album. But one wonders if Brian knows where the uneasy line between he and his character begins and ends.

The truth, if Brian goes looking for it, is that pain fosters a false sense of intimacy. Pain is a simulacrum of vulnerability, a hook in a young girl's heart. Too often, the seed of some sad, sweet dream.

---

[2] By contrast, Darkness attempts to seduce Princess Lili with a black bridal gown; its neckline plunges below her belly button. When Lili accuses him of stealing her dreams, he offers wise counsel. "The dreams of youth," he says quietly, "are the regrets of maturity."

ON THE ESSAY:

I didn't choose to write this essay with the hope I would win March Faxness. I considered my selection an act of sabotage, which isn't to say I thought I'd be changing the hearts and minds of Marilyn Manson's "true fans." Mostly, I wanted to dispel an illusion that had gripped me longer than it should have, and I turned to loads of research, as I often do. There's nothing better than discovering places where space and time align. The difficult part is transitioning from research to writing, of knowing when you've got more material than you can hold. That's usually when I turn to my non-writer husband, who's happy to tell me when and where he's confused by a tangent I've followed. If I don't have a good enough reason for including something—even if I liked the *idea* of writing about the color orange as a minor motif—I know it's a good place to cut and redirect my energy elsewhere. In this case, I wanted to leave plenty of space to write about Scott Putesky, the green-haired guitarist who never made it into my goth-girl dreams.

THERE ARE MANY ATLANTIC CITIES, AND ONE BELONGS TO LEVON HELM:

Erin Keane on The Band's Cover of "Atlantic City"

My father, a liar and a son of New Jersey, believed so deeply in his own powers of resurrection that he made judges believe in them, court-appointed lawyers believe, rehab doctors believe, my mother believe—for a while—and especially me believe, long after his death. He saw himself as a man who should have been one of life's winners—even when he found himself ever south of that line, his time, he assumed, was surely just around the corner. I know too much now to buy this story anymore, but old prayers die hard. What is a fitting hymn for a man who wished a mythological version of himself into existence? He died in 1982, and I wasn't there to sing "Amazing Grace" at his funeral, so now I light my candles to "Atlantic City" instead.

Bruce Springsteen's "Atlantic City," off his 1982 brooding solo album *Nebraska*, is a desperate man's ballad. I have always understood the protagonist as an underworld wannabe caught up in the gang war who would not make it out in one piece. Our guy is not a player, not really, but the game is deathly serious to him. He has money troubles, girl troubles, and now he's in a cursed town intent on turning his luck, and if you've been around any block at all you know how this probably ends. Here is a man who has told himself a story he needs to believe in. If he can just do this one errand for this one important man, he'll earn his second chance. The old him can die, and all of his mistakes too, and he'll be a new man, a better man. You'll want to stick around for the big miracle, baby. You just watch him turn this burned coffee into wine.

But we're not with him for the magic trick at the end; it's earlier in the day, maybe nearing dusk, in the phone booth outside the diner where he left the newspaper folded on the counter for the next guy as he fumbles for change in the pocket of his inadequate jacket, when he opens the call to his girl with the news of the day, the headline digest and the word on the street: the mob boss murdered in his Philadelphia home, the cops up in arms, the crime families gone to war over the casinos and all they can offer. Implied in his recap: the opportunity he senses for his fortune to turn.

When I drop the needle on this record, I am the girl worrying a bus ticket in her worn-out gloved hand, wondering if I should bother putting my face on this time. Because he believes what he's saying, every word of it, I have to work not to fall for it, to be the one who knows better. His attempt to bridge that distance between us, the tension of the wire he must cross, the yearning for redemption that may or may not be granted, that's what makes the song work.

Because the first rule of the cover song is to do no harm, "Atlantic City" can only work in the hands of a believer. The second rule of the cover song is the artist has to make it their own. Otherwise, it's karaoke, which is a different kind of sacrament. A cover must be willing to tear down what we think the song must be, to plant a revised version of the truth in its ashes and let it grow into something else. Not better, necessarily, but different. It's dangerous alchemy; if you follow the second rule, you always risk breaking the first. For me, with "Atlantic City," the stakes are high. I am putting a broken hymn to my father in your hands. What will you do with it?

When The Band covered "Atlantic City," Levon Helm transformed Springsteen's aching solemnity into an anthem for a living wake. Their cover was recorded for *Jericho*, released in 1993, when I was seventeen years old. (I was born right before The Band's 1976 farewell concert, which Martin Scorsese immortalized in *The Last Waltz*.) The Band had reunited the year after Springsteen's *Nebraska* came out, without Robbie Robertson, and began recording in 1985, but the next year vocalist/pianist Richard Manuel died by suicide while on tour. The comeback album would wait. We can hear Richard sing lead in "Country Boy" on *Jericho*. All of this is to say that *Jericho* is a fitting vehicle for a song that contemplates what it means to die and to return.

The first time I heard Levon sing this song I did not suddenly start believing in the resurrection or anything, but I swear I could feel myself levitating about a quarter-inch off the ground.

Levon, son of the Mississippi Delta, the low flat water that keeps secrets as well as any ocean swell, which is to say, it's always only a matter of time before the truth washes up, no matter the shore. As soon as Levon starts singing this Jersey song in his Arkansas accent, we recognize his character as an outsider, this country boy a long way from home, here where the sands are not quite turning gold—a promise he knew better than to believe in the first place, coming as he does from a land of old lies.

An outsider can see clearly what a man who has spent his whole life with his nose pressed against the glass cannot. Levon's man is not, perhaps, especially reverent of this South Jersey mythology and its various gods and spoilers. Cops are the same in every town, more or less. Crooks, too. A smile teases his lips as he delivers the news from this strange land to his girl on the other end of the line: *The Chicken Man, baby! And his house too!* It's as foreign to him as the night cryptid said to be dragging its forked tail through the Pine Barrens' sugar sands, but what patch of dirt on this earth isn't home to its own monster?

I hear my father's longing to be a bigger man in Bruce Springsteen's haunted vocals, his dazzling harmonica. Levon's mandolin changes the tone, turning a boardwalk séance into a barn jamboree. The expansive lift when Levon sings, "put your *makeup* on," makes it hard to sing along without a hopeful smile. The Band's version strips the song of just enough of its despair and balances it with a modest allotment of acceptance—self-forgiveness, even. *There wasn't any other way to play it*, Levon's voice conveys. *If I'm a dead man walking, we'd better party on the way to the grave.*

Which is not to say his "Atlantic City" is a joyful place. The resurrection chorus is still as menacing as it is hopeful. Everything dies, and it could be someone's turn tonight. There's no moving on from what's to come. Or it's an apology for what happens next, or doesn't. Bruce's lyrics have *maybe* doing an awful lot of work in this song. In Levon's performance I also hear twinges of Hank Senior, singing praise with one breath, only to stop Minnie with the next, telling her no, in fact, *there ain't no light*. It doesn't pay, our man making this phone call to his girl seems to know, on some level, to believe your own best lines. Nobody ever got my father to believe that.

I don't know if I believe in much, in this world or beyond, but I believe in the truth as Levon and Bruce tell it. The more desperate we are for transformation, the more the stories we tell ourselves can keep us in a fixed state. Some nights you're going to hear a ghost laugh on the line. There's not always much distance between a promise and a threat. Grace is where you find it—sometimes that's the harmonica wail, and sometimes it's sheer mandolin pluck.

When throat cancer took Levon's voice, he nursed it back to strength and won three Grammys. On the thirtieth anniversary of my father's death, we lost Levon too. The cancer came back. "Atlantic City" is my reminder that second chances are only what we decide to make of them. Grab hold of the waning light. Someone tune the mandolin. Play us a song for our comeback hearts. Let's get to dancing while we still have moving feet.

ON THE ESSAY:

For a while I thought you had to be in a secret cool-kids club to write for March Xness, then I paid attention and saw I could just put my name into the lottery myself. For my first tournament, I picked the song I felt the strongest personal connection to, figuring the extra passion would win me votes. I wanted to write short for the internet's attention span. I was knocked out in Round 1. Now, after a few more brackets with this delightful community of music nerds who volunteer to do homework for each others' amusement (about as far from a secret cool-kids club you can get) under my belt, I know it's a stronger move to pick a song with a higher nostalgia appeal—preferably to elder millennials and young Gen Xers, if I'm being candid. Still, this essay, my losing debut, remains my favorite. Honestly, I wrote it mostly for myself.

I THINK WE'RE ALONE NOW

Justin St. Germain on Tiffany

If I'd known that when I wrote this I'd have Covid, I would've picked a different song. Under the circumstances, "I Think We're Alone Now" feels a little on the nose. You have to understand that I chose my song in that halcyon summer of 2021, when everyone was getting vaccinated and cases were down and there were no new variants and it seemed like this was almost over. Some things were, it turns out, but not the pandemic.

I'm writing from the pit of an Oregon winter, in the throes of Omicron, during what they're calling the worst days. It's been the worst days for weeks now. Yesterday I went to the county fairgrounds to get tested inside my car inside a barn, and today received my positive result. It did feel sort of positive, almost like an accomplishment—after all that waiting, all those times I thought my relationship stress or existential dread or seasonal allergies were Covid, I was finally right. I looked on the county website at this week's orange bar, five times taller than any other, and found it oddly reassuring: at least I'm not alone. The feeling didn't last.

*

Recently—yesterday, last week, who knows—the algorithm delivered a headline to my device. Our robot overlords have noticed how much I've been listening to "I Think We're Alone Now"; I can't look at a screen these days without seeing ads for dating apps or boner pills or suicide hotlines. This intrusion was, thankfully, more specific to my interests: Tiffany, née Tiffany Darwish, whose cover of this song is arguably the best-known version, was in the news.

Tiffany took "I Think We're Alone Now" to number one in 1987, twenty years after the Tommy James original. She was sixteen at the time. She's fifty now, and had recently taken the stage in some minor Florida burg to sing her biggest hit. The article linked to a video on TMZ. I clicked. Such is the age in which we live.

The clip starts as Tiffany is in the middle of the song. She seems lost, disoriented, possibly drunk, pretty much the way we all seem at this point. Her voice breaks. She forgets the lyrics, growls a few *oh yeah*s to stall. (Speaking of 1987, she sounds sort of like Macho Man Randy Savage.)

It's sad. Tiffany is all alone up there. Not literally—some dude on a stool strums a guitar stage left, and a fiddle fires up offscreen for the chorus. But nobody came to see the fiddler. They came to hear Tiffany sing this song, and she's disappointing them. Someone boos. She stops and points at them.

"Fuck you guys!" she yells.

Instantly, every time—and I've been watching this video a lot—I think: *Yeah, fuck those guys!*

"This is my hit!" she yells. "I'm going to sing it right!"

She tries her best, remembers and screams: *running just as fast as we can. Holding on to one another's hand. Trying to get away, into the night. And then you put your arms around me and we tumble to the ground and then we s*— The clip cuts off mid-syllable, but you know the rest. You sang some of it right now, didn't you? Or are you one of those people who lies about not liking this song?

Tiffany caught some shit online, but to me, that performance was perfect. To get up on stage in November of the worst year we can remember and totally botch a song about being alone, a song she didn't want to sing in the first place thirty-five years ago, but is now stuck with forever, because it reminds us all of a past we're desperate to return to. Or maybe it's just me. The fuck-you-guys fiddle version of "I Think We're Alone Now" is my favorite one, and that's saying something, because I love this song.

A few days after the controversy, Tiffany posts an apology video to Instagram. She starts by singing the chorus again. It sounds better, the song re-recognizable, but you wonder why she's doing it. To prove that she still can? Is she covering herself? What does that even mean?

Tiffany says she had a panic attack, lost her voice: "I got up there and it just wasn't there." She appreciates the support. "I'm vulnerable," she says, "and I'm human."

You and me both, sister.

*

My chest constricts, I cough a lot, my face hurts. But most of it's mental: I feel dumb and unstable, keep forgetting why I walked into rooms and nearly falling over. I wear a mask around my house. I'm trying not to infect my wife, who's packing boxes in the living room as I write this. I probably should've mentioned that I'm also getting divorced. If I had known I'd be getting divorced, I would definitely not have picked this song.

I wasn't going to write a personal essay. My criticisms of the genre have been documented. But have you ever been around someone who's getting divorced? Not just divorced people—a lot of them are happier—the ones who are getting one. Everything is personal; I lost it last week during an episode of *BoJack Horseman*.

Still, that doesn't mean it's worth writing about. One of the first things you realize when you start getting divorced is that nobody gives a shit, just like you didn't when all those other people you knew got divorced. Besides, the world is ending, divorce is not that big of a deal. For my parents, my soon-to-be-ex-wife's parents, Tiffany's parents, and all the other parents of the '80s, divorce was like Omicron, everybody got it. My parents got divorced six times between them. Seven if you count theirs twice. Eight if you count the murder. If you think divorce is some kind of tragedy, you've never seen one. But I have brain fog and a deadline, so here I am, writing about it.

As I often try to remind myself, divorce isn't all bad. Sure, it's scary: all that emptiness ahead, the fear and loneliness and fear of loneliness. But being married sucked—that's why we're getting a divorce. I once heard a recently divorced acquaintance say that when someone says they're getting one, you shouldn't say you're sorry, you should say congratulations. I never understood that until now. The calmness, the freedom, no more compromises or resentment or tension. It's almost a relief that there doesn't seem to be anyone around.

The tape dispenser screeches. I crank up the volume and try to focus. A while back I made a playlist filled with like thirty different versions of "I Think We're Alone Now"—there are more, I just gave up—which I've now been listening to for a solid month, as its title has gotten truer and truer. I've been trying to figure out why people don't like it.

For example, when I picked this song, our friendly tournamentmongers responded: *oh god, really? Tiffany?* They're not alone in that sentiment: the single currently has a 2.8/5 on rateyourmusic.com. Last year, as part of a series reviewing every American number-one hit, Stereogum gave Tiffany's version of the song a 5/10, saying, "It's a perfectly digestible pop product, but it never sounds like anyone's world exploding." I beg to differ—right now, it sounds exactly like my world exploding.

Which brings me to a question I've been asking perhaps too often lately, in a variety of contexts: am I wrong here? Because I want to be clear about this, and communicate my honest feelings in the way I've been told I often fail to: I fucking love this song. I didn't pick it ironically or cleverly or for some contrarian reason, or even because I thought it could win. (Although I do—I think it *should*.) I just love it. Especially now.

Every time I hear "I Think We're Alone Now," any old version, even the shitty ones, it makes me happy. Well, happi*er*. I catch myself singing it all the time. I don't dance as a policy—it looks like I'm being defibrillated—but sometimes when Tiffany's version comes on in my headphones I find myself trying to imitate that heel-intensive thing she does in the video, in my kitchen, with limited success. This last month, as I've been listening on repeat, it's become one of my favorite songs.

I've recently learned that I need to be more empathetic, so I'm trying to understand why so many people are so wrong about this song. I guess the lyrics don't make a lot of sense. Even the title's full of contradictions. Wouldn't you know whether you were alone? If someone is saying all that stuff, how could the beating of their hearts be the only sound? Can you even be alone together? Don't answer that one: the tape dispenser just did.

I admit, the production value of Tiffany's version is not fantastic. Tommy James had a whole band, the fungible Shondells: backup singers, drums, guitars, a tambourine, maybe a marimba there at the end. His producer included that deeply strange but technically innovative sample of crickets. The original has texture and weight. Tiffany's version seems slight in comparison, just her and a Casio keyboard; its most daring move is a synth solo.

Maybe it's Tiffany herself. The culture underestimated her, for reasons that were readily apparent: young, female, pretty, most famous for a cover song. You don't hear so much the story of a child prodigy who started performing in clubs at the age of ten, killed *Star Search* at fourteen, and recorded her first album a year later, the self-titled one that would soon top the charts, making her the youngest female artist ever to do so. Nobody talks about how she had *two* number-one hits: "I Think We're Alone Now," which wasn't even supposed to be a single, and the ballad "Could've Been." Or that she's released ten more albums since, voiced Judy in the Jetsons movie, has a handful of other film and TV credits—and sure, *Mega Piranha* isn't exactly *Citizen Kane*, but she got top billing, and how many movies have you been in? She has an active fan club, tens of thousands of followers, more than a million monthly listeners on Spotify. Thirty-five years after this song came out, she's still one-name famous.

Maybe it's not Tiffany at all—maybe people don't like the original, either. Like Tiffany, Tommy James has not been taken seriously enough. Is it because his first hit, "Hanky Panky," was a cover? Or because he's been covered so much? (This tournament includes two Tommy James covers, and could've easily had a third, Billy Idol's "Mony Mony.")

Consider the man's resume. He made two number-one hits—not including "I Think We're Alone Now," which reached #1 on some lists, but not Billboard's—and, in the late '60s, released eight albums in four years, charting a whole artistic evolution from bubblegum pop to psychedelic rock; *Crimson & Clover* is a stone-cold classic. He helped pioneer the concept of a music video by making one for "Mony Mony" fifteen years before MTV debuted. He's been touring steadily for sixty years. He once dosed a presidential candidate with amphetamines on the campaign trail. He was so mobbed up in the '70s that he had to flee New York so he didn't wind up with concrete shoes. One time, before a concert, he got so high that he collapsed onstage and was pronounced dead. Fifty years later, he put out an album called *Alive*. That guy is punk as fuck.

Maybe it's the video? I should probably talk about the video. Four and a half minutes of pure, uncut 1987. Teenaged Tiffany dances alone in stonewashed jeans by some train tracks. She hangs out the window of a moving car, like people did back in that gloriously reckless era. The synth solo hits, and she does her signature dance. Gumby makes a cameo. God, I love this video. Most of it takes place in a mall in Ogden. A mall in Ogden! Tiffany's manager sent her on a nationwide tour of malls to promote her album, and it worked. "I Think We're Alone Now" shot to number one because of malls. Is that why people don't respect it? Do you have something against malls?

If you still have a mall nearby, like an honest to god food-court-and-atria mall, you should go now, before it's gone. Until I got Covid, et cetera, one of my plans for this essay was to go hang out in a mall all day and see what happened. There is no better place to meditate about how much has changed since this music video came out, the death drive of consumer capitalism and social media's fragmenting of our shared reality blah blah blah. A mall used to be the kind of place Tiffany could pack so full of fans that some bros in tank tops had to hold them back, as they do, somewhat unconvincingly, in the video. Now malls are the loneliest places in America.

*

Nobody wants to read about the pandemic anymore nearly two years in, but humor me for a moment: "I Think We're Alone Now" has become the pandemic anthem. A few weeks into the first lockdowns, Billie Joe Armstrong, the lead singer of Green Day, recorded a cover of this song and posted it to YouTube, along with the following note: *I figure if we have to spend this time in isolation at least we can be alone together.* Remember that? When we were all going to be alone together?

Armstrong sang it again a week later on *The Tonight Show*, then released another version with his kids on drums and bass. Half a dozen other bands have released cover versions since the pandemic started, and someone made an 8-track sorta-cover that's better than it has any reason to be.

Like everything else, this song has changed in the last two years. At first, "I Think We're Alone Now" was clearly about sex: we all know what they're tumbling to the ground for. *Children, behave*? *Watch how you play*? Those kids are fucking.

But meaning changes according to context. I could quote Roland Barthes or something, but it's pretty obvious: everyone's singing this song now because the pandemic has made us lonely. In an interview about Billie Joe's cover of her cover, Tiffany said as much: "There are people out there that need a little pick-me-up." This song might have been about sex in 1987, but now it's about loneliness, and we can't stop singing it.

Neither could its two best-known performers. Tommy James has made a few different versions, not including his minor hit "Mirage," which according to legend—more specifically, a really old and shitty website—contains the same chord progression as "I Think We're Alone Now" in reverse; apparently he accidentally played it backward while he was fucking around during a songwriting session. James cut a pandemic version of his own, an acoustic self-cover released in 2020.

Tiffany has done at least four different versions, as far as I can tell, and possibly hundreds; Spotify lists 213. This song has been in so many movies and TV shows and '80s compilations, not to mention re-covers and remixes, that it's impossible to say which ones should be considered independent versions. There's probably some profound essayistic observation to be made about that, quoting Baudrillard or Benjamin or some shit, but give me a break here.

Her latest was in 2019, so wasn't technically a pandemic version, but it is about loneliness. It's longer, more rock than pop, and Tiffany's voice is husky, soulful, more mature.

She was getting divorced at the time. That's not my business. I'm only mentioning it here because she discussed it publicly in interviews, and because I wonder how much getting divorced informed her decision to record this song again. Maybe I'm projecting.

Divorce certainly shows up in her other recent songs. A few months into the pandemic, Tiffany released an EP of acoustic self-covers, *Pieces of Me Unplugged*. My favorite, "Starting Over," begins with the lyric: *I wish that I could just be free / from the loneliness in me.*

*

The good news about being alone is you get used to it. That's also the bad news. I've been alone a lot. I was the son of a single mother who worked, and I grew up on the outskirts of a pissant town in Arizona where I was sometimes the only human in sight. And I read and write, both of which involve a lot of time alone pretending that you're not. When the pandemic started, my wife and I joked that I'd been preparing for it all my life. Turns out it wasn't so funny. Soon we were lonely together.

Now, in my first days of being alone again, it sometimes feels lonely and sometimes feels natural, inevitable, the way it is. Nothing lasts forever: someone leaves or someone dies. That's why so many people are lonely. Nobody admits it, not out loud, not in a conversation. But search for loneliness on Spotify, read the lyrics:

Look at all the lonely people.
At my window, sad and lonely.
I've got my own loneliness.
Can't get away from loneliness.
Loneliness is the worst thing in the world.
I think we're alone now.

*

There are at least three movies called *I Think We're Alone Now*. One came out during the pandemic, a slasher film I didn't bother to watch, the trailer for which plays Tiffany's version of the song. Another came out before the pandemic but is about a pandemic. Tyrion Lannister lives alone in a library by a lake after everyone dies in some kind of plague. Nobody talks for the first twenty minutes. It doesn't include the song.

The documentary does. It's from 2008—which looks longer ago onscreen than 1987 does—and it follows two people who are obsessed with Tiffany. One of them is the most sympathetic stalker you'll ever see, and the other radiates so much pain and loneliness you can feel it through the screen. Together they go to Vegas to see Tiffany live. After the concert, they take pictures with her, and that night, in their hotel room, these two broken people exaggerate that interaction until they're arguing over who's better friends with Tiffany. The next morning they go back to their grim little lives. It's a great documentary, smart and subtle and more sophisticated than it seems. It's the loneliest movie I've ever seen.

*

I once spent a week alone in Belgium, touring breweries and battlefields and researching a novel I was writing as far as the IRS was concerned. I went because I was lonely at the time, the last of my book money was burning a hole, and I'd been listening to the Camera Obscura song "Let's Get Out of This Country" so much that finally I said to myself: *let's*.

So I flew into Brussels, rented a Nissan, and drove out to the German border, to a hamlet called Winterspelt that the German writer Alfred Andersch once named a novel after. The book is about a German officer near the end of World War II who wants to surrender, but nobody will let him. Well, that's the plot—I don't really remember, but want to say it was about loneliness. Andersch was a German deserter, and he spent time in Dachau and American POW camps, so he knew a thing or two about the subject. I liked his book. My war novel was sort of an homage, although I never actually wrote it.

I did spend a night in Winterspelt, in a German bed and breakfast where nobody spoke any English except for the owner's teenaged son, who showed me to my room and asked why I was there and ended our conversation rather quickly when I said to see where Americans died in the war. It was hard to sleep in all that German quiet, and the next day, after a breakfast of sliced cheese and indeterminate sausage, I returned for good to the Belgian side of the border.

In Bastogne, where Americans died in the war, I went to museums and memorials and a brewery or two, alone, drawing glances and stares and the occasional polite inquiry in languages I didn't speak. One day I drove my Nissan into the Ardennes to find some battlefield I'd read about online. I got lost on a switchbacked forest road, and the computer lady announced I'd entered Luxembourg—lonely, neutral Luxembourg—which I then left imperceptibly. Soon enough, I was back in Belgium, at my destination, a museum in a barn beside a field where an Army platoon was ambushed during some peripheral skirmish of the Battle of the Bulge.

I parked and followed signs down a path blazed through a field of shoulder-high grass, probably barley, for all the beer. As I groped through the gloam the signs petered out, and in the fading light I couldn't read the garbled English on the pamphlet. But I didn't need to be told what had happened or where. There are benefits to being alone. Soon I found myself pulled like a witcher's stick to the spot where the ambush happened, a clearing where I just knew. I stood there, staring into the dim treeline, imagining an enemy out there in the forest, waiting for the terror to descend before they started shooting. It was the loneliest place I've ever been.

*

I'm off the rails here. Nobody cares about my divorce or the pandemic, and why the hell am I writing about Belgium? I should've picked Limp Bizkit. This is due tomorrow, but it's just not there.

Fuck you guys. It's my essay.

*

Today my wife and I went down to the courthouse and sat knee-to-knee in a cubicle as a clerk slid forms through a hole in the plexiglass and we signed them one after another, cracking jokes, trying to keep it light and quick. Behind the clerk, above her desk, hung a sign with one of those quirky office slogans, something about the beach. There isn't a real beach in five hundred miles, nowhere you'd want to swim or drink a margarita, just the cold and lonely places people around here call beaches, all dead kelp and outcrops. That's not true: there's a nice one about an hour's drive west, a halfway secret you have to climb down stairs to get to, where a big rock out in the water makes for a pretty sunset. That's where we got married.

Ten years together, over in ten minutes. The clerk said we'd get the papers in a week, depending on the mail, and wished us luck. Outside, it was freezing. We gave each other one last married hug and walked away alone. In the car, while I was Venmoing my half of the divorce fee—in the note field, emojis of a husband, a wife, a skull and crossbones—my phone's Bluetooth connected, and guess what song came on. The original. Tommy James. Crickets.

ON THE ESSAY:

This was my third time writing for March Xness, and I probably wouldn't have written this essay for any other context. By then, I'd read and loved so many weird, delightful tournament essays, and knew it was a whole community of smart, generous readers and writers, so I felt like I could risk publishing something that felt a little bit unhinged. This essay didn't win, but it helped me through some shit, and I'm grateful to the Xness for that.

MARCH FADNESS '80s

THE SITUATION THAT THE BASS IS IN: "IT TAKES TWO" & THE BIRTH OF THE AUTHOR

Dave Griffith on "It Takes Two" by Rob Base and DJ E-Z Rock

For the first 47 years of my life, I believed that Mike Ginyard, aka MC Rob Base, was celibate.

In 1988, when Base and his childhood friend DJ E-Z Rock's single "It Takes Two" dropped, I was thirteen and did not know of anyone, besides the adults in my life, and *maybe* Tanya, the hot-as-hell sixteen-year-old daughter of my paper route client, Mr. Yarbrough, who was having sex.

And so, every time I listened to "It Takes Two" in the basement of our split-level ranch in Decatur, Illinois, on my father's capable system—Pioneer receiver with 5-band graphic equalizer, JVC CD player, with a hand-built '70s HeathKit turntable, and Pioneer speakers with 15-inch woofers—the line "...don't smoke buddha can't stand sex [sic], yes..." struck me funny.

The only people I knew that did not have sex on principle were the priests and nuns at Our Lady of Lourdes Catholic Church, and I would come to find out, years later, that I was even wrong about that.

I was naive about a lot of things—I was thirteen years old and living just off a cul-de-sac in the heart of the heart of the country in the Soybean Capital of the World—but especially sex and drugs. It wasn't hard for me from context clues to understand that "buddha" was weed, but the syntax and flow of the line, "don't smoke buddha, can't stand sess, yes" made it seem these were separate activities. Like, don't drink, don't smoke, what do you do?

Thanks to Urban Dictionary, now I know that "sess" is short for sensimilla, a word that I actually did know (even back then) due to uncles who exposed me at a young age to *Caddyshack*: "This is a hybrid," groundskeeper Bill Murray lisps. "This is a cross of Bluegrass, Kentucky Bluegrass, Featherbed Bent, and Northern California Sinsemilla. The amazing stuff about this is that you can play 36 holes on it in the afternoon, take it home and just get stoned to the bejeezus…."

At thirteen I had yet to smoke (or drink) anything that would send me into an altered state, unless you count RC Cola, but I was discovering that music did something to me—for me.

I had been playing trombone since the fifth grade and had just that year joined the Mound Middle School jazz band, led by Mr. Jim Walker, a balding, spectacled clarinetist, who led a Dixieland group that played street festivals and wedding receptions. Somehow, amidst all the distractions of middle schoolers playing grabass, Mr. Walker taught us the rudiments of swing: "*Doo-va-Doo-va-Doo-va-Doo-va*," he would drone, tapping his foot, and twirling his index finger, coaxing us forward into that new musical, alchemical idiom in which two eighth notes become a dotted eighth, sixteenth.

There are times even now, 35 years later, that I will spontaneously begin singing the melody to Glenn Miller's "A String of Pearls" or Count Basie's "Shiny Stockings," big band standards that groove with a deceptively deep, almost tidal force.

And yet, for all my exposure to some of the swingingest, most danceable music ever written, dancing is not something I did. Not my family, nor any family I knew, did it. Maybe my dad would have a little too much Cold Duck on Christmas Eve and would get to bouncing around and twirling my mom, but that was it. We were Midwest Catholics (my mom was actually raised Seventh Day Adventist, a sect that frowns upon dancing) with no strong ethnic identity—some Irish, some Welsh, some German and Dutch—but not a high enough concentration of any of these to influence the food laid on the table, or our holiday rituals.

In the absence of these influences, I was a blank slate. I would lay on my back on the basement floor and listen to Zeppelin and Edgar Winter albums from my parents' collection but also a stray Donald Byrd fusion album, and a completely whacked out Emerson, Lake, and Palmer album with a cover featuring battle tanks in the shape of armadillos; I sang in the choir at the Methodist church because that's where many of my friends worshiped; I did a brief stint as a trombonist at our Our Lady of Lourdes because the music director discovered a Vatican II hymn that squarely ripped off Brubeck's "Take Five" called "Sing of the Lord's Goodness," which was excruciating because all I could imagine while playing this abomination was the angelic, crystalline tone of alto saxophonist Paul Desmond.

But by far the biggest influence on my sense of musical possibilities was my neighbor, Chip. Chip was four years older, had Tony Hawk bangs, and a fake radio station, WPIG, in his basement.

WPIG was basically a podcast 30 years before podcasts were a thing. We had a whole crew of guest DJs: my younger brother would sometimes show up and be allowed to choose a few tracks; Chip's girlfriend, who I would later date after Chip went off to college, appeared on mic a few times under the alter ego Lois Lane; even my friend Cory, whose voice and reporting now regularly appear on National Public Radio, had a cameo.

Each show took up the space of a 90-minute cassette. Most of the 90 minutes was music, but what made it different from your run-of-the-mill '80s mixtape was that we would take turns introducing the tracks in our best, most sincere imitations of the slacker college radio DJs broadcasting from the local WJMU: *And that was [long pause] 10,000 Maniacs [long pause] "About the Weather,"* I would say in a high pubescent voice, trying desperately to sound world weary.

Every third or fourth song there would be a recap: *You…just…heard INXS "Mediate," the Beastie Boys "Brass Monkey" and [long pause] U2 "Bullet the Blue Sky…."* There were segments where we read articles directly verbatim from *Rolling Stone* or gave a rundown of the Top 40 albums, but there were also skits and interviews with invented characters from the neighborhood, like the hard-of-hearing Granny Fudrucker, played by my brother, in a caterwauling, dragged-up Terry Jones falsetto.

It was in the summer of 1988, in Chip's basement, WPIG station headquarters, that I first heard "It Takes Two." By that time, the song had already peaked. It spent three weeks in the Top 40 in mid-April and then spent 19 weeks slowly sliding down the Top 100, but continued to hold steady on the dance charts through 1989, ascending as high as number 3. In 1989 *Spin* magazine ranked "It Takes Two" as the No. 1 single of all time. In 2021 Rolling Stone ranked "It Takes Two" No. 116 on its "Top 500 Best Songs of All Time." Eventually, it would be certified Platinum many times over.

I didn't know any of that at the time. I just knew it was unlike anything I'd heard before.

It's one of those songs, like Zeppelin's "When the Levee Breaks," or George Clinton's "Atomic Dog" or Peter Gabriel's "Sledgehammer," where there's a rhythmic tease, a few bars to set the tone; a little prelude to get your attention. But the first several bars of "It Takes Two"—a sample from the Galactic Force Band's 1972 "Space Dust"—isn't so much a tease as a pronouncement; it's giving a prelude to a grand space promenade; like you're at a block party with hundreds of people: grills are smoking, the sun is beating down, everyone is out and looking good; everything and anything is possible, and then, out of nowhere a portal in the sky opens and this synth fanfare erupts, but not one of those soaring, medieval fanfares with piercing trumpets, but a bottom-heavy, descending line pulling you down, pulling you in like some kind of trance-inducing deep space transmission, like some kind of tractor beam; something you've heard and felt standing wedged between Galaga and Space Invaders in the crowded mall arcade. You just can't place it. But before you can think, a voice enters your consciousness, a voice that has been there since before time, waiting. The booming voice of god speaks the song into existence:

> *RIGHT ABOUT NOW...NOW...NOW*
> *YOU ARE ABOUT TO BE POSSESSED*

[A platform bearing two men in tracksuits—deus ex machina style—lowers them to the stage]

> *BY THE SOUNDS OF MC ROB BASE*
> *AND DJ EZ ROCK...ROCK...ROCK...*
> *HIT IT!*

The basement was carpeted and had a low drop ceiling. At the far end, just outside the laundry room, was a tiled dance floor backed by a mirrored wall, so without even trying, the acoustics were bright without being muddy, like the school gyms where Chip and I would later DJ. The bass hummed in the tile and shimmied in the marbled mirrors, sending vibrations up through my feet, into my chest and teeth. It was a good, alive feeling.

And that was just the first 12 seconds of the song.

What follows is one of the most memorable downbeats in music history: a low frequency bass kick that cannot be produced on any actual acoustic instrument because it's not a sample—a digital recording of an actual drummer playing an actual kick drum—but a completely synthetic sound created by the Roland TR-808 drum machine. The beat hits, then rumbles—sound engineers call it "decay." Only the 808 has that specific kick and decay; a gauzy thud, like a heartbeat.

And then, we all know what happens next, a funky, janky, clattering Mardis Gras march of synth snare, hi-hat, and clap track:

Whoo! Yeah! Whoo! Yeah!
It takes two to make a thing go right
It takes two to make it outta sight

I didn't know it at the time, but these few bars snatched from Lynn Collins' 1972 feminist funk-soul hit "Think (About it)" is one the most famous and most sampled breakbeats in all of hip-hop. It's hard to hear, but down there underneath all that synth is Jabo Starks, the drummer for the JBs—James Brown, the Godfather of Soul's, backing band.

Starks' meticulous 8-on-the-floor style isn't showy. He was known for holding it down so others could be free. JB bassist Bootsy Collins and trombonist Fred Wesley have both said as much. "I could just blow free," Wesley said in one interview. Starks' impeccable groove-making allowed others to not just be fully themselves, but the confidence to transcend their limits. Which is exactly what Rob Base does when he finally begins to rhyme:

I wanna rock right now
I'm Rob Base and I came to get down
I'm not internationally known
But I'm known to rock the microphone
Because I get stoopid, I mean outrageous
Stay away from me if you're contagious
'Cause I'm the winner, no, I'm not the loser
To be an M.C. is what I choose 'a
Ladies love me, girls adore me
I mean even the ones who never saw me
Like the way that I rhyme at a show
The reason why, man, I don't know
So let's go, 'cause
It takes two to make a thing go right
It takes two to make it outta sight

The circumstances in which I first encountered "It Takes Two" are comically different from the circumstances in which the song was created: Decatur, Illinois, a sprawling prairie city (47 sq. miles), population 94,000, versus Central Harlem, over 100,000 people crammed into 1.4 square miles. But what was similar is that the late '80s was a moment when everyone was learning how to copy, sample, and remix. I didn't own turntables or a mixer, like DJ

E-Z Rock, or even any LPs of my own, but I had a dual cassette deck hooked up to a CD player and a brick of blank Maxell cassettes, a VCR, and a closet full of blank VHS tapes with bright orangey yellow labels. I made mixtapes for friends and, later, girlfriends. I learned to program our VCR so that I could record episodes of *Monty Python's Flying Circus*, which came on every Saturday night at midnight on the local PBS station.

For a school project on *Romeo and Juliet*, my buddy Joe and I figured a way to connect two VCRs together to create what we considered to be masterpiece of video art, in which we intercut video of our classmates performing scenes from the play with clips from *Yo! MTV Raps* and Python-esque interludes in which we referenced stupid inside jokes from *Late Night with David Letterman*.

When we weren't making fake radio shows, we were taking Polaroids of ourselves skateboarding and then cobbling them together into a handmade zine, employing the photocopier in the business office of the local Kmart, where Chip's dad was the manager. There we taped the Polaroids to pieces of copy paper, captioned the images with a Sharpie and then laid them against the warm glass, a process that turned the washed out color photos into grainy gray-scale tableaux depicting me and my brother and Chip ollying off curbs and leaping from (unseen) stacks of landscaping ties to create the impression of catching massive air, a la the Tom Petty "Free Fallin'" video.

This is all to say that I grew up making copies of things, sampling things, then stitching them together with other things. But I did not grow up dancing. There was a lot of chin-out head nodding, eyebrow raising, and maybe some slight up-and-down shoulder action, but otherwise the arms, legs, and hips did not get involved. Dancing always seemed so risky, so deeply personal—so visible. The copying and sampling and stitching and dubbing was out of sight—all anyone saw was the finished product. No one saw me sitting in my parents' basement late at night obsessing over the sequence of songs, worrying whether the selections were too bald, my emotions and intentions too easy to spot.

This all changed with "It Takes Two." Prior to that summer, the big hip-hop hits weren't things you could even play at the Mound Middle School dances. I mean, there was LL's "Going Back to Cali" and Kool Moe Dee's "Wild Wild West," songs you could hear on the radio, songs that even our teachers would admit to knowing, but we all knew the real stuff wasn't for public consumption. I'm talking NWA, 2 Live Crew, Too-Short, Ice-T, Slick Rick—even Public Enemy was seen as too political.

If you wanted to listen to any of that, you had to know someone who could drive—an older brother or sister, or a neighbor, and then you could catch a track or two while catching a ride home from school, take in lyrical scenes and situations that my white, Midwestern, thirteen-year-old self had never even dreamed.

But in the end, the lyrics weren't the thing that stuck with me—it was the beats and the bass pulsing through my back, rattling the windshield and trunk lid. This wasn't the Bronx, where hip hop and Rob Base were born, or Harlem where he moved in fourth grade, met DJ E-Z Rock, and first heard the Crash Crew playing at block parties; this was Montgomery Hills, Decatur, Illinois, a quiet warren of hilly, curving streets punctuated by cul-de-sacs. There were no block parties, no one used their porches or stoops for anything more than pumpkins and rustic benches that no one ever sat on. No, the music was confined to basements and cars—stereos that were only played loud when parents weren't home, kicker boxes locked inside the trunks of Honda hatchbacks, volume turned down when we rounded the corner into the neighborhood.

"It Takes Two" was an exception. It played well with others, and not played well with others in a palatable Fresh Prince way, but in a way that brought generations together. I remember my mom, a Baby Boomer, who came up with the Mamas and the Papas, James Taylor, and the Moody Blues, coming down into the basement, catching the beat, bobbing her head, and half joking, half not, shouting along with the "Whoo! Yeah!" break.

At the time I didn't know where that sample came from, but I have to believe that my mom, who graduated from college in the early '70s, would have known Lynn Collins' "Think (About It)." Maybe she recognized it, maybe she didn't. It doesn't matter. What matters was that it made her move, made her shout.

Flash-forward a few years to post-football game dances in the galleria of Stephen Decatur High School, and "It Takes Two" became the great leveler of the dance floor. All of a sudden, it wasn't just the cheerleaders and the pom squad out there doing "Da Butt" or "The Percolator," which required a startling, cold-sweat inducing level of coordination and ass-moving. Rob Base had come to democratize the breakdown. When he commanded us, on the count of three, to "1, 2, 3…Get loose now!" We listened. It became something we could all do—we needed to do—a welcome release from the 1-2, 1-2 foot shifting of slow dancing to "Running to Stand Still" or Sinead's "Nothing Compares 2 U."

The popularity of "It Takes Two" shouldn't be so much of a mystery, and it definitely shouldn't be seen as a fluke, or a fad. What Rob Base and DJ E-Z Rock did was tap into the essence of hip-hop itself. Only fifteen years earlier, on August 11, 1973 in the Community Room at 1520 Sedgwick Ave in the Bronx, DJ Kool Herc, an eighteen-year-old immigrant from Jamaica did something no one else had done before. He'd been watching the crowds at dance parties, and noticed what got people on the floor were the breakbeats, the funky, groovy instrumental sections between choruses. So, DJ Kool Herc, using two turntables, like the disco DJs in Manhattan (to keep an uninterrupted flow of music going), began mixing together just the breakbeats: a break from James Brown's "Give It Up or Turnit a Loose" would slide into "Bongo Rock" by the Incredible Bongo Band, then back to Brown, and then over to Babe Ruth's flamenco guitar inspired "The Mexican." The result was a party where the DJ kept the audience guessing, finding more and more unexpected combinations of rhythms, and flavors, and genres, which led to more people on the dance floor and, eventually, later, a method of laying down a rhythmic foundation for MCs to rap over. Herc called this the "Merry-Go-Round."

"It Takes Two" doubles down on the Merry-Go-Round, looping Lynn Collins' "Think" ("Whoo! Yeah!") break over and over and over throughout the track, then layering on top an 808 confection: a deep bass hit on the one and a clap track pattern that is a direct rip-off of the 1984 disco sensation "Set it Off" by Strafe, a beat that all but obscures Jabo Starks' snare and hi-hat, so while you can't hear it, you can feel it down there.

Which is what makes "It Takes Two" so singular, so itself, a classic, not some gimmick. If you really listen, you can hear and feel all its antecedents, all the layers of rhythm. You can hear the whistle of the drum major summoning the band in the Mardi Gras parade. You can hear the hi-hat and snare of Jabo Starks, who grew up in Alabama listening to the loose but military style of the Mardi Gras parade drummers. You can hear the tambourine from the original Lynn Collins track, and on top of that—doubling it— the ricocheting high hat and clap track of Strafe; all these generations, motivations, and situations of sound on stage at once.

In other words, what makes "It Takes Two" so infectious, so readily, irresistibly danceable, is that it's basically a five minute long Frankenstein's-monster of a breakbeat.

Again, I say this all as though I knew it then back in the summer of 1988. All I knew was what it did to me; how it made me move my shoulders from side to side; how it put a hitch in my hips; what the bass did to the air around my body.

But there's more.

In a 2018 interview with *Rolling Stone*—four years after DJ EZ Rock's death—Rob Base revealed that the creation of "It Takes Two" took place over the course of one night in a studio in Englewood, New Jersey, right across the George Washington Bridge from Manhattan. They didn't have an album yet or a record deal, so their manager told them: "Yo, we need to get in the studio, knock out a song or whatever."

And so they did.

They started listening to records, throwing around ideas, eventually putting on *Ultimate Breaks & Beats Volume 16*, the latest installment in a series of albums put out by Bronx DJ "Breakbeak Lou" Flores for use by other DJs, in which he compiled jazz, funk, and rock tracks with especially tasty, groovy, funky, or original sounds and beats. Side one of *Volume 16* features tracks by the Commodores and Marvin Gaye. Side two, as luck would have it, features Lynn Collins' "Think," followed directly by the Galactic Force Band's "Space Dust."

Rob Base told *Rolling Stone*: "Basically, it's just like, it was right there. The hit was right there in our face. And we just took it."

That fall, my eighth grade year, Chip started a DJ business. Not exactly his business partner, I was enlisted to help schlep equipment and page CDs and cassettes. I really only remember one gig: a dance at John's Hill Middle School, and those memories are vague and dark: a steamy gym, the stench of Drakkar Noir, Janet Jackson's "Rhythm Nation" and Technotronic's "Pump Up the Jam." But what I remember clearly is the moment when I pressed play on the CD player and that godly voice filled the room: *RIGHT ABOUT NOW...* There were screams followed by dozens of tweens in pegged jeans sprinting from the dark edges of the gym onto the dance floor. Up until then I had been a dabbler, a spectator, but at that moment I became hooked on the power of making others move their bodies.

Now, thirty-five summers later, I am clearing the fog from the bathroom mirror and preparing to shave my face. "It Takes Two" is blaring from the iPhone on the back of the toilet tank. As I lather my face, I begin to bob and weave and rap, "...my name's Rob, the last name Base, yeah, and on the mic I'm known to be the freshest..." As I bring the razor down my jaw I think of Chip. I haven't seen him since—I have to think hard on this—the summer of 1996 or '97 at a house party in a bad part of town, but we're Facebook friends, so I know he's out in Portland and a DJ.

I'm thinking of him because last night as I was writing I wondered if he had any of our old WPIG tapes—I thought I had one, but can't find it anywhere—a casualty of so many moves. And so I messaged him on Facebook: *Hey, working on this thing about "It Takes Two" and WPIG...You have any of those tapes still?* And to my surprise, he responds: *Have to take a look.*

A few minutes go by and a photo pops up in the chat box. It's Chip's hand holding a vinyl copy of "It Takes Two."

A few more minutes go by. Chip writes back: *Damn. I think any tapes that old got melted in my apartment fire in Decatur in the 90s...*

I return to the keyboard and reread all that I've written. I am having that spectator feeling again. All these words and sounds are just sitting there on the page pointing to something, pulling me *toward* something: a desire to be both in my body and loose of it.

I get up from the table, walk to the stereo, and push play on the CD player:

RIGHT ABOUT NOW...NOW...NOW...

I turn the volume up as loud as I can stand it. My old speakers crackle a bit, but then settle in.

YOU ARE ABOUT TO BE POSSESSED...

I'm looking for that exact frequency.

BY THE SOUNDS OF...MC ROB BASE...AND DJ E-Z ROCK... ROCK...ROCK...

I want to feel it again for the first time—in my feet, my chest, my teeth, and, most of all, in my nearly fifty-year-old heart.

HIT IT!

ON THE ESSAY:

I'd been wanting to write about my time as a fake radio DJ for a long time, ever since I found a copy of one of the WPIG cassettes in a box of old stuff from high school. Listening to my pubescent voice introduce songs that I loved back then (and now) transported me back in a startling way. And so when the March Fadness tournament came around, and I realized that "It Takes Two" technically qualified as a one-hit-wonder, I figured it was now or never. The resulting essay is a kind of ars poetica. Writing it, and researching how the song came to be, helped me to own just how formative music and mix-tape culture was to me–a landlocked, Midwestern kid who grew up far away from the places and situations where hip hop was born. In the end, this essay became a kind of homage to the awe that art inspires and how it set me off on a journey to make things that also moved people in some way.

FRANKENSTEINMAN'S MONSTER:

a Duet by Mark Butler and Laura Lorson on "Rock and Roll Dreams Come Through" by Jim Steinman

Pop music leans hard on dreams...dreams of love, dreams of getting out and going anywhere but here, dreams of a different life. The combination of dreams and a beat that makes your heart race is potent. Everything about it is thrilling and immersive. It's hot, it's big, it's wild, and when it's done well, it's addictive. "More," you think. "I want more of this feeling."

Jim Steinman, the architect of Meat Loaf's *Bat Out of Hell*, is all about "more." He was rock's resident bigger-better-faster-more impresario. Beneath the Dionysian excess of choirs and codas and angst, his work whispers, "Hey, kid...there's something amazing out there waiting for you. Go on, take a look. First taste is free."

How could the restless youth of Reagan's America not be drawn in by a lurid carnival of teenage hormones, celestial choirs and American guitars? Certainly, the two of us succumbed. We were kids in our respective middles of nowhere—Mark in Kansas, Laura in Kentucky—who were feverish for pop songs, American Top 40, and anything big and loud. We did have rock and roll dreams. Accordingly, we understood that someone (namely, Jim Steinman) must have blessed us when he gave us his songs.

The two of us decided to tackle the giant, wonderful behemoth of a song that has rewired our brains, cemented a friendship, and made us question our own dreams by putting it into context, through a record of the time and the zeitgeist. And yeah, it's rock and roll, so this is a duet. The why of this approach will become clear as we move forward. Laura and Mark's solos are helpfully labeled for your reading pleasure. Everything else (like this segment) is in unison. So...settle in. Surely you didn't think a meditation on a six minute and twenty-three second magnum opus was going to be the sort of thing you could read in four minutes?

But stop right there, before we go any further... behold the one-hit wonder who also sold 100 million records by eclipsing hearts, making all the stadiums rock, and doing (almost) anything for love. It's Jim Steinman and "Rock and Roll Dreams Come Through."

Part One: Objects in Mirror Are Closer Than They Appear

Laura, 1981, Kentucky

I'm listening to the American Top 40, like I always do, on a Saturday. I'm 13. I hear a song that is definitely NOT by Stars on 45. It is also not "Gemini Dream," which is the song I'm actually waiting to hear. I have plans to tape it. But this song is vaguely ominous, and enormous. It's too big for my GE clock radio speaker. I have no idea what it is. I hear Casey explain it's by Jim Steinman. I write down the name in my special American Top 40 notebook. (You don't understand how challenging it was in the pre-internet world to find out what a song you heard in passing on the radio was called, or who it was by. I took copious notes every week. I made flow charts. Capsule reviews.) "Jim Steinman," I think. "I wonder who that is." I underline the name. I wonder if I'll hear it again next week.

I hear it again next week. This song is...and I distinctly remember thinking this...completely hilarious, and awful, and absolutely wonderful.

I hear it on the radio, NOT on Casey Kasem, the following week. It's gaining traction. That means I can look for it at Musicland.

I find it at Musicland. I buy the 45 with some of my birthday money. I bring it home and put it on the record player in my bedroom. My dad let me put his old Voice of Music stereo in my room when they bought a new walnut cabinet console for the living room. It's old, the motor smells like dust cooking, but it plays just fine. It has a fascinating spindle adapter. I put it on the turntable, lower the single onto it, start the record, and listen. I am thrilled by this. The song continues to feel enormous. I listen to it again, a little louder this time. I want to fill up the entire space with it, with the weird choir of angels at the end. I have no idea what this song is supposed to mean, but it is big and majestic and about rock and roll coming through... for you...in a world of things that never come through for you. I listen to the song three more times before my mom comes upstairs to find out why I keep playing this song. I stop, and do my algebra homework. I listen to it again before I go to sleep. "You can't run away forever," I sing along in my head, "...but there's nothing wrong with getting a good head start."

Mark, 1981, Kansas

In 1981...I was on the verge of being lost. I was a lonely kid with a brain that was sizzling all day long. I was flying fast, but with no destination. My old friends couldn't keep up with my boundless curiosity and my "why so many questions" parents gave up on trying to understand me. I was smart enough to know that adolescent troublemakers get all the wrong attention and compliant weirdos get left to their own devices. That gave me hours every day with The Music, which I remember with vivid clarity.

For a curious kid in the middle of Kansas, "somewhere else" was my destination and the radio was my only mode of transportation. I could goose that engine to get me to Topeka and Wichita, or even Chicago, if I held the antenna just right. No matter where I traveled, I found the same thing: a steady diet of meat and potatoes rock. The best stations gave me more, pushing me towards what I really needed without knowing it: a guru, a curator, and something close enough to a friend—the DJ.

The smart, funny, excited adult voices of the DJs afforded me companionship, enthusiasm and old-fashioned gospel-style sermonizing, but minus all that church stuff. You better believe I made note of those sermons: rock and roll is what you need, and possibly *all* you need.

My sizzle brain was thrilled that for once I could not keep up with this endless stream of music curated by my new friends. Like Laura, I took notes on breakouts and picks to click. I taped stuff...fingers hovering over the Record button. I hoarded Billboard Hot 100s and started memorizing that week's AT40.

The charts sent a vital signal to this lonely kid. If I like a song on the countdown this week, there must be others like me because lots of people like it too. And here was this guy Jim Steinman putting his all into this song that was telling me everything I needed to hear at the end of the summer of seventh grade. So, of course, I remember the music. What else was there?

Laura and Mark, 1986, Kansas

It's 1986 and we have both ended up in Lawrence, Kansas, adrift among endless possibilities and brimming with curiosity about everything. We might have cooled on the tired old rock and roll dreams of classic rock radio — but we are absolutely feverish about each and every next big thing.

Laura is a sophomore at KU, and feeling a bit lost. Most of her friends from freshman year had been seniors and graduated. Aside from the social isolation, it means that her source of free jazz and art rock has dried up. Her other friends from high school had evolved into big Windham Hill fans and were spending a lot of time with each other, which seems to her to be kind of a waste of the college experience. She spends a lot of time reading NME and Spin and Melody Maker, because everyone else she knows seems to be utterly fixated on the Grateful Dead or Hot Tuna, with the one weird Andreas Vollenweider contingent. It's fine, but it just feels like…there must be something more out there. She visits a record store on her first day back in Lawrence, and the store is playing "Virginia Plain" on the PA. "This," she thinks. "This is what I want. I want to be the sort of person who goes places where the staff plays glam-era Roxy Music." She buys a King Crimson album, to the approval of the guy at the counter. The future felt enormous, and like there ought to be more to it, musically speaking, than her new roommate's fixation on Nu Shooz's "I Can't Wait" and Michael McDonald. There's a time and a place for the popular, but right now, she's on fire for arcana, apocrypha, incunabula.

After a very unengaged and random college search process, Mark has uprooted himself for the first time in his life, a whopping 90 miles down the interstate, largely due to The University of Kansas offering a high saturation rate per capita of very with-it record stores.

In the years leading up to college, he had carefully cultivated a seismic shift in his musical tastes. He didn't need *Foreigner 4* and *Eagles' Greatest Hits* when he had Let's Active and The Damned. This makeover wasn't calculated for social status. He was doing this for himself, no longer wishing to shoulder the burden of big, obvious rock. He'd discovered weirder, edgier, more deeply felt stuff and couldn't get enough of it. As a 17-year-old freshman, he hadn't mastered high school social dynamics, so he certainly did not know how to attempt a college reboot.

New town, new people. He hadn't exactly thought that through, schlepping into college with an uncool haircut, no sense of purpose, and an inability to instigate a conversation with anyone. Thank god for the John Hughes approach (obsess over good stuff, put up tons of posters, wear band shirts, and organically find your real tribe) and their uncanny ability to broadcast a signal to the folks you want to reach.

Mark: I don't know if I was wearing my beloved fuchsia R.E.M. Little America shirt when my roommate William introduced me to "Laurel Orson, who is also weird like you." (He might have said "cool" but we both know he meant "weird.") But that shirt with the cruddy bicycle on it definitely sparked a connection. I had found a key person in my tribe, so much so that she's here in this very essay. Smart AF and ready to dig into anything. We instantly and constantly sparred and bonded over philosophy, religion, literature, and yeah, music.

Laura: I don't remember William being there at all—I remember looking for him and you were, rather thrillingly, putting up posters, cheat codes to the as-yet-unknown puzzle of you. Cocteau Twins. Kate Bush. I remember thinking, "This is a person who likes the sort of music I like." I don't make friends easily, so this whole meet-cute would usually be my cue to flee the scene, but it turned out you were funny, and clever, and smart. We ended up talking music, of course, and we talked a long time, because you were putting up posters for bands that I liked, or had read about, and you were handling albums like they were precious, like they meant something almost religious to you. It was a long time ago. Either way, the die was cast.

We spoke in tongues as one must in those formative early days of early days.

"This Mortal Coil?"

"Of course. That Petrol Emotion?"

"Alex Chilton?"

"The song or the guy?"

Music and friends who loved music sustained us more in that year of college than any beer and pizza ever could.

Part Two: Out of the Frying Pan (And Into the Fire)

In these times of curious and cool, there was little room to air guilty pleasures, because the genuine pleasures of the new, the weird, and the transgressive gave no room for the oldies of yore.

Mark: So... Laura, if I'm vague on specifics about how we met, I also don't remember how we outed ourselves on the least cool thing that you or I liked. My guess is that it was "Total Eclipse Of The Heart," a song that continued to leak out of dorm rooms, car speakers, and house parties (for squares, natch.) And it was probably an involuntary response to Rory Dodd (take note, foreshadowing fans) and his falsetto "turn around" and you and I excitedly blurting out "every now and then I fall apart!"

Laura: The conversation somehow got around to me asking "what is the

worst popular song you have ever heard" and to be honest I think this was because someone was probably blasting Boston's "Amanda" just down the hallway. You said, "You probably won't know this song, it wasn't a massive hit, but it's by this guy, Jim Steinman, the producer? It's kind of simultaneously wonderful and terrible. Have you heard of a song called 'Rock and Roll Dreams Come Through'?" and I suddenly knew with complete certainty and absolute clarity: I am going to be friends with Mark Butler for the rest of my life.

We both wanted to keep the cool kid conversation focused on random NME cover stars and Julian Cope and the 4AD design aesthetic, but it kept creeping back to this overblown, overwrought AOR rock dude who kept putting his name on the front cover of other people's records—"Songs By Jim Steinman."

Mark: Forget about Bonnie Tyler. What about "Making Love Out Of Nothing At All?"

Laura: Oh, the one that can make all the stadiums rock? Didja know there's a Streisand one?

Mark: Oh yeah, and a Manilow one.

Weirdly (or deeply on brand for this fast-forming friendship), we almost NEVER bring the conversation back to Meat Loaf and *Bat Out Of Hell*, where Jim Steinman made his name, his reputation, and his fortune. No, we return to "Rock and Roll Dreams Come Through," the song where Jim Steinman became the center of gravitational pull in his own universe… where he became in his mind a true auteur, an ur-songsmith. This song became our touchstone, the codex that we need to crack to understand this singular and puzzling body of work. And as it turns out decades later, "Songs By Jim Steinman" feed the current of a continuing obsession of our friendship.

What are these songs?!? For one thing, they're our songs. They've bonded to us. The absurdist statements built out of non-sequitur titles. The bombastic swells of choristers. The forever-teenage angst. It's saturated all the way down into us. And somehow, it's bonded us together. We didn't know this at that moment and we may not have fully realized it until a litany of social media posts made it impossible to ignore that we couldn't stop talking about Jim Freaking Steinman.

Mark: I'd much rather talk about Love's *Forever Changes*—the heartbreaking masterpiece that still reveals new secrets even today. (The best birthday present a kid ever wanted, by the way. 1987. Thanks, Laura.) But maybe—ok, definitely—*Forever Changes* is perfect even in its imperfections, and how long can you talk about perfection before you get bored? Go listen to the perfect thing and hush up. The oeuvre of Jim Steinman is far from perfect. It's a hot mess, frankly, of mixed metaphors and constant sonic overkill. And that mess is one of the things that brings us back.

In fact, it's fair to say that we have many of the same questions today as we had on the night we first met.

If someone's been through the fires of hell, would they really save the ashes to prove it?

When he wants " to wrap myself around you like a winter skin," is it as creepy as you think?

Who among us has truly made love out of nothing at all or suffered from a partial eclipse of the heart?

Wouldn't you rather have a rock and roll dream come true instead of come through?

C'mon, Jim, we love you, but make better choices. Religions were built on lesser inscrutability. When we praise these songs, we also want to bury them. But much like the generic American teen dude that seems to loom large throughout so many "Songs By Jim Steinman," we never stop coming back for more.

Part Three: Left in the Dark

Laura: To really get at the core of that endless attraction, we're going to need to digress for a minute. In retrospect, one extremely weird thing about culture in the late '70s and early '80s is that nostalgia was big. REALLY big. Kids like us were swimming in it, the whole '50s revival thing. But we were kids. It wasn't OUR nostalgia. It was our parents'. We didn't even know it was nostalgia. We thought it was just...culture. *Happy Days* and its attendant spinoffs were just kind of what you watched, because they were there, like Mount Everest. So as a kid, my popular culture was actually nostalgic comfort food schlock for my parents, who did not in fact even watch it themselves, because they were busy generating new experiences to create more content for the military-industrial-entertainment complex. This sort of thing is probably why I ended up in grad school.

Anyway, all that aside, nostalgia was everywhere, it's just that it wasn't nostalgia for which I had any frame of reference...except in music. If you grew up with a radio, you heard '50s songs. You heard '60s songs. So I

could recognize "nostalgia" as a broad category in songs being produced in the '70s and '80s. Plus, the songs were largely about recapturing a kind of youthful insouciance of which I had absolutely no experience. I realized at the time that clearly I was missing out, because I was certainly not hitting winning home runs or having someone walk right up and ask me if I wanted to dance, or having some guy pull up in front of my house waiting for me to slam the screen door (as my dress swayed) so we could pull out of this town full of losers. It was only later that I figured out practically none of the people for whom these nostalgic songs were written actually had those experiences, either. All that rock and roll "glory days" Americana was fundamentally reliant upon archetypes that had no basis in reality for the vast majority of the listening audience, but collectively they Meant Something. Pure simulacra.

The important part of this, aside from establishing how insufferable I am, is that at a very young age I became aware that the whole enterprise, once you get to the center of the Tootsie Pop, turns out to be hollow. Which brings me to my actual point about rock and roll dreams. Steinman was an astonishingly effective dream merchant because he understood what made dreams addictive to a kid in a mid-size town, or at least a town that wasn't New York City or LA. He left a trail of breadcrumbs in his work—that Hal Blaine heartbeat drumline? Check. Non-specific dramatic tension? Check. Big guitars? Check. This is such stuff as dreams are made on: nostalgia, longing, and the promise of the new. This is a composer and lyricist who understood the nature of fame, and how if it's anything, it's the proverbial monkey's paw. You want to be famous? There is a cost. You want to be fulfilled artistically? There is a cost. But that doesn't make the dream any less beautiful. Rock and roll dreams are particularly beautiful when you're a teenager, because you still buy the whole package. Years pass before you understand how the sausage is made. Spangles look tawdry up close; stage cosmetics up close are vaguely repellent; what looks like heaven from the cheap seats turns out to be smoke and mirrors. I think this is why even as a kid at ground zero of the MTV era, I always preferred the radio to video—music as mindscape felt limitless, whereas music videos always felt limited, bounded, ultimately claustrophobic. "Here's our approved vision of the song," said the Machine. "Whatever you were thinking, consumer...uh, I mean, uh, kid...that's not it."

Anyway...back to the issue of the rock and roll dream, a la Jim. The song is frankly a strange interlude. It taps into the pain of isolation, but

in a way that you don't realize it 'til you zoom in tight. It's about escaping into a kind of fugue state, propelled by bass and guitar and drums that make you forget for a minute that you are sitting on your bed listening to a radio. Jim Steinman's rock and roll dreams put our little lives on pause for a moment. And however cynical you end up becoming about rock and roll, or dreams...that's not nothing. That's straight-up magic.

Mark: With a clearer view of that nostalgia factory that we grew up in, it made me question what my rock and roll dreams were. Even if rock was starting to be consumed by focus groups and corporate earnings, the dreams were real and they could still bring dreamers together. In 1981, those dreams were basic and colossal: Be in a band. (Guitar, obviously.) Be really loud. Buy every good record. Be a DJ that played only the best of those songs. Make out with someone. Work in a record store. Be a big deal.

Nothing fancy here and nothing complex for a lonely kid. Just basic double-necked guitar and Marshall stacks. At 12, though, these felt like unobtainable lifelong goals, born of growing up in a household governed by a slowly smothering mantra of "that's not a good idea." A steady diet of "no" would have sparked rebellion, but I found myself choosing stealth and harboring my rock and roll dreams in my secret rock and roll lair of 45s and music magazines.

But then... wow! Within the next five years, thanks to Jim Steinman or possibly despite Jim Steinman, my rock and roll dreams did come through (with the exception of the last one, where I learned I have a severe allergy to being anywhere near the center of attention). Rock and roll dreams were... easy. A bit of a letdown, to be honest.

By the time I met Laura in 1986, the only rock and roll dream that hadn't been crossed off was "buy every good record," a dream which remains naggingly unfulfilled even today. I wanted to find out about the amazing redemptive and inspirational powers of rock and roll, but I wanted to find out on my own. Or...even better...with kindred spirits to join me on hunts through the record racks. Music could still be a solitary experience, but now by choice—it suddenly tasted more rich and flavorful with friends.

Once I discovered the possibility of frenetic interactions with fellow music fans, my obsessions intensified. I needed the new, the innovative, the never-before-heard, the weird. I could not stop and play one record over and over for the rest of my life. I couldn't even play one genre of music exclusively for a day. Rock and roll was meant to be intensely exciting. Every return to an old favorite drained a little more blood from it until I would find those songs almost empty. Nothing could replace the first time you heard your new favorite song.

Laura: Oh, exactly, I was trying to explain this not long ago, about why it's so hard to write a truly great pop song. The best I could come up with was "it's extraordinarily hard to write a song that makes someone fall in love with it every time they hear it, whether it's time one or time 87." You become a different sort of listener, the more you add tools to your toolbox. I have a very different sense of DJ Shadow's *Endtroducing*... now that I have 25 more years of listening intensively to more records under my belt than I did back in 1996. Then, it was just this big aural soundscape with interesting moments, and now that I actually really recognize the beats and breaks, it's a much different kind of experience. But you were saying....

Mark: I'm always intrigued when a song can be reinvigorated. Sometimes, it's as simple as hearing it under new circumstances, but often, it's who you hear it with. In 1986, we'd share new finds and beloved oldies that found new life and new affection when the enthusiasm of a fellow believer would reawaken them. And yes, even the ridiculously oversized works of Jim Steinman took on new meaning when I found someone to share it with. The two of us would talk feverishly about those Steinman Events where a song of ginormous proportions would be a guaranteed hit. (Of course, we did not know that Jim's imperial phase had already wound down by 1986. Neither did Jim, I would wager.)

You could not shut the two of us up when we found out our Jim was working with The Sisters Of Mercy. Mister Magnum Opus was going to work with those morose mopesters! "This is going to be amazing," we'd exclaim to anyone who'd listen. "Yeah, well, is it going to be good?" they'd ask. And we'd yelp back in delight, "That literally doesn't matter!" And yes, "This Corrosion" was great and ridiculous and ridiculously great, but it felt like a dead-end. He'd gone from Manilow to Goth in a matter of years...where else could he go? ("Broadway!" was our long-running answer to this rhetorical question.)

Jim Steinman and the 12-year-old me had done big already—bombastic and grandiose and widescreen spoke volumes to me in my early R&R dreaming. Signs were indicating that Jim had taken big as far as he could, but he kept going. I, however, couldn't. His songs became wings of the Winchester Mansion... he had to keep building forever to fend off evil spirits. I realized I'd rather hang out with the ghosts instead of contending with constant construction and convoluted results. I needed new thrills and a regular dose of them.

These songs that always opted for overload became too much for me. So, I moved on. Most people did. But just like we praise intrepid pioneers of yore, we still celebrate the audacity and the scope of Jim Steinman's epics.

Laura: Now that you mention audacity and scope, this seems like a decent place to get into the nuts and bolts of "Rock and Roll Dreams Come Through." It's profoundly odd. That's what makes a song that doesn't necessarily have a hook as big as a house memorable and noteworthy. Love it or hate it, it makes an impression (much like Wile E. Coyote slamming into the side of a cliff. Perhaps "indentation" is a better term here). The whole enterprise is designed to make an impression. One does not simply walk into Bearsville Studios, my friend. Take a look at the lineup. There's only room for E-Streeters, most of Utopia, Elton's guitarist, and even some Blues Brothers.

And all this is before you get to the producers, who were John Jansen (Britny Fox, reprazent!), Todd Rundgren (well, sure), Steinman (duh), and…wait for it…Jimmy Iovine (needs no explanation).

It's just one more way that this song managed to compile all the components of the cultural movements that were brewing at the time. I actually think of it as an example of what made postmodernity—in philosophy and the social sciences anyway—so appealing as writers started to develop a new kind of cultural criticism. Steinman took a form that relied on cultural synthesis (i.e. rock and roll) and then went ahead and threw everything but the kitchen sink at it (i.e., multiple historic undercurrents in rock that had been perceived as outdated and old-fashioned, using Tin Pan Alley song structure and Brill Building hookiness, combined with cabaret intimacy and Broadway theatricality and arena-rock excess). It's pastiche, it's synthesis, it's commodification. But why is THIS song from the Steinman oeuvre the one I just can't quit poking at, like a sore tooth? What is it about THIS one that made it such an odd touchstone? I, of course, have a theory.

It's impossible to talk about Jim Steinman without at least considering one Marvin, later Michael, Lee Aday, which is to say Meat Loaf. He had an enormous physical presence, and an enormous voice. He was, in short, perfect for performing Steinman's work. *Bat Out of Hell* was such a cultural juggernaut that it, and the songs ("by Jim Steinman," we are once again helpfully reminded) it comprised, took on a life of their own.

For better or for worse, it cemented the two men together creatively and artistically. But if you listen to Meat Loaf's recording of "Rock and Roll Dreams Come Through" from 1994, it seems pallid and unmemorable. So what's missing? I would have loved to hear a circa-1977 Meat Loaf give it a go. Watch one of those old, grainy video clips of the band out flacking *BOoH* at the time—known as the, uh, Neverland Express, if you can believe it. You probably saw some of this footage at least once in the earlier incarnations of MTV, or maybe on USA Network's Night Flight. I have an absolutely terrifying clip of them tearing up "Paradise by the Dashboard Light" on The Old Grey Whistle Test. This staggering chaos was aggressively pure performance. It felt genuine. That drama, that passion, that *theatre* is what is missing from the 1994 remake, which felt lazy and languid like a massive, over-indulged cat, sprawled on a Victorian settee. A performance of "Rock and Roll Dreams Come Through" requires a kind of theatrical, adolescent recklessness if it's not just going to be seen as ludicrous in every way. Shades of the Pamchenko Twist from *The Cutting Edge*, right? If you don't commit to it completely, someone's gonna get seriously hurt. The key to a Jim Steinman song is not so much the phony rock-and-roll dramatics or the subtextual violence and sexuality. It's the danger of the performance. Everything about it is so highly strung that it could just snap at any moment—a Jim Steinman composition is literally the staged experience of teen angst. And this song, honestly, is the Steinmaniest.

Mark: By the way, I think it's vital to point out here that Jim didn't sing on his one and only Top 40 entry. Those credited "featured vocals" mean that Rory Dodd took the lead. (You all know Rory. He also sang the "turn around, bright eyes" hook on "Total Eclipse.") This fact still shocks me. It suggests that Jim was either fully committed to the all-star performance strategy to get this song onto the charts—or he felt like his own voice paled next to that of his partner/nemesis Meat Loaf. If you listen to the rest of *Bad For Good* where Jim sings, it's a bit of both.

Laura: The thing about this song is that it starts from the presumption that you, the listener, are well-versed enough in the history of rock and the mechanics of performance that OF COURSE you are going to get all the references. Just the act of listening to it made you part of the club. OF COURSE you are familiar with the 32-bar A-A-B-A structure of Tin Pan Alley songcraft. OF COURSE you understand operatic pacing, *recitative*, and the dramatic coda. OF COURSE you are familiar with Grand

Guignol. *Of course* he does not need to spell this out for you, you're in the club. For those of us who were of the right age and know-it-all temperament when this thing came out, it wasn't just a song—it was bait.

But the best bait in the world won't work unless the fish are in the mood to bite. There was something in the air at the time, something this song tapped into. There was a whole lot of "rock is redemptive" going on. A whale-ship might have been Herman Melville's Yale College and his Harvard, but ours was rock and roll radio. Chapter and verse of our common scripture was Bruce Springsteen No(t) Surrender(ing), Bob Seger still liking that old time rock'n'roll, Joan Jett not giving a damn about her bad reputation. The Sex Pistols...not that you ever got to hear them on the radio in the American heartland...wondered if we ever got the feeling we'd been cheated, and the answer was yes. Something fascinating was always going on just over the horizon, and you were worried that you might miss it. But rock radio was a periscope, a pair of binoculars.

Radio isn't like it used to be in the '80s. While a short stint listening to Midwestern broadcast commercial radio right this minute might lead one to believe that "no, in fact it is almost precisely like it used to be, right down to the very songs being played," it's really not. There's way more information available. There's streaming, there's social media, decades of music articles online—back in the '80s, you had to work hard to find out anything, anything at all about a song you heard once and might have liked. You had no idea what was in the pipeline. You might have some sense of what was up and coming and what people in the big cities were listening to via induction, when you saw a sketch on a variety show or maybe someone made a reference to something on *Saturday Night Live*. This is how I learned about punk rock. I was lucky enough to grow up in Louisville, with a quirky set of AM stations and a thriving AOR FM scene...I vividly recall the launch of a quadraphonic station and hearing Funkadelic for the first time over the commercial airwaves, which now seems impossible. I remember hearing "Ça Plane Pour Moi" on WAKY-79 AM and thinking, "This is INCREDIBLE, how can I get more of this?" But by the time I was a teenager, mostly it had all stratified into Rock Stations and Lite Rock Stations and the obligatory community radio station with that one grizzled announcer who was really into Ornette Coleman.

As a kid first hearing "Rock and Roll Dreams Come Through," there were already articles of faith within the Church of Rock: you can check out any time you like, but you can never leave; baby, we were born to run;

and music could save your mortal soul. We believed these things in the same way our parents believed in the strength of the U.S. dollar and the superiority of American V8 automobiles that ran on leaded gasoline. We knew that on any given broadcast countdown of the Top 100 Rock Songs of All Time, "Stairway to Heaven" would be Number One. What we did not know, what would remain unwritten, was...where do we go from here?

Mark: From here? For you and me, it's *everywhere*, not just where classic rock radio takes us. I've come to realize that the true fuel for my rock and roll dreams is not big anthems or overblown bluster. I love the wild knife's edge of music. I want stuff that explores the darkness within us. I need transgression. I crave something new. I am counting on younger bands, laptop punks, jazzy freaks, and budding weirdos to come kick the ass of the old school. You won't actually harm the classics but you'll write a whole new chapter. And you know what, there's always room for the next Jim Steinman. We won't know that he or she has arrived until we collectively say, "What the hell was that all about?" in the most affectionate way. And of course, "Play that insane one again."

I often wonder if Jim Steinman forgot that dark edge of rock and roll dreaming and instead fixated on rock and roll excess. If he'd thrown a smoke bomb and disappeared through a trap door on the stage in 1984, he'd be the mythical rock beast that appeared on the cover of *Bad For Good*. "He wrote these insane epic hit singles and then one night, at the stroke of midnight in the middle of a thunderstorm, he was gone." Instead, he's also the guy that became the proprietor and CEO of the *Bat Out of Hell* franchise. *BOoH2*! And parts of *BOoH3*! And the musical! The laurels of his original record with Meat Loaf are some fancy digs to rest upon, but when his whole body of work started sounding familiar, Jim's legacy got significantly diluted.

Nonetheless, as a moment frozen in time, as someone with my own rock and roll dreams, there was something irreplaceably captivating about hearing Jim (or...Rory, whatever) tell you about his own dreams. It felt like he wrote that song for me, and every other adolescent or still-clinging-to-adolescence person out there.

Laura: This gets at a kind of epiphany I had about Jim when I was working at NPR headquarters in the '90s. I was working on a radio feature about Kander & Ebb, trying to find a way to trim it to eight minutes and I was thinking, "This music is too much of an intimate experience to just axe this way," and it hit me all at once, for no good reason: Jim Steinman was writing cabaret. I headed down to the reference library

and discovered that he had worked with Joseph Papp with the idea of producing a piece of musical theater that Steinman had developed in college. Suddenly, all the pieces fell into place. The '70s were the pinnacle of arena rock excess. Part of the experience of arena rock at the time involved physical distance from the performers. So when you're trying to break new ground, how do you overcome that? By dramatically (pun intended) reducing the emotional distance from the musicians. That's what Steinman did: he upped the emotional intimacy logarithmically, to compensate for the lack of physical proximity. He was writing cabaret, and staging it as rock and roll. Once you posit that it's all designed with the physical constraints of musical theater in mind, it suddenly isn't awkwardly grandiose. It's intimacy turned up to eleven. This is perfectly in line with the kind of emotional drama of the American Teenager, when you feel like every moment is...well, momentous. Steinman songs are designed to preserve every perceived slight or minor drama in amber, eternal and meaningful and fever-pitched, adding to the sense that you'll always feel this way about whatever it is that's bumming you out as a teen, whether it was loneliness or getting a bad grade or wishing you were someplace else more thrilling.

Mark: Absolutely. Jim's compositions were all siren songs for angsty teens. Objectively, Steinman wrote much better songs than his one hit and absolutely everyone who sang them did a much better job than him. But listen, this is rock and roll we're talking about. Objectivity does not rock. "Rock and Roll Dreams Come Through" was the perfect song for my absolutely imperfect dawn of adolescence—and all of the 31 other songs that outranked it when it peaked on the charts were not. This song spoke about chasing away loneliness with music, hitting me where no other song had yet hit—and that's all you need for perfection when you are a lonely kid looking for hope—and for other rock and roll dreamers.

Laura: That tracks with my tween experiences in Louisville, with the particulars just being a bit different. Funny how it turns out in our culture that endlessly capitalizes on "You are special! The most special! No one in the world is like you! Your drama is the most dramatic!" when most of everyone's experience of that time is, at the core, more or less the same. Where we diverge, in the end, is that you ended up going deeper into the vaults to find something a bit more stripped-down. I, on the other hand, wanted more of that glorious, unashamed excess. Fortunately for me, there exists such a thing as progressive rock, and much of it was available

at astonishingly reasonable prices at used record stores and garage sales. There was certainly quite a bit of Steinman on the airwaves, but none of it had that snap and weirdly wired flair of "Rock and Roll Dreams Come Through." The possible exception to this was "Total Eclipse of the Heart," which is equally bonkers lyrically (though for my money no Steinman lyric is as weird as "and the angels had guitars even before they had wings," which aside from its theological shakiness is just strange). All of this is the long way 'round of saying: "Rock and Roll Dreams Come Through" was a springboard into weird rock, the rock that was not being played on the radio in the '80s, the rock that had vision with a capital VISION, so I owe Jim for opening the floodgates of prog rock for me. I wanted big, I wanted complex, I wanted music that required footnotes and a minor in Comparative Literature. Hello, Van der Graaf Generator. Hello, Amon Düül II. Hey there, Queensrÿche. Which is not to say that I was ignoring everything else—I certainly loved punk and garage, indie and Top 40 radio play hits, dumb schlocky arena rock and Madchester as much as anyone. But I believe that "Rock and Roll Dreams Come Through" was the song that pushed me into being the sort of person who wanted to hear more, who wanted to try everything, who ever after wanted to recapture that sort of immersive thrill that I got from that initial Steinman-esque hit of excess. And that's the magic of what on the surface is admittedly one extremely perplexing moment in 1981, and why it's a song I keep revisiting. If I hear it come up in a shuffle mix or a feed, I will listen to it, and be vocally judgmental if it's the radio edit. I will not leap to get it off the speakers in the same way that I would, say "I Love You" by Climax Blues Band or that Vitamin C graduation song. I unapologetically like it, and it's a part of what shaped my musical taste.

I may be going out on a pretty shaky limb here, but it's possible "Rock and Roll Dreams Come Through" pushed me toward textual analysis as an academic. I spent a lot of time by myself as a teenager, not popular but popular-adjacent, busy but not exactly sought-after. I'd listen to records in that alone-time. I spent an inordinate amount of time mentally dissecting the lyrical nuances of this song. Who is this song for? The singer is singing to someone…who is that person? Is it a girlfriend or boyfriend? Is this a person the songwriter knows? Is it a person at all? I believe that at the core, this is a song about loneliness. It was a song about being young and being lonely, and having rock and roll music be your friend.

Mark: At 12, I was desperate for a friend who understood me. Being told that "you have your entire future ahead of you" is no solace for the lonely. The best I could do in 1981 was find friendship on the radio—and even though it feels foolish to say, Jim Steinman found me when I needed him the most.

Laura: I think Jim pushed me to figure out WHETHER I had rock and roll dreams, actually. My dreams were never "write a hit song" or "perform on a giant stage to a sold-out crowd where everyone loves you"—those both sounded like a trap to me. My dreams were more along the lines of "someday, I will have all the records I want" or "someday, I'll meet someone I can talk about records with for hours. I will also have amazing speakers." Those particular rock and roll dreams came through, by the way.

Mark: Yay for that. I realize now the best dreams are the ones that change your life—and when our individual dreams brought us together to talk about pop music (and Talk Talk), our lives got better. Our enthusiasm for music and everything remains fierce and diverse. And yet, we come back again and again to Jim Steinman, giggling over the big bluster of Jim Steinman's teenage dreams, obsessing over his bold confidence and unshakeable faith in the redemptive power of music that "Rock and Roll Dreams Come Through" promised.

Laura: He was really good at trapping and preserving that "lonely teen" feeling and spinning it into gold, like Rumpelstiltskin. This is a guy who understood his audience, and understood pop music under the hood, as it were. It's made up of thousands of little spinning cogs and wheels that have to sync up just right or the whole thing will seize like an indifferently-maintained 1982 Iron Duke Camaro and self-destruct. The point of the performance is for us to see past what we think we want, for it to show us something we never imagined we'd see. The point of the spectacle is to create new dreams, rock 'n' roll or otherwise, petering out or coming through. That's why we keep returning to Steinmania. In the end, he was able to channel dreams through ink and paper and pour them out through massive guitars and amps. He's captured, in music, that whole Lewis Carroll dreamy wistfulness about youth that you find in *Through the Looking Glass*—just doing it with session players and a production suite the size of a city block: "In a Wonderland they lie, Dreaming as the days go by, Dreaming as the summers die; Ever drifting down the stream—Lingering in the golden gleam—Life, what is it but a dream?"

Part Four: The Beat Is Yours Forever. The Beat Is Always New.

Jim Steinman's dreams were a big bombastic celebration of rock and roll excess, a Lost Boy seeking deliverance through music. But unlike Peter Pan... and unlike Jim Steinman...we grew up. Yet, even though we knew better, it turns out the two of us never completely left Jim's Neverland.

What kept us in his thrall long after his songcraft and his success slowed? We clung to one unexpected dream sprung fully formed from Steinmania: the dream of being audacious, ridiculous and weird. Jim, we cherish your WTF-ness, not your high-rent pickup band, not your clumsy and confusing wordplay, not your choral reprises. (OK, yes, maybe we do love the choral reprises.) And we cherish that you had the world singing along.

It took guts to make records as epic and odd as these. It also took guts for the two of us to 'fess up to obsessing over these songs in 1986 as the sun had set on Jim's empire. Steinmania goes beyond guilty pleasures, for us. We shared dreams with Jim Steinman long enough to forge an indelible Mark-and-Laura bond, strong enough that we can always find our back to each other. That's the true golden nugget...a gift from a wannabe god.

We'll never go to the mat trying to convince you that "Rock and Roll Dreams Come Through" is some kind of pinnacle of anything. But this song was a key to a locked door for us. It independently wedged itself into the mind palace of two kids stuck in separate-but-similar places made up of shopping malls, cineplexes and chain restaurants, where the guiding principle for music was "everyone else likes it, so therefore you do, too." What the song did, in all its six-minute, twenty-three second overproduced glory, was tap something inside both of us that said: "There is more out there for you, if you want it." Turns out, we did.

We've moved on to more brilliant corners and surreal landscapes. Mark became absolutely encyclopedic on rock, garage, punk, dance, electronica, and alphabet pop (J-pop, K-pop, and all that). Laura became a person who gravitated toward energy and excess, which probably explains her love of disco and soul and psychedelia and prog rock, but she also became addicted to the idea of intensity in performance and songcraft, so that led her to experimental jazz, post-rock and extremely gloomy trip-hop, the darker and sparer the better.

No matter how our preferences have evolved, Steinman was a big enough deal then that he is actually kinda inescapable now. When we bump into him on the waiting room speakers at the Toyota dealership or as we wade past a pack of sorority pledges screaming "turn around, bright eyes," it all comes back to us, and our Steinmania easily reignites.

It's increasingly rare, as you age, that you can pinpoint things that have to do with your personal aesthetics. But those musical moments, for each of us, are the ones we continually mentally revisit: there is something happening in this song. Objectively, it's ridiculous. Subjectively, those moments of Weird Artistic Transcendence, that moment of sublime connection with a product for which there is an extremely niche market, are incomparable. "Maybe there's more of that odd thing," you think. "I would like more of that," you think. You will now look for that beneath the layers of corporate veneer. You get, on an intrinsic level that you cannot yet name, that the entire enterprise is a kind of commodification of desire. Maybe the thing you're looking for from art, that lightning-in-a-bottle moment of connection, is not on the highway. Maybe it's in a cul-de-sac. Let's go find out.

This one song, from its initial blast of castanet-laden intro, basically opened us up to the possibilities of music, popular and otherwise. Jim Steinman didn't make us weird, but he opened our eyes to the infinite potential of weird. "Rock and Roll Dreams Come Through" gave us something to work with—a big, overblown reference point, something that years later, inspired you to ask, "Do you remember this song?" and when that person said yes, you knew you'd found your tribe of weirdos like you, whether they said yes and smiled or said yes and grimaced. There's always something magic. There's always something new. This is how rock and roll dreams come through. The violins swell. The beat is yours forever.

ON THE ESSAY:

Every song has a secret history and sometimes the best histories are from the listeners rather than the creators. We spilled just enough secrets to each other in 1986 about our secret-ish love of Jim Steinman to become friends for life. Decades later, dueting on this essay gave us the chance to meet younger versions of ourselves whose history might've been forgotten—and to add to our stories today.

After growing up...with multiple moves, and jobs, and life milestones, this project gave us the opportunity to remember how fun it still is to see where the stream-of-consciousness would take us, even if that end destination is the world's most wack-a-doo '80s-coded Excalibur-themed video and the Choral Reprise to End All Choral Reprises.

This bout of Steinmania reminds us that awkward, "oh god, what is this?" shared songs form the true bonds between friends. The beat is **ours** forever.

RAP ON THE RADIO

Steph Brown on "Rapper's Delight" by The Sugarhill Gang

Have you ever went over a friend's house to eat
And the food just ain't no good?
I mean the macaroni's soggy, the peas are mushed,
And the chicken tastes like wood?
So you try to play it off like you think you can
By saying that you're full
And then your friend says, "Mama, he's just being polite.
He ain't finished, uh-uh, that's bull!"
So your heart starts pumpin' and you think of a lie
And you say that you already ate
And your friend says, "Man, there's plenty of food."
So he piles some more on your plate.
While the stinky food's steamin', your mind starts to dreamin'
Of the moment it's time to leave
And then you look at your plate and your chicken's slowly rottin'
Into something that looks like cheese.
Oh so you say, "That's it, I gotta leave this place.
I don't care what these people think.
I'm just sittin' here makin' myself nauseous
With this ugly food that stinks."
So you bust out the door while it's still closed
Still sick from the food you ate
And then you run to the store for quick relief
From a bottle of Kaopectate.

—"Rapper's Delight," 9:30-10:21

That's it. Those 51 seconds *are* the argument for the greatness of "Rapper's Delight."

I could tell you that this song represents a watershed moment in the history of American music, the moment when hip hop crossed over into the top forty for the first time, and that that tells us something profound about American culture, about popular aesthetics, about the evolution of our shared history and sensibilities.[1] But if you've made it through this tortuously-cadenced verse that describes trying to hork down "chicken slowly rottin'/ into something that looks like cheese"[2] and concludes by rhyming "food you ate" with "Kaopectate," and your hand isn't drifting towards the "vote Sugarhill Gang" button, I may have already lost you.

This verse is also the moment in which the song becomes a metaphor for the experience of listening to "Rapper's Delight": in 2023, submitting to the entirety of the track feels like nothing so much as 14 minutes and 38 seconds of being forcibly fed an overlarge serving of dried-out chicken. White meat only.

*

> "The hip hop community was like 'What the...who the fuck is that? Like who the *fuck* is that? What *is* this *shit*? What are they doing to our art form? You know what I mean, it's like, this is the first introduction they're gonna get to, like, what we do, to what we've been doing for like seven years?'" —Grandmaster Caz, interview in *Hip-Hop Evolution*

> "We hated it. That was the worst piece of shit stupid ass song that every-fuckin-body liked, and then people would come to us and say 'you know, y'all need to make a record like that' and we'd be like 'Well how we going to make a piece of shit like that?'" —Melle Mel, interview in *Hip-Hop Evolution*

The Sugarhill Gang should win this tournament because this song is simultaneously crucial to the trajectory of 40 years of hip hop and popular music *and* because it could only ever be a one hit wonder. It is in its essence a one hit wonder, and more importantly it *deserves* that fate. Had Sugarhill Gang ever again hit the Hot 100, it would have irreversibly unbalanced some cosmic scale.

"Rapper's Delight" appeared in the fall of 1979, and in early January of 1980 it hit #37 on the Billboard Hot 100 (securing its future place in the

March Fadness tournament by a mere five days). Its place in music history is cemented by its status as the first rap record to cross over to radio, as well as the first to chart. It's also notable that although there was a shorter radio release, the song got radio play in its 14-minute-plus entirety. And if you know anything about the song beyond "Ho-tel, mo-tel, Holiday Innnnnn," it's probably the anecdote about Sugarhill Gang being made up of three guys—Big Bank Hank, Master Gee, and Wonder Mike—who weren't experienced rappers, who had never performed together, who were pulled from a pizzeria, thrown in a studio, and cut that entire track in a single take, in a bid to be the first to monetize the emerging sound of the South Bronx for a mainstream audience.

It worked.

At least in part. "Rapper's Delight" showed that rap could sell—it remains the best-selling 12-inch single of all time. Its success destroyed '70s rappers' contention that the unit in which rap was best appreciated was the nightlong party, or failing that, the 90-minute cassette. The question, for those rappers, was not how such a long single track could succeed commercially, it was how anyone could get at rap's complexities in such a short slice.

Decades later, the indignation of Bronx-based rappers Grandmaster Caz and Melle Mel at the success of "Rapper's Delight" remains palpable. *Hip Hop Evolution* is worth watching for Caz intoning "who the *fuck* is that?" alone. But "What are they doing to our art form?" is the better question for my purposes: in this moment, Caz's horror is real. Sugarhill Gang were, in the words of hip hop historian Jeff Chang, "rap amateurs, a no-name group using partly stolen rhymes—the very definition of a group with no style." If style emerges organically through the process of integrating separate personalities into a coherent whole, it is unsurprising that "Rapper's Delight" sounds like an assemblage of disparate parts scattered over a Chic sample.[3]

Hip hop works by working the break beats, or breaks—the moments between verses in which most of a song's vocals and instruments drop out, leaving a percussion line that emphasizes the ongoing rhythm. DJs carefully cultivated and guarded their archive of breaks, going so far as to soak their labels off their records to prevent other DJs from identifying them and stealing their breaks.[4] DJs' reputations were made by their skill, but also by their catalogs. Laying down vocals over a studio band rather than over a DJ mixing removed the DJ, and his archive, from the production process. Demoting the DJ and his on-the-spot mix of breaks made the MC's work easier, and paved the way for the dominance of rapper-producers in later decades. It led to the homogenization of studio rap's sound, at least temporarily. The DJ's curated archive of breaks let him introduce contingency not only into the timing of the performance, but also into the material it incorporates, generating an unpredictable sonic environment to which the MC had to creatively adapt. All this changed in the studio at Sugar Hill Records. Sugar Hill's use of a band instead of a DJ, as Loran Kajikawa notes, gave Sugarhill Gang the "stability and symmetry" of a verse structure that was "strictly regularized… to rap over." Ideally, this would give an MC the ability to introduce narrative and stylistic complexity in their lyrics. Lyrically, what Sugarhill Gang did with that structure on "Rapper's Delight" was negligible.[5] The casual misogyny is casual, and "leave" rhymes with "cheese."

This brings us to the woman who is, by some accounts, the villain of the piece: Sylvia Robinson, the Sugar Hill Records producer who put the group together after hearing Lovebug Starski rap and failing to persuade him to record what he was doing for commercial release. Robinson stepped into hip hop's path and undeniably set rap on a new trajectory. (Whether you thought that was a good thing may have come down to whether or not she owed you money.) Robinson made rap a moneymaker, but she also fundamentally changed the power dynamics that had given it its previous form. Pre-Sugar Hill, the DJ drove rap from his position behind the turntable. Sylvia wrested that control in the direction of MCs and producers. This fundamental alteration to rap's structure is Sugarhill Gang's primary contribution to the genre's history.

Of course, there's a version of this story that finds in Robinson a profoundly sympathetic young female musician trying to make a career in the '50s and '60s, who as the talented head of a celebrated independent label in the late '70s and '80s was never quite given her due as an influential rap producer, because of her gender and Sugar Hill Records' sketchy business practices. There's the story of Robinson producing Grandmaster Flash and the Furious Five's *The Message*, which in the wake of Ronald Reagan's visit to, and horrified flight from, the South Bronx in 1980 became the first rap album to carry a serious political critique. This essay isn't that story. Reading Sylvia through "Rapper's Delight" only ends one way, even though we might want to accept *The Message* as her penance, if we were the ones in charge of adjudicating such things. We're not. *Exit Sylvia.*

The commercial success of the studio band format on "Rapper's Delight" ensured that the DJ's ear for the more eclectic breaks would be sidelined in the studio recording process. Some people also point to the moment of this success as the "death of hip hop." If pre-1979 hip hop DJs had the musical appetite of an omnivorous beast and the gut PH of a turkey vulture, then "Rapper's Delight" envisioned a hip hop culture that was just eating the same dry chicken, over and over for as long as the money lasts.

Maybe you think I'm being unfair. It's probably true that I'm underplaying how much *fun* the Sugarhill Gang demonstrably had in live performances of this song. While writing this essay, I talked to Liz Lindau, an ethnomusicologist and professor who teaches "Rapper's Delight" in her popular music history class at Cal State Long Beach. She tells me that her students see humor as one of the continuities between this track and contemporary rap, and that one thing the song implicitly did was allow radio rap to be funny, even goofy. To quote her description of the song, "There's a groove, it repeats, I don't know. But 'Wet Ass Pussy' is funny." It might be true that I can't hear this track at this distance without hearing it across *Illmatic*, across "Fight the Power," "Fuck Tha Police," or "C.R.E.A.M.," Lauryn Hill's "Lost Ones" or even *The Message*—across all the history that this song, you might argue, made possible. To that I'd say: if Big Bank Hank was looking to be judged with scrupulous fairness, he should have cut the line "I can bust you out with my super sperm."

Hip hop died before I was born, but of course, hip hop will never die. Even "Rapper's Delight" couldn't kill it.

*

What does it mean to *deserve* to be a one-hit wonder?

Strangely enough, as I'm writing and thinking and living inside the 14 minutes of this song, it's a few lines from the early 20th-century Irish poet W.B. Yeats that turn up out of nowhere to illuminate the essential nature of "Rapper's Delight," and by extension The Sugarhill Gang, for me. At the end of his poem "No Second Troy," after ruminating on an aging Helen of Troy's diminished capacity for destruction, the poet looks at Helen and asks:

> Why, what could she have done, being what she is?
> Was there another Troy for her to burn?

It's the "being what she is" that matters here: the Sugarhill Gang weren't built to be a group, let alone a crew or a gang. They were a conjuncture, a technology through which some of the forms of hip hop culture, shorn of its soul and style, could enter the mainstream. This is clear in how people talk about them: no one is ever going to try to argue for their technical skill or collaborative artistry. It's why listening to them now feels vaguely embarrassing, why you feel more than a little embarrassment *for them.* It's why they could never have been anything *but* a one-hit wonder. They had been designed to perform a particular function, and having completed that function, there was nothing left for them to do.[6]

What could they have done, being what they were? Was there another Bronx for them to burn?

[1] I actually don't know a lot about these things, which I suppose makes my decision to write this essay presumptuous. My attempt to convey the context for this song relies on a lot of recent reading, most notably Jeff Chang's *Can't Stop, Won't Stop: A History of the Hip-Hop Generation* (2005) and Loren Kajikawa's *Sounding Race in Rap Songs* (2015), as well as the *Drunk History* episode about the song that, at a slim six minutes, somehow clocks in at less than half length of the song itself.

[2] An Escher-ish image that I cannot, despite repeated attempts, actually picture.

[3] The extensive history of litigation around "Rapper's Delight" includes Chic, whose 1979 song "Good Times" was the source of the initially-uncredited sample over which much of the song was built.

[4] Rap legend DJ Cool Herc's father, who had run a sound system back in Kingston, referred to soaking off the labels as "Jamaican style" DJing: "Hide the name of your records because that's how you get your rep. That's how you get your clientele. You don't want the same people to have your same record down the block." (Quoted in *Can't Stop Won't Stop.*)

[5] And, notoriously, mostly lifted from Grandmaster Caz's cast-off notebooks.

[6] Even if it took them multiple albums to realize it, including a 1999 children's album, *Jump on It!* Clocking in at 5:06, "Kids' Rapper's Delight" is, true to form, the longest track on *Jump on It!* It swaps in a verse about how "I don't mean to brag, I don't mean to boast/But we're like hot butter on your breakfast toast" for the chicken dinner verse. The substitution is probably a sound artistic decision.

ON THE ESSAY:

When my name was pulled for the 2023 Fadness draft, I scanned the options for a song that had *done something* to popular music at a particular juncture. I pulled up at "Rapper's Delight," because it had recently shuffled into a mix while I was doing yardwork in Tucson's late spring heat, and when the chicken verse hit, I was briefly convinced I was having heatstroke—I hadn't remembered the song's narrative at all. I had maybe never heard it in its entirety. So I wanted to think about what it meant for rap to reach radio audiences through this anomaly, one that we would never, today, talk about as emblematic of that culture, that time, if it hadn't been the first.

In hindsight, I feel a little regret at my take on the Sugarhill Gang: they *were* having fun in a grim place (on the eve of Reagan's America), and just now, I'm less inclined to run that down.

SEARCHING THROUGH EVERY OPEN DOOR:

James Charlesworth on "(I've Had) The Time of My Life" by Bill Medley

Bill Medley is not a one-hit wonder.

I begin with this clear and obvious statement of fact not because it is a drum I intend to beat incessantly throughout this essay (though I do plan to whack it a couple good ones), nor do I start here because of some beef I have with the committee over the eighty-two-year-old Righteous Brother's inclusion in the roster of this tournament.

Nope, I'm admitting this here at the outset because it is a concession pertinent to other assertions I intend to make. Namely: that despite the aforementioned incontrovertible truth—and, for that matter, the corresponding verity of the non-one-hit-wonderness of Jennifer Warnes (it *is*, after all, a *duet*, people)—the number one seed in the top-right quadrant of your tournament bracket, "(I've Had) The Time of My Life," which climbed to number one on the Billboard Hot 100 charts in November of 1987 and took home an Oscar, a Golden Globe, and a Grammy the following year, nevertheless deserves your vote in this contest of Fadness.

But the reasons for this have little to do with Medley—and to get there will take a little bit (okay, maybe a lot) of explaining.

I. "Let's Just Get This Piece of Shit Over With"

It bears mentioning up front that the whole thing reads like a Hollywood script. The story of "(I've Had) The Time of My Life" is complete with down-on-their-luck characters and flawed protagonists chasing dreams into dead ends. There are rising tensions and moments when all seems lost and dramatic last-minute salvations—and perhaps there is no better place to begin telling this tale than with songwriter Franke Previte, who was forty years old with $100 in his checking account when he got the phone call that changed his life.

"Franke, it's Jimmy. How ya doin'?"

The eponymous former front man of the pop rock band Franke and the Knockouts—who'd achieved fleeting notoriety when their 1981 song "Sweetheart" rose to Number 10 on the Billboard charts and then was promptly forgotten by history—Previte had been selling used cars out of his driveway in New Jersey to make ends meet for the past couple years since the Knockouts broke up. He was therefore thrilled to receive this phone call out of the blue from the president of his former record company—his excitement waned, however, once Jimmy Ienner got around to the reason for his call.

"I'd like you to do a song for a little movie I'm working on called *Dirty Dancing.*"

Oh no, Previte thought, his flattened palm hitting his forehead. *Poor Jimmy's doing pornos.*[1]

This was late summer 1986, and though Ienner had not in fact resorted to doing pornos, he was likely privately regretting the agreement he'd recently signed with a small-time video distribution company out of Stamford, CT, called Vestron Pictures, who—in hopes of saving themselves from bankruptcy—had made the rash decision to begin producing low-budget movies for straight-to-video release. The first script chosen for this endeavor was one that had been floating around Hollywood for years. For a time MGM had held the rights, but a series of managerial regime changes had put the script by the largely unknown screenwriter, Eleanor Bergstein, in production hell for half a decade before MGM finally unloaded it. When Vestron made their offer, Bergstein had been happy to accept, even if it meant a budget of less than 5 million dollars at a time when most films ran budgets of 15-25 million—even if it meant filming not in the Catskill Mountains of upstate New York, where Bergstein had spent her summers as a youth and where she had set her largely autobiographical screenplay, but in the cheapest location the scouts had been able to find and book. Specifically: a former Boy Scout camp in rural western North Carolina called the Lake Lure Lodge.

Of course, Franke Previte was not yet privy to any of this backstory, and Jimmy Ienner wasn't inclined to disabuse him of any delusions that might already have begun to bloom in the former Knockout's noggin. When Previte, grasping for excuses, or perhaps being coy, said he didn't have time, Ienner told him to make time. "This movie's gonna change your life," he said.

"That's the good news," Ienner continued. "The bad news is the song has to be seven minutes long. And I need it in two weeks."[2]

*

"To tell you the truth," Patrick Swayze would say later of the days he and other cast and crew members spent at the Lake Lure Lodge that late summer of '86 filming *Dirty Dancing*, "at that point we all hated the movie, so we were like, 'let's just get this piece of shit over with.'"[3]

By the time Jimmy Ienner placed his phone call to Franke Previte, a litany of problems had already befallen the underfunded production. A relentless deluge of rain had caused heavy flooding to block the roads to the set; a principal cast member had fallen ill and had to be recast; a rehearsal space had been burglarized and, among the cast and crew, there'd been a serious fall from a ladder, a broken toe, a fractured wrist, and several severe bouts of food poisoning. When the rain finally let up it was followed by a sudden cold snap, then a heat wave that sent temperatures over 100 degrees for a week straight, the interior of the Lake Lure Lodge where the final dance scene was being filmed rising to well over 120 degrees, causing ten professional dancers to pass out in twenty minutes on one particularly taxing day.

It was into this maelstrom of misfortune that 26-year-old Jennifer Grey had stepped off a plane from JFK, fresh off a week of waitressing shifts. For this, her first starring role after gaining minor notoriety as a supporting cast member in the previous summer's biggest hit, *Ferris Bueller's Day Off*, Grey had been paid a flat rate of $50,000. She'd also brought with her a justified disdain toward her co-star, Swayze, based on his behavior during their time filming together a few years previously on *Red Dawn*, when he had captained the mostly male cast in a midnight hazing ritual consisting of an M80 duct-taped to Grey's hotel room door and set off.

So who could blame her, really, for not trusting Swayze enough to perform the difficult "lift" maneuver that was Bergstein's script's culminating moment? Sure, it was a move Swayze, a former professional ballet dancer, had done thousands of times, but that did not mean Grey was enthusiastic to trust the former firecracker wielder to be standing open-armed as she raced across the hardwood floor of the Lake Lure Lodge and leaped into the air, aiming for the chandeliers, at which point he would supposedly grasp her at the waist and deadlift her, balancing her above his head while she held out her arms, crossed her ankles, and pointed her toes. And so, despite the urging of fellow cast members and crew, despite the encouragement of her dance instructor, Kenny Ortega, despite the knowledge that at some point they *have* to film this scene, Grey will not even rehearse it.

And yet even *that* is *still* not the biggest problem. Because although Eleanor Bergstein has already selected nearly the entire soundtrack—composed mostly of old standbys of the 1960s—she is still searching for a song to play over the final scene, something that will evoke the past while still feeling contemporary to the current age. Every night, after long days of shooting, she gathers Swayze, Grey, Ortega, and director Emile Ardolino in her hotel room and pops recently submitted demos into a boombox. "We didn't like anything," she'll say later of the first 149 demos they received. "They were terrible songs…like listening to a drink of water."[4]

You can see where this is going. As the final day of filming in North Carolina approaches, the heat wave persists. Tension mounts. But in New Jersey, a down-on-his-luck songwriter is hard at work—and it is on the penultimate day of the lease at the Lake Lure Lodge, precisely two weeks after Jimmy Ienner's phone call, that salvation arrives like a campy first plot point in our saga. A padded mailing envelope is torn open, and a cassette tape containing the very last of the 150 demos they have received is snapped into the sound system. For a moment all is still. And then into the sweaty gloom of the Lake Lure Lodge comes a sleek high-pitched male tenor. (Not Bill Medley's indelible baritone—that will come later.) For now it is the voice of Franke Previte himself, singing the opening vocals of the song that will change his life and the lives of everyone involved in this small-budget film from a no-name production company.

Now I've… had… the time of my life…

The next day, Jennifer Grey races across the hardwood floor, aims for the chandeliers, and leaps into the air.

II. We Seem to Understand the Urgency

According to legend (i.e., Wikipedia), Franke Previte was taking his ticket at Exit 140 of the Garden State Parkway when inspiration struck.

"Now, how I write is through phonetic melody jamming," the songwriter says. "A *G* chord will make a certain sound in my mind and an *A* chord a vowel sound."[5] On the day in question, Previte was "grunting nonsense" while listening to the instrumental track of the new song he was working on for Jimmy Ienner when a certain phrase came unbidden into his mind. Perhaps it was a call back to Ienner's comment that this movie would change his life, or maybe—as Previte believes—it was "the man upstairs" reaching down to bestow inspiration. Regardless, Previte seized the moment by digging around on the floorboard of his vehicle until he excavated a pen and an old envelope, upon whose torn-open flap he scrawled the phrase "time of my life."

It will surprise no one to learn that the remainder of the lyrics were pulled together over the course of an afternoon. These are not sentiments that inspire or deserve a deep textual analysis.

I've been waiting for so long, now I've finally found someone, to stand by me
Saw the writing on the wall, and we felt this magical, fantasy
Now with passion in our eyes, there's no way we can disguise, secretly
So we take each other's hand, cuz we seem to understand, the urgency...

By the second verse, even the AABCCB rhyme scheme loosely employed at the outset has lazed into a simpler AABB. This is not to imply, however, that the song's composition is without its elements of brilliance. Promptly upon hearing from Ienner, Previte had called up his old songwriting partner John DeNicola, with whom he'd previously collaborated on dozens of songs (including one called "Hungry Eyes" that had been recorded for but not included on the Knockout's 1984 album, *Makin' the Point*). "It's kind of a boy-meets-girl upstairs-downstairs type story," Ienner had explained on their initial call, and it was armed with little more than this cryptic synopsis that Previte went to work, envisioning a duet, two voices representing the two main characters. "Let's start it in half-time," he told DeNicola, who called up their mutual friend Don Markowitz, proud owner of a 12-track in his tiny Upper West Side apartment and willing to help them pull together the backing tracks. "We'll put the chorus up front," Previte brainstormed, "then double-time the verses to give it a dance beat."[6]

It is, of course, that evocative half-time opening that invites the listener into the intimate world of the song, but "(I've Had) The Time of My Life's" primary gift is the way it remains continuously surprising. The arrival of the female vocal halfway through the intro and the sudden movement to the dance beat both succeed in keeping the listener delightfully off-balance. Even the chord progression is subtly deceptive and non-repetitive, a series of unexpected movements that complicate and beguile before coming full circle. It opens with the classic "minor fall"—moving from the root (E) to the relative minor (C#m)—but then counters our expectations by sliding up a semitone to a flattened seventh (D). When the dance beat kicks in, the verse alternates between the seventh and the root before resolving strangely to the sub-dominant (A) as we move to the prechorus, where we then tumble down a full step to a minor third interval (G), despite the fact that we are in a major key. And it is only then, with our expectations unbalanced by all this modal interchange, that the second half of the prechorus hits us with the A to B movement our ears have been unconsciously anticipating since that opening minor fall, a classic IV-V tension builder that resolves cathartically at the root as the chorus opens up triumphantly and we can't help but sing and dance along. Add to that a resounding saxophone solo that builds to a climax before a sudden and dramatic return to the calm intimacy of the intro and you've got a perfectly encapsulated structure, a flawless pop song that also manages to be something a little more convincing, a little more moving.

That day at the Lake Lure Lodge when she heard the initial demo, which Previte recorded with his friend Rachele Cappelli performing the female vocals, Eleanor Bergstein was convinced they'd found their song. What she wasn't so sure about were the voices. Though Swayze would always maintain that Previte and Cappelli's original version was his favorite, Bergstein implored Jimmy Ienner to find a voice that would be more recognizable. While principal photography wrapped in North Carolina and then later at a second location in Mountain Lake, Virginia, Ienner again stretched out his tentacles of connection. Donna Summers was asked first to do a duet with Joe Esposito, then Daryl Hall of Hall & Oates for a pairing with Kim Carnes of "Bette Davis Eyes" fame, but neither combination worked out. Maybe what they needed, Bergstein theorized, was a voice that could transport the listener back in time simply through the depth and quality of its sonic profile, a voice that would evoke Bergstein's own memories of her childhood as the youngest of two daughters of a Brooklyn doctor, who every summer packed up the family and drove them a hundred miles north of the city for weeks of swimming and golf and relaxation at Grossinger's Catskill Resort—in whose basement night club, the Terrace Room, Eleanor Bergstein as a teenage girl (who happened to go by the nickname Baby) had learned to mambo in the summer of 1963…

When Ienner approached Bergstein with his next idea, she was immediately supportive—though getting it done would take some more Jimmy Ienner magic.

III. The Indelible Baritone

Among the drive-ins and malt shops of late '50s Orange County, Bill Medley came of age: possessor of a slicked pompadour, clad in a plain white tee shirt with a pack of Camels tucked inside a rolled-up sleeve on his deltoid, a leather jacket slung over the opposite shoulder. "Bill *was* Fonzie," a childhood friend said of him. He also happened to boast a baritone as sonorous as some vast canyon of the west. Upon dropping out of high school (or getting thrown out, depending on who tells the story) he joined a barbershop quartet, learned to play a few chords on guitar, and, by the time he was twenty-one, had a lucrative songwriting and recording deal with Atlantic. All this before he joined forces with fellow Californian Bobby Hatfield in Righteous Brotherhood and recorded ten Billboard Top 40 hits between 1964 and 1974, including two that made it all the way to number one.

In the early winter of 1986, when he received a phone call out of the blue from Ienner, Medley was forty-six years old and had been a millionaire for over half of those years. One of the Righteous Brothers' number one hits, 1964's "You've Lost That Lovin' Feelin'," was in the midst of a rejuvenation of popularity after appearing in the summer's highest grossing domestic film, *Top Gun*. You remember the scene of course: Maverick and Goose and a gaggle of ogling wingmen serenading their ambivalent aerospace-professor-slash-Maverick's-love-interest-to-be, Charlie, at a douchey bar in Miramar. Though the song was omitted from the *Top Gun* soundtrack, and was not rereleased in any formal way, it nevertheless reemerged on the radio waves that summer, bringing the long-broken-up Righteous Brothers back into the public eye. It was no surprise that, when Eleanor Bergstein expressed her desire for the final song of her film to be sung by a canonical voice of bygone decades, Ienner soon got around to Medley. The ensuing conversation went something like this: "Bill, we're doing this movie and I want you to sing the title song for it." "Oh yeah? What's the movie?" This, of course, was the moment Ienner had come to dread. He sheepishly whispered the title.

"What??" Medley said. "That sounds like a bad porno movie!"

Medley had other reasons for declining beyond the film's salacious moniker. In addition to the fact that his most recent foray into movie soundtrack contribution had resulted in disaster in the form of an unsuccessful duet with Gladys Knight for the Sylvester Stallone box-office bomb, *Cobra*, there was also a certain unbreakable promise he'd recently made to his second wife. "Not only do I not want to do it," he informed Ienner. "I can't do it because I promised Paula I'd be there when our child was born."

Nevertheless, all through the winter, Ienner pushed. Phone call after phone call. Was the kid born yet, or what? But Medley stood his ground.

"Jimmy, listen to me," he said, hoping for the firm finality that addressing someone by name can carry. "I'm not...gonna...do it."[7]

*

When Jennifer Warnes was a sad, uncool teenager with glasses and a heavy backpack full of geometry and social studies textbooks, her bus ride home from school took her every day past a dilapidated dance bar called the Flamingo, whose surrounding fields and vacant lots would fill up with Ford Fairlanes and Chrysler Imperials whenever the marquee read *Righteous Brothers – Tonight!*[8]

Born in 1947 in Seattle and raised in Anaheim, Warnes was offered her first recording contract at age seven, sang in church choirs throughout her early teens, and earned an opera scholarship at Immaculate Heart College in Los Angeles, which she turned down in favor of a brief stint at a convent. In her twenties she'd recorded four albums, notched a Top 10 hit with 1976's "Right Time of the Night," and toured and recorded extensively with her close friend Leonard Cohen. In her thirties she'd won two Golden Globes and Academy Awards for Best Original Song—first for "It Goes Like It Goes" from the 1979 movie *Norma Rae* and later for her 1983 duet with Joe Cocker, "Up Where We Belong," for the soundtrack of *An Officer and A Gentleman*—and became the voice of American after-school evenings by way of her duet recording with J.B. Thomas of "As Long As We Got Each Other," theme song for the wildly popular television sit-com *Growing Pains*.

Still, Warnes recalled those after-school bus rides and the young girl who dreamed of the tall, sexy Bill Medley. So when Jimmy Ienner reached out in early 1987 and told her that Medley had expressed an interest in recording a song for a movie they were working on and wanted *her* to do a duet with him, Warnes immediately requested the demo. Driving in her car with her boyfriend, she popped it into the tape player with a simmering excitement that had settled to lukewarm by the time the song ended. The boyfriend asked, "How much did you say they offered to pay you?"

The answer was: a lot. Somehow, principal photography had come in well under budget and Jimmy Ienner had found himself with some cash to throw around. Reassured by the monetary figure, the boyfriend suggested Warnes take it. "What do you have to lose?" he reasoned. "You get to record a song with one of your idols. So what if the song's lousy and the movie's a bust? Probably nobody will ever hear it."[9]

Having thus secured Jennifer Warnes by implying that Bill Medley had already agreed, Ienner went back to the still-refusing Medley and told him Jennifer Warnes was enthusiastically on board, but only if Medley agreed to do it with her. Plus they could do the recording in L.A., so he wouldn't even have to travel. Plus they only needed him for an hour, two tops. When his daughter McKenna was born that February, Medley at last agreed.

In the video, embracing in an overexposed sunbeam, backdropped in black and white against an ethereal dance rehearsal space with wide windows, Medley and Warnes seem happy to be there, exuberant even, perhaps almost in love themselves. But it's an act. By all accounts, the time they spent together recording was limited to an hour in an L.A. studio in February or March of 1987. At Warnes's request, a rough cut of the film's final scene was played so she could match the emotion of her vocals to moments from the film. Medley seems not to have concerned himself with such details, though it's hard to argue with his performance. "I went up to the studio and learned it enough to throw a bunch of stuff on about fifteen tracks," he recalls. "Jennifer and I were trading melody and harmony lines, answers, shouting lines, lots to choose from. 'There you go,' I said. And we left."[10]

It would be hard to blame them for any perceived lack of enthusiasm. As the spring of '87 slouches toward summer, as *Lethal Weapon* and *Beverly Hills Cop II* dominate the box office, even Vestron Pictures seems less and less committed to making their romantic debut with the smutty-sounding title a priority. "(I've Had) The Time of My Life" is originally slotted for a June release concurrent with the film, but Vestron pushes back the premiere date to August and either forgets or doesn't bother to let RCA know, so Medley and Warnes' passionate but anachronistic duet is launched naked and without context into a void and forgotten amidst a Billboard Hot 100 topped by Whitney Houston and U2 and George Michael and Heart. The same rough cut of the film used by Jennifer Warnes for vocal inspiration is circulated for professional consumption with almost unanimously negative responses. Jennifer Grey's own agent, exiting the Magno screening room in Manhattan, tells her she's "just going to have to get something else in the can as soon as possible" because "nobody is *ever* going to see this movie."[11] One well known director, asked by Bergstein what they could do to improve the film, suggests that they "Burn the negative, and collect the insurance."[12]

If this essay were a Hollywood script, this would be the second plot point, the moment when all seems lost, when all of our protagonists' efforts toward a happy ending have left them at the end of their rainbows and their ropes. A music-accompanied montage shows them going their separate ways: Franke Previte returns to his front-yard used-car dealership; Bill Medley and Jennifer Warnes forget entirely about the duet they reluctantly recorded in less than an hour and go back to more fruitful endeavors; Patrick Swayze flies to the Namib Desert to film another future flop, *Steel Dawn*; and Jennifer Grey spends a week in Ireland vacationing with her boyfriend, Matthew Broderick, where they get in a serious car accident and break up.

And on the night before the movie hits screens, Eleanor Bergstein ushers Emile Ardolino and Kenny Ortega out the doors of a party in Manhattan and leads them on an anxious walk north up Broadway. Tomorrow, this story of her childhood that has been her baby for five years will become the property of the world, will be exposed to critics and unforgiving viewers. At a bodega, Bergstein spontaneously buys three yoyos, and for the next twenty blocks, as the city's bright apartment towers give way to intermittent views of the park, they play with the yoyos. And Bergstein, optimistic in the face of what seems unavoidable failure, veteran of half a decade of disappointment—but remembering now a line her reassuring father used to say back when she was a girl—reminds them: "We've had ups and we've had downs. We've had ups and we've had downs. We've had ups and we've had downs..."[13]

IV. "Just Remember!"

Of course you know what happens next. You've seen enough movies to spot a happy ending coming. You don't need me to tell you that Eleanor Bergstein's autobiographical story strikes some mysterious nerve in the zeitgeist of the moment. You don't need me to inform you that this small-budget film from a first-time production company, produced well *under* its paltry budget of 4.7 million dollars, hits theaters and conjures an unprecedented word-of-mouth craze. People watch the movie and step outside in a gleeful daze, only to do an about-face and walk back into the theater to watch again. You don't need me to tell you that it grosses over $200 million worldwide during its four months in theaters and becomes the first film to sell more than a million copies to home video (back when *that* was actually a thing), or that its legacy will inspire a touring rendition and at least two sequels with a third on the way: a collaboration between Eleanor Bergstein and Jennifer Grey—with the latter returning to reprise her role as an all-grown-up Baby—that is currently slated to hit theaters in the summer of 2025.

And you certainly don't need me to tell you that the song, contextualized forever in the emotion of that magical last dance and its cathartic lift scene, will climb to the top position of the Billboard Hot 100 in November and take a clean sweep at the major awards ceremonies, will become over the years the closing song of countless wedding receptions and anniversary parties, will be interpolated by the Black Eyed Peas in 2010 and performed on the hit television show *Glee* later the same year, will remain a staple on the setlist of Bill Medley wherever he plays, with the female vocals now sung, fittingly, by his daughter McKenna, whose birth he years ago tried to use as an excuse to avoid recording the song in the first place.

"The stars were aligned for this one," Franke Previte says now of the song that has gifted him with endless "mailbox money," a check that arrives periodically and has long since kept him from considering a return to the front-yard used-car dealership business. "If you separate anything from the equation, I don't think you have the same phenomenon."[14]

And so I guess the only question left to answer then is... *why?* Why exactly has this song lived on through the years and—more pertinently—why does it deserve your vote in this tournament of one-hit wonders? Maybe the answer lies not in criterial technicalities or chart rankings or sales statistics but in its embodiment of the very spirit of one-hit-wonderness itself, in all of its inscrutable glory and mystery, the intense magic that springs from a combination of circumstances and luck, from dedication and dreaming and hard work and happenstance: a screenwriter holding out hope for her script and its hard-won success over half a decade, a phrase scrawled on the flap of an envelope at Exit 140 of the Garden State Parkway, the very last of 150 demos arriving at precisely the right moment to save a floundering film, and a young yearning actor racing across a hardwood floor and aiming for the chandeliers with faith and hope despite doubts.

For Jennifer Warnes, the answers are simple. It's not something complex or puzzling but a more fundamental force that has made this song and this movie lasting touchstones of their era. "I've thought about it," she says, "and I've wondered why the whole world loves it so much and I think the answer is because it's real joyful. If you take the joy out of that song, it's not a hit."[15]

And so now let us come together in service of that joy. Now, as we cast our votes in this tournament of Fadness, let us take each other's hands. Because we seem to understand.

The urgency.

NOTES

[1] Yates, Henry. "How We Made Dirty Dancing's (I've Had) The Time of My Life". *The Guardian*, 9 April 2019. https://www.theguardian.com/music/2019/apr/09/how-we-made-dirty-dancing-ive-had-the-time-of-my-life

[2] Dye, Robert. "Behind the Song: "(I've Had) The Time of My Life". *American Songwriter*, updated 2 August 2021. https://americansongwriter.com/behind-the-song-ive-had-the-time-of-my-life/

[3] Yates.

[4] Kring-Schreifels, Jake. "How '(I've Had) The Time of My Life' Saved 'Dirty Dancing'". *The Ringer*, 20 August, 2020. https://www.theringer.com/2020/08/20/movies/dirty-dancing-song-time-of-my-life-history

[5-6] Dye.

[7-8] Medley, Bill, with Mike Marino. *The Time of My Life: A Righteous Brother's Memoir*. Boston, Da Capo Press, 2014.

[9] Yates.

[10] Medley.

[11] Grey, Jennifer. *Out of the Corner: A Memoir*. New York, Ballantine Books, 2022.

[12-13] Rickey, Carrie. "'Dirty Dancing': Panned as a dud, but dynamite". *The Philadelphia Inquirer*, 19 August 2012. https://www.inquirer.com/philly/entertainment/20120819__Dirty_Dancing___Panned_as_a_dud__but_dynamite.html#loaded

[14] Kring-Schreifels.

[15] Warnes, Jennifer. "Interview with Jennifer Warnes". Carl Wiser, Interviewer. *Songfacts*, 13 April 2018. https://www.songfacts.com/blog/interviews/jennifer-warnes

ON THE ESSAY:

I never know what I'm going to write about when I choose a song for March Xness. "Time of My Life" is not a personal favorite, and when I selected it I had seen *Dirty Dancing* once, as a kid, and remembered nothing. For me, the interesting thing is not choosing a song I want to cheerlead for but one that provides the material to throw a lot of balls into the air and juggle them and then try to catch them all with a graceful "tada!" There often comes a time in the writing, with the deadline looming, when it seems I have more balls in the air than I can possibly catch. In that way, writing this essay was a bit like Jennifer Grey's moment of trepidation before racing across the floor for her fabled leap. Thanks, March Xness fans and committee, for playing Swayze to my Grey.

AT THE CRACK OF THE WHIP

Cameron Carr

In the 1932 horror film *Island of Lost Souls*, Dr. Moreau, a scientist experimenting with transforming animals into something close to human, cracks his whip. This is what separates him from the other beings on the island.

The film, adapted from H.G. Wells's novel *The Island of Doctor Moreau*, is a lesser-seen but much-acclaimed document of early horror cinema. It's best remembered for a repeated line that Moreau's creations recite at the prompting of the whip: "Are we not men?" He wants them to become something other than what they are. He wants this one response to become their definition. They have no freedom to object. So they repeat: "Are we not men?"

This question, and its answer, had little impact on me when I first saw the film. It was 2010, I was going on sixteen, and sitting in a high school classroom. More interesting to me was why my English class was watching yet another movie instead of reading. I wanted art and all the world around me to be full of meaning, but I didn't see any in my obligatory viewing of a near-century-old black-and-white film. I fidgeted in the plastic seat of my combination chair and desk.

Outside school, in my suburban piece of middle America, I didn't see meaning either. It's a well-known but unspoken fact that every city is famous for something. But usually that something is someone else's interpretation of nothing.

The maybe-famous-nothings are documented by plaques honoring old buildings and the forgotten people who lived in them. The businesses take on local myths and titles in their names. Pizza parlors hang up signed pictures of athletes, newscasters—anyone who made it out but then came back long enough to enjoy a slice.

The purpose of these photos is never clear to me. The people are novel because they started here and went so far and because they have gone so far but still come back. The photos seem to promise the chance of escaping to somewhere better at the same time as they swear this is a place worth staying. I don't find them convincing. To visitors and outsiders, it all looks somewhat pitiful. But interpretations are often a matter of distance.

What I mean to say is that we all have false notions of importance, and at the same time we all ignore so much importance. I am guilty of it too—Ohio alternately impressing and depressing me.

Six and a half miles from the house where I grew up, a music store hung signed records, drumheads, and setlists above the door and tried to convince the shoppers that real art could come from here. There were signatures from the Dayton band Guided by Voices, but I'd fled from Catholic school a few years prior and had no interest in being guided by the voices of a trinity or any other group. I remember, perhaps falsely, signatures from Kim Deal of the Pixies and Chrissie Hynde of the Pretenders. But the Pixies were from Boston and the Pretenders from England; it would be years before I learned the musicians were born in Ohio. None of it convinced me.

I saw Ohio instead for all its ugly blemishes, a home to only minor flukes and oddities. I didn't believe that Ohio was a place of no hope, but I believed that all things truly worthwhile in my Midwestern home came from quiet secrets we made for ourselves—the songs we wrote and sang in basements. I believed that life would be better someday because life—the real life, the one I was expecting—would take place somewhere else, in a place where better things come from. That life could start in an instant, at the snap of fingers or the click of heels.

Because of this, I left.

I fled to the coast, 610 miles to a record label in New Jersey, with an office looking across the Hudson River into New York City. On my first day, one of the two full-time employees turned to me and said, *Who's the best band in Ohio.* I tried to answer, but I'd misinterpreted. He was not asking me, because it was not a question. The answer, he informed me, was Pere Ubu. I did not know who Pere Ubu was. But he allowed one possible alternative: *You know Devo, right?*

I don't know when, but at some point, probably in the sixties, Gerald Casale and Mark Mothersbaugh watched *Island of Lost Souls* too. They saw in it a direct reflection of a theory they were developing about the state of humanity: human-like creatures progressing toward some human ideal, then regressing backward; the human species itself a false ideal; meanwhile, some greater power keeping everything in strict obedience.

They heard the whip crack and they listened closely to the question: "Are we not men?"

This was before Casale and Mothersbaugh knew what to do with their ideas. But the answer to the question was on the tips of their tongues. It wasn't a matter of evolution, becoming more human, it was the opposite: de-evolution.

You likely know Devo for their 1980 hit single, "Whip It."

"Whip It" peaked at number fourteen on the billboard charts the week of November 15, 1980. It's often remembered as a novelty song. In some ways, that's true, but in others it's not. "Whip It," one might say, is novel as one of the only hit songs to document presumptions of ope-ing Midwestern manners: The guitar chatters with robotic enthusiasm but freezes for a synthesizer's opulent reply. The vocalists, Casale and Mothersbaugh, squeal in turns. One voice, then another—inhuman, but polite. I don't mean the Midwest is inhuman, but Devo certainly is, and "Whip It" certainly is. It's expressively rigid, emphatically cartoonish. It's a caricature of misinterpretations. It's possibly about masturbation. It's all of this in a little over two and a half minutes.

A healthy resting heart beats sixty to one hundred times per minute. "Whip It" moves at one hundred and sixty beats per minute, the heart rate of a twenty-year-old exercising vigorously. (And the drummer is doing exactly that.) The Number 1 song when "Whip It" reached its pinnacle of popularity—"Lady," written by Lionel Richie and performed by Kenny Rogers—moved at only half the pace and clocked in a minute longer.

"Whip It" seems to want things to progress faster than possible. It documents a call and response. The whip cracks and no one replies to "Are we not men?" but suggestions are given: Straighten up. Keep moving. Forward. It's not too late.

The track is a common, offhand example of a one-hit wonder. But I'd like to remind you that interpretation is a matter of distance. I would like to remind you that every few Halloweens you still see someone in a black turtleneck and a red geometric dome hat. I would like to remind you that Devo did chart two other songs, "Working in a Coal Mine" and "Theme From Doctor Detroit," though neither broke the top forty, and neither were available on a studio album.

The argument against the one-hit wonder label is an argument of misinterpretation. It's an argument about failing to see what Devo truly is.

In 1978, the "dean of American rock critics" ventured out of the hallowed castle of New York to investigate a new sound leaking out of a barren, distant land called Ohio.

"What's going on in Akron-Cleveland right now is probably an accident," Robert Christgau wrote in the *Village Voice*. "There's even a possibility that bands in other cities are making rock and roll every bit as good and not recording it—but I doubt it."

If you are not from Ohio, you might not know anything about Akron, you might not have even heard of Akron. If you are from Ohio but not from Akron, you might know it as the rubber city. It is the birthplace of Goodyear, Goodrich, Firestone, General Tire, and not much else. (Cleveland, though historically more focused on steel and other industry, is home to the world's largest rubber stamp.) This made Christgau's (noncommittal) claim, and Devo's unexpected rise, all the more impressive and perplexing.

As the scene's major acts—Devo, Pere Ubu, and the Dead Boys—spread beyond their corner of declining middle America, they offered an answer to punk that was eclectic, unpretentious, and bordering unhinged. While the New York post-punks were art school kids adopting the confrontational qualities of punk rock, the northern Ohio sect were rubber factory children experimenting with further strangeness. The Talking Heads debuted in collared shirts, Devo debuted in hazmat suits.

By the time Christgau visited the Buckeye State, the key bands had already made their most influential albums and the scene was moving to a new stage of life. The Dead Boys had relocated to New York, pioneering punk label Stiff Records was preparing to release *The Akron Compilation*, and Devo would immigrate to Los Angeles that same year.

This is where the challenge of the one-hit wonder label begins. The title implies that were it not for one song, an artist would leave the cultural memory untouched. But that's not true for Devo. For many, the band's importance comes from before "Whip It" rather than after.

Devo birthed from the end of the sixties into the shadow of the 1970 Kent State massacre. The band's founders were Kent State University students at the time and knew at least one of the four unarmed students killed by the Ohio National Guard. The young musicians saw the shooting as ominous support for their nascent theory of a de-evolving humanity willing to submit to loss of freedom.

As much a conceptual art project as a band, the group's real debut was the 1976 film *The Truth About De-Evolution*. It took first prize at the influential Ann Arbor Film Festival the following year and established, in absurd visual form, Devo's view of humanity. David Bowie and Iggy Pop took notice and helped the band land a record deal with Warner Bros., though Bowie ultimately relinquished most production duties to Brian Eno for the band's 1978 debut album: *Q: Are We Not Men? A: We Are Devo!*

The album, in the words of a contemporary *Rolling Stone* review, is "a definitive restatement of rock & roll's aims and boundaries in the seventies." It's replying to the question "are we not men?" but the answer isn't yes or no. It's an attempt to answer something else entirely. It's a vision of a new path for humanity, or at least popular music. Check the near unrecognizable cover of the Rolling Stones' "(I Can't Get No) Satisfaction." The band performed the track on *Saturday Night Live* (the week after the Rolling Stones served as the musical guest, no less), debuting their yellow safety suits and animatronic stage presence to a dumbfounded American audience.

Are We Not Men is the greatest challenge to the one-hit wonder pigeonholing. It is, in a critical sense, Devo's high point. The album sets a path forward from punk that counters the jagged, gray posture of big city post-punks and the fluorescent commercialism that new wave (de-)evolved into. When Devo is given as a musical reference point, this is almost always the Devo in question.

The high-speed, angular, yelping sound has become the base of legions of bands since, especially in the Midwest, even prompting a wave of twenty-first century "devo-core" acts such as the Coneheads, Booji Boys, and D.L.I.M.C. And the Devo members' arty pedigree has earned them a slew of film scoring gigs including almost half of Wes Anderson's filmography, *Rugrats*, *Happy Gilmore*, and *The Lego Movie*.

Before it had Devo, Ohio had Dean Martin, Doris Day, the Isley Brothers. Joe Walsh attended Kent State at the same time as some of Devo's members. Maybe what Devo did was demonstrate a way to make art that didn't rely on attention or success. Devo showed that creating could be important even in the distant land of middle America. And maybe this is more important than any one hit.

But distance is a matter of interpretation, and Devo didn't see that much space between one thing and another. In his *Village Voice* article lauding Akron and Cleveland as the birth of a "real new wave," Christgau recounts a story where "a Warners exec told [Devo] that he liked to sign one 'art band' for every act he knew was going to sell three million, he was politely asked what art band would balance off Devo." At least some of the band was happy to imagine a future where Devo might be a mass success.

The band moved to Los Angeles in 1978 and released another album—*Duty Now for the Future*, a middling entry in the group's legacy—before *Freedom of Choice* and "Whip It." Till then, the executives who made decisions knew Devo for music videos, coordinated outfits, and heavy use of synthesizers—future staples of the eighties, but arty oddities at the time.

Following the commercial flop of their sophomore album, Warner warned Devo that without a hit, the band's next album would be their last with the label. When Devo finished *Freedom of Choice*, Warner selected "Girl U Want" as the lead single, seeing its "My Sharona"-like guitar riff as the clearest path to success. This was, of course, a misinterpretation.

"Whip It" became one of the first hit songs to use a synthesizer as a lead instrument and propelled *Freedom of Choice* to become one of the first major new wave albums (it peaked at Number 22 on the Billboard 200 chart). MTV wouldn't launch for another year—"music video" wasn't even a term yet—but when the channel did join the airwaves, Devo already had a "Whip It" video ready that played up controversial misinterpretations of the song's meaning. MTV helped the song chart for a second year in a row.

This is the Devo that most everyone knows.

The beauty about "Whip It" is that it's not an outlier but rather a concentration of Devo. The mechanical drive, the vocals squeezed from Mickey Mouse, aphoristic double entendres. The lyrics contort and subvert meaning on par with anything else in their catalog. (*Is* it about masturbation? Sadomasochism? Supporting presidential candidate Jimmy Carter? Imitating Thomas Pynchon?) If you've listened to and enjoyed "Whip It," you'd likely enjoy much of *Are We Not Men*. Maybe not quite as much, but enough.

"Whip It" is the brief glimpse the rest of the world took of Devo. Though it has so much of what made the band great and influential, on its own it calls more attention to other things: the costumes, the silly music video. But listeners can interpret as they want. As Devo says, it's their freedom of choice.

The whip cracks and the question repeats. How to define the thing?

"Are we not men?" became a central rallying cry at the foundation of a Midwestern band of misfits. What did it mean to see the sixties combust, the eighties looming, the factories closing? They asked the question again and again. But the answer was never yes or no: They're Devo.

The whip cracks again and the question repeats: "Are we not men?"

But what's more important, the crack of the whip or the way we reply?

ON THE ESSAY:

In college, I tried to teach myself to write about music like it was something I could win. The day an album came out, I'd put it on and walk around campus, sometimes through the scattered leaves of a cool Midwestern fall and sometimes stepping carefully across patches of black ice. I'd replay it till I found myself back in my dorm, the album an ambient reminder while I wrote. When I finished, I compared my attempts to the big music pubs. I wish, now, I'd sometimes set myself against something else: the black ice patches, psychology lecture notes, my hot takes about what *Rolling Stone* got wrong. If writing about music is a competition, then the opponent is what is lost between the experience and the writing down. The best music writing—or maybe any writing—does more than tell what's there: it gives shape to what is lost.

MARCH DANCENESS '90s

SERIOUS JOY:

Sejal Shah on "1 Thing" by Amerie

What I remember is dancing to this one song in the house in the northeastern corner of Iowa, the driftless area. I rented it for the academic year from a professor who was away in Copenhagen and in their little buttercream-colored house I danced at night. I was lonely. *Na-na-na-na-na, oh (ah-ah).* Was I going to find an academic job? *It's this one thing that got me trippin'.* Is an academic job the way to happiness or a book? *This one thing you did.* For me it was neither, but I didn't know that at the time. *This one thing, I want to admit it.* This one thing, but I'm not telling you what it is—and it's the secret ingredient in the secret sauce—the secret ingredient is what makes the secret house.

I was dating the professor's younger son. *Ooh-wee, it felt so serious.* I had also been out on some dates with a painter/chef at the local bistro. *This one thing and I was so with it.* It was hard to figure out. This was a town of 8,000. Blink and twenty years go by. *Na- na-na-na-na, oh.* Days go by. That was another song I was thinking about. What gets you tripping? The past is a head trip.

This one thing—what is it that makes a person right for another person? What's the thing that makes a relationship last? What's the thing that you can't get over? And it's exactly what I would say is not working in a student poem or story. Or one of mine. Here's what I would write: *"Thing" lacks specificity. It's a* thing. *Can you be more specific?* And yet, there is something about the thinginess of a thing. What's your thing? What's mine?

LOOKING AT SOME OF THE LYRICS:

Trying to let it go

(this is me, in everything I write, this one thing, trying to let something go)

This one thing, your soul made me feel it

(What thing is it?)

Hey, we don't know each other well

(No, that's what makes it interesting)

Memories just keep ringing bells

(a song unhooks those memories, unfastens them, silvers them, sounds them)

I'm hoping you can keep a secret

(What's the secret except this one thing?)

This one thing you did—when it's something that someone has done to me, it has the whiff of the unforgivable. But what if no one did anything and dancing is only another way to write?

While working on my story collection, I found myself listening to songs on repeat and dancing alone again in my house—it was the pandemic—and who could have imagined this one thing that kept us afraid and apart was also this one thing that drew us together as we tried to figure out what the next best step was.

I danced once to "Days Go By." This is an essay, though, about "1 Thing." I danced to many songs including "1 Thing." *This one thing, I want to admit it.*

Amerie singing at the top of the hill and I sat and danced in the yellow house on the hill, wondering what one thing it would be—a job or a person or event waiting to happen, which would give my life direction, a ballast. Things did happen. I got a job in New York. I didn't marry either the painter/chef or my landlord's son (also a painter), though he said he would have. I didn't realize for a long time that he was serious (the landlord's son). It's not that I wasn't serious, it's just that I didn't think of myself as having that 1 thing for someone else, seeing that it was easier to be aware of that 1 thing in someone else.

I didn't realize for a long time how much I admired painters. *This one thing and I was so with it.* They say if you admire it then you should try it. I've been trying (this one thing) painting some watercolors. I didn't get tenure.

The times we never even got to speak. I left New York.

It took me a long time to see this one thing is whatever you make it. I couldn't find it outside of myself. The song always surprised me, made me wonder—what is everyone else thinking the one thing is? Or is it just the hook and the beat and the danceability of it and no one really cares what that 1 thing is or is it that there's some mystery and anyone can fill it—magic, that you are a painter or a chef or a 6'1" teacher or that dancing alone in a house on a hill can bring you some magic and that can be the one thing that keeps you going when you don't know what comes next in your life—and let's be real, not one of us does. Dancing can keep you going when you are writing a book, and you don't know if someone is going to ever publish it. It's a romance. I did marry. Not the chef-painter, not my landlord's son, but a middle school teacher, years later. He coaches tennis and champions my writing. What is the 1 thing? It's the turning toward each other instead of turning away when it gets harder. I think that's the 1 thing. That's a thing, anyway.

What are some things I will remember?

Dancing at night in the house, before there was wi-fi so I was near my laptop, which was plugged in.

Oh, been trying to let it go

Why is it so hard to let anything go?

Trying to keep my eyes closed

Should it be closed?

Trying to keep it just like before

Before, before, I can see before (painter/chef)

The times we never even got to speak

The time before you know it's going to work out with someone—

Don't wanna tell you what it is

Then when you know when it's not going to work out, no matter how much you want it.

Do you even know what that 1 thing is?

I'm here to argue that we don't. We just come up with reasons after—

Ooh-wee, it felt so serious

These things are serious! Even dancing alone is serious, because dancing is serious joy—

Got me thinking just too much

What is writing, but a different way of thinking?

They, we, are all of us married now. One to a psychiatrist, one I don't know.

Na-na-na-na-na, oh (ah-ah).

I am writing this essay about a song, about how there was some joy in dancing even when lonely.

More than writing a book, but if you are dancing while writing a book—

Hear voices I don't wanna understand

Here I am talking about some thing

My car keys are jingling in my hand

Here I am telling you a story about two painters and a story collection

My high heels are clicking towards your door

And a tennis coach. It wasn't a door, the way out is always on the dance floor, dancing, or toward a window, your eyes looking up

It's this one thing that got me trippin' (you did)

This one thing and I was so with it

Dancing with myself on a January night, not knowing what comes next, not knowing what the 1 thing was til I became the 1 thing—

Trying to keep it just like before

There is no going back, but there's always dancing, let me say that's one thing that won't forsake you.

Dancing is the secret house, is the way to write your secret book, is the way to make it real.

ON THE ESSAY:

This is from an email (March 9th, 2024) I wrote to Ander, the day Amerie and "1 Thing" and I beat Outkast's "Hey Ya!" in our first round, 492 to 488. Four points! I couldn't believe it. (Amerie and I went on to win the championship and the championship ring!)

> I've read essays and sometimes voted in the past [March Xnesses], but didn't even really know what a bracket was or how to fill one out. It's been a pretty depressive time for me of late and just reading all these essays and listening to these songs has brought me some serious joy and out of a serious depression…My goal was just to not get creamed like 10 to 5,000, which is how I thought it might go down (or, you know, 10 to 250)...so this was an absolute delight. I even texted my cousins in California this morning and asked them to vote. They are not writers. I hesitated, thinking how do I explain this tournament?
>
> Thank you again for making up such a fun game. I had forgotten how much fun it is to *play*. That's a joy right there, too.

"KE$HA DOES NOT EXIST":

J. Nicholas Geist on "TiK ToK" by Ke$ha

> *"Wo-oh-oh-oh-oh-oh,*
> *There's a party at a rich dude's house;*
> *Dananana nuh nuh nuh nuh DA NA NA NUH NUH*
> ...
> *I threw up in the closet."*
> —Ke$ha, 2009

> *"If you asked me then where I wanted to be,*
> *It'd look somethin' like this, livin' out of my wildest dreams*
> ...
> *But if you ask me now, all I've wanted to be is happy."*
> —Kesha, 2023

It is 2010, and Kesha does not exist.

Ke$ha does, of course. In fact, it feels a bit like Ke$ha is all there is. She dropped "TiK ToK" at the end of 2009, and by the end of 2010, it will become the best-selling single worldwide. And it is a song *about Ke$ha.* In her first single, she tells us exactly who she is: a woman who wakes up in a place she has no plans to return to, who brushes her teeth with Jack Daniels, who drifts from party to party and boy to boy with a clearly defined—but also seemingly quite generous—boundary as to exactly how gropey a guy is allowed to get before she takes offense.

That this is who Ke$ha *is* seems unquestioned, here in 2010. She sits down for an interview with *Billboard,* and the interview is called "Ke$ha: The Billboard Cover Story." Describing the woman he sees on the red carpet at the 2010 Grammys, Bill Werde explains,

"Everything in her body language, expression, and posture perfectly

> conveys one thought: 'I'm not sure, but I may still be drunk.' It's not so different from the look on her face when she climbs out of the bathtub in the video for her breakthrough song 'TiK ToK.'"

The woman on the red carpet, the woman in the bathtub: they are the same; they are Ke$ha.

*

It is 2024, and I am researching for this essay, and so for the moment, Ke$ha is all there is.

My wife, Megan, and I are getting ready for work. Somewhere in the house our two children are wreaking unknowable havoc, but we allow that to remain undiscovered until we both have pants on.

"There's a track on *Animal*," I say, "where she rhymes the words 'pimps,' 'Trans Am,' and 'handbag.'"

"Those words don't rhyme," Megan says.

"I didn't think so either, but I'm not from Nashville."

Megan leans toward the mirror, checking her lipstick. She doesn't seem as interested in this as I feel she should be.

Because in a way, this *is* Ke$ha: an entity who would see a need to rhyme "pimps," "Trans Am," and "handbag," and who would even arguably succeed. *Animal* is fascinating to listen to because it simply cannot be separated from Ke$ha.

On paper, it seems like it *should* be possible to separate this particular art from this particular artist. Dr. Luke, Ke$ha's producer, was perhaps *the* bona fide hitmaker of the late aughts and early teens, and he cultivated a fairly deep roster of female pop stars. One might imagine, with a producer like that, which track goes to which artist might be at least a little bit arbitrary. And when I listen to "Your Love Is My Drug," the first track on *Animal*, it is for a moment very easy to swap out Ke$ha for, say, Kelly Clarkson. I can imagine Katy Perry singing "what you've got boy / is hard to find / I think about it / all the time." The same goes for "Kiss N Tell"—I can very easily imagine a circa 2009 Miley Cyrus singing "do I make your heart beat / like an 808 drum."

But I cannot imagine anyone but Ke$ha singing "my steeze is gonna be affected / if I keep it up like a lovesick crackhead." I cannot imagine anyone but Ke$ha singing "before I leave, brush my teeth / with a bottle of Jack." I cannot imagine anyone but Ke$ha singing "I'm down to get faded / I'm not the designated / driver." In order to explain Ke$ha as an entity, one must be able to define both "faded" and "enjambment."

To listen to *Animal* in 2024, knowing the story of the last ten years, is to ask: what *was* Ke$ha? Was the entity Ke$ha a role that the woman Kesha was playing? A performance of an exaggerated self? Was Ke$ha a prison from which Kesha had to escape? Or an *Animal* into which she transformed? If Ke$ha is a construct, who constructed her?

I try again to explain this to Megan: "Later she rhymes 'smashed,' 'cans,' and 'mess,' but it doesn't work as well."

"Hm," she says, as if the ways in which our performance of our identity can come to consume us from within hold no terrors for her whatsoever.

"The hook for that track is 'there's a place in France where the naked ladies dance,'" I tell her.

"There are times," Megan says, "when the distance between two people—who share a life, and a house, and a bed, and a bathroom, and two children, and most of a career—seems so great as to be almost insurmountable."

"It's Henry's favorite song now, so heads up. I told him not to sing it at school."

*

It is 2010, and Kesha does not exist—at least, in the eyes of the media. Ke$ha is trying to tell Bill Werde about Kesha, but Werde doesn't seem particularly interested. Everyone asks if she's a party girl, Ke$ha says. Her answer, and Werde's response, are so disconnected that it is worth reproducing them in full:

> "If you mean 'party girl' like, at a club with a short skirt on with no underwear," Ke$ha says, "then no. I've gotten drunk before but never gotten a DUI. I don't go to clubs. I try not to let my vagina hang out. I don't do drugs, but I think I'm a walking good time and I talk kind of funny, so people think I'm messed up all the time. I'm not."

But Werde does not hear this. "You can see where those people might get their ideas," he says, and barrels into a conclusion he had clearly reached before starting, "The Ke$ha you hear on her songs is the Ke$ha you get in person."

Except.

Except that two paragraphs previously, Werde told a story about the red carpet at the Grammys, where Ke$ha was worried that her complex designer dress was leaving her a little too exposed, and had to have a handler make sure she was covered to her liking.

Except that Ke$ha seems to keep trying to bring the conversation back to her intelligence. She tells Werde that she was in an International Baccalaureate program. He puts it in quotation marks as if she made it up. (Twice.) She tells him that she got a 1500 on her SATs. He tells us that she was on *The Simple Life*. "The point being," she tells him, "I'm not just a little pop moron." He tells us what her burps are like.

Except that despite Werde's foregone conclusion, this is the interview where I first learned that Ke$ha and Kesha were two different people. It is where I first heard Ke$ha trying to introduce the world to Kesha, where I first heard a media voice actively suggest that there was no line between Kesha the woman and Ke$ha the construct, and most powerfully, where I first heard the story of the unsettling alchemy by which Ke$ha was constructed.

I am coming down hard on Bill Werde here, but as I said, in 2010, Ke$ha seems to be all there is. Scan the references list of her Wikipedia page and look at the titles from that time:

- "Ke$ha tells us all kinds of awesome, crazy stuff: 'Have I made out with chicks? Hell yeah.'"
- "Party Animal: Behind Ke$ha's Big Debut."
- "Kesha—from Band Geek to Life of the Party."
- "Pop sensation Ke$ha gutsy, fearless."
- "Kesha and the Not-Quite-72 Virgins in Her Own Personal Heaven."
- "Kesha: Crazy, Sexy, & Too Fuckin' Cool."
- "She's a walking, talking, living dollar."
- "Make it $top."

They don't all include the $, but it's there even when it's not. That Kesha is Ke$ha, that the person and the per$ona are coterminous—in 2010, everyone agrees.

Only Ke$ha seems unsure.

*

It is 2020, and—at least in my car—Ke$ha does not exist.

My daughter, Violet, is an incredible force of will. When she wants something, she will not be impeded. If, in her toddlerhood, she decides a pair of pants are itchy—which she does on nearly a daily basis—the pants are gone. There will be no compromises about her outfit and no quarter granted to any parent so foolish as to try to reason with her. If she must crack the Earth to its very core and cast us all into the roiling mantle, so be it.

ITCHY.

But that is later. For now, it is 2020, Violet is six months old, and for her, Ke$ha does not exist. We are in the car, and she does not want to be in the car, and so, in a polyphonic train-whistle scream jazz singers sometimes spend a lifetime learning, she wordlessly bellows her infant misery.

Megan reaches into the backseat and grabs Violet's hand. Her brother, Henry, has headphones on, but absently pats her on her screaming head.

"You're okay, Violey," I say. It's strange: we've never really called Henry anything but Henry, but Violet became Violey—which looks a lot weirder written out than it sounds when I say it—almost at birth.

"It's okay," I say, but it is not okay. There is only one path to calm for my cacophonic daughter.

We must play "Flik Flok."

"Flik Flok" is not a toddler's mispronunciation of "TiK ToK," but rather a mashup of the beat from "TiK ToK" and the vocals from Dizzee Rascal's 2007 track "Flex" which, unless you are an aficionado of the mid aughties UK garage scene, you have not heard.

I have heard it, though. Thousands of times, I would imagine. On the drives across the desperately boring country between my house and my in-laws, Violet wails endlessly and unignorably until the last fiber of our resolve snaps and we put on "Flik Flok," and she finally settles—only and exactly as long as "Flik Flok" plays, over and over, for hours and miles and an endless eternity of identical highway.

For whatever reason, "TiK ToK" on its own does not work for Violet. We try playing the original, but the instant she hears Ke$ha wake up in the morning feeling like P. Diddy, Violet makes her disappointment known to us at impossible volumes. Nevertheless, the backbeat of her infancy is the boxy synths and relentless bass of "TiK ToK," looped and pounding and always. Ke$ha simply does not exist.

*

"Flik Flok" was created by the Kleptones, also known as DJ Erik Kleptone, the mad scientist (and singular plural) of the illegal music scene. Their special genius is their ability to put things in conversation with one another, and "Flik Flok" is, to my mind, among the greatest of their dialectics. We know, I hope, what "TiK ToK" is, but Dizzee Rascal's "Flex" is its own fascinating contradiction.

"Flex" is a sort of horny ekphrasis: Rascal spends three and a half minutes celebrating the details of a woman dancing. He praises her timing, the way she controls her body. "Pure skill," he says. He pauses to appreciate the movement of a drop of sweat. He catalogs her moves: the bogle, the butterfly. Drop it like it's hot. Dip. Rock. Grind. Flex. "Your figure," he says, "is so pleasing to the eye."

And yet, woven in among the aesthete's paean, Rascal makes sure to tell us he has a boner. "Got my tings rising," he says, with only minor abashment. "What do you expect, that ain't surprising." Rascal's appreciation is artistic, but it is also clearly *visceral.* It is about *bodies.* The wiggling. The jiggling. My heartbeat. My temperature. My blood pressure. "You could kill like that," he tells her.

"Gosh," he says, "you make a rude boy so shy."

It is this dualism that makes "Flex" such a good fit for "TiK ToK." Rascal and Ke$ha are both attempting to live out the same superposition of states. They are club kids and they are not club kids. They are animalistic and they are academic. They are themselves and they are not themselves. Even the names—Dizzee Rascal, as you might imagine, is not the name on his library card, and in "Flex" he briefly refers to himself as "Dills," a portmanteau of his "real" name, Dylan Mills. They create a space in the sweaty melee of the dance floor where they unquestionably belong, and yet keep themselves distant. It is easy, listening to "Flik Flok," to imagine a sort of astral Dylan Mills and Kesha Sebert standing in the steamy haze above the crowd, watching Dizzee and Ke$ha dance.

This is why "Flik Flok" is so good: the braiding of these two artists, each of whom are already twinning with themselves, creates a helix of connection that is as meaningful thematically as it is musically.

Also, it fucking slaps.

*

It is 2005, and Ke$ha does not exist.

There is a 17-year-old girl in Nashville with a single mom who knows some folks in the music industry. Her name is Kesha, but be careful: most of what we know about her—about how she snuck into Prince's house to give him a demo, for instance—comes from stories Ke$ha will tell later. She thinks she might go to Barnard. She is studying the Cold War. Sometimes, her mom brings her along to the studio, and she records something, not really expecting anything to come of it.

One of those demos winds its way into the hands of Łukasz Gottwald, better known as Dr. Luke, who is well on his way to becoming a god of pop music production (the power of Dr. Luke: when the time comes, and she writes the line "Wake up in the mornin feelin like P. Diddy," Dr. Luke will get on the phone, and Diddy himself will *that same day* come to the studio to record a couple of voice lines for the debut single of an absolute unknown).

On that demo, Dr. Luke hears two different people. Years later, he will play these two tracks for Bill Werde, who will write about it for Billboard, and I will learn about the utter fragility of identity. Werde:

> "At Conway Studio where Luke works in Hollywood, he plays me two songs from the Ke$ha demo, each striking for different reasons. The first is a gorgeously sung, self-penned country ballad that hints at what could've been had Ke$ha pursued a different path. The other is a gobsmackingly awful trip-hop track. But at one point toward the end, Ke$ha runs out of lyrics and starts rapping, for a full minute or so: 'I'm a white girl/From the 'Ville/Nashville, bitch. Uhh. Uhhhhh.'"
>
> Luke and his producer friends were smitten by this bit of screwball-gangsta improv. His face lights up even now as he remembers. "That's when I was like, 'OK, I like this girl's personality. When you're listening to 100 CDs, that kind of bravado and chutzpah stand out."

This is how I remember the story—how I think about Kesha, and about Ke$ha: a girl gave a man two versions of herself and asked him, "who do you want me to be?"

*

It is 2023, and Violet is three years old.

She has started giving us concerts at bedtime. Once she has her pajamas on, she will go into the playroom and fish out an old toy guitar that I have had for 25 years, and she will bring it to the living room. She will ask us to put on Train's "Drops of Jupiter" and she will stand in the center of the room, strumming the guitar, and singing the lyrics, which she almost knows. It is always "Drops of Jupiter." There are other songs that she loves—"Flik Flok" still among them, and now that she has the more developed palate of a toddler, "TiK ToK" as well—but for the concerts, it is always "Drops of Jupiter."

I watch her dance, graceful and proud, and I think about "Drops of Jupiter," and Violet, and Kesha. "Drops of Jupiter" is a song about a woman who leaves, drifting unmoored from earthbound stability, to try to find herself (the song is best if you imagine it is about Elizabeth Gilbert circa *Eat, Pray, Love*). The speaker asks this woman about her travels: whether she found what she sought, whether she escaped being scarred, whether she flew, Icarine, too close to the sun, and what it cost her to do so. And because it is a song that is written and sung by a man, the speaker of the song feels that the woman owes him answers to all these questions, and that the most important question among them is *did you miss me*, despite the fact that he estimates his own value as a human being as approximately equivalent to that of a really good soy latte.

Violet's little voice sings out an approximation of this story, this man who feels he has a right to tell a woman who to be, and then we say prayers, brush teeth, and settle in the rocker in her bedroom.

This week, she has been playing with nicknames—among other peculiar experiments, she is trying to get Megan to call me "Mump," for reasons nobody really understands—and so today, she has had an argument with her brother, who insists always and only on being called Henry. She wants to call him Hens. Personally, I think that is the cutest thing in the whole damn world, but Henry is insistent: his name is Henry.

I sing to her as I rock her, and as I sing I call her Violey.

"I don't want to be called Violey any more," she says.

"You don't? I've called you that your whole life," I say.

"No. Just Violet."

This makes me instantly sad. It feels as if I am losing something, a connection with her I have had since she was born. But, like, what am I, the guy from Train? Should it be up to me to decide who she is? Of course not.

I don't want to let go of "Violey," because Violey is my daughter. But she will spend the rest of her life deciding who she wants to be, and I never want that to be contingent on what anyone else thinks—least of all a man worth little more than a cup of coffee.

So sitting here, holding this tiny blonde dynamo who is already so many women when she is still only barely a big girl, I say, "Okay, Violet," and I let her take one of the million tiny steps she will take in her life away from the image of her I hold in my mind, and toward the person that *she* wants to be.

*

I do not think we can know each other.

I don't just mean that I cannot know Kesha, or Ke$ha, that two people as distant as a pop star and a listener a decade and a half later cannot know each other. I don't just mean that I cannot know Violet, or that the churning storm of mystery at the heart of a three-year-old is beyond the comprehension of my meager dad brain. I do mean those things, but that is not all I mean. I mean you and me. I do not think that any two people can know each other.

Here: can you tell me who you are?

Not "can you tell me things about you." Can you communicate your completeness? Put your entire self into words that I can understand? Can you put your entire self into words that you can understand?

A friend has read this essay, and she keeps saying: *Violet will tell you who she is, you just have to listen.* Kesha, after all, tried *so hard* to tell us who she was, but we could not—or at very least did not—listen to her. But if Bill Werde had listened, had struck the $ from the title of "Kesha: The Billboard Cover Story" and told us without ambiguity that this woman was not the character she was playing, would we have known her?

I am afraid that Ke$ha was born because a man named Łukasz heard a woman sing two songs on a demo, and thought "I can understand this person." And "I can understand her" led to "I understand her," which led to "I know her better than she knows herself," which led to "I know what's best for you," and this is how Ke$ha was made.

I do not know this with certainty. But I do know that Ke$ha was born because Kesha trusted that Dr. Luke knew what was best for her, and Dr. Luke did not deserve that trust.

Listen.

*

It is 2008, and Ke$ha does not exist, but be patient: she is about to be born.

Kesha has signed with Dr. Luke, and he has already told her which of the two girls from her demo he wants to sign: he wants the party girl. Flo Rida is in the studio recording "Right Round" with Dr. Luke. Luke tells Flo that he thinks a female vocalist would round out the mix, and he has just the person.

Kesha comes into the studio, lays down a vocal track, and Flo likes it. Likes it enough, in fact, that he'll use Kesha again on "Touch Me" in 2009.

Here's Dr. Luke, moving his artists like chess pieces. Here's Flo Rida, who's already been in the Top 40 several times. And here's Kesha, young and broke and nameless.

"Right Round" spends six weeks at #1.

Kesha doesn't get a credit. Kesha doesn't get a dime.

"I was so broke and on the No. 1 song and it was being played everywhere all the time," she tells *Vibe.* I imagine her working a register somewhere, hearing her own voice over the store sound system, and watching someone use her tip jar to break a $5. Kesha changes her name to Ke$ha. "Just kinda making fun of myself," she says.

*

Here is my question, the question of the father of a daughter who is so strong, so sure of herself, so unstoppable, but who is nevertheless only three, and who will someday be 17, and 21, and 27, and who will enter a world where women do not always get to decide who they are, or who they will be; the question of a father who has never been a woman, and who somehow has to help this small fireball decide who she is going to be when she is 17, and 21, and 27, and being pushed against by men who have their own ideas about who she should be; the question of a father who will, inescapably, *be one of those men*; here is my question:

how do I help her decide who she is?

*

Not long after "Right Round" topped the charts, Ke$ha would release "TiK ToK," which would spend *nine* weeks at number one—half again as long as

"Right Round," thank you very much—under her own name. Ke$ha would become what Ke$ha became, and Kesha would fade, and Dr. Luke would help her launch not one but *three* #1 singles—which, incidentally, is the same number Flo Rida has. The version of Kesha Rose Sebert that Dr. Luke chose was incredibly successful, even if he kinda ripped her off with "Right Round."

Except.

Except the thing I have not yet said: ripping her off is not the worst thing Dr. Luke ever did to Kesha.

In 2014, she filed a series of lawsuits against Dr. Luke, accusing him of "sexual assault and battery, sexual harassment, gender violence, civil harassment, violation of California's unfair business laws, intentional infliction of emotional distress, negligent infliction of emotional distress, and negligent retention and supervision." She said he drugged her, raped her, and caused her eating disorder, among other things.

The lawsuits were not settled until 2023, but they were settled—nine years after they were filed, but only a month after Kesha released *Gag Order*, her last contractually mandated album on Dr. Luke's label, Kemosabe. I do not and cannot know what happened—about Kesha's allegations, about the settlement, or about any of this. I am just another man trying to say who Kesha is, and was, and speculating about the shape of her authentic self, and how well it fit the container that was Ke$ha, and who built that container, and if she chose to get into it or if she was put into it by Dr. Luke, and I do not and cannot know *any* of that.

But I have listened to "Praying," and it seems obvious to me that it was written by a woman who was deeply, profoundly hurt, who is healing, and who is trying to forgive someone who has done her incredible harm. And, while this is perhaps an unusual standard of evidence, I know that at time of writing the Wikipedia page for "Praying" features a picture of Dr. Luke next to the words "fuck you."

I do not know Kesha, and I do not know Ke$ha. I do not know Łukasz Gottwald, and I do not know Dr. Luke. I do not know Dylan Mills, and I do not know Dizzee Rascal. I do not know Eric Kleptone, and I do not know the person who bears the name on Eric Kleptone's birth certificate (although I do have a pretty high degree of confidence that that name is not "Eric Kleptone").

What I know are the stories that are told about them, the stories that they tell about themselves, and the story I piece together from those stories.

*

It is 2024, and the Kesha/Ke$ha superposition fills my car. She hasn't used the $ for nearly a decade now, and Apple Music knows this. They have dutifully removed it from the artist name in her metadata. But the album art cannot be so easily changed, and so it is that Kesha and Ke$ha both ride with us as I take the kids to school.

We pull into Henry's school, listening to "Take It Off" for the third time. We both get out, and I sign him in, give him a kiss and send him on his way. When I turn back to the car, Violet is gesturing frantically at me from the backseat.

"Henry," I holler, "did you forget to kiss your sister?" One of Violet's many insistences: if she does not get the affection she believes she is due, there will be *problems*. He runs back to the car, climbs into the backseat, and is instantly rebuffed.

"She doesn't want a kiss," Henry says. "She wants you to pick her a flower."

So, of course, I do. The school garden butts up to the parking lot, and some of the marigolds they have planted to keep bugs away have grown through the fence. I pluck the prettiest bloom from among those scraggly stems, and I hand it to Violet as I get back in the car.

"You got me an orange one?!" she says, and it is unclear to me if this is surprise, delight, or disapproval. By now, "Take It Off" has given way to "Kiss N Tell," which is not Violet's favorite.

"Not this," she says. "Something else." I push the previous track button twice.

"Wake up in the mornin," Ke$ha says, "feelin' like P. Diddy."

In the backseat, Violet slowly, deliberately, raises her hands in triumph. "TiK ToK," she says quietly.

She has grown and changed in the last three years, and has come to love "TiK ToK" as much as, if not more than, "Flik Flok." Because she is a person, she is new and different every day; tomorrow, she will respond to the same song with "NOT TIK TOK, I DON'T WANT TIK TOK." Today, though, "TiK ToK" merits this small celebration.

We arrive at her school, and I unbuckle her seatbelt, and she takes her flower and tucks it into the cupholder in the backseat. "I don't want to tell anyone about my flower," she says. "I'm going to leave it in the car."

*

It is 2041, and Violet is 21 years old. She is in college in Montana, and she texts me during her boring night classes to make fun of her professors, but I do not know her.

Or it is 2041, and Violet is 21 years old. She calls me on her commute from San Francisco to Manteca, to tell me about how Galinda is leaving the production of *Wicked* she's been understudying, and how she's pretty sure she's going to get to move up, and she's so excited and I am so excited for her, but I do not know her.

Or it is 2041, and Violet is 21 years old. She collapses onto my bed in tears because of a fight she had with her partner about something her partner's cousin said about her brother, and I have no idea what she is talking about, but she is so upset, and so with one hand I rub her back while she cries, and with the other I text Megan to see if she can make sense out of any of this, and she says she cannot, so we agree to sit down later and make a flowchart or something, and I ask Violet if she wants to get some air, and we sit on the front porch in the dark and the fog and the cold and she leans against my chest and I remember when she was three and she would sit on my lap and play with my earlobe until she fell asleep, and she says "Dad can we go inside? It's fucking freezing," and I start to say something but don't because I know that she's old enough to use grown-up words now, and we go in and she goes to bed, and when I come to check on her later she is asleep with a book in her hand, and I remember all the nights before she could even read when she couldn't fall asleep unless there were at least a dozen books in her bed, and I love her every bit as much as I did then, but I do not know her.

It is 2024, and Violet is three years old, and I know Violet as well as it is possible to know a three-year-old, but I suspect that is not very well. She is miserably sick, and she is hungry, and she is so, *so* mad, because her mother and I have made her peanut butter sandwich, but she wants us to cut it like a clock, and I have tried to cut it like a clock but it is *wrong, no, that is not like a clock, NOT A CLOCK, I want it like a clock*, so Megan tries, *no, Josh, it's not a circle, a clock is a circle*, and she cuts a circle, and Violet becomes incensed, *NO NO NO NOT LIKE A CIRCLE LIKE A CLOCK CUT IT LIKE A CLOCK*, and she shoves the sandwich across the table, and Megan asks *ok, honey, I'm sorry, we're trying, would you like daddy to make you a new sandwich and cut it like a clock?* and Violet sniffles, pitiful, exhausted, feverish, and says *uh huh*, and so I make a second sandwich, and I take it to the table with the knife, and I let her direct me cut by cut, *do you want me to cut it like this? and then here? like this? okay?* and step by step I cut the sandwich, first vertical, then horizontal, across the diagonals, until it is divided into eighths like pie slices, and she sniffs and says *see, daddy, like a clock*, and I say *I see, honey*, because this is exactly how I cut the first sandwich twenty minutes ago, but she is three years old, and I *do not know her*.

All of these Violets exist in my imagination. Even the one I dropped off at school this morning, who made me sit in the parking lot until we got to the end of "TiK ToK." I have been with her since the instant she entered this world, and I will share with her every moment she will let me (although for transparency I must disclose that at this particular moment she has been sent to bed early because she threw a book at me for unclear reasons). But still, I cannot hold her completeness in my mind—even now, when her completeness is not quite tall enough to ride Jumping Jellyfish at Disneyland.

I can hold her in my heart, though. Not perfectly, but completely. There's room in there for all the people she might ever decide to be.

*

"Bring it back," Dizzee Rascal says at the end of "Flik Flok." "Bring it back."

*

It is 2014, and Ke$ha does not exist. Kesha is 27 years old. She has just left rehab for her eating disorder, and she decides that she is done with the front. "I let go of my facade about being a girl who didn't care," she'll explain at SXSW next week. "My facade was to be strong," she'll say, "and I realized it was total bullshit. I took out the $ because I realized that was part of the facade."

But that is next week. Today, she is getting off a plane at LAX.

She is wearing a sweatshirt that says "IMA SURVIVOR," and she looks so unfathomably *young*. If you told me she was 17 and not 27 in this picture I would believe it without question. There is something about this young woman, who is deciding so intentionally who she wants to be, who is deciding to leave Ke$ha behind and to become again the person she was ten years ago, someone I do not know and someone she might not know that well any more either, that I cannot help but love a little tiny distant bit.

I do not know her, and I have no right to feel any kind of way about her, and she is not 17 or 27 but almost my own age, but none of that matters to my dad heart. I cannot help it. I am so, *so* proud of her.

*

It is 2023, and Ke$ha does not exist. Kesha still performs "TiK ToK," though, because why wouldn't she? It is today what it has always been: an absolute banger. Two days ago, though, singer Cassie Ventura filed a suit against Diddy alleging that their musical partnership was fraught with years of abuse, emotional manipulation, controlling behavior, and even rape. It is not hard to understand why Kesha would take this very seriously.

The Ke$ha of "TiK ToK" is eternally 21, one boot on the floor of a stranger's bathroom, emerging half drunk from the tub like a scrungly Venus, cheap jewelry on her wrists and a cockeyed trucker hat on her soul. The first thing the Ke$ha of "TiK ToK" tells us about herself is that she wakes up in the morning feeling like P. Diddy. And why not? The Ke$ha of "TiK ToK," after all, doesn't mind a little light groping. But it is 2023, and Ke$ha does not exist. She has been gone for a long time now.

Kesha must have decided the instant she heard: tonight, she will not say his name.

The synths haven't changed, boxy and wobbly at the same time. The bass is no different, round and rough and boneshaking. But this is not the same woman.

"Wake up in the morning," she sings, "feeling just like me."

ON THE ESSAY:

Everything I learned in researching this essay has made me appreciate and admire Kesha more than I would have guessed at the start. Go listen to her new stuff; it's actually *hers*. She has her own label now. She changed the opening to "TiK ToK" again, this time permanently. Now she sings, "Wake up in the morning like FUCK P. DIDDY."

My anxiety that Violet would be overly concerned with my opinion of who she should be has, happily, proved unfounded. This morning, she couldn't decide what to wear in her hair: a classic black headband, a bright blue headband with an enormous bow, or a glittery gold bowler fascinator with a yellow feather that the Notre Dame leprechaun might wear to the MET Gala. I told her to choose one. She wore all three to school.

NEW YEAR'S EVE, 2009:

Raquel Gutiérrez on "Blind" by Hercules & Love Affair

As a child, I knew
That the stars could only get brighter
That we would get closer
Leaving this darkness behind

2008 was a year that felt over the day it began. Celebrating its end with a party, in hindsight, was an empty gesture. It was the third year you worked at a Southern California university as a mid-tier departmental administrator. By the end of that fall semester you were told the position you had ruefully assumed to be secure had to be whittled down to 17 hours a week. It was devastating but you still had your benefits which made it easy to stay and weather whatever storm lay ahead.

At least you had seen Anohni and the Johnsons' god-tier concert at the Walt Disney Hall back in October of that year. It left you and the rest of the audience that night astonished. What had you witnessed? You hoped to be greeted by Anohni's voice, accompanied by a 20-piece orchestra, whenever you finally left this earthly plane. Hers was probably the closest to a siren call you would ever experience, and you would gladly swim away from shore towards it. Her cover of Beyoncé's "Crazy In Love" was spiritual sustenance. And you needed that. You weren't sure what was coming next but whatever happens you have this feeling, like protection, following you wherever you go.

You got through the holidays dissociating as per your typical yearly script. Your person at the time had marked NYE on the kitchen calendar for your return from her family holiday gathering in the Central Coast of California. There was a new queer club waving its flag and the new year would prompt its inaugural party. It was in a neighborhood on the other side of the river from LA's Chinatown. It was at a rehabbed warehouse and the floors were polished concrete. All these details you note because rent is going up and your paycheck is reducing thanks to the housing crash and you wonder how people are affording their new art centers in the making, even if it *is* a good time for art. You couldn't see where the money was coming from but it was making a dent in Queer Los Angeles. *Did academia really pay that well?* You kept all of your wondering close to your chest, like you did in grad seminar. Ideas are always too scared, too skittish to leap from the diving board of your mind, to exit through your mouth. God forbid you said the wrong thing.

It was an era when drag kings had exited the cultural arena and audiences were finally emboldened to normalize their respective gender performances. Butches and studs were finally clearing their throats. You could now wear thrifted Brooks Brothers madras shirts and shaved-in parts in public now, out of the club and into the classroom. As if a goth phase never existed. As if gender liberation meant we could now be boring bros and it was perfectly acceptable. Maybe even welcomed. It was a moment that coincided with everyone you knew suddenly wanting to go to grad school and be a professor in a big metropole somewhere. And here. In Los Angeles.

And you don't begrudge anyone for carrying those ambitions. Performance art in Los Angeles was a hot commodity—er, rather, a radical site of inquiry. And it has always been a site of innovation thanks to underground institutions like Highways Performance Space in Santa Monica and Los Angeles Contemporary Exhibitions in Hollywood. Places you had been involved with, paid to organize and visit with care.

But there was something about the current economic crisis that invited artists in your respective creative ecosystem to think more thoroughly about its radical possibility. Performance had slowly but surely begun to lure its interdisciplinary brethren to the City of Angels from the East Coast. You had been back from New York for a few years now, having completed an expensive Master Of Art degree in Performance Studies, but somehow didn't get the Wonka golden ticket to do the PhD program. No bueno because you had amassed quite a bit of debt trying to keep up with your large cohort cavorting around the West Village and then the East Village watching late night performances at La Mama and drinking through the Avenues, ending up at either The Cock or The Hole, walking home several times a week between 4 and 5 a.m. You wince at the thought of having to pay your loans back so soon. Your advisor urged you to stay in New York another year and try again for a coveted spot. Instead, you took your covetousness (and boy, did you have plenty to spare) back to Los Angeles, missing its sprawl, its sunshine and the default familiarity you had automatically in place. You couldn't see yourself in New York anymore. You rejected the reinvention of self everyone who went to New York longed for because you were tired of being challenged by a catalog of critical theory that would take years to read, let alone understand. And to do so without any real fiscal support made the endeavor that much more untenable. The stack of books stared at you from across the thumbnail living room in the Prospect Heights 2-bedroom you shared with another roommate, a wonderful Hondureña raised in the Bronx who took you under her wing (and to her family parties) when you first arrived to New York in the summer of 2003.

You were competing with graduates from the Ivy League and loving language wasn't enough to power you through anymore. Foucault. Derrida. Weber. Butler. *This shit was hard, man.* You thought you could handle "hard." You liked Los Crudos. And Ornette. And Alice Coltrane. And Vaginal Davis. But your vinyl collection and pre-Pauline Oliveros deep listening hadn't prepared you for grad school as well as you had hoped. No one had prepared you. And you couldn't see how it was all connected.

This was back before trigger warnings and questions about why you used the D-word became a thing. This was back in an era where our generation reclaimed slurs and repackaged them as the language of radical reclamation. You wore your KICK ME signs proudly.

This was also a moment when sapiosexuality was enacted so openly, and thus the cruising was essentially a hodgepodge of academic ranks moving in and out of the dating circle like the hokey-pokey of advanced degrees. And being in the humanities meant having to wade in this strange soup of big brained eros. It was an orgy of nerd sex. And you knew this because it was also the late dawn of social media so everyone used MySpace as a clarion call for sex and to broadcast their predilections for theory. We all tailored our DIY HTML to signal our attractions for radical affinities, for object fetishists. You had such a boner for obsolescence. Didn't we all? Your MySpace background was a scrolling landscape of dead cassette tapes in a range of colors.

You went out a lot in your early 30s, more than any other time. More than you did as a high schooler lucky enough to encounter a few all-ages clubs where many of our favorite bands would come through Los Angeles to play.

Going out feels like an artifact from an analog past. As a younger person, all ages meant paying $5 for a show at Jabberjaw. That was the spot, on

Pico Boulevard near Crenshaw. It's where you picked up a caffeine habit. Back when lattes were served in beer mugs. Back when gas was $1 a gallon. In *Los Angeles.* It's true. It was once possible to traverse the canyons and concrete rivers on another five dollars a week. The Clinton era. *Reality Bites*. And the Los Angeles Riots. We were all living high, even those of us not riding the hog. Going out feels like an artifact because back then you did it to find expressions of ideas that resonated with your curiosities and desires for a bigger world.

But then sex became a thing and no one told you about it but you knew you had to experience it. You burn down the closet, a feat in 1994. There was no going back. Your 20s were spent chasing dead ends at the club. You searched for ways to express desire. Everyone there knew that you were there to hook up, and that wasn't so bad because no one had broadcasted their thoughts about your methods the way they do now on their little self-reporting surveillance machines. These places were frequented by mostly gay men and a smattering of lesbians anyway. What harm could they do? This was back when you kept your sneering out of earshot. The usual *ooonce-ooonce* bouncing off the walls and into your innards. The bass was thick for an era where lesbians felt nothing for house music. Not to suggest queer historical revision—there *were* plenty of lesbian clubs, if one knew where and how to look. Or rather, there weren't. Not really—because you weren't looking. The concentration of lesbian clubs were in West Hollywood and they were okay. Just club remixes of whatever was popular. A soulless Top 40 and Lauryn Hill's "That Thing" on a loop. It kept your sad excuse for desire at a 11% color saturation. It was fine.

A graduate degree in Performance Studies obviously helped you see quickly why and how you had been doing nightlife all wrong. And when the economy crashed just as you settled into your work routine, going out was the only thing that helped. Job insecurity gave way to a YOLO mindset that you're still paying for today. And all because you didn't know how to want what you wanted, or how to name an economic desire. How could you know how to inhabit economic stability as a young, queer, transmasculine butch dyke? How (and from whom) would you learn to wear down the brick wall of capitalism, one oily fingerprint at a time?

And you tried to bid farewell to 2008, but it should have been an exorcism. And the queer gentry's art center's New Year's Eve party was awash with lighting that would one day be known as bisexual lighting. And you drank too much when you definitely shouldn't have, but it would be years before you realized that your inhibitions would save your life. And in those years many lives couldn't be saved. People with more resources than you took their own lives because the economy tanking shattered everyone's dreams and delusions. But before the inhibitions took the wheel, before you could see their rightful purpose, there were the DJs that saved your life on the regular. And that night, that last night of 2008, a DJ played your life and the bouncy, untroubled opening beats of Hercules and Love Affair's "Blind" began and you rushed as coolly as you could to the dancefloor. And sure, you still had to share that space with those who were rightly composing their own *Le Grain De La Voix* essays in their heads as they, too, surrendered to the ethereal allure of Anohni's voice, interfering with any shred of ability to dance on beat. But not you. You sure as shit never wrote essays in 2008.

ON THE ESSAY:

I generally jump for joy when my number comes up in the March Xness lottery. And more so when the songs that are authentically meaningful to me are last to be chosen. That is typically the indicator of my niche tastes. Oh well, more for me. I know I will never win my bracket because generally it feels like the popular song always wins. And that's fine by me. However, I am always just grateful for the chance to ruminate in public on the poignant outcomes and miserable consequences in the life of my younger self scored by the songs in question. I chose this song because Anohni's voice was the salve my soul needed during a harsh post-2008 economic hangover. And the beat helped me forget my broke butch blues. The extended mix was the rip in the time-space continuum I didn't know I needed.

SONG FOR THE LONELY

Drew Krewer on "Song for the Lonely" by Cher

A few short weeks after leaving rural Georgia to start college in New York City, I looked out a window on the fourteenth story of my dorm to watch the Towers collapse a mile away. My eighteen-year-old brain tried to explain away the danger, that fires would be extinguished, that a city as big as New York had an infrastructure in place to take care of this before the nightly news would air. Seeing the first tower collapse quickly changed the way my brain felt and completely silenced my thoughts. It was an experience that I would later come to characterize as "numinous."

Rudolf Otto, a German Lutheran theologian, posited that all great religions are an attempt to experience the "numinous." This concept forever changed the way I would view religion and has woven its lessons throughout my life. If we are to simplify things, the numinous is said to be "wholly other," something not experienced in ordinary life, something beyond ourselves, beyond language. It is experienced as a stupor, an overwhelming power, a terror that illuminates how nothing we are. But even for all its horror and bluster, it is merciful, gracious, alluring.

As the glass buckled on top of glass and sparkled in the sun, as the sparkle gave way to smoke, as the force of the fallout had no defined trajectory, I was caught in a moment of not knowing if I was in immediate danger, but I couldn't look away. My body and consciousness were suspended somewhere between panic and mercy.

*

When you are a rural, teenage queer, with self-hatred of the femme, with no sense of fashion, with no context for your desirability, trust the city gays to guide the way. The small group of quick friends I had made were comprised of theater queers, and they were incredibly welcoming, even though most of my clothes came from a now-defunct chain of Southern department stores, appropriately called Gayfers.

"If you don't have your first kiss from a man by the time this year is over, we will line up and each of us will kiss you."

Me, later that night: upstairs at the Limelight, necking some blond dude who looked vaguely like an *XY*-model, candy kid, probably on ecstasy?

*

Seeing a community face an event like the Towers in real-time was a striking lesson on how trauma is processed in wildly different ways. I saw dorm-mates and orientation buddies shift their behavior in a matter of hours. A photographer acquaintance asked me to follow her to document the evening of the 11th. She talked for hours about giving blood. Things took an uncomfortable turn when we entered a bar and she started jabbering at a rescue worker, who was buried in a drink. He had left his station out of self-preservation, and he kept crying and expressing that he just couldn't do the work. My acquaintance asked him if she could take his photo. He was processing at the bar, she was roaming feverishly with a camera, and I was numb.

*

Shortly after the first dude kiss, I faded away into school work, leaving new queer friends behind, and attempting at all hours to avoid my roommate, who was evidence campus life roommate questionnaires often turn into failures of self-reporting. Any conversation became an act of emotional labor, and I turned to online journaling as a cheap (and satisfying) alternative to therapy. I spent most of my time in the library basement, a jungle of public computers and study cubicles. I often slept on the floor. I only stopped by my room to shower, change clothes, and occasionally sleep.

Late at night in the library basement, an older woman would appear, slightly disheveled, almost ghostly, but with the spirit of an academic. She was there most nights, sitting at a large table, mumbling to herself and either reading or staring at the *New York Times*. The building had security, and entry was restricted to those with university ID. Seeing her there frequently made me wonder if she saw me as a regular basement-dweller and called into question the decisions I was making for myself.

*

As my life shifted to being documented online, and as I was stranded in Georgia over the holiday break, I discovered the now defunct Gay.com, complete with chat rooms and dating profiles. I was taught early on to explore quick fixes first, so it seemed natural to deal with the rural fairytale of my undesirability by flirting carelessly with strangers in a huge city, where both my successes and failures would remain secret.

One of the first guys I dated came in second place to Leonardo DiCaprio for the lead role in *The Basketball Diaries* and he gave me a hard cover copy of *The Prophet* on our first date. We also ended up sitting behind Kurt Loder, eating popcorn, while watching *In the Bedroom*, starring Sissy Spacek—which turned out to be one of the most depressing movies I've ever seen to this day; totally inappropriate for an early date. He was maybe 33, and I was 18, and he was extremely shaken after the movie; it was hard for him to speak. My distance from the emotional component of the film left me questioning my own responses (or lack-thereof)—is this my disposition, a result of PTSD, or the miracle of antidepressants?

*

That winter I emerged from the library basement, studying an appropriate amount, and filling my life with strangers. Kurfew, an 18+ club night coining itself as "America's Largest Young Gay Dance Party," had recently relocated to a bar in Chelsea; when one of my orientation queers canceled on me one Friday, I decided to go by myself, which became a frequent occurrence.

Over the loud soundscapes of Jonathan Peters remixes and dimmed lighting, I saw a man approaching me. Definitely a bad-boy vibe—a cross between Hot Topic and the Snow Queen, someone I might have seen in a young gay magazine at the time. He called me beautiful and asked me intellectual questions and stuck his tongue down my throat. He was an intern at MTV, so he gave me swag, burned me Belle and Sebastian CDs, and told me that I needed new clothes.

I became his three-week Eliza Doolittle, and with very little money at the time, I was guided through buying some of the nicest jeans and shoes I had ever owned. He took me thrifting along St. Mark's Place to find fitted vintage shirts. He taught me how to appropriately use lime and salt for a tequila shot, and he culture-jammed me with queer favorites like *Grey Gardens*. He was 21 and obsessively called himself (and anyone over 20) "old," and he lived in an empty condo his father owned on the Upper East Side, which meant nothing to me at the time. He was an asshole, treated people like napkins, and consistently had the worst breath I've ever smelled in my life. But for a brief moment, he thought I was attractive, and collecting brief moments seemed to be where I was at.

*

For extra money, I signed up to participate in a psychological study that asked students within a certain radius of Ground Zero to read statements and to rate their emotional response on a Likert scale. It offered quite a bit of cash, as it involved an initial in-person session and subsequent phone calls spaced out over the year. Filling out the inventories was challenging, and emotionally distressing, as I often found it difficult to measure how I felt. Was I supposed to be anxious about the future? Do I not care? Should I be ashamed of riding the serotonin wave of eliciting desire while others are struggling?

*

Even with the light drizzle that March evening, the air continued to have an ongoing odd metallic quality. I was holding an umbrella and waiting for a DJ acquaintance of mine to pick me up in a taxi to head to the Roxy—he had heard that Cher was going to perform, and I was fresh off the MTV intern. I was in front of my dorm, donning one of my "outfits," when I saw a man in the distance walking from the park across the street, through the slow traffic, to ask me if he could stand under my umbrella for a moment.

The volume of traffic was heavy enough—anything was very visible—so, I hesitantly obliged.

"You looking for some money tonight?" he whispered.

It took me a few Georgia moments to get this.

"I think you have the wrong idea."

He nodded, turned around, and left the umbrella's cover to weave his way slowly back through traffic, into the darkness of the park.

The Roxy was overheated and uncomfortably packed, and my earlier encounter had left me uneasy and throwing retinal caution to the wind, staring directly into the club lighting for long stretches of time.

At the Roxy, at Kurfew, at Twirl, it was almost guaranteed that the final song of the night was going to be Cher's "Song for the Lonely," with some of its final lyrics of the evening loudly insisting over and over that things would be alright. Being surrounded by community, by lights, by Cher—a warm queer cocoon—enriches, supports, distracts. When we encounter something that is larger than ourselves, we can't fight our experience, but we can be careful observers. How do we glow in the lights without living in them? How do we teach ourselves to dance through territories of enchantment and nothingness to mastery?

I had hopes Cher was going to perform at least a tiny set of songs, if she performed at all. Showing up near closing time, and singing the one song I knew she would sing, Cher was small and beautiful, blocked by the crowd.

ON THE ESSAY:

I initially chose "Song for the Lonely" because Cher is always correct. As I watched the music video, and its images of NYC being rebuilt, I remembered how important the song was for me during 9/11 in NYC and its aftermath. In doing research for this essay, I saw that Cher had a small, post-9/11 gay club tour. It felt familiar somehow, so I instinctively looked up *Photo Cher Roxy March 2022*. Photographs surfaced, and I remembered that I was actually at that show--Cher was so hard to see from the 18+ section that I had not connected my memory of the Roxy with the Cher performance. I have also been trying for years to write about my 9/11 experience, and I'm grateful that the structure of the March Xness tournament helped me recover these threads, and that the music allowed me to find an angle, an appropriate distance.

THE MIDDLE OF EVERYWHERRE:

Katie Moulton on How Nelly's "Hot in Herre" Defines Millennial Dance Pop

I do not know much about gods; but I think that the river
Is a strong brown god—sullen, untamed, intractable,
Patient to some degree, at first recognised as a frontier;
Useful, untrustworthy, as a conveyor of commerce;
Then only a problem confronting the builder of bridges.

—*T.S. Eliot*

I was like—
Good gracious!

—Nelly

Start with the hook, in pieces. A kick-boom, a couple of frisky organ notes, a heraldic hi-hat. A half-phrase shouted from somewhere in the back: *HOT in!* For a breath, it's the sound of a band assembling on stage, but the shambolic stance is a facade—this outfit tightens up so fast it'll snap your neck. The guy on the mic clarifies—*So hot in HURR!*—but what is *that?* A complaint, maybe, but not a thesis. This is Sam Cooke warming the crowd, if Cooke had a tenor like sandpaper and was a loudmouth in the bleachers—somebody already sweating and ready to touch the ceiling. The sharp snare and funky top-line kick in, and the guy on the mic wants you to taste *that.* From the first perk of *ah, ah*—your shoulders: shrugging, your hips: twitching, upper lip: curling—*just a little bit* —because *oh!* that *is* tasty, and it's just beginning to boil.

This is the opening of "Hot in Herre" by St. Louis rapper Nelly. It's the double-platinum first single off his second album, and arguably his most enduring and influential hit. Released in early May 2002, it's been the quintessential song of summer for more than two decades now.

But more than that, "Hot in Herre" is a bridge. It's a bridge from the humble middle to points in all directions. It's a bridge in hip-hop, between late-'90s throwback tunefulness and the suburban hip-pop that would define mainstream music for the rest of the 2000s. It's a bridge in youth-pop itself, spanning the retrograde Britney-boy-band era and launching us beyond. It's a bounce from the belly, shooting into every tip of nerve. Sometimes it doesn't matter what's on the other side of the bridge, just that we get there.

"Hot in Herre" quickly dominated across platforms—radio (remember radio?), sales charts, and nascent downloading and streaming services. The record garnered Nelly the inaugural Grammy for Best *Male* Rap Solo Performance, its general unassailability proven by the Recording Academy's simultaneous ghettoization of the song and inability to ignore it. Nelly was not the first melodious or singing rapper (not even from the first from the Midwest, shout out Bone Thugs-n-Harmony), but we can draw a line connecting Nelly's popularity to the rise of iconic, non-coastal emcees who incorporated singing (hello, Kanye, Chance, Drake), as well as the pop interpolations (howdy, Jack Harlow) that dominate across genres today. He even preempted hip-hop-inflected "bro country," Lil Nas X, and Beyonce's current conquest of the country.

The song may have been aiming for pop dominance—and struck a bullseye right in the inclusive middle—but it's a weird song. Its creation was the product of risk, timing, and a willingness to be offbeat. As on Nelly's 2000 breakout debut, *Country Grammar*, most of *Nellyville* was produced by fellow St. Louisans. But just before release, the team felt something was still missing; they didn't "have the fuse for the bomb," Nelly said. He had just featured on NSYNC's final single, "Girlfriend," which was produced by the hottest rising duo, The Neptunes. Nelly sought to harness his momentum to that of the man who would be crowned the most influential producer of 2000s dance pop: Pharrell Williams.

Pharrell offered that tasty, space-funk groove—a track built around a re-working of 1979's "Bustin' Loose" by Chuck Brown. Brown was a DMV-based musician known as the "Godfather of Go-Go." Go-go is a profoundly regional subgenre of funk, characterized by its syncopated bass, snare and hi-hat, and audience call and response. In an interview with *The FADER*, Nelly said that once they were in the studio, he caught the vibe off the beat and riffed the hook first—*It's getting hot in herre*— Pharrell offered two pieces of advice: First, "You gotta have the girls answer, 'I am, getting so hot—,'" and second, "Whatever the verses, that first line's gotta be something everybody's gonna wanna say."

And what did Nelly say, for that all-important first line?

"Good gracious—ass is bodacious!"

Somehow, in 2002, one of the biggest rappers in the world combined the least-cool exclamations of my Midwestern grandma *and* Bill and Ted. Nobody, I mean nobody, who takes themselves too seriously can write a line like that. And nobody can take themselves too seriously once they've shouted it aloud on a crowded dance floor. It's a cure for pretension, for self-consciousness. It's the enactment of that Midwestern commandment: *Thou shalt get off thy high horse.*

"Me and Pharrell...we both think there's no such thing as a 'dumb' record," Nelly told *Maxim* in 2017. "We created a *moment* for people."

That moment arises from a half-baked pickup line that sounds like it was cooked up by adolescents: "It's getting hot in herre...so take off all your clothes!" He's talking to a potential paramour, but he's also talking to the whole room, his crew, himself. What unfurls from that brilliantly silly opening is a swift pile-up of rhymes and jokes, which Nelly delivers in a singsong sideline holler:

I'm waitin' for the right time to shoot my ***steez***
Waitin' for the right time to flash them ***keys***
Then, uh, I'm ***leavin', please believin',***
Me *and the rest of my* ***heathens***
Check it, got it locked at the top of the Four ***Seasons***
Penthouse, rooftop, birds I'm ***feedin'***
No ***deceivin'****, nothin' up my* ***sleeve and***
No ***teasin'****, I* ***need ya****...*

He can't help himself! But he's also *trying*. He's your clever uncle, the class clown, the courtside cut-up; he wants you laughing with him. He may have a twang, and the stakes may not be dire, but there's nothing *slow* here. And despite the sexual innuendo, the language is naughty but technically clean, toeing the line.

"It's more the *story* of a party record," Nelly said. "People can relate to the *process* of the club...as opposed to the typical 'everybody throw your hands up,' and that's why it lasts longer." I buy this conception of the song because of the fleeting but careful frame Nelly gives at the top of the song.

The first line is not, in fact, "Good gracious!" but rather, "I was like—" In this "story-song," we start mid-conversation, mid-party, and our pal Nelly is about to regale us. The narration then is separated ever so slightly from the action. Incident becomes practice, becomes ritual and community—and awareness of a memory even as it's being made.

On May 7, 2002, I'm red-faced in the blaze of 4 p.m. sun, peeling myself off my high school's flaking rubber track after practice. The Mississippi is two miles dead east. In St. Louis, you always know where the river is, even if you can't see it or feel a breeze off the bluffs. The night before, I'd seen my heroes Green Day and Jimmy Eat World at Riverport Amphitheatre, where security made me leave my CDs on the gravel outside the fence. I'm fifteen for a few more weeks. The bridge into true teenagehood is rushing fast under my feet. I've been *waiting* for more Nelly. And I'm bracing myself for the kind of disappointment that can only be delivered by your hometown.

In 1999 and 2000, we'd passed around middle-school hallways a burned copy of the "Country Grammar" single as it hit local, then regional, then national radio. We lived in a redlined metro defined by City and County, North and South, and here was somebody named Nelly saying we were all *Country*. We spent the summer before high school memorizing every lyric from Nelly and his crew the St. Lunatics, catching every reference. So many references were already our own: *STL, 314, M-I-crooked-letter-crooked-letter-O-U-R-I*. We, too, loved the Cardinals, the Blues, the Rams—bootleg jerseys that were always in style. We drove past all the same exits Nelly called out: Jennings, Hanley, Kingshighway, Natural Bridge. The malls that Nelly name-checks in his upward mobility—"Face and body Frontenac, don't know how to act, without no vouchers on her boots, she bringin' nothing back"—as in *Plaza Frontenac*, the shopping center in the wealthy suburb named for a colonial French governor of Canada—those were the same faraway fancy places where we could afford to walk around but never buy anything.

Me and my friends were white from South County. Nelly and the 'Tics were Black from University City (U. City), which was actually Mid-County. Their suburb was more urban than ours, older, first accessible by streetcar in the last century. The old streetcar line is Delmar Boulevard, running east-west through an entertainment district called the Loop, anchored by Blueberry Hill, the landmark restaurant where, up until he died in 2017, Chuck Berry—Father of Rock and Roll—still played the basement club once a month. Delmar Boulevard is also a long-standing racial dividing line of the city between the white south and the Black north. On the other hand, my suburb sprung up around the old telegraph line running north-south along the river, and by our time, there was no way to get there but by car. And nothing, by design, to draw anybody there who wasn't just heading home.

Still, Nelly was technically a *suburban* kid, too, and we could hear it—not like us, but also, *like* us. More specifically than anything else we'd seen or heard. In a hollowed-out city like St. Louis, there's a tendency to claim both your particular pocket and the whole metro area. We know kids at every Catholic high school in town. We gather in large crowds downtown, and we have to travel a ways to get there. I ran track against the U. City team, often lost to them in the 400. Even his name—*Nelly*, short for Cornell—wasn't tough but diminutive, familiar, belying deep-seated confidence. When Nelly landed a record deal, his friends and collaborators were working at the airport, the barbershop, McDonald's, and Office Max. Nelly had been a serious high-school athlete and low-grade dealer, who'd considered three paths to adulthood: ball, streets, or music. Soon enough, I would sit on gym bleachers as a guidance counselor told us to divide ourselves into our post-grad plans: state school, community college, military, or job. No choice that quite fit.

In the music video for "Country Grammar," the setting is a block party, the street between humble red-brick houses near Natural Bridge and Kingshighway jam-packed with tricked-out Cutlasses and revelers in booty shorts and Cardinals jerseys. The lighting is a little gray, made to look "real," and there's no question this street and the people in it, if not the level of festivity, *are* real. The video opens and ends with the camera positioned on the ground, aimed up at a lone Nelly against a clear blue sky, standing framed by the Gateway Arch monument above his head.

In St. Louis, we talk a lot about the Arch. We talk about the river below and measure floods by how many steps the brown water rose to lap at its great steel feet. We talk a lot about 1904. Our public park is bigger than Central Park; our museums are world-class and they're free—all built for the World's Fair in 1904. Constructed as a temporary pageant for outside visitors, to welcome the world to the river city. Once the Fair was over, it was all meant to be torn down. Instead, we kept it. Kept the limestone buffed, certain avenues shaded with trees. We mention that we were once bigger than Chicago, but they bet on the railroads, and we bet on the river. We always bet on the river.

I was a kid who loved St. Louis and hated my suburb, who dreamed of leaving because I believed there was *more* for me someplace else. We were a gateway, after all. St. Louis may be a place to return to, but first it was a place to leave. To stay meant to be concentrated in your smallness, to be doomed to asking, "Where'd you go to high school?" for the rest of your life. The artists left as soon as they could or when they couldn't take it anymore: T.S. Eliot, Maya Angelou, Josephine Baker ("Friends, to me for years St. Louis represented a city of fear, humiliation, misery, and terror"), Tennessee Williams, who called the city "cold, smug, complacent, intolerant, stupid, and provincial."

But Nelly didn't just represent St. Louis; Nelly *claimed* St. Louis. As Nelly burst onto the national stage, it was precisely this uncategorizable "Midwest Swing" that was being celebrated. Uncategorizable and idiosyncratic, perhaps not because it was *outside* the dominant culture but because in the middle, we have to take a little bit from everything flowing through. We have to study the maps. We have to know about you, elsewhere. But we figured that elsewhere, people must not have a damn clue what Nelly was talking about.

Yet coming of age at precisely that moment likely gave me and my friends a miscalculation of our centrality to the larger world. We considered ourselves to be the truest of *Millennials*—those who came into adolescent consciousness right at the flip of the year 2000. And suddenly, everybody had heard of our city. When we met kids in other places (leadership camp, student newspaper conferences—yes, hometown escape velocity takes many forms), they always said, "St. Louis? Oh, do you know Nelly?" Our answer was always: *Of course.*

Later, when I get to college on the East Coast, my roommates from Queens say, "Missouri? That's one of those square states that votes for Bush, right?"—and then, "Do you know Nelly?" Studying abroad in England, I flirted with a bartender who called *me* "Nelly" rather than my name, and asked if I owned a gun back home.

Because even though Nelly rarely rapped about violence or even carrying weapons (with the notable exception of "Country Grammar" where "street sweeper, baby, cocked" was edited to "boom, boom, baby, uh, uh" for radio), this was another thing people heard about St. Louis: It was dangerous. People got shot there. According to *U.S. News & World Report*, St. Louis was the "Most Dangerous City in America," based on the FBI analysis of violent- and property-crime rates from 2003 to 2009—another dominant statistic of the decade. And that's where the lie—*I know Nelly*—breaks down. The median income isn't that different between U. City and my suburb, but the crime rate is unfathomably higher. Same county, different planets. What did I know but what I heard and occasionally witnessed? I always got in my car and left again.

It seemed possible in those years that St. Louis could be respected and influential on culture at large. That in so doing, our local culture could be shared among us at home too. That the city's long standing inferiority complex, "glorious potential," racial injustice, and provincial terror could be brought into the light because it mattered. That all the industry, civilizations and people who had been lost and who remained mattered. Mattered and spoke. And when they spoke, sometimes they lilted and purred not quite like anyplace else.

So in 2002, when I listened to "Hot in Herre" for the first time, I was anxious whether the hometown hero would deliver or melt in the glare. Or worse—abandon us. But there were reasons to be optimistic: The album is titled *Nellyville*, which we assumed would be another elevation of this city, sharing his crown. And the first single insisted on its peculiar accent.

He stuck the accent right in the title: "Herre," meaning "here," is pronounced *HURR*, a kind of drawl punctuated by a hard *R*. For Black St. Louisans, other words that may rhyme closely with *here* include *her, there* (as in the Chingy hit "Right Thurr"), *hair*, *year*, and even *mayor*. "Everything collides linguistically in St. Louis," says Dr. John Baugh, a Washington University (WUSTL) professor specializing in social stratification of linguistic behavior, and linguistic variation among African Americans. "It's where the South meets the North. It's where the East meets the West." The "urr" sound likely traveled north along the more rural Mississippi, where it collided with the Inland North Vowel Shift of people moving south from Chicago. Within this national crossroads, St. Louis's history of extreme racial segregation likely isolated the dialect. That's what happens in our "once-great," long-overlooked American cities, cities like Nelly's St. Louis, like Chuck Brown's Baltimore. If you don't leave, you become more and more yourself.

In 2002, the sound felt new—or rather, old, more organic, warmer. But sure enough, there was Nelly's voice—a stringent, friendly, party-starting rasp, linking go-go and Midwest swing, bridging the underestimated in-betweens. Nelly still shouted out "the Lou" once and his own Vokal-brand tank top. The language is a translation, another kind of bridge between Nelly, his roots, and the rest.

"Hot in Herre" both echoes and subverts Nelly's first hit, "Country Grammar," from the emphasis on local linguistics to the opening shout of

Hot—! and edgy hooks cloaked in playground chants. Both songs are eternal turn-up anthems, and the music videos depict fantastical parties for the ages. Instead of a derrty-summer block party, "Hot in Herre" is a club scene, highly stylized, shot in glossy oranges and blues, featuring immaculately sweaty women who just happen to be wearing bikinis under their halter tops—and who are distinctly no longer the same girls from the neighborhood. Still, everybody is elbow-to-elbow, getting down. At one point, the ceiling billows with actual flames, but the clubgoers mistake the DJ's warnings as a party-starting tactic, chanting back, "We don't need no water—let the motherf*cker burn!"

In the video, Nelly wears what became his temporary trademark—a white Band-Aid on his cheek. This may be an absurd fashion affectation or may be a tribute to City Spud, his friend, producer, and fellow St. Lunatic who has a show-stealing verse on "Ride Wit Me" and who was incarcerated just as their careers were about to blow up. It wouldn't be until 2008, just in time for the wane of Nelly's imperial period, that City, or Lavell Webb, was released from prison.

It turns out, we were wrong about "Nellyville." The title track does not proclaim a lush homecoming. Instead, it's a conception of utopia—"where all newborns get a half-a-mill'" and "nobody livin' savage, errybody got change" and "ain't nobody shot, so ain't no news that day." The bridge, in true country songwriting fashion, punctures the dream, as Nelly keens, "I just want to go and look/Won't you please take me on in." "Nellyville" is definitively not St. Louis. It's not where Nelly is, or where he can even get to.

The official "Hot in Herre" video was not the first. The original, rarely seen video, is another club scene. But this party is happening *inside* the Arch. The link is literal: The world's first image of Nelly is him tapping on the camera from the ground below the Arch, and now he's at the very top of the symbol of his city. That room, of course, doesn't exist as such. As St. Louis schoolchildren, who get bussed there on a field trip every single year, *know*: Once you ride the glowing-egg elevator up a click at a time up one grand leg of the Arch, the "top" is a narrow hallway covered in industrial carpet. There's nothing to do but peer down from cloudy windows to see just how puny our city looks from up there. (As one KMOX reporter put it, "Something great happened here, but it's over now.") But *that* scene, of a club full of real bodies draped in recognizable glamor, at the top of our small world, is a powerful fantasy of belonging.

I was like—"Hot in Herre," then, is both a bridge and a compromise. We from the middle know about these things. We can't make you know us, how it feels to grow up with a river above your head, watchful of how it rises and falls. We can't stick you in the wild heat of the downtown fair on the Landing, sweat stains on the concrete, fire rocketing from the barges in the dark. You can't be with me all those summers, driving the highways from South County to my job in Ferguson off Natural Bridge, windows down because the AC busted again in my inherited 2002 PT Cruiser, hot wind buffeting you in the face as we speed under the Arch's gleaming shadow, under and around without stopping the neighborhoods where kids still get shot, for no reason and every reason, all the time, the river on our right in the morning, and on the left headed back again.

Listening to "Hot in Herre," I could tell right away that Nelly was now talking to more than just "us"—whoever he imagined as his home-team crowd—that he's spreading his arms, goading everyone to peel off their defenses. We can dance to it; we can repeat the jokes. The jokes are so corny we'll still be telling them in twenty years. And I thought, briefly, that maybe Nelly had figured out a way to make it out and make it home. He proved he could create a moment for folks to step into, shake their ass inside, return to. That a song, somehow, can be for all and for *us*, and maybe that the flow between can expand our definitions of both.

ON THE ESSAY:

This essay turned me from Mi*nelli*al into full-blown Nellyologist: I recently delivered a talk titled "Nelly's Band-Aid: Physical Vulnerability as Pop Fashion Statement." The small white bandage Nelly wore on his left cheek was an idiosyncratic adornment, blemish cover, tribute to his incarcerated friend and collaborator, a silent protest. In any case, it signifies a wound. What makes the symbol stick in cultural imagination, however, is its almost radical smallness and how it defies easy interpretation. The Band-Aid is like this song, like the hometown I can't quite return to—accessible yet illegible, and therefore utterly our own. Songs may evoke nostalgia, the pain of trying to go home and never getting there. But silly dance songs are channels: The dance floor is where time and distance can truly collapse. Where we can not only remember but embody our loves, losses, those small, deep cuts we protect and carry.

HIDDEN TRACK

Hello Book Readers. If you're like me, CDs trained you to look for secrets: Nine Inch Nails's, "Physical," on the back end of the *Broken* EP; Nick Cave & The Dirty Three covering *The X-Files* theme cleverly hidden as track 0 on the *Songs in the Key of X* soundtrack, Cracker's absolute classic "Eurotrash Girl," track 69, lol, on *Kerosene Hat*; Nirvana's "Sappy," hidden on *No Alternative*; Green Day's "All By Myself" at the end of *Dookie*; Janet Jackson, "Whoops Now" at the end of *Janet*; Eels, "Mr. E's Beautiful Blues" crowning the end of *Daisies of the Galaxy*; and on and on. I know this practice predates the CD era: of course the Beatles did it (accidentally) in 1969, well before CDs, and in 2012, in the declining days of the medium, Beach House delivered "Wherever You Go" 13 minutes after the end of "Irene," the magnificent track that apparently ends *Bloom*. I mean that searching for, buying, occasionally shoplifting, scrutinizing, and obsessively listening to physical media on repeat showed me how artists play with media, how the song isn't the same as the medium on which the song is inscribed and distributed to you.

My favorite is the end of the track "Runnin' Down a Dream" at the midpoint of Tom Petty's CD release of *Full Moon Fever*, where after that song finishes and a few seconds of silence we hear Petty's distinctive voice: "Hello CD listeners, we've come to the point in this album where those listening on cassette or records will have to stand up or sit down and turn over the record or tape. In fairness to those listeners, we'll now take a few seconds before we begin side two. Thank you. Here's side two." Behind Petty's voice you can hear some barn noises, clearly human-made, a guy yelling "neigh neigh" or "nay, nay" (if there's a difference), and some bird sounds or something, maybe they're real maybe they're not, and then someone saying, deep in the mix, "come on you bastard."

Only in 2025 I found confirmation that this version remains on the streaming version of *Full Moon Fever*, which I just verified on Apple Music and Spotify. What a strange oddity, to be streaming an album that addresses you as a CD listener, and for this, not the vinyl, not the cassette, to be enshrined as *the* version of this song that most casual listeners will henceforth ever encounter. Maybe you're old like me and remember CDs clearly. Maybe you collect them, as Megan and I do, because you're skeptical of the cloud and the promise of unlimited availability, which is only as good for its promises as capitalism is, and when your wifi goes down or Apple Music for some reason glitches "Gimme Sympathy" off Metric's *Fantasies* album and your kid freaks out because she loves the track (so do I) and it's freaking *gone???*, you can hand her the CD like a secret, you've been waiting for this moment your whole life. Anyway, it's kind of the same difference between reading essays on a website and reading essays in a book object like this one is, is my point. So hey, come on, you bastards! —Ander

CONTRIBUTORS

Erin Belieu is the author of five poetry collections, all from Copper Canyon Press, including 2021's *Come-Hither Honeycomb*. Recent work has appeared in the *New York Times*, the Academy of American Poets' *Poem-A-Day*, and *Kenyon Review*. Belieu lives in Houston where she teaches for the University of Houston's MFA/Ph.D. program in Creative Writing.

Matt Bell is the author most recently of the novel *Appleseed* (a New York Times Notable Book) and the craft book *Refuse to Be Done*, a guide to novel writing, rewriting, and revision. He is also the author of the novels *Scrapper* and *In the House upon the Dirt Between the Lake and the Woods*, as well as the short story collection *A Tree or a Person or a Wall*, a non-fiction book about the classic video game Baldur's Gate II, and several other titles. A native of Michigan, he teaches creative writing at Arizona State University.

Steph Brown is a professor (professional) and rock climber (very amateur) in Tucson, Arizona.

Mark Butler is a writer, editor, and karaoke enthusiast in Seattle. Alongside his family, he worked on the development team for the hit card game, Taco vs Burrito. He previously wrote about Kirsty MacColl for March Fadness. He still can't believe that Jim Steinman got away with writing a nine-minute song called "Objects In The Rear View Mirror May Appear Closer Than They Are."

Megan Campbell is one half of the Official March Xness Selection Committee.

Cameron Carr is a writer from Ohio. His essays have appeared in *The American Scholar*, *Longreads*, *The Missouri Review*, and elsewhere.

Dan Chaon is the author of eight fictional books, including the novels *One* *of Us* (2025), Sleepwalk (2021), and *Ill Will* (2017). Other works include the short story collection *Stay Awake* (2012), a finalist for the Story Prize; the national bestseller *Await Your Reply*; and *Among the Missing*, a finalist for the National Book Award. Chaon's fiction has appeared in the *Best American Short Stories*, the *Pushcart Prize Anthologies*, and the *O. Henry Collection*, and he was the recipient of an Academy Award in Literature from the American Academy of Arts and Letters. Chaon dwells in Cleveland.

Brooke Champagne is a native New Orleanian and the award-winning author of *Nola Face: A Latina's Life in the Big Easy*, named a Best Book of 2024 from Kirkus Reviews. Her work has been selected as Notable in several editions of the *Best American Essays* anthology series, and she is the recipient of the 2023-2024 Alabama State Council on the Arts Literary Fellowship in Prose. Champagne also serves as Book Reviews Editor for *River Teeth: A Journal of Narrative Nonfiction*. She lives with her husband and children in Tuscaloosa, where she is Assistant Professor of Creative Writing in the MFA Program at the University of Alabama.

James Charlesworth grew up eighty miles east of Pittsburgh and lives in Boston. He is the author of a novel, *The Patricide of George Benjamin Hill*, and has contributed four essays to March Xness.

Steven Church is the author of six books of nonfiction, most recently the collection of essays, *I'm Just Getting to the Disturbing Part: On Work, Fear, and Fatherhood* and the book-length essay, *One With the Tiger: Sublime and Violent Encounters Between Humans and Animals*. His essays have been anthologized in "best of" anthologies from *River Teeth*, *Brevity*, *Essay Daily*, and *Fourth Genre*. He's a founding editor and nonfiction editor for the literary magazine, *The Normal School*, and he teaches in the MFA Program at Fresno State.

Danielle Cadena Deulen is the author of a memoir, *The Riots* (U. of Georgia Press, 2011), and three poetry collections, most recently *Desire Museum* (BOA Editions, 2023), winner of a 2024 Lambda Literary Award. She's an associate professor in the graduate writing program at Georgia State University and co-host of the literary podcast, "Lit from the Basement." You can find her on Instagram: @dcdeulen, or on her author site, danielledeulen.net.

Danielle Evans is the author of two short story collections, *The Office of*

Historical Corrections and *Before You Suffocate Your Own Fool Self.* Her first collection won the PEN American Robert W. Bingham Prize, the Hurston-Wright award and the Paterson Prize; her second won the Janet Heidinger Kafka Prize and was a finalist for The Aspen Prize, The Story Prize, The Chautauqua Prize, and The Los Angeles Times Book prize. She has also been awarded The New Literary Project Oates Prize, a National Endowment for the Arts fellowship, and a US Artists Fellowship. Her stories have appeared in magazines and anthologies including *The Paris Review*, *A Public Space*, *The Sewanee Review* and *The Best American Short Stories.* She lives in Baltimore, where she is an Associate Professor in The Writing Seminars at Johns Hopkins University.

Melissa Faliveno is the author of the essay collection *Tomboyland*, named a Best Book of 2020 by NPR, New York Public Library, Oprah Magazine, and Electric Literature, and recipient of a Literary Achievement Award from the Wisconsin Library Association. Her work has appeared in *Esquire*, *Paris Review*, *Kenyon Review*, *Brevity*, *Bitch*, *Lit Hub*, *Diagram*, *Essay Daily*, *Prairie Schooner*, and *Brooklyn Rail*, among others, and in the anthology *Sex and the Single Woman: 24 Writers Reimagine Helen Gurley Brown's Cult Classic* (Harper Perennial, 2022). She teaches creative writing at the University of North Carolina in Chapel Hill, and her debut novel, *Hemlock*, is just out from Little, Brown.

T Fleischmann is the author of *Time Is the Thing a Body Moves Through* (Coffee House) and *Syzygy, Beauty* (Sarabande).

Elisa Gabbert is the author of seven collections of poetry, essays, and criticism, including *Any Person Is the Only Self*, *Normal Distance*, *The Unreality of Memory*, *The Word Pretty*, and *The Self Unstable.* She writes the On Poetry column for the *New York Times*, and her work has appeared in *Harper's*, *The Atlantic*, *The Paris Review*, *The Believer*, *The Yale Review*, and elsewhere. She lives in Providence.

J. Nicholas Geist is an essayist. Josh's print essays have appeared in *Ninth Letter*, *Creative Nonfiction*, and the much-mourned videogame journal *Kill Screen.* His extracurricular essay for March Fadness 2023, "The Essential Whiteness of One-Hit Wonders," was included in *Sight and Sound Magazine*'s list of the Best Video Essays of 2023.

Danielle Geller wrote a book (*Dog Flowers*, One World/Random House 2021) and regrets giving up her toy horses, especially that little gray colt.

Ryan Grandick has had work published in the *Seneca Review*, *Diagram*, *Dirty Chai*, *ScissorTale Review*, and *Public Books*. He has an MFA from the University of Arizona and is currently a mailman.

Camellia-Berry Grass is the author of the lyric essay collection *Hall of Waters* (The Operating System, 2019), and her essays appear in *DIAGRAM*, *Barrelhouse*, the *Texas Review*, and *Waxwing*, among other publications and anthologies. She has served as Nonfiction Editor for *Black Warrior Review* and for *Sundog Lit*. She holds an MFA in creative writing from the University of Alabama, and has taught most recently at Rutgers University, University of the Arts, and in the MFA program for creative writing at Rosemont College. Her essay "Battle Vest" was a 2019 nominee for the Krause Essay Prize.

Jennifer Gravley writes mainly short prose, watches mainly bad television, and thinks Excel is really very useful. Her first book, *The Story I Told My Mother: Poems and an Essay*, was published in 2023. Find her online at jennifergravley.com.

Dave Griffith is the author of *A Good War is Hard to Find: The Art of Violence in America* (Soft Skull).

Raquel Gutiérrez is a critic, essayist, poet, performer, and educator. Gutiérrez's first book *Brown Neon* (Coffee House Press) was named as one of the best books of 2022 by The New Yorker and listed in The Best Art Books of 2022 by Hyperallergic. *Brown Neon* was a 2023 recipient of The Publishing Triangle Judy Grahn Award for Lesbian Nonfiction. Gutiérrez was recently named a 2025 recipient of the United States Artist fellowship as well as a 2025 recipient of the Foundation for Contemporary Arts fellowship. Their new poetry collection, *Southwest Reconstruction*, will be published in fall 2025 on Noemi Press.

W. Todd Kaneko is the author of *The Dead Wrestler Elegies* (Curbside Splendor 2014) and co-author with Amorak Huey of *Poetry: A Writer's Guide and Anthology* (Bloomsbury Academic 2018). His recent poems and prose can be seen in *The Normal School*, *Barrelhouse*, *Gulf Coast*, *The Rumpus* and many other places. A Kundiman fellow, he is co-editor of *Waxwing* magazine and lives in Grand Rapids, Michigan where he teaches at Grand Valley State University. Catch him online at www.toddkaneko.com.

Erin Keane was born in New Jersey and lives in Kentucky and knows both places are misunderstood. Her debut memoir, *Runaway: Notes on the Myths That Made Me* (Belt Publishing) was named one of NPR's best books of 2022. She is also the author of three collections of poems, including *Demolition of the Promised Land*, inspired by Bruce Springsteen, and editor of *The Louisville Anthology*, also from Belt Publishing. She is Chief Content Officer at Salon and teaches creative nonfiction and poetry in the Naslund-Mann Graduate School of Writing at Spalding University.

Porochista Khakpour is the author of the novels *Sons & Other Flammable Objects* and *The Last Illusion* and the forthcoming memoir *Sick*. Her work has appeared in several sections of *The New York Times*, as well as *The Los Angeles Times*, *Bookforum*, *The Wall Street Journal*, *Elle*, *Spin*, and many others. She currently teaches at Bard College, Columbia University, and VCFA.

Drew Krewer is author of the chapbook *Ars Warholica* (Spork Press) and co-editor of *The Destroyer*. His work has appeared in *Troubling the Line: Trans and Genderqueer Poetry and Poetics*, *DIAGRAM*, *Afternoon Visitor*, and *Dream Pop*, among other publications. He holds an MFA from the University of Arizona and lives in the desert.

Laura Lorson is a news editor, radio producer, and announcer at Kansas Public Radio in Lawrence. Her husband owns and operates Love Garden Sounds in Lawrence. They spend an inordinate amount of time listening to new music, arguing about optimal speaker positioning, and the relative merits of tube amps.

Lela Scott MacNeil was born in Los Alamos like the atomic bomb. Her work has been published in *Gertrude*, *Essay Daily*, and *Trouble in the Heartland: Crime Fiction Inspired by the Songs of Bruce Springsteen*.

Kristine Langley Mahler is the author of three nonfiction books, *Teen Queen Training*, *A Calendar Is a Snakeskin*, and *Curing Season: Artifacts*. Her work has been supported by the Nebraska Arts Council and Art at Cedar Point and twice named Notable in *Best American Essays*.

Karyna McGlynn is a queer writer, visual artist, and educator. She is Director of Creative Writing at Interlochen Center for the Arts, and was the 2023-24 Visiting Distinguished Professor of Poetry in the Helen Zell Writers' Program at the University of Michigan. She is the author of three poetry collections from Sarabande Books, including *50 Things Kate Bush Taught Me About the Multiverse* (2023 Lambda Literary Finalist), *Hothouse* (a New York Times Editor's Choice), and *I Have to Go Back to 1994 and Kill a Girl* (Kathryn A. Morton Prize in Poetry). Their writing has appeared in *Poetry*, *Missouri Review*, *Ninth Letter*, *New England Review*, and *Kenyon Review*.

John Melillo is a professor, writer, and musician who lives in Tucson, Arizona, and St. Joseph du Moine, Cape Breton. His first book, *The Poetics of Noise from Dada to Punk*, was published by Bloomsbury in the Fall of 2020. Melillo teaches/researches at the University of Arizona and performs under the name Algae & Tentacles.

Ander Monson is one half of the Official March Xness Selection Committee.

Katie Moulton is the author of *Dead Dad Club: On Grief & Tom Petty* (Audible 2022). Her essays and criticism appear in *The Believer*, *Oxford American*, *New England Review*, *Sewanee Review*, *Salon*, *Village Voice*, and elsewhere. You can find links to more of her work at katiemoulton.com. She teaches at Johns Hopkins University and the Newport MFA. She makes her home in Baltimore, but she remains, forever, *so St. Louis (ask my tattooist)*.

Laura C. J. Owen is a writer living in Tucson, Arizona.

Elena Passarello has written essays for March Sadness, Fadness, Shredness, Vladness, and Badness. She is also the author of *Animals Strike Curious Poses* and *Let Me Clear My Throat*.

Kathleen Rooney is a founding editor of Rose Metal Press, a nonprofit publisher of literary work in hybrid genres, and a founding member of Poems While You Wait, a collective of poets and their typewriters who compose commissioned poetry on demand. She is the author of the novels *Lillian*

Boxfish Takes a Walk, *Cher Ami and Major Whittlesey*, and *From Dust to Stardust*, and her latest poetry collection *Where Are the Snows*, winner of the XJ Kennedy Prize, was released in Fall of 2022 by Texas Review Press. Her picture book *Leaf Town Forever*, co-written with her sister Beth Rooney, is forthcoming in Fall 2025 and her latest novel, *Man Overboard!*, will be published in Summer 2026. She lives in Chicago with her spouse, the writer Martin Seay, and teaches at DePaul.

Amy Rossi lives in and writes in North Carolina with her partner and two rescue dogs. Her debut novel *The Cover Girl*—which explores rock music excess in the 1970s and 80s—is available from MIRA/HarperCollins.

Jim Ruland is an old punk who lives by the sea. He is the author of the novels *Make It Stop* and *Forest of Fortune* and the short story collection *Big Lonesome*. Jim is also the *LA Times* bestselling author of *Corporate Rock Sucks: The Rise & Fall of SST Records*, which was named a best book of 2022 by *Pitchfork*, *Rolling Stone* and *Vanity Fair*. Ruland is the co-author of *Do What You Want* with Bad Religion and *My Damage* with Keith Morris. Jim is a frequent contributor to *Razorcake* fanzine and the *LA Times*. He is a veteran of the US Navy and lives in San Diego.

Martin Seay's debut novel *The Mirror Thief* was published by Melville House in 2016. His March Xness contributions include essays on Michael Penn, Yngwie Malmsteen, A Certain Ratio, Scott Walker, Sonic Youth, Peter Gabriel, and Scritti Politti. Originally from Texas, he lives in Chicago with his spouse, the writer Kathleen Rooney.

Sejal Shah is a writer, interdisciplinary artist, and educator. She is the author of the story collection *How to Make Your Mother Cry: fictions*, which includes images, ephemera, and a soundtrack. This hybrid book came together through a lot of dancing. Her award-winning essay collection *This Is One Way to Dance* was an NPR Best Book of 2020 and named in over thirty "most-anticipated" or "best-of" lists including *Literary Hub* and the *Los Angeles Times*. Winning March Danceness is one of her all-time favorite accomplishments. Sejal lives in Rochester, New York; find her online at sejal-shah.com and @sejalshahwrites on Instagram.

Aaron Smith is the author of five books of poetry, most recently *Stop Lying*.

He is an associate professor of creative writing at Lesley University in Cambridge, Massachusetts.

Justin St. Germain wrote the memoir *Son of a Gun* and the book-length essay *Bookmarked: Truman Capote's In Cold Blood*. He dressed a lot better back in '87.

J. Max Stinson is a recovered ne'er-do-well, stay at home dad, and podcast co-host at LitFromTheBasement.com. On Twitter: @VitaReadings. On Instagram: @litfromthebasement.

NOW AVAILABLE FROM SPLIT/LIP PRESS

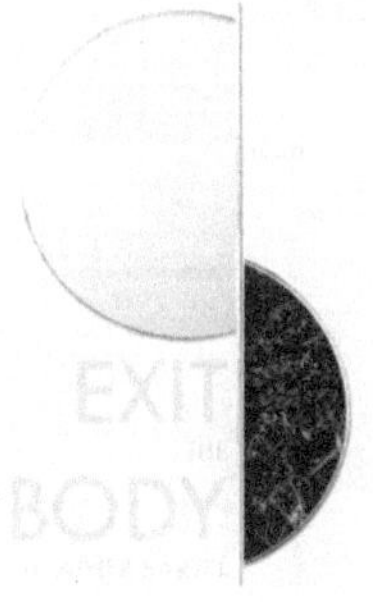

For more info about the press and titles, visit us at www.splitlippress.com

Follow us on Instagram and Bluesky: @splitlippress

www.ingramcontent.com/pod-product-compliance
Lightning Source LLC
LaVergne TN
LVHW041102080826
845145LV00007B/1668

* 9 7 8 1 9 5 2 8 9 7 4 9 8 *